Macroeconomics and the Phillips Curve Myth

JAMES FORDER has been a senior teaching member of Oxford University since 1993 and is Andrew Graham Fellow and Tutor in Political Economy at Balliol College, where he is also Vice Master (Executive). He has taught at La Sorbonne and for Stanford University, and is Managing Editor of *Oxford Economic Papers*. He has previously researched on European integration and the economics of central bank independence. He was Senior Tutor of the Oxford University Business Economics Programme, and a member of the Council of *Business for Sterling*, in the days of the debate over British membership of the euro.

T0320837

Oxford Studies in the History of Economics

Series Editor: Steven G. Medema

This series publishes leading-edge scholarship by historians of economics and social science, drawing upon approaches from intellectual history, the history of ideas, and the history of the natural and social sciences. It embraces the history of economic thinking from ancient times to the present, the evolution of the discipline itself, the relationship of economics to other fields of inquiry, and the diffusion of economic ideas within the discipline and to the policy realm and broader publics. This enlarged scope affords the possibility of looking anew at the intellectual, social, and professional forces that have surrounded and conditioned economics' continued development.

Macroeconomics and the Phillips Curve Myth

James Forder

OXFORD
UNIVERSITY PRESS

OXFORD
UNIVERSITY PRESS

Great Clarendon Street, Oxford, OX2 6DP,
United Kingdom

Oxford University Press is a department of the University of Oxford.
It furthers the University's objective of excellence in research, scholarship,
and education by publishing worldwide. Oxford is a registered trade mark of
Oxford University Press in the UK and in certain other countries

© James Forder 2014

The moral rights of the author have been asserted

First published 2014
First published in paperback 2018

Published in the United States of America by Oxford University Press
198 Madison Avenue, New York, NY 10016, United States of America

British Library Cataloguing in Publication Data
Data available

Library of Congress Cataloging in Publication Data
Data available

ISBN 978–0–19–968365–9 (Hbk.)
ISBN 978–0–19–881987–5 (Pbk.)

ACKNOWLEDGEMENTS

First, I must thank Irene Lemos, who, as well as reading some of the drafts, has been following the progress of the work with what is politely called 'interest'. She would be entitled to feel the Phillips curve has been wrapped around her neck much too long, but it would all have taken much longer without her encouragement.

Vivienne Brown, Peter Oppenheimer, Terry Peach, and Mary Robertson made valuable comments on all or much of the text. Several parts of the work were presented at conferences. I can hardly record everyone who commented over a number of years, but John Aldrich, Roger Backhouse, Richard van den Berg, Mauro Boianovsky, Tony Brewer, Hugh Goodacre, Geoffrey Harcourt, Peter Kriesler, Steven Medema, Renee Predergast, John Vint, and Michel de Vroey all made contributions which in one way or another stuck in my mind. The same is true of David Laidler, Richard Lipsey, and John Nevile in correspondence, and Wilfred Beckerman, William Coleman, Andrew Graham, John King, and Terry O'Shaughnessy in conversation. Bob Solow and David Vines commented on a version of Chapter 2. John Anderies, Thomas Baranga, Robert Leeson, Jonas Prager, and Nancy Wulwick helped with finding otherwise inacessible materials. Max Dalton, Marc Pacitti, Joe Spearing, Caroline Thurston, and Sophie Tomlinson all gave very good research assistance as well as making a number of useful comments. Angus Hawkins and George Charlson similarly helped with this project by speeding other projects along.

CONTENTS

NOTE TO THE READER

The following are identified by their last name only: Stephen Bailey, James Ball, Daniel Bell, John M. Clark, William Dickens, Irving Fisher, Crauford Goodwin, Robert J. Gordon, Robert E. Hall, Alvin Hansen, A. G. Hart, David Hume, Terence Hutchinson, John Kenneth Galbraith, Christopher Gilbert, Neil Jacoby, Harry Johnson, Robert G. King, H. Gregg Lewis, Daniel Mitchell, Arnold Packer, A. W. H. Phillips, Joan Robinson, Arthur Ross, Tibor Scitovsky, David C. Smith, Jim Taylor, H. A. Turner, Richard Wagner. Others sharing those last names are further identified when necessary.

At no point have I felt it helpful to change the emphasis in quotations, so any emphasis is the quoted authors' own.

Where I have quoted from reprints, the original dates of publication and the quoted edition are indicated in, for example, the form 'Keynes (1946/1972)', rather than the 'Keynes (1972)' form that has become commonplace.

Introduction

There is one story about the history of macroeconomics that seems to be known to everyone who has studied the subject for more than a few weeks. It puts varying interpretations of the Phillips curve at the heart of the development of policy-orientated thinking from the 1960s to the 1980s, and its motif is the idea that economists of that period initially failed to appreciate the importance of expectations of inflation. Details of this story vary but the central points are these. In what quickly became a classic paper, Phillips (1958) discovered a negative relation between inflation and unemployment; then, either under the influence of Samuelson and Solow (1960) or otherwise, policymakers treated it as offering a selection of inflation-unemployment combinations from which they could choose, depending on their—or their voters'—aversion to the two evils; much work was done investigating this tradeoff and, because of it, inflationist policy was pursued until Phelps (1967) and Friedman (1968a) revolutionized thinking by pointing out that continuous inflation would change expectations and thereby shift the Phillips curve so that there was no long-run tradeoff; and although this was initially disputed, in due course it was accepted.

One point I hope to make in what follows is that each component of that story is false. They should all simply be dismissed, and that should be the end of it. That, however, is a minor point. The more important point is that the orientation of this story—its general implication, trend, or tendency—is wholly misleading as well. The story offers a picture of an economics profession that was still, well into the post-war period, struggling to articulate the simplest ideas, and disputing the obvious even when it was stated. It describes an interlude in which either economics was bizarrely primitive or its practitioners were extraordinarily slow-witted. That picture needs not just to be dismissed, but also replaced. Supposing that I can achieve those things, there will obviously be a further question as to how this story ever came to be told, believed, and become conventional, and responding to that issue is therefore a third objective. Indeed, it could reasonably be said that offering some account of the emergence of the story is almost a condition of making a persuasive case that it is only a myth.

Although I cannot, in advance of all the arguments, explain the acceptance of the story—even dating its appearance precisely takes some effort—I can perhaps say that the best-known early statement of it is found in Friedman (1977) – that author's Nobel Lecture. I hope that I have dissected that particular source sufficiently in Forder (2010a), but a reprise of Friedman's story is in order here. He stated it as an objective to show that, despite widespread scepticism, it was appropriate for there to be a Prize for economics because, like the sciences, economics progresses by hypothesis formation, testing and rejection, and the formation of further hypotheses. He then took the story of the Phillips curve as his example and said that up to that time professional opinion had been through two stages of which the first was one of,

> the acceptance of a hypothesis associated with the name of A. W. Phillips (1958) that there is a stable negative relation between the level of unemployment and the rate of change of wages—high levels of unemployment being accompanied by falling wages, low levels of unemployment by rising wages. (Friedman, 1977, p. 454)

And that,

> This relation was widely interpreted as a causal relation that offered a stable trade-off to policymakers.

So that,

> Economists then busied themselves with trying to extract the relation…for different countries and periods, to eliminate the effect of extraneous disturbances, to clarify the relation between wage change and price change, and so on. In addition, they explored social gains and losses from inflation on the one hand and unemployment on the other, in order to facilitate the choice of the 'right' trade-off. (p. 455)

Then, citing four of his own statements from the 1960s concerning the idea that expectations would adjust to continuous inflation, thereby eliminating the tradeoff, he said,

Some of us were skeptical from the outset about the validity of a stable Phillips curve...

and

What mattered for employment, we argued, was not wages in dollars or pounds or kronor but real wages—what the wages would buy in goods and services.

He proceeded to explain the idea that behaviour would adjust to anticipated inflation so as to shift the Phillips curve, and in due course, summing up, he claimed,

The age-old confusion between absolute prices and relative prices gained a new lease on life. (p. 469)

And,

In this intellectual atmosphere it was understandable that economists would analyze the relation between unemployment and *nominal* rather than *real* wages and would implicitly regard changes in anticipated *nominal* wages as equal to changes in anticipated *real* wages.

So that,

The hypothesis that there is a stable relation between the level of unemployment and the rate of inflation was adopted by the economics profession with alacrity. It filled a gap in Keynes's theoretical structure...In addition, it seemed to provide a reliable tool for economic policy, enabling the economist to inform the policy-maker about the alternatives available to him.

But he said that, as time went on, inflation rose, the inflation–unemployment relationship seemed to disappear or change, and

Many attempts were made to patch up the hypothesis by allowing for special factors such as the strength of trade unions. But experience stubbornly refused to conform to the patched-up versions. (p. 469)

The failure of those patched-up versions was, at the time he spoke—so he said—bringing acceptance that there was no stable tradeoff, meaning that macroeconomic policy could have no durable effect on unemployment.

Whilst I appreciate that the claim that this story is fictitious may at first seem startling, I take it that is not true of the claim that the story is important. It is, after all, a story which is widely repeated—it features in textbooks and lectures, and in brief reports, as well as more elaborate accounts of history. In all these it is treated as a piece of commonly understood wisdom. Sometimes it is the basis of further arguments, sometimes just recited as background. More than this, though, the events described in the story are also treated as a key part of the development of the post-1980 consensus. It is thus a major part of the rejection of Keynesian economics and of the story of the origins of early twenty-first-century policymaking presumptions. As a piece of history—or fake history—then, its importance can hardly be doubted.

In considering something which has become so central to what is believed about macroeconomics, and yet is so misguided, there initially appears to be a dilemma as to whether to try to write an alternative history of the thought of the period, from which it would emerge that the conventional story has no basis; or to address directly the constituent parts of that story, dispensing with each in turn, and hope that a better history emerges from that. A problem with the first course is that it would be an attempt to dismiss the story substantially by ignoring it: the Phillips curve is simply not prominent enough in the economics of the 1960s for that approach to lay bare the extent to which the things subsequently said about it are definitely false. It would also make it very hard to explain the emergence of the conventional story. On the other hand, the second approach is not easy to execute because appreciating what was meant when the Phillips curve and related matters were discussed does involve breaking away completely from the ideas of the conventional story. That is hard to do without something to put in its place.

So, attempting to steer between these difficulties, I proceed as follows. Each of the first four chapters addresses some aspect of the conventional story—first the significance of Phillips (1958); second, the role of Samuelson and Solow (1960); third, the content and objectives of the econometric 'Phillips curve literature' of the 1960s; and fourth that of the 1970s. In those last two cases, the idea of the 'Phillips curve literature' is a broad one, encompassing all the varieties of work that have later been included under that heading and hence many discussions of the relationship between inflation and unemployment (or the lack of it) which the authors did not describe using the language of the 'Phillips curve'. In all four cases the chapter is organized so as to highlight the real concerns and character of the literature in question rather than to revolve around the rebuttal of specific claims about the Phillips curve. But the rebuttals of those claims, when they are taken individually, do, I hope, emerge very clearly.

A summary of the findings about the Phillips curve story emerging from these chapters would be that Phillips' paper ran counter to what was commonly believed, but the finding of a negative relation between wage change and unemployment was not original, and, in any case, his work impressed few. Samuelson and Solow were not advocating inflation, and practically no one thought they were. The idea that they had been highly influential in promoting an inflationist view is a later invention. The econometric Phillips curve literature of the 1960s was hardly influenced by Phillips at all and certainly was not an attempt to refine his work. With few exceptions, the authors concerned showed no hint of believing their work indicated that inflation would be a sensible policy, and the few who were exceptions mostly had sensible reasons for favouring inflation. The expectations argument was very widely known before Friedman or Phelps stated it. There is virtually nothing in the literature of the period to suggest it was ever doubted. To describe the literature of the 1970s as an attempt to 'patch-up' Phillips work is quite mistaken—that objective was almost no part of it since a variety of much more serious objectives were being pursued. And reality was certainly not stubborn enough to make it impossible for the econometricians to find relations to which it conformed. As to inflationism, there is again very little of it although, if anything, there is slightly more after Friedman's (1968) intervention than there was before it.

With the conventional story at least in abeyance, in the first five sections of Chapter 5 I turn to sketching an account of how matters concerning inflation and its relation to other outcomes of interest were viewed. The Phillips curve is more or less absent from this discussion because it was more or less absent from the analysis of the times. These sections serve, I hope, to indicate the actual structure of thinking, to show that the non-econometric literature does not bring the Phillips curve to centre stage, any more than the econometric literature did, and to show how easy it is to understand the coherence of thinking of the 1960s and 1970s without interpreting everything in terms of the Phillips curve. The sixth section of the chapter seeks to identify what was said about the Phillips curve in the non-econometric literature. By emphasizing how little of it there was in the 1960s especially, I hope again to indicate how misleading the usual story is in its grand vision as much as in its specific details. Certain contrasts between the non-econometric 'Phillips curve' of the 1960s and the 1970s do, however, deserve separate attention and these are also discussed.

I am not primarily concerned with policy and policymaking, but accounts of what have been said about it do contribute to my story. Chapter 6 gives a brief account of what occurred, just to sketch how policy can readily be described without recourse to the Phillips curve (or an inflation-unemployment tradeoff under any other name). What is more interesting, though, is the easily identified tendency of the Phillips curve to appear more and more prominently in historical accounts of the policymaking of the 1960s and 1970s as time goes on. Apart from offering general support to my case that the Phillips curve did not greatly feature in contemporary thinking, this also serves to date the appearance of the conventional story fairly accurately.

The picture of changing historical accounts is then part of the background of the discussion in Chapter 7. That concerns how it came about that the story told by Friedman (1977) or others a couple of years earlier, came to be believed. It is slightly speculative, but by this time I hope it will be clear that the Phillips curve story is not correct, and that there must be something to be said about how it gained such credence. Chapter 7 contains my suggestions as to what that might be.

The principal conclusion of this book is, in a sense, the new picture of thinking about inflation and unemployment in the early post-war period that I am able to offer, piece by piece, and most of all in Chapter 5. But there are other things to be said. Chapter 8 begins with a summary account of an alternative history of the Phillips curve, and a few further reasons that story should be preferred to the conventional one. Beyond that, though, there are conclusions about the consequences of the acceptance of the usual story and about seeing the contribution of Friedman in its proper historical perspective, and lessons that might be learned about the development of economics, and perhaps even about the best view of the substance of the relation between inflation and unemployment.

In seeking to make my argument I do refer to a large amount of literature, and at certain points I am aiming to be as near to comprehensive as possible. There are three distinct reasons. One is that I am anxious to make my case. The conventional story is so widely believed, and as I have often discovered in conversation, so firmly believed, that I feel it takes as full a coverage as possible to prove my points. A second is that by presenting a large amount of evidence I can be confident in saying that certain viewpoints were unusual or others were very common, or even that some were, for practical purposes, non-existent. Although some of these are strong claims, I believe they are supported by the data I have, and, as will become apparent, they offer important insights. Thirdly, the wide coverage makes it possible to be sure about some things about which one could otherwise only guess, such as exactly how the expression 'Phillips curve' was used at various times. Fussy as that may seem, it is—so I argue—important in explaining how the conventional story emerged. Still, since there is a large amount of information, I have confined much of it to endnotes, so that the trusting reader, if such there be, may make reasonably rapid progress.

Whilst I have aimed at wide coverage of the literature, there are some specific limitations. I have, with only a couple of exceptions, confined myself to the discussion of fully published works in English. If anyone finds the conventional story alive and well in working papers and other languages, then so be it, and we shall have to discuss the significance of that finding. I also make no motion towards offering my own assessment of the econometric technique of the authors under consideration. Santomero and Seater (1978) and Qin (2011) both do that specifically in relation to the Phillips curve literature, but apart from anything else, such matters are far removed from my objectives. I am sure there is much to be said about the deficiencies of the econometrics of the 1960s and 1970s, but none of it touches on questions such as whether the authors were promoting inflation, or had failed to understand the idea of expectations shifting the Phillips curve, or any of the rest of it. Whatever may be said of the econometrics, the theoretical orientation and the policy ideas of the authors can be assessed without regard to it. Those are the issues I am addressing. A further limitation is that numerous of my brief mentions of works are so far from doing justice to them that it would be possible to be embarrassed to be mentioning them at all. That is, unfortunately, a feature of the facts that there are specific points I am trying to make, and that I am trying to make them by reference to a very wide array of writings. The breadth of literature I am considering is essential, and the narrowness of what I say about many things cited is therefore inevitable.

As to my time frame, I have sought to take the story up to about 1979, with only occasional reference to later developments where they have some relevant connection. That was the year of the election of Prime Minister Margaret Thatcher and the appointment of Paul Volcker as Chairman of the Federal Reserve, and although policymaking is not my main concern those events do also mark a change in outlooks generally. That in itself would make it a natural stopping point, but there is also Lucas and Sargent (1978), in which the authors made their famous denunciation of Keynesianism for having been based on a naïve faith in a simple, exploitable Phillips curve, and of this as having led to what they called 'econometric failure on a grand scale' (p. 57), so that the task for macroeconomics had become that of 'sorting through the wreckage' (p. 49) of the Keynesian era. They have been criticized before, although usually for their lack of moderation or the shallowness of their appreciation of Keynesian theory, rather than for their failure to comprehend the history they were dismissing. In any case, theirs is perhaps the most emphatic landmark in the acceptance of the Phillips curve myth and for that reason marks the end of my principal period of investigation.

In all this there are a few points which should become evident as my account progresses, but which it is probably helpful to make explicit at the beginning. One is that certain ideas which I suppose now are only dimly perceived and in any case regarded as the outcome of muddled thinking, possibly as the inevitable result of verbal reasoning, were once perceived with easily enough clarity to make them useful, and much of the time—so I shall argue—concerned entirely reasonable points. The most important of these is the distinction between cost-push and demand-pull inflation. There are problems in drawing this distinction precisely, as discussed in Chapter 5. But that is no reason to dismiss it since there are problems in drawing a precise distinction between plenty of the ordinary and useful concepts of economics—consumption and investment, capital and labour, monetary and fiscal policy. We find out whether the distinction is useful, not by checking the dictionary, but by applying it to analysis and seeing where it leads. Fellner (1959) captured the point precisely. Noting the difficulty of precise definition he said the 'intuitive content' of the distinction was clear. That is correct: demand-pull inflation is caused by excess aggregate demand; cost-push inflation is caused by the exercise of market power in conditions where demand is not excessive. In the end, these may or may not be helpful ideas, but one cannot understand the attitudes of the 1960s and 1970s to inflation and its relation to unemployment without appreciating their importance then.

Another important point concerns the numerous ways the expression 'Phillips curve' is used. There is not even consistency as to whether it is a relation of wage change or price change to unemployment. (The idea that they amount to the same thing, allowing for productivity change, is a later perception—there are real issues at stake in the earlier literature.) If forced to define it as it has actually been used in the 1960s and 1970s, I would have to offer something like 'a depiction of the general idea that there is a negative relationship between unemployment and either wage or price increase'. Even that does not really cover all the cases since there is an occasional 'positively sloped', or 'horizontal', Phillips curve. But, more importantly, to rely on such a vague definition would conceal the fact that particular authors all had something much more specific in mind when they wrote about 'the Phillips curve'. One cannot offer a *general* assessment of the things said about the Phillips curve because the expression means so many crucially different things.

This ambiguity of usage of 'Phillips curve' joins the lack of clear perception of the character of the difference between cost-push and demand-pull inflation in a way which is certainly part of the problem of unpicking the historical story, but also instructive in appreciating the confusion that has arisen. The relation in Phillips (1958) is between wage change and unemployment and—as I shall argue in Chapter 1, despite some controversy—it is certainly a depiction of demand-pull inflation. But, in the first textbook appearance of the expression 'Phillips curve', which comes in Samuelson (1961a), it is a price-change relation, and the outcome of cost-push forces. In due course Modigliani (1977) said that in Phillips it had been a wage-change relation, but his discussion treated it as important because it described a relationship between price change and unemployment, and he expressed the view that one of the attractive things about it was that it had laid to rest the 'sterile' debate between cost-push and demand-pull inflation. They all have quite different ideas of 'the Phillips curve'.

I can do no better on the question of whether it is a statistical or a theoretical relation. For Phillips, the curve emerged from studying historical data on unemployment and wage change—the curve was a representation of a particular empirical insight. For many others it was a label for an empirical relation of some other kind. But then, for others again it was a name for an assumption made in modelling something. Then there is the issue of whether it is taken to depict a policy tradeoff menu, and if so whether that is a long-run or short-run tradeoff. Yet another issue arises over the direction of causation. Friedman (1975a) said Phillips had made a mistake in treating unemployment as cause when it should be an effect. Well, Friedman had a theory to make inflation the cause of temporarily low unemployment, but that is just one theory. It hardly justifies dismissing the thought that high employment causes wages to rise. That was the theoretical idea behind Phillips' view. But there is no point in asking which is the real Phillips curve. There are numerous empirical relations, and numerous theoretical ideas. In each case they offer competing views, and the application of the label 'Phillips curve' reveals almost nothing about what issues were at stake, whilst introducing a false impression of uniformity of view.

All that helps understand—but only helps—how it could be that when Routh (1959, p. 304) became the first actually to use the expression 'Phillips curve' in print, it was entirely mocking—he thought Phillips' work ridiculous. He stuck with that view—in Routh (1986) he offered one of the more intuitive reactions to econometrics and perhaps also one of the more insightful ones about the Phillips curve, noting that Phillips' scatter diagram looked less like a hyperbola than an ostrich. Next were Samuelson and Solow (1960, p. 186), who conveyed a very different impression with the expression 'Fundamental Phillips Schedule', and later, Johnson (1970, p. 110), who judged it 'the only significant contribution' of Keynesian thinking to the theory of economic policy. But they too all had different ideas of what they were talking about.

Despite the occasional protest over whether 'the Phillips curve' ought to be exclusively a demand-pull relation, none of these issues has been clearly perceived as leading to a problem in understanding what was said—or even as being issues of much importance at all. Even those who have set themselves to write histories of the Phillips curve, or surveys of the literature, have passed over them, as if they were unaware that there was a problem. And they have, thereby, of course, compounded it. Whilst I can identify the problems, I cannot spirit them away. There is nothing for it, but to accept that different authors are writing about different things and there is no point in trying to begin this book with definitions, and certainly not to try to proceed on the basis that there is some Platonic form of the Phillips curve which needs to be identified so that historical truth in the writings about the 1960s and 1970s can be found. Equally, to start with a treatment of previous histories or surveys of the Phillips curve literature would be unavailing. They have added far more confusion than clarity so that when they appear in my account, they are part of it, not alternatives to it.

There is some temptation to think that the work of Phillips (1958) might be similarly relegated to a secondary position. Certainly, it is a great mistake to suppose that the way of understanding what has unfortunately come to be known as 'the Phillips curve literature' is to start with a close study of Phillips (1958). The inclination to start with that work flows primarily from the ideas that Phillips was the discoverer of the negative relation of wage change and unemployment, which he was not; or that he was the inspiration of the econometric literature of the 1960s, which he was not; or that the inflationist attitudes of that decade drew their inspiration from him—but there were no such attitudes. The fact is that Phillips himself, despite a couple of exquisite papers (Phillips 1954, 1957), had practically no influence at all, and Phillips (1958) in particular was a negligible paper. In understanding the development of economic thought, if one were commencing with a clean sheet, Phillips' famous paper would be ignored. On the other hand, in studying the history of what has been said about that Phillips curve literature, the claim that Phillips' paper should be ignored is itself something needing to be established. And so, for my purposes, that is the place to begin.

CHAPTER 1

The Curve of Phillips

One of the great misapprehensions about the Phillips curve literature is the belief that Phillips (1958) either discovered or was instrumental in promoting the idea of a negative relationship between wage or price change and unemployment. That would make 1958 the year in which these enquiries began. In Section 1.1 I argue that the idea was far too well known before Phillips wrote for this to be reasonable, and in any case his presentation of it was widely regarded as poor. What he did do, although it is scarcely noted in the economics literature, is suggest that that relation was much more consistent through time than would have been expected. That gave his work an attraction, for reasons considered in Section 1.2. It also, however, was an idea very much in conflict with prevailing views. Two aspects of those views—the character of the relation of inflation and unemployment, and the theory of wage bargaining—are considered in Sections 1.3 and 1.4, and it becomes apparent that the curve certainly did not fill any gap in prevailing theory, and, for most economists, did not point in an appealing direction at all.

1.1 PHILLIPS' WORK AND ITS RECEPTION

Of all the things authoritatively said about the Phillips curve, the one that is easiest to dismiss is that it offered the first intimation of a negative association between inflation and unemployment. The basic relation was suggested by Hume (1752/1987, p. 286), and continuous statistical relations also pre-date Phillips by decades. Fisher (1926) found such a relation between the change in prices, rather than wages, and unemployment, but Tinbergen (1937, p. 16) commenting on the work of the Netherlands Central Statistical Office (1933), described a similar relation, noting that the main effect on wages was employment about a year earlier.

Fisher's work on this topic for some reason disappeared from view until it was rediscovered—along with various other so-called precursors of Phillips—in the 1970s. Weighty tomes in Dutch were perhaps not widely read, but Tinbergen's discussion of his work was in English, and he also explored Phillips-type relations in English-language publications in 1939 (Tinbergen, 1939, ch. 3.1) and 1951 (Tinbergen, 1951, pp. 49–50). Tinbergen shared the Nobel Memorial Prize for Economics in 1969—the first year it was awarded—so it is hardly credible that the economists of the postwar world knew nothing of his work. In any case, plenty of other people were exploring the same thing before Phillips—Klein (1950) and Klein and Goldberger (1955) both estimated wage equations as functions of unemployment (before Klein, too, won the Prize—in 1980), but it was Colin Clark (1957, p. 181) who, conducting a multi-country study, said that, 'as common sense' would suggest, 'the rate of increase of money wages rises when employment is exceptionally high'. Indeed, it is common sense. Of course people had that idea before Phillips. So it is not only that this idea was not new in 1958, as has, indeed, often been noted,[1] but, more significantly, that there is not the remotest possibility that such an idea would ever have surprised anyone.

It has also been suggested that somehow it was Phillips' particular calculations that were important. He suggested (1958 p. 299) that price stability would be achieved with unemployment 'a little under 2½ per cent' (or about 5½ per cent to stabilize wages, allowing prices to fall as productivity rose). Some have regarded 2½ as very modest—Parkin (1998, p. 1015) goes too far when he says that figure was 'far more favourable' than 'people had dared to expect'—but others certainly found it acceptable, and it was better than the 3 per cent Beveridge (1944) had thought a reasonable target. On the other hand, in Britain, as Blackaby (1976) recounts, during the 1960s such outcomes were certainly thought unsatisfactory, with policy clearly aiming at lower levels, while Stewart (1967/1972, p. 196) thought that at that time nothing worse than an average of 1.5 per cent was politically acceptable. More importantly, though, that sort of numerical estimate of what could be achieved was nothing very new and nothing special either. That again calls into question the impact of Phillips' paper.

Another idea that can be rejected almost as swiftly is that Phillips himself might have felt that he had found evidence for what came to be called an 'exploitable tradeoff' between inflation and unemployment, so that it provided a whole range of policy options, including lower unemployment at higher rates of wage increase and hence inflation. This suggestion is more often hinted at than made overtly, but Chapple (1996) thought both that it was conventional wisdom that this had been Phillips' view and that the conventional wisdom was correct. He argued that in the 1958 paper Phillips had contemplated that the policymaker might aim either at price stability or at wage stability with falling prices—and therefore that he must have felt there were choices to be made; and also that in other writings—notably Phillips (1962)—he had implied that policymakers might accept a persistent inflation. Consequently, says Chapple, Phillips should be understood as having believed the whole range of inflation-unemployment options was available. Then, perhaps, it was his advocacy of this 'tradeoff view' of the curve that distinguished him.

Although that idea fits later accounts of history nicely, there is too much against it. To begin, reliance on the relation of the 1958 paper to Phillips' other work is dangerous. Blyth (1975, p. 306) quotes him as saying 'It was a rush job', and in Blyth (1987, p. 857) glosses this as an admission by Phillips of 'excessive haste' in publishing it. Similarly, Schwier (2000, pp. 24–5) says that Phillips told her the curve was a 'quick and dirty' analysis arising from his 'playing around' with some data, and says that he lost interest in it very quickly. Bollard (2011, p. 7) has Phillips regarding it as 'a wet weekend's work'. Certainly there is precious little suggestion in Phillips' later work that he regarded his 1958 paper of much importance—he hardly refers to it. None of this, then, makes the article sound like an integral part of anybody's life's work.

In any case, it would be puzzling why Phillips—having considered wage stability and price stability as possible options—made no mention of the possibility of policy pursuing inflation. Chapple took the view that Phillips simply had a 'normative policy preference' for price stability. But that just raises further questions—why would someone who believed that unemployment could be materially lowered by a couple of percentage points of inflation have such a preference, and why would he not even consider that the possibility of raising inflation should be mentioned? He would surely have expected other people to think it a good idea. On the other hand, the proposal of a falling price level, which he did consider, would have been easily recognized as an alternative standard of monetary stability. (Although it disappeared from discussion in the 1960s, before being revived by Selgin (1997). Amongst others, Hawtrey (1930) supported it, and his treatment led Keynes (1930b) to call the choice between it and price-level stability a 'vitally important question'. It was considered by Lundberg (1952) and Robertson (1957), and it was presumably under Robertson's influence that it found its way into the First Report of the Council on Prices Productivity and Incomes (1958a, ch. 4, especially para. 109), of which he was a member, just months before Phillips wrote. Most likely, then, it was only the topicality of the idea that led Phillips to include a line on it. In contrast to this possibility of falling prices, there is no indication that he gave any thought at all to inflationary policy, or what would happen if it were pursued. *That* was not a topical idea, and there is no sign it was on Phillips' agenda.

Another possibility might just about be that Phillips noticed that, in addition to the long-term relation of wage change and unemployment, falling unemployment was (up to 1913) associated with points above the curve—that is, wages rising faster than would have been expected on the basis of the curve alone—whereas rising unemployment was associated with slower wage increase. These 'loops' around the curve, as Phillips called them, have attracted an inordinate amount of attention from those writing surveys on the Phillips curve literature, and there has been a certain amount of theorizing about them. But, with the exception of Lipsey (1960), the empirical literature does not particularly associate them with Phillips, although, as will become apparent in Chapter 3, the idea that the rate of change of unemployment is a determinate of wage change has certainly featured. Whatever the interest in this point, the loops can hardly be central to the story—they are not even features of the curve but auxiliary ideas, and it is certainly not the 'Phillips loops' which fill conventional historical or pseudo-historical stories.

Nor was any attraction of the work to be found in Phillips' methods of establishing the existence of the relationship. First, considering only the period 1861 to 1913, he grouped his data points according to the level of unemployment, and took the average rate of wage increase for each group—so, for example, he found that in the years when unemployment was below 2 per cent, the average rate of wage increase was just over 5 per cent; in the various years when unemployment was between 2 per cent and 3 per cent, wages rose on average by a little less than 2 per cent. He constructed six such groups according to the level of unemployment, and the curve was estimated from the six resulting points. The method of fitting the curve perhaps seems peculiar as well: Phillips selected a functional form involving three parameters, estimated two of them by least squares in relation to four of the points, and the third by trial and error to make the curve pass as closely as was possible to the remaining two points. For the period from 1913 to 1957, he performed no estimation at all, but simply compared the raw data points with the curve from the earlier period. Some points were close, and for the others he made ad hoc suggestions as to what made the difference. These were usually based on the then-fashionable line of thinking deployed by Maynard (1955) and Dow (1956) to the effect that import prices were crucial in determining the cost of living and hence wages. The satisfactory identification of such factors led him to conclude that the underlying relation from the period of his actual estimates persisted up to the 1950s.

Desai (1975)—rather later—identified the methodology as a clue that Phillips had in mind a deep theory that made the curve itself a stationary path in a two-variable phase space. Desai himself worked out the rest of the model and as a piece of theory it has attracted some interest, but as Gilbert (1976) noted, Phillips' paper gives no indication at all that Desai's model is what he was thinking about. Gilbert must be right: Desai's interpretation is so different from anything current when Phillips wrote, and so different from anything else that Phillips wrote, it is impossible to believe he would have said nothing at all about it—even if, for some reason, he had stopped short of working out the whole model himself. All told, there are plenty of reasons to reject Desai's interpretation,[2] and in any case, it had no impact on the rest of the Phillips curve literature.

Otherwise, the six-point methodology has mostly been seen either as an obvious weakness, or mysterious curiosity. For Lipsey (1960) it was the former, and a weakness that he wanted to remove. Even in a volume evidently intended to raise Phillips' reputation, Lipsey (2000 p. 236) said that Phillips' attempt to demonstrate his hypothesis was 'rudimentary', whereas he himself had

> applied standard statistical procedures and tested a number of *ad hoc* hypotheses that Phillips had formulated.

Santomero and Seater's 1978 article was a major review of work on the Phillips curve, and surely the most highly regarded one. Further aspects of it will be considered in due course, but its strength is surely the authors' assessment of econometric technique in the literature, and it offered another clutch of statistical complaints. But when the authors came to the six-point approach, they could conceal neither their bafflement nor their wonder, describing it (p. 502) as 'bizarre, though perhaps clever'. Even then they did not seem to think it made the paper in any way remarkable.

It is a curiosity of the whole discussion of Phillips' method that only Wulwick (1989, p. 175) noticed that procedures like Phillips' were—in the days of very limited computing power—often used as a rough-and-ready method, even being included in statistics textbooks of the time, such as that by Allen (1949). Even here, most of the authors concerned were out of touch with the history they were writing, but Lipsey was right—it was not bizarre, not puzzling; simply rudimentary.

The quality of Phillips' data and his handling of it attracted no commendation. Turner (1959) seems to have been doubtful about the value of most available statistics and included Phillips amongst those he feared had been misled by their imperfections. Routh (1959) was very much a sceptic, offering a detailed criticism of the wage data used by Phillips, and added criticism of the unemployment data. He moved on to criticize Phillips' treatment of the data as inconsistent, and argued that had it been consistent it would not have been true that the post-war data lay close to the 1861–1913 curve. He finished with a reassertion of the importance of changing institutions and clearly felt that he had left Phillips' analysis in ruins. Knowles and Winsten (1959) pointed out that inspection of the data revealed that a very large range of wage outcomes were compatible with various unemployment rates, so the relation could certainly not be expected to be reliable. They were particularly critical (p. 119) of Phillips' failure to take price changes properly into account, and his failure to recognize the importance of 'wage drift'—the tendency of actual wages paid to deviate from agreed rates. His neglect of these things, they said, gave him 'the handicap of appearing something of an anachronism' (p. 120). Similarly, Colin Clark (1960), notwithstanding his earlier comment on the common sense of the general idea, said 'The apparent demonstration' (p. 287) of Phillips' claim, was an illusion created by his choice of data sources. All in all, there was a great deal of hostility to Phillips' work.[3]

The same sort of worries appear in Lipsey (1960). That paper was itself a very significant one which, like Phillips', found a negative relationship between wage change and unemployment, but offered more detailed theoretical analysis, standard econometric technique, and much greater care. It is sometimes regarded as the true origin of the 'Phillips curve literature' and considering its careful attention to all the matters immediately at hand—both theoretical and econometric—it is easy to see why. Still, well disposed as he was to Phillips' idea, Lipsey can hardly be said to have approved his methods, since he drew attention to a number of further specific failings, including (p. 5) noting the remarkable point that at one place Phillips substituted one data series for another just because it achieved a better fit for the hypothesis.

Other early criticisms presaged later arguments: Kaldor (1959a) thought Phillips' idea wrong and dangerous. In his opinion, Phillips should have considered profit as a variable explaining wages: if policymakers were to take Phillips' advice they would find that demand policy would prevent inflation only if it lowered profit, and if it did that it would damage growth.

Griffin (1962) said that Phillips' data fell into two blocks—the pre-war data where there was no support for the theory, and the post-war period where unemployment had been consistently low, but wages increases had been between 2 and 11 per cent per year. And so, he said, rather than look for a single curve it would be better to accept that the two periods were different and, in particular,

> [W]ages in the more recent historical periods appear to be insensitive to changes in the level of unemployment. The 'Phillips curves' shift systematically as percentage unemployment is reduced. (p. 381)

That, in fact, was easy to see from the data, if one were inclined to look at it that way. Griffin went on to investigate the existence of a similar relation in post-war American data. He too used what must be admitted to be a rather basic econometric technique but formed the view that there was no useful relationship and, in particular, that his data did not allow him to say what level of unemployment would stop wages rising. And he ended up by suggesting that incomes policy had a better chance of controlling inflation than did unemployment, in both Britain and America. Later assessments, when they really focused on Phillips' work rather than subsequent developments, were no more charitable. In the same volume as Lipsey (2000), Klein (2000, p. 290) noted his 'loose and very approximate reasoning', and Holt (2000, p. 309) called Phillips' paper 'conspicuously sloppy'. Sleeman (2011), noting these sorts of problems, is led to worry over why Phillips even allowed it to be published.

All this does, then, raise the question of what it was about Phillips' work that was thought interesting. It is apparent that there was some interest in the paper since Yamey (2000, p. 336) tells of how, as editor of *Economica* at the time, he accepted Phillips' paper within a day of submission, and even rearranged the forthcoming issue to make it the lead article. Lipsey (1997, p. xix)—who saw the draft version—reported recalling his astonishment at the speed of the process, saying that after considering the paper over a weekend, he brought his copy to Phillips 'bestrewn with comments'—only to be told he was too late, because the paper was already in proof. And in later treatments, again and again it is simply presumed that Phillips' work was special and important, and authors set about its examination with the idea of discovering why. Again, of all the surveys and historical treatments in this vein.[4] Santomero and Seater's is most notable. Determined that Phillips should be the inspiration of the literature, but unable to see why, they ask why it was that his 'competitors and their insights were ignored at the time' (Santomero and Seater 1978, p. 500). The simple answer to that is that Phillips' so-called competitors and their insights were not ignored at the time. It was Phillips who was disparaged immediately and later, while others were much more highly regarded. Still, Santomero and Seater offer three suggestions: that it was only Phillips who drew the 'eye-catching' curve; that Phillips' work appeared just before two other wage-change equations—those of Dicks-Mireaux and Dow (1959) and Klein and Ball (1959); and that it was Phillips who had his work picked up and developed in what they quite understandably called the 'brilliant' paper by Lipsey (1960).

The first will hardly do—even if pictures did make the man Brown (1955, p. 99–103) had already presented scatter graphs and a discussion, and Sultan (1957, p. 555) had drawn a curve showing a theoretical relation between price change and unemployment. Actually, as noted by Lipsey (1978), Phillips (1954) had drawn a similar curve—but Santomero and Seater mention none of them. If the drawing of the graph was such a breakthrough, that is not easy to explain. As to the second point, once it is appreciated that the negative relationship was so well known, it is difficult to see that a few months' difference between these particular papers matters much. Here Santomero and Seater are surely misled by their presumption of Phillips' originality since they nowhere mention Hume, Tinbergen, anything by Klein before 1959, or any of those identified as Phillips' precursors in endnote 1. If the fact that Phillips was a matter of months ahead of Dicks-Mireaux and Dow (1959) and Klein and Ball (1959) makes a difference, what of Klein and Goldberger (1955) and Tinbergen (1937)? Just as they were by Santomero and Seater, they have tended to be ignored in the later literature. But what would explain that?

The third suggestion is one of more interest. Lipsey's 1960 paper was one that impressed. Both the paper itself and Lipsey's later comments show that he was very much inspired to write it by reading Phillips' paper. But as an answer to Santomero and Seater's question this takes us only so far. The further issue would have to be why it was that Lipsey chose Phillips' paper as his starting point. From all those on offer, why choose the one that was quick and dirty, rudimentary, conspicuously sloppy, of loose and approximate reasoning, based on impaired and incompatible data, written in a wet weekend, and rushed prematurely into print?

1.2 POPPERIANISM, 1958

A line of thinking that leads to the best answer was identified by de Marchi (1988a). He argued that at the end of the 1950s, a group of particularly talented, young economists at the London School of Economics and Political

Science—Lipsey notable amongst them—became attracted to the scientific methodology based on what came to be called 'falsificationism', embodied in Popper (1959), but which they learnt slightly earlier. Science advances, according to the picture in question, by the framing of bold hypotheses, and subjecting them to severe tests. Theories took their value from the survival of sincere attempts to reject them. They remained mere conjectures in that at any moment some further test might disprove them. Progress was made, so long as hypotheses for testing were well designed, by devising new hypotheses which explained what the earlier ones explained, but survived more attempts at refutation.

The attraction of this, suggests de Marchi, lay in its contrast with and possibility of escaping the aprioristic approach of Robbins (1932/1984). The quest was probably hopeless, and as de Marchi's argument develops it concerns principally the eventual failure of a fairly thoroughgoing Popperianism to provide a satisfactory methodology. Nevertheless, we can appreciate the attraction of the general line of thinking to Lipsey and his colleagues.

Robbins' approach maintained that economics advanced by drawing inferences from indisputable facts of experience, but that because of the infinite variety and changeability of circumstances could never hope to establish universal laws. He created (Robbins, pp. 108–9) a character called 'Blank', who convinced himself the elasticity of demand for herring was 1.3. How becoming it would be to have such results, thought Robbins, since it would put economics on a level with other sciences. But, he continued, the demand for herring,

is not a simple derivative of needs. It is, as it were, a function of a great many apparently independent variables. It is a function of fashion; and by fashion is meant something more than the ephemeral results of an Eat British Herrings campaign; the demand for herrings might be substantially changed by a change in the theological views of the economic subjects entering the market. It is a function of the availability of other foods. It is a function of the quantity and quality of the population. It is a function of the distribution of income within the community and of changes in the volume of money. Transport changes will alter the area of demand for herrings. Discoveries in the art of cooking may change their relative desirability. Is it possible reasonably to suppose that coefficients derived from the observation of a particular herring market at a particular time and place have any *permanent* significance—save as Economic History?

It is a good question, as well as a fine blast against econometrics. Economics was made kin to geometry with a coherent body of maxims, many, admittedly, with a clearly apparent application to practical questions, but could never match physics in the development of tested laws of motion. The frustration that this outlook could engender should be clear. The organization of logical relations and the taxonomy of cases with no means to tell which pertain is hardly a recipe for effective policy; and even if one knew the direction in which one wished to travel, Robbins' approach offers no opportunity to determine how far to go.

It might also be noted that the works of Snow (1956, 1959) were very widely read and discussed, and despite inducing the unintentionally comic fury of Leavis (1962) were often highly regarded. Although ostensibly deploring the partitioning of learning, the weight of Snow's pieces was really on evangelizing for Salvation by Science. Much of the argument was concerned with the plight of the developing world, and Snow seemed to think that science and technology would rescue it from poverty; but it is not hard to see that economics might play a role, and the general sense he conveyed of science being the means to betterment must have encouraged some to want to be scientists—or, if they were already something else, to have that profession join the sciences. Again, a frustration with Robbins' view would be easy to understand.

Nevertheless, some degree of caution about the exact role of Popper's approach is in order. It is far from clear that the LSE economists ever appreciated the details of it. Just how he should be interpreted and applied to economics are substantial issues,[5] and as Popper's 1959 work was largely concerned with the devising of hypotheses for testing it is hard to see what Lipsey and his colleagues took from that. The approach was, in any case, intended to distinguish 'science' from pseudo-science, not from exercises in logic. Astrology, psychoanalysis, and vulgar versions of Marxism were Popper's paradigmatic targets, and their common weakness lay in the fact that whatever happened could always be explained away—nothing was ever disproven. Robbins was not presenting propositions of economics like that. And in any case, since the tests of ideas in economics were only ever statistical, a definite refutation was not really to be expected.

What is clear, though, is that the general idea of a 'falsificationist' approach became part of the outlook of Lipsey and others. It is visible all through Lipsey (1960) and Lipsey and Steuer (1961). And, as de Marchi says, the same thing is more than evident in his textbook—(Lipsey 1963)—and in Lipsey's (1964) commentary on it. Certainly, the general point that Lipsey was anxious to see economics develop as an empirical science, seems perfectly clear. Equally, it is clear that such a development would be at variance with Robbins' approach, as Lipsey clearly intended it to be.[6]

Indeed, this possibility—of making economics into an empirical science—was directly addressed by Lipsey (1962) in one of his less well-known papers, called 'Can there be a valid theory of wages?' It is clear enough what he was trying to achieve since, in explaining his approach, the echoes of Blank's problem could hardly be more distinct or more obviously deliberate. Lipsey said that if one were to seek to predict wage bargains in a particular year,

> we find not only individual behaviour which is difficult to predict, but also changing institutional circumstances so that, even if wage negotiations should show stable reactions to things like the level of unemployment in, say, the 1890s, we would hardly expect it to show the same reactions in the 1930s, let alone the 1950s. Surely the rise of unions and employers' organizations, the change in the level of negotiations (from the plant to the nation-wide bargain) and the increasing concern of government through such means as compulsory arbitration must mean that wages react to given circumstances in a very different way now than they did in the past. Thus, it is argued, each historical period is unique and we cannot hope to get a theory applying to more than a few years at a time. (p. 106)

And the answer to this, as he put it—and one notes the two appearances of the word 'stable'—is that the

> question about the possibility of finding stable, hence predictable, patterns of human behaviour in the economic sphere must be sought from empirical data…We therefore frame the working hypotheses that group human behaviour shows stable patterns and that these patterns do not change in response to institutional variations. We then test this hypothesis against the data…(p. 106)

And so to Phillips.

The striking thing about Phillips' work is the length of the period he analysed—from 1861 to 1957—and the point that he found the *same* wage change – unemployment relationship prevailed. He allowed minor variations in the relationship—such as what he seems to have taken to be the temporary effect of the pay freeze achieved by Chancellor of the Exchequer Stafford Cripps in 1948. But his central story was that the laws of the labour market were unchanged over that very long period.

None of those usually cited as Phillips' predecessors considered anything near 100 years; and Phillips' results could hardly be less concordant with the fate that Robbins anticipated for Blank. The crucial thing was that if Phillips were correct, it would mean wages remained unaffected by much more even than Lipsey mentioned—none of the political, social, institutional, or technological change brought by two world wars, the creation of the welfare state, the spread of unionism, and the universal franchise would have had an effect. Even memories of the Depression, so often thought to have had such a formative impact on the post-war world, apparently had no effect on wage bargaining. In the period from the invention of the bicycle to the flight of the Sputnik, wage bargaining remained unchanged. Even the acceptance of Keynesian economics itself, according to Phillips' curve, did not affect the impact of unemployment on wage bargaining. The world of *Great Expectations* and that of 'You've never had it so good' shared the same labour market laws.[7]

This was a remarkable claim—a bold hypothesis. It might well be doubted whether Phillips' paper, with its all-too-evident flaws, really subjected his idea to a severe test, but it is not too much to say that he gave an indication that there might be something in it. It was an idea much more than it was a proof; and the idea was not a triviality about wages going up when employment was high, nor anything as silly as making a case for continuous inflation, but a suggestion that there might be a discoverable law of motion in the economic universe. Nothing was settled by it; but something important was suggested. And if it were properly tested, and if it did survive those tests, that would be something. It would be, indeed, the beginning of a new kind of economic science. It is easy enough to see why that would be of interest, and why Lipsey or Yamey might have been excited by it; and indeed why it might even warrant a quick acceptance and the reordering of a journal issue to give it prominence.

1.3 THE 'L-SHAPED' AGGREGATE SUPPLY CURVE

That was the point of Phillips' paper, but it was not just a striking claim that might excite the young. In its historical context, it was also a shocking claim, which flew in the face of standard theory. That is because, whereas to say that the *idea* of a negative relation of wage change and employment was nothing new, that is not to say that such a thing was accepted, and certainly not that a high degree of regularity in such a relation would seem plausible. The point has been lost because of discussions of the Phillips curve which so routinely present it as a clear and substantial advance over previous understandings of the Keynesian system.

For example, as Friedman (1971/1974, pp. 31–2) put it—in an expression later often used—the Phillips curve provided the 'missing equation' to link output and prices. Lipsey (1978) developed the point at more length, referring particularly to Phillips (1954). He said that Phillips' great interest was in the theory and estimation of models of short-run macroeconomic stabilization, and that,

> When he began his work in the early fifties the prevailing macroeconomic model with which he was presented was one that made a strict dichotomy between behaviour at full employment and behaviour at less than full employment: at less than full employment, the price level was fixed and disturbances to the system affected only real variables (real income and employment in particular); at full employment, real variables were fixed and expansionary disturbances to the system affected only monetary variables (the price level in particular). Phillips wrote down the relation that subsequently became famous as the 'Phillips curve' and built it into his early models in order to remove this dichotomy. It was obvious to him that any disturbance to the system had both real and monetary effects in the short term. (p. 49)

Although this sort of thing is widely believed, it should be apparent that something is seriously wrong. For one thing, it is simply unarguable that in terms of writing down an equation to split the impact of disturbances into real and monetary effects, Phillips contributed nothing. Neither his empirical nor theoretical work contributed an original idea at that level, nor a significant methodology, nor empirical results that were better regarded than others: Tinbergen and Klein, to name just two, were there before him. But more than this, Lipsey's proposition would appear to be that, for something like two decades after *The General Theory*, Keynesian economics lacked an essential component that no one was able to supply, and when it was supplied, it turned out to be as simple as the idea that demand disturbances have both price and quantity effects. Can anyone really believe that?

Lipsey has, I suggest, misstated the point about the 'strict dichotomy', and his remarks do not reflect the real character of what is sometimes called the theory of the (reverse) 'L-shaped aggregate supply curve'. Certainly it would have been agreed that excess demand—that is, demand greater than supply capacity at full employment—would cause inflation. But at lower levels of demand, the point was not that prices were fixed, but that there was no determinate link between them and demand. Viewed thus it encapsulates the idea that all the while there is unemployment due to a deficiency of demand, an increase in demand results in a fall in unemployment and an increase in output, with that relationship entailing nothing about price change. Or a fall in demand would result in a fall in employment, again with nothing needing to be said about prices or wages. That was no one's idea of the literal truth, but it captured something that was seen to be an essential—namely that output and employment were demand determined—whilst treating other aspects as inessentials. That is, after all, the kind of basis on which much theory is accepted.[8]

Two kinds of detail might be highlighted at this point although both will be more fully discussed later. One would be that at high levels of employment, and particularly when employment rose, various factors might cause an increase in prices even though full employment had not been reached. For example, specific shortages ('bottlenecks' as they were called) might result in temporary price rises in certain sectors; or a decline in the marginal product of labour might mean the price level was higher at full employment than at lower levels of employment. Bach (1941) discussed the first point, and Keynes (1936) both of them. There was no 'strict dichotomy' but merely the view that for some purposes such things would be ignored.

A different sort of issue was raised by the possibility that the actions of trade unions or producers with pricing power might affect the price level independently of the level of employment. There ended up being various versions of this idea, a sample of which are considered in Chapter 5, but the main idea in the simple, early versions was that if policy offered a guarantee of full employment, that would empower and incite trade unions to seek large wage increases. Some thought the full employment policy was deeply flawed just because of this. At that extreme was Viner (1936, p. 149)—no friend of Keynesianism, of course—who disparaged Keynes' proposals as promoting a 'race between the printing press and the business agents of the trade unions'; and in Viner (1950, p. 391) he criticized the thoroughly Keynesian proposals of Clark et al. (1949) saying, in terms obviously pre-dating the worst of the post-war inflation,

> The sixty-four-dollar question with respect to the relations between inflation and full-employment policy is what to do if a policy to guarantee full employment leads to chronic upward pressure on money wages through the operation of collective bargaining. The authors take a good look at the question—and run away.

Other economists took a variety of different views. A few economists—perhaps most notably Friedman (1951)—denied that unions had much power to raise average wages at all and more—Clark (1948) and Chamberlin (1951) would be two—thought that the danger could be controlled by limiting unions' power and special rights. On the other hand, others were simply more optimistic about the behaviour of unions. Robinson (1937) hoped for responsible trade unionism, Beveridge (1944) thought it could be encouraged by price control, and Hansen (1947, p. 246) even thought that the commitment to full employment would itself induce responsible behaviour, in contrast to the irresponsibility that naturally arose when policymakers disregarded the level of employment.

What distinguished these views (except Friedman's) was that they differed about the likely or possible attitudes of unions—not about any strictly economic forces. The optimists hoped that unions would see wage moderation as in their own interest, so that the full employment policy would be consistent with price stability. The pessimists saw no such hope. The same sort of thing could be said about attitudes to industrial pricing. It may be that in retrospect the optimists seem to have been naïve, although arguments have been made—by Eichengreen (1996), for example—that amount to saying they were, up to a point, correct. The first point, though, is that—like it or not—it was this combination of views which underlay the hope that full employment and price stability could be achieved, as well as the recognition that there were significant difficulties with that plan, albeit difficulties that were not of a strictly economic kind.

A second point is that, whereas the concerns over union behaviour were initially focused on the consequences of full employment, or of guarantees of full employment, there could be similar concerns about lower levels of employment. Once it is accepted that organized labour might have the power to raise wages or prices and thereby confront the policymaker with the choice of inflation or higher unemployment, there is no reason to think that power exists only at full employment. So wages might rise even when there is less than full employment. In due course, that concern developed into the idea of 'cost-push' inflation, on which there would be many variations, but at least up to the 1970s the predominant lines of thinking preserved the sense of the cost increases being substantially independent of the level of employment. Unions might, of course, refrain from raising wages, or employers might resist them, at moderate levels of unemployment; or they might not. Equally, they might so refrain at full employment. So the occurrence of cost-push inflation would, at least as an approximation, be substantially independent of the level of employment.

What emerges, then, is that the L-shaped theory is a depiction of the unconnectedness of inflation and unemployment. It is not, as Lipsey seems to suggest, a primitive way of presenting a connection, later to be improved by the discovery of the Phillips curve. Nor is it an idea that was accepted because no one had the brains to devise a non-linear relation. Nor was it ever supposed that the price level could not change at less than full employment. Rather, it was a proposition about the exogeneity of nominal wages and prices to the level of employment. The argument was that there was no essential reason wages should change because of variations in demand and, just as importantly, that they might change without such variations. Wages and prices were no more *fixed* in that model than technology was fixed in Solow (1956).

It is a strange thing, it might be said, to have a theory to describe the fact that two things are not related. But there is an easy response to that. It is that there was, in the 1950s, barely such a thing as 'the L-shaped aggregate supply curve'. That terminology is almost exclusively a later invention. It dates from the era when the Phillips curve was treated as a standard approach, and looking back on the 1950s the question was asked as to what economists had before they had the Phillips curve.[9] Indeed, the theory of the 1940s and 1950s had no need of a 'curve' of any shape to link inflation and unemployment. They were simply seen as separate problems.

1.4 THEORY OF WAGES, 1958

All this might seem to suggest that there was something of a vacuum in the area of the theory of wage determination. That is not correct, and this point is important in order both to appreciate the sense of the L-shaped supply curve and the development of the Phillips curve literature considered in Chapter 3.

The issue of wage determination was intensively explored in an empirical literature that pre-dated *The General Theory* and continued on very much the same lines long after it. Certainly the authors of that literature tended to reject comprehensive treatments of the issue. Lester (1941) was particularly emphatic about this, but most of the leaders of the field in that period agreed broadly with his view: none of the old theories—from subsistence theory, to the wages fund approach, and on to the marginal product theory—could explain wage determination. The last of these—the only one with any real currency in the 1940s and 1950s—was the theory that was most firmly rejected by students of wage bargaining. Lester ridiculed it, almost abusively, and later—in a 1946 article—started the general attack on marginalism that led to his famous clash with Machlup and Stigler, later surveyed by Lee (1984). Dunlop (1957/1966)—a cooler head perhaps, and certainly someone generally better disposed to economic theory of a conventional type— made it clear that there had been a phase of history when the marginal productivity theory of wages had been adopted, but interest in it had declined as it proved inadequate, and a better approach was required.

And Samuelson (1951, p. 312)—hardly someone inclined to dismiss theory—said,

> I fear that when the economic theorist turns to the general problem of wage determination and labor economics, his voice becomes muted and his speech halting. If he is honest with himself, he must confess to a tremendous amount of uncertainty and self-doubt concerning even the most basic and elementary parts of the subject.

He went on to survey various theories, finding none of them satisfactory. That was a widely shared view.[10]

In view of this failure of such theory, the approach to wage determination that was adopted was, as summarized by Lester (1952, p. 485), an exploration of the middle ground between

> the narrowly based traditional theory and the all-inclusive confusion of the German historical school or the American institutionalists.

and that

> Any theoretical formulation that allows for multiple motivation and includes numerous economic, psychological, political, social, and institutional factors must necessarily be eclectic and unprecise, devoid of simple solutions and subject to zones of indeterminacy. (p. 485)

That idea—of there being indeterminacy in wage bargaining—appears again and again in the literature of the time. Economic theory could set some limits to what wages might be agreed, but within those limits it was a matter of bargaining.

Just what that means is another thing that can be hard to grasp from the perspective of modern theory, although Usher (2012) has surely seen the point, saying that understanding bargaining requires an assessment not just of self-interest but also of compromise. 'Compromise' is then not just another way of talking about self-interest, and social, political, institutional, and psychological forces are not merely masks for the imprecision of reasoning about rational action—they are the fundamental determinants of decisions. In this view, the full analysis of rational behaviour led to indeterminacy, and other 'non-rational'—or non-economic, anyway—considerations had to resolve it. To this approach Nash (1950)—the beginning of game theoretic approaches to bargaining—and its progeny had nothing to offer (and went unnoticed by the labour economists). Such theoretical ideas as those were neither the starting point nor any staging post on the road to understanding how negotiation worked. The bargain to be struck was, as it were, a *genuine* bargain, a human bargain, not something ever to be discovered by the mathematician. The whole process, one might say, is in part 'volitional', rather than purely 'mechanical' as it would be in conventional economic theory.

On precisely this point Samuelson can be quoted again, this time from the third edition of his textbook—(1955). This, let it be recalled, was the volume that introduced the 'neoclassical synthesis' with the effect that, as he put it, closely following Keynes (1936, pp. 378–9), of course,

> mastery of the modern analysis of income determination genuinely validates the basic classical pricing principles. (Samuelson 1955, p. 360)

Yet even in a work with that orientation, he accepted indeterminacy of the wage, saying that the result of collective bargaining,

> depends on psychology, politics, and a thousand other intangible factors. As far as the economist is concerned, the final outcome is in principle indeterminate— almost as indeterminate as the haggling between two millionaires over the price to be paid for a rare oil painting. (p. 547)

In this context, research focused on conducting a large number of studies of actual wage determination. Some of these, perhaps, were tarnished by overemphasizing the limitations of marginal productivity theory, but constructive results did emerge. In particular, again and again some conception of the fairness of the wage emerged as being important in the reaching of an agreement, and there three things stood out as relevant: changes in the cost of living, the profitability of the employer, and the relative position of different groups of workers.

One striking finding, which was often treated as furthering the rejection of the marginal product theory of wages, was that there could be a wide range of wages paid for the same job by different employers, even when all allowance was made for the skills of workers, non-wage benefits, and the like. Kerr (1950) noted this very clearly. Reynolds (1951), for example, left no doubt about the general salience of fairness, and noted (p. 99) the particular importance of adjustments of wages to compensate for changes in the cost of living. No one questioned that that was an important part of wage bargaining. Slichter (1950/1961) pointed to the role of profits and the importance simply of management policy in wage determination. Dunlop (1947) noted that certain 'key bargains' could establish a norm which would then readily be followed in other bargains, since the maintenance of relativities was one of the characteristics of a fair bargain. In his works of 1948 and 1957/1966 he developed this into the idea of 'wage contours' whereby workers in different occupations could see their wages as rightfully linked, while Ross (1948, p. 71), introduced the idea of what he called an 'orbit of coercive comparison' whereby the moral force of wage comparisons with other workers would affect bargained outcomes. In due course it became widely believed that these sorts of things led to the occurrence of 'wage rounds' whereby one wage increase could spark others and lead to a general movement.

So Hicks (1955)—someone else who was hardly afraid of theory—was in good company and only stating what was widely understood when he said,

> It has never been the general rule that wage-rates have been determined simply and solely by supply and demand. Even on pure grounds of efficiency, it is desirable that the wage which is offered should be acceptable, acceptable both to the worker himself and to those with whom he is to work. There has in consequence always been room for wages to be influenced by non-economic forces—whether by custom...or by any other principle which affects what the parties to the wage-bargain think to be *just* or *right*. Economic forces do affect wages, but only when they are strong enough to overcome these *social* forces. (p. 390)

And in due course (p. 394) he listed the cost of living, differentials between groups of workers, and the profitability of the employer as three natural considerations. Those ideas were to go out of fashion in mainstream economics, although their merits have sometimes been rediscovered.[11] But the important point is that these were the ideas motivating wage theory at the time of Phillips' curve.

One consequence of this kind of thinking is that it makes it easy to see the case for incomes policy (or prices and incomes policy). Later treatments have tended to regard prices and incomes policy as attempts to overrule market forces, and therefore as basically foolish. Schuettinger (1978, p. 25) offers a clear and robust example. He started his analysis with ancient Sumer saying,

> For the past forty-six centuries (at least) governments all over the world have tried to fix wages and prices from time to time. When their efforts failed, as they usually did, governments then put the blame on the wickedness and dishonesty of their subjects, rather than upon the ineffectiveness of the official policy. The same tendencies remain today.

He then gave an account of the breakdown and failure of a whole succession of such policies, treating those of the modern world as late instances of the same mistakes.

Such responses miss the point since if, as was the case, wages are understood to be determined by a broad range of factors so that bargaining is a matter of decision and agreement and only at the periphery of market forces, then all forms of persuasion, including setting an agreed standard of fairness, co-ordinating actions on a fair outcome, influencing expectations, or perhaps even providing a clear standard of compliance, incomes policy obviously included, might have a role.

On the other hand, unemployment was seen to have little impact on wage determination. Dunlop (1944, ch. 4) went further than most in suggesting that trade unions might be treated as seeking to maximize the wage bill. Ross (1948) disputed that, and the so-called Dunlop–Ross debate became something of a cause célèbre of the time, with Reder (1952) noting that at his time of writing there had already been a considerable number of contributions. Most economists probably sided with Dunlop but the points Ross was making were accepted as having force. But even this was a debate about the employment of those in a particular union, not the general level of employment—a consideration that received even less attention. Reynolds (1951, p. 231) said,

> The level of unemployment has nothing directly to do with the time at which wage increase begin or with the speed of the advance.

It is because all this was part of the understanding of the time that one of the leaders of a subsequent generation of labour economists, Freeman (1988, p. 219) could say,

> I vividly remember John Dunlop pounding the table against the Phillips curve in a graduate labor economics course: he, Reynolds, Kerr, Lester, and others who based their assessment on firsthand knowledge of wage setting came away with a very different picture of the role of unemployment than that given by 1960s macroeconomists enamored of the Phillips curve.

In these ideas, then, we can see a source of hostility to the Phillips curve. In this aspect, the importance of Phillips' work in 1958 was the challenge it presented to a vision of macroeconomics. Phillips questioned the prevailing wisdom on wage determination precisely because he made it a matter of supply and demand, and invariant to institutional change. This is indeed apparent from the opening lines of his paper. He said:

When the demand for a commodity or service is high relatively to the supply of it we expect the price to rise, the rate of rise being greater the greater the excess demand. Conversely when the demand is low relatively to the supply we expect the price to fall, the rate of fall being greater the greater the deficiency of demand. It seems plausible that this principle should operate as one of the factors determining the rate of change of money wage rates, which are the price of labour services.

Those words have later been seen as thoroughly unadventurous, or even facile, but they were anything but that. His point was that the established view of wage determination was incorrect and there was nothing in all the work of the labour economists because the labour market was just like any other. The laws of wage change had remained the same for 100 years, so labour was nothing special at all. The macroeconomics of wage change, in Phillips' revolutionary claim, owed nothing to the special status of labour, to psychology or social forces, or indeterminacy and fairness. Wages worked just like everything else—according to supply and demand.

Wage-change equations like those of Tinbergen or Klein would certainly not have been accepted by the labour economists but nor, because of their short data sets, did they imply that all matters of social relations must be irrelevant. So Phillips' suggestion offered not only a way for economics to take a step towards a scientific status in the manner sought by Lipsey; but also threatened to reveal that wage determination owed nothing to its apparent human aspect. A great many deeply held views about wage bargaining would have to be abandoned. Indeed, many people would have had to change their vision of economics.

There is more than this, even. If Phillips were right, or even approximately right, it would have meant that wage bargaining was subject to economic law, and hence the achievability of full employment with price stability was at the pleasure of that writ. It was not, if Phillips was right, a matter of the attitudes of unions or the politics of industrial relations. It was either possible or it was not. That, clearly, would have been another great blow to established thinking.

1.5 CONCLUSION

But Phillips, of course, was wrong. One does not need to adjudicate the criticisms of his data and approach that were made by his many detractors. Even Lipsey (1960, p. 25), although he may have emphasized his positive finding of Phillips-type relations, noted that they were different in different periods. Not many of those following Phillips even investigated the possibility of the same relation holding over a long period, but of four who did, only one found it. Bhatia (1961), using twentieth-century American data, found the 'relationship has varied from one period to another'; France (1962), starting in 1890, found that unionization made wages less sensitive to business conditions, and Bowen and Berry (1963. p. 165) specifically divided the 1900–58 period into three 'to facilitate historical comparisons', and found the coefficients different in each of the periods, observing that this would not surprise those who emphasized institutional changes. Only Bodkin (1966), using American data for 1899 to 1957, felt he had found such a relationship (but he made no test of the effect of considering sub-periods).

In any case, very soon the econometric literature lost any understanding of the importance of the unique aspect of Phillips' work. The idea of an enduring relation—a relation that was stable through institutional change—ceased to be part of what was being investigated. It might very well be said, therefore, that the story of *the curve of Phillips* ends here. It was a bold hypothesis indeed, and a deep challenge to the presumptions of the time. But it was quickly rejected, and once rejected had no further influence on the development of economics. It was implausible, wrong, and forgotten. On the other hand, the story of 'the Phillips curve' has hardly begun.

CHAPTER 2

The Role of Samuelson and Solow, *American Economic Review* 1960

Samuelson and Solow (1960) have frequently been cited as the first advocates of the view that the Phillips curve suggested that inflationary policy could lower unemployment, and been held responsible for leading the general opinion of economists in that direction. Neither of these claims stands up to scrutiny. I begin this chapter by arguing that, from reading the paper itself, it is clear that they did not believe the relation to be stable and, although there might be some doubts, in the end it is also clear that they did not advocate inflationary policy. Then, however, I consider several later discussions of the paper by Solow, which make it clear that there was no inflationary intent—although others have quoted his later work (and the original paper) in ways which give a different impression. One notable point is how little Solow refers to the original article at all (and Samuelson even less). As I show in Section 2.3, he does not appear to have regarded it as the path-breaking paper it is supposed to be (or terribly important in any other way). A different sort of point emerges in Section 2.4 from an extensive study of commentary on Samuelson and Solow's article before about 1977. I consider a large number of discussions and comments about the paper, and it appears that none of their contemporaries took an inflationist message from it. However one reads the paper itself, the lesson its early readers learned was not what the usual story says. On the other hand, in Section 2.5, I consider later comments on their paper. Again, from a large sample it is clear that they have an interestingly, and mysteriously different, colouring. The weight of evidence is important to substantiate these claims but also turns out to pay further dividends in Chapters 7 and 8.

2.1 DID SAMUELSON AND SOLOW ADVOCATE INFLATION?

It can hardly be doubted that Samuelson and Solow (1960) is important in the continuing story of the Phillips curve, since the authors are so often said to be the source of the idea that the curve offered a stable schedule of policy options. When that claim is made, it is often also claimed that they advocated a policy of inflation in preference to accepting the level of unemployment necessary to stop it. And hence they are, in this view, the parents of the Phillips curve inflationism of the 1960s and 1970s.

For example, Frisch (1977, p. 1293) (and similarly Frisch, 1983) drew a diagram with a Phillips curve and a community indifference curve supposedly showing society's preferences between inflation and unemployment, and claimed that Samuelson and Solow 'propagated the Phillips curve as an instrument of economic policy' and that,

> According to their suggestions, a trade-off exists between the rates of inflation and unemployment, so that the government has the possibility of choosing alternative points on the Phillips curve with alternative rates of inflation and unemployment.

Leeson (1997b) offers another example of this kind of thing. Although at some points in his paper he notes numerous doubts about this expressed by Samuelson and Solow, in his summary of his own argument, no qualifications are mentioned when he says,

> Samuelson and Solow believed that they had uncovered evidence that suggested that tolerable and stable rates of inflation were associated with high employment. (p. 145)

Similarly, Sargent (1999),

> In 1960, Paul Samuelson and Robert Solow found a Phillips curve in the U.S. time series for inflation and unemployment. They taught that the Phillips curve was exploitable and urged raising inflation to reduce unemployment. Within a decade, Samuelson and Solow's recommendation was endorsed by many macroeconomists and implemented by policy makers. (pp. 2–3)

Despite the impression all this sort of thing might create, there is simply no argument that Samuelson and Solow felt they had discovered a curve which was 'stable' either in the sense that made Phillips' idea so interesting, or in the sense that policy could be set on the basis that the curve would not shift.

Samuelson and Solow's was a conference paper presented as part of a discussion of the 'Problem of achieving and maintaining a stable price level', and their own title was 'Analytical aspects of anti-inflation policy'. It would be strange to find them advocating inflation. They ranged widely over theories of inflation and in due course presented a scatter diagram of inflation and unemployment—with little information about what data they had used—and drew by visual estimation a relation pertaining to the recent past. They noted that what made Phillips' paper interesting was the long period it covered, and used the expression 'Fundamental Phillips schedule', but it is also clear that their use of his name owes nothing to his particular idea of a long-enduring relation, since they say, of the United States,

> There may be no such relation for this country (p. 817)

And later, in connection with a close scrutiny of the data,

> What is most interesting is the strong suggestion that the relation, such as it is, has shifted upward slightly but noticeably in the forties and fifties. (p. 189)

That this was the 'most interesting' point is itself not something to be ignored, but the fact that they had the curve shifting (if it existed at all) meant they could be listed with Routh (1959), Griffin (1962), and the rest, as people rejecting the key point of Phillips' study. Certainly, it is impossible, reasonably, to treat them as taking the view that the curve is stable, whatever later commentators believe or say.

Samuelson and Solow did point to policy alternatives, presenting a diagram captioned as displaying a 'menu of choice' and saying,

> Our own view will by now have become evident. When we translate the Phillips' diagram showing the American pattern of wage increase against the degree of unemployment into a related diagram showing the different levels of unemployment that would be 'needed' for each degree of price level change, we come out with guesses like the following:
> 1. In order to have wages increase at no more than the 2½ per cent per annum characteristic of our productivity growth, the American economy would seem on the basis of twentieth-century and postwar experience to have to undergo

something like 5 to 6% of the civilian labor force's being unemployed. That much unemployment would appear to be the cost of price stability in the years immediately ahead.

2. In order to achieve the nonperfectionist's goal of high enough output to give us no more than 3% unemployment, the price index might have to rise by as much as 4 to 5% per year. That much price rise would seem to be the necessary cost of high employment and production in the years immediately ahead. (Samuelson and Solow 1960, p. 192)

Whilst they offer no adjudication, they do go on to suggest (p. 193) that the likely outcome of the 'tug-of-war' of politics will result in something in between the two. After this they emphasized—again—that these 'guesses' related only to the 'next few years'. Then they suggested a whole range of ways in which policy might move the curve, such as, for example, that a low-demand policy might either improve the tradeoff by affecting expectations, or worsen it by generating greater structural unemployment. Then, considering an even longer run, they suggest that a low-demand policy might improve the efficiency of allocation and thereby speed growth, or, rather more graphically, that the result might be that it 'produced class warfare and social conflict and depress the level of research and technical progress' (p. 193) with the result that the rate of growth would fall. None of these ideas were terribly original in themselves and some of their antecedents and developments will be considered in Chapter 5, but if, in virtue of being the last point, the dangers of a low-demand policy has a slight emphasis, then that is the nearest the authors come to advocating expansionary policy, and even that relates to achieving growth not to reducing unemployment per se.

But before Samuelson and Solow are convicted of being the source of Phillips curve inflationism, even on these slender grounds, there is another point. When they read off possibilities from their 'menu' there was no indication as to which policy they preferred—the presentation of the two policies is perfectly balanced, even down to the repetition of 'in the years immediately ahead'. It was only after this, when they discussed the range of possible longer-term considerations—those that they thought might move the curve—that even a hint of favouring expansion arose.

So when they said in the discussion of the data that the 'most interesting' thing was that the relation had shifted upwards in the 1940s and 1950s, what they must have had in mind was that what goes up might also come down; and their expansionist case rests heavily on that possibility. It is not merely that Samuelson and Solow did not think the curve stable, but much more than this—and quite contrary to the later stories—it is the possibility of its moving that must be the crucial finding if they are to be construed as proposing any particular policy.

2.2 SAMUELSON AND SOLOW'S REAL OBJECTIVES

None of this, though, even approaches the heart of the concerns of Samuelson and Solow's paper. As argued in Chapter 1, the macroeconomic theory of times—the 'L-shape theory' as it was later labelled—invited the idea that, with sufficiently good control, there was no fundamental impediment to the simultaneous achievement of full employment and price stability. Whether in fact it was going to be possible to achieve that outcome with any consistency was, of course, another matter, and in the late 1950s, it was not easy to tell.

One simple reason was that there was little useful data. Only the post-war period could be relevant in the assessment of peacetime Keynesianism. That period was short in itself, but the period of reconversion up to 1948 or so was easily recognized as atypical, whatever the exact explanation of the high rates of inflation that briefly prevailed. Then the Korean War (1950–3) clouded the picture further—there was clearly an excess of demand arising from military expenditure and perhaps purchases by the private sector in anticipation of price rises or shortages. But there were also price controls, so nothing very decisive could be learned about the free-market system from that period.

On the other hand, some things could be said. The worst fears of Viner—the race between the business agents of the trade unions and the printing press—had not been borne out; but nor had there been the high level of employment and price stability for which some had hoped. In America, that latter point became particularly clear after the period 1955 to 1957. Then, there was continuous, albeit very modest, inflation, despite unemployment not being low. It was possible to see that as evidence that 'full employment' left more people out of work than had been expected, but this was by no means the only reaction. Another was to say that demand was deficient—hence the high unemployment—but that something else caused the inflation.

There were many explanations of what that other cause might be. In so far as these are remembered at all they tend to be distinguished as a group from the conventional theory by the label 'cost-push' theories of inflation. At the time, however, more emphasis was placed on the variety of explanations. Bowen (1960a) was having a bit of fun when he said,

> It is no longer fashionable to speak simply of 'inflation'; instead, one must specify whether he means 'cost inflation', 'demand inflation', 'excess-demand inflation', 'wage inflation', 'money inflation', 'structural inflation', 'log-rolling inflation', 'buyers' inflation', 'sellers' inflation', 'mark-up inflation', 'administered price inflation', and so on. (p. 199)

But Samuelson and Solow were perfectly earnest when they said that economists had been debating the merits of

> demand-pull versus cost-push; wage-push versus more general Lerner 'seller's inflation'; and the new Charles Schultze theory of 'demand shift' inflation. (1960, p. 177)

So there were many theories, and not much data, few key facts, and one important question. That question was whether full employment and price stability, or, as it was sometimes put, whether full employment, price stability, and an absence of wage and price control, were compatible in the America of those times? This is the environment in which Samuelson and Solow wrote.

Their response was first (1960, pp. 182–5) to say that there was no a priori basis to favour one explanation of inflation over another, and that the possibilities would be hard to distinguish using historical data. They contemplated (p. 191) an experimental reduction of demand, saying that if a small reduction stopped inflation, it would suggest it had been due to excess demand, but if it took a large one, it would suggest it had not. Such an experiment, they noted, would be very dangerous.

It is after having reached the conclusion that it is hard to tell which of the explanations of inflation is correct, but having considered the scatter diagram of inflation-unemployment combinations in the American economy, that Samuelson and Solow make the remarks quoted earlier in this chapter—'Our own view will by now have become evident...'. What has become evident is not, as the quotation above and other remarks by Leeson, suggest,[1] that their view is that they have discovered that satisfactorily low inflation yields an improvement in employment. Rather, it is that they could not readily distinguish the various sorts of inflation but that, nevertheless, inflation could be seen to have happened, and the relationship between it and the level of unemployment could be roughly quantified. That quantification was quite overtly applied only to the circumstances of the time and was intended to characterize the extent of the problem at least as much as to offer choices about it. Samuelson and

Solow's conclusion, therefore, was not an optimistic one about how little inflation was required to achieve full employment, but the pessimistic one that there was a serious difficulty in achieving full employment and price stability at the same time. And then their paper ends, unsurprisingly, with an expression of hope that something can be done to rectify the situation.

2.3 SOLOW'S LATER COMMENTS

An interesting aspect of the later life of this article is that Solow made a number of further, fairly extensive comments about it—and, as it happens, these provide further evidence that later commentators have misconstrued the intentions of Samuelson and Solow. Certainly, if one is predisposed to the inflationist interpretation even the title of Solow (1978)—'Down the Phillips curve with gun and camera'—might give that impression. And the fact that there Solow says, 'Any time seems to be the right time for reflections on the Phillips curve' (1978, p. 4) suggests an all-pervasiveness of the curve in his thinking which is not otherwise evident. Reading the whole paper, it is clear that both the title and the remark are intended to be light-hearted, and the actual content of the article is mainly a discussion of the role of expectations and the question of how one might respond to Friedman's (1968a) argument about them. The 1960 paper by Samuelson and Solow is described as having offered a 'guess' which turned out to be reasonably accurate for a few years, and suggests that that is all that should be expected. That period—a few years after 1960—saw expansion without rising inflation, so even here there is no suggestion that they had proposed inflationist policy.

Another comment which has been quoted—in this case, more than once—more or less for the purpose of suggesting Samuelson and Solow had inflationist ideas comes from Solow (1979a). Discussing the development of their work, Solow said,

> I remember that Paul Samuelson asked me when we were looking at those diagrams for the first time, 'Does that look like a reversible relation to you?' What he meant was 'Do you really think the economy can move back and forth along a curve like that?' And I answered 'Yeah, I'm inclined to believe it' and Paul said 'Me too.' And thereby hangs a tale. (p. 38)

When just those words are quoted in the context of an argument that Samuelson and Solow took an inflationist position, it might not be immediately apparent that it is clear in the Solow paper that the diagrams originally under discussion were those from Phillips (1958), not Samuelson and Solow's 1960 paper—and indeed there seems to have been little acknowledgment of that amongst those using the quotation.[2]

It certainly would not be clear that Solow immediately drew the contrast between this and the American data, which he said did not reveal stability of the curve. He went on to say that, for the post-war years, he and Samuelson had found something that looked like a Phillips curve, labelled it as a menu, and that its relation performed reasonably well for a period 'given that we only intended this as a schematic thing, not the result of formal statistical work' (p. 39), but that after that the relation changed. He could have added that they specifically said,

> It would be overhasty to conclude that the relation we have been discussing represents a reversible supply curve for labor along which an aggregate demand curve slides. (Samuelson and Solow 1960, p. 189)

As the 1979 paper then develops, Solow describes (again) his scepticism about literal-minded versions of the expectations hypothesis, and offers a number of ideas about the causes of inflation at less than full employment and the relation of inflation to unemployment in the post-war period. There is no further reference to Samuelson and Solow (1960).

Solow's 1979 article is from the alumni magazine of the Massachusetts Institute of Technology and is obviously intended to be informative and entertaining for an intelligent, non-expert audience. It also shows signs of being quickly written, and there is nothing surprising in the fact that it contains the occasional offhand remark like that at the end of the quoted conversation with Samuelson. The discussion of the 1960 Samuelson and Solow paper is very brief, and in so far as there is any discussion of whether the authors thought the curve stable, it clearly says they did not. Reading the whole piece, it is difficult to see what specifically Solow had in mind as being the 'tale', but it was certainly not to say that this paper was the origin of Phillips curve inflationism.

Another point is that the importance of Samuelson and Solow's paper in Solow's mind is questionable—as it seems to have been in Samuelson's.[3] Solow (1962) was a discussion of the need for expansionary policy, and was published shortly after the author left the staff of the Council of Economic Advisers; Solow (1964a) was a deeper discussion of the causes of unemployment at the time, but was still very much concerned with the practicalities of policy; while Solow (1973) was written in a similar vein with regard to later developments, and also gave a retrospective treatment of the early 1960s. None of these papers mentions either the Phillips curve or Samuelson and Solow (1960). Obviously, if Solow had thought that they had, as Leeson claimed, 'uncovered evidence that suggested that tolerable and stable rates of inflation were associated with high employment', he would have referred to it. Solow (1964b) does discuss the Phillips curve, and there he said that if demand restriction had its main effect on employment and output rather than inflation 'policy faces a nasty dilemma' (p. 151), and that it was yet to be seen whether institutional change could resolve it—but even there he makes no mention of Samuelson and Solow (1960). Solow (1968) does refer to that paper (p. 4), but only to say that he and Samuelson had discussed the cost-push–demand-pull debate, and that he does not want to go into the details again. Solow (1975) refers to it briefly to quote its price-stability level of unemployment, before embarking on a discussion of issues around the tradeoff that go well beyond what was said in the 1960 paper.

There is no discussion of the paper in Klamer (1984), but in Solow's later conversation in Snowdon and Vane (1999), there is. There, Solow explains that he and Samuelson had been attracted to Phillips' work because of the long run of data it dealt with, but had found that there was not the same stability in the American data. The authors were, says Solow, 'just curious', and in considering American economy in the 1950s they felt it provided 'some help in understanding slow inflation' (1999, pp. 284–5). That sounds about right for a conference paper. Solow also noted that he and Samuelson had been aware that there was an issue about expectations, and he specifically rejected the picture painted by Leeson (1997b), part of which was quoted above.

A further point emerges from Solow (1988/2005). There he again notes how cautious the paper was, but also reports that Assar Lindbeck had said to him that, notwithstanding the qualifications, it was written in a tone which was too optimistic, and it was this that led to its being so influential in promoting inflationary policy. To this, Solow seems to assent, saying, 'I had to admit the justice of that observation' (1988/2005, p. 166). Perhaps he had this conversation in mind when he wrote Solow (2002). That paper was specifically a retrospective view on Samuelson and Solow (1960)—it is a notable point that the latter was, by that time, thought worth such a treatment. Solow again points to the numerous nuances of the discussion, but says that the expansionist inclinations of the authors are visible and that they were later proven to have been too optimistic. All that may be true.[4] But what of Lindbeck's view that the paper had the effect of encouraging inflationist attitudes?

2.4 RESPONSES TO SAMUELSON AND SOLOW

There is, therefore, another question about what message was taken from Samuelson and Solow's 1960 paper. In part that turns on appreciating the point from Section 1.3: that the hope of achieving both price stability *and* full employment was perfectly real. Then, it becomes apparent that substantial point made by their paper was that it appeared that these hopes were, in fact, going to be disappointed. Their illustration of the existence of the Phillips curve was, therefore, a problem, not an opportunity. Thus, for example, Hansen (1960, p. 4), who noted Samuelson and Solow's results, although he considered them 'tentative', said:

> It may be doubted, however, that we can achieve both a satisfactory level of employment and price stability without major improvements in our anti-inflation weapons.

and drew from this the conclusion that

> We are suffering from the serious delusion that there is a harmony of interest between the various goals we seek.

Hansen's views on what explained that problem and what should be done about it raise further questions, but it is clear that the message he took from Samuelson and Solow was that the problem existed; several others also referred specifically to them as authorities for the same point.[5] Another group of authors were not far from that position in being impressed by Samuelson and Solow's arguments for the possibility of the existence of cost-push inflation. As Kindleberger (1967, p. 217) put it, they 'dispose of the a priori belief that wage push is impossible', and the same point was made elsewhere.[6]

Those who cite Samuelson and Solow specifically as authorities for the view that the Phillips curve or the American Phillips curve was *unstable* comprise a large and interesting group. For example, Bronfenbrenner and Holzman (1963) was, for a long time, the authoritative survey of the theory of inflation. The authors say that Samuelson and Solow's paper is the best-known study of the American 'Phillips curve' and that they found the curve had shifted in the post-war period (p. 620)—and that is all they say about it. Shonfield (1967, p. 436) said that Samuelson and Solow constructed a Phillips curve for the United States and showed that 'there is no long-term stability of the curve', and suggested that the explanation for this was that the expectation of high employment had made employers more willing to grant wage increases. And Kuh (1960, p. 333)—who was not an enthusiast for Phillips' argument—went even further than this and, rightly or wrongly, attributed to Samuelson and Solow a 'candid exposé' in the form of 'a scatter diagram indicating no relation for the aggregative data'. Again, there were plenty of others who saw Samuelson and Solow's work like this.[7]

Others from this period could just about be understood as reading Samuelson and Solow's paper as suggesting the existence of a stable trade-off, but respond to them by rejecting that view. There might be those who even think Samuelson and Solow were proposing inflationary policy, but they certainly reject that idea. Either way it can hardly be the case that these instances show that Samuelson and Solow were the source of the belief in a stable tradeoff. For example, Chandler (1960, p. 213) and Lerner (1960, p. 217)—both conference comments on Samuelson and Solow—made the point that if one did try to lower unemployment with inflation, the required inflation rate would not be stable. There, they were specu-lating more broadly and not really criticizing Samuelson and Solow, who had made the same point. Beyond that, neither showed any sign of believ-ing that proposing inflationary policy was an objective of Samuelson and Solow's paper. Chandler noted the caution they had used in advancing their 'guesstimates' as to possible policy outcomes, and Lerner remarked that the most interesting thing in their paper was the discussion of the difficulty in empirical distinction of cost and demand inflation. He also said (1960, p. 216) they 'questioned' the view that high output cannot be maintained if accompanied by inflation, although exactly what direction his think-ing took is perhaps not clear, at least from that piece.[8] Scott and McKean (1964), citing Samuelson and Solow, said the Phillips curve described 'the relationship between rates of inflation and rates of unemployment, and each point on the curve represents a combination of these two rates that policy makers might choose' (p. 1). They suggest that Samuelson and Solow 'apologize' for inflation on this basis, but their own piece is thoroughly anti-inflationary (because inflation was associated with growth).

A variety of miscellaneous comments on Samuelson and Solow's paper can also be found in the 1960s. But many of them are not really discussing the inflation problem at all, and none give any sustenance to the view that the authors were believed, by the economists of that decade, to see a stable Phillips curve, or if they did, that this was accepted as making a case for inflation.[9]

Whilst it is hardly likely—well, it is hardly even imaginable—that my catalogue of those citing Samuelson and Solow (1960) up to about 1968 is complete, it does not appear that there is *any* author in that period who could be said to have adopted the idea that inflation is beneficial because of Samuelson and Solow's paper, nor any who could be said to have found in the article inspiration for inflationist policy. Most see the authors as propounding the instability of the Phillips curve, or of describing the requirements of anti-inflationary policy, or simply pointing to a problem; or, if they are seen as suggesting inflationary policy, the authors in question reject that proposal. The nearest to finding an inflationist message in the paper which he is prepared to accept may be—strange to say—Phillips (1962). In a passage which clearly presumed that policy would not be set to stabilize the price index, he referred to Samuelson and Solow's estimates as if they might guide American policy. But he also said that he thought those estimates were too optimistic and further noted that they depended on the assumption of the 'continuation of the conditions of the post-war period', so even he was not really treating their curve as stable. Whatever Samuelson and Solow meant, the idea that they were the inspiration of inflationism seems definitely to be a fiction.

2.5 LATER COMMENTS ON THEIR PAPER

But a little later, the principal themes of the literature started to change. One thing, which might perhaps seem just to be an oddity, is that Samuelson and Solow's paper became frequently cited for the reason that, whereas Phillips' work had been about wage change, they described specifically a relation of price change and unemployment. Gray (1968, p. 58, n. 1) may have been the first to emphasize this, citing it as the source for a 'derivation' of a 'modified Phillips curve' of this kind. And Smyth (1971, p. 426, n. 1) picked the paper out as his sole example supporting the claim that 'The Phillips curve has been widely interpreted as providing a relationship between the rate of inflation and unemployment.' The point that Samuelson and Solow applied Phillips' name to an inflation relation receives no emphasis in the earlier period, but in the later one became commonplace, and persistent.[10] Peston (1971) stands out from this group because he is critical of Samuelson and Solow over the same point, observing that they were amongst the first to 'take the two dangerous steps' (n. 15) of drawing a smooth Phillips curve without a scatter of points, and to draw it as a price-change relation.

Perhaps there is also—in the early 1970s—a slightly greater tendency to see Samuelson and Solow as propounding a tradeoff. But by no means all the authors concerned accept that idea themselves. Ian Hume (1970, p. 241) uses the term 'trade off', citing Samuelson and Solow, and says that with the Phillips curve it is 'supposedly possible to find the degree of deflation of demand...which...would be consistent with any particular rate of wage-caused inflation.' He is clearly sceptical about it himself, as the word 'supposedly' reveals, but in any case, after a brief consideration of arguments, he says, 'so the use of the Phillips Curve as a basis for anti-inflation policy prescriptions can be misleading' (p. 241). There is no indication that he thinks it might be used as a basis for pro-inflation policy prescriptions— his point, along the lines of the L-shape theory, is that he doubts the power of unemployment to stop inflation. Lohani and Thompson (1971) say that Samuelson and Solow suggest the possibility of trading-off inflation and unemployment. They immediately deny such a possibility, pointing to the importance of changing expectations.

Rothschild (1971) said that Samuelson and Solow considered a relationship between price change and unemployment, and said,

> after the publication of Phillips' article Samuelson and Solow (1960) carried his analysis fully into the sphere of inflation policy. They shifted the Phillips curve to a price change-unemployment diagram . . . and named this construct a 'menu of choice' for policy decisions. Since then the 'trade-off' question has been continuously discussed in general and quantitative terms. (p. 270)

Similarly, Goldstein (1972), in a substantial review of the Phillips curve literature which has been much less noted than Santomero and Seater's, reported some of Samuelson and Solow's guesses about possible policy choices and described these as applying to 'the postwar period', but did not report any of the words of caution or indicate the emphasis given to 'the years immediately ahead' (p. 653). On the other hand, he did note that they found the curve to have shifted and did not say they suggested any particular policy. Rothschild and Goldstein both give some impression of being willing to tolerate inflation themselves, and the reasons for that deserve further attention (in Chapter 5), but they give Samuelson and Solow no decisive role in forming those views.

It is later still that the idea emerges that Samuelson and Solow had been instrumental in convincing economists generally of the exploitability of the tradeoff. Almost simultaneously with Frisch (1977), Nobay and Johnson (1977, p. 479)—giving an historical account of the debate over monetarism, identifying the Phillips curve as the 'missing equation' in the Keynesian system, and clearly presuming it underlay inflationary policy—said that it

> gained widespread acceptance as the 'trade off' between prices and unemployment through its use in this respect by Paul A Samuelson and Robert Solow.

They say no more about the role of the Phillips curve, who specifically is supposed to have followed Samuelson and Solow in this view, nor the views of Samuelson and Solow themselves. But they do try to acquit Phillips of any misunderstanding of the relation between real and nominal wages, and thereby clearly suggest that Samuelson and Solow and those who (supposedly) followed them were wanting in that area. Perhaps it is a coincidence that this happens in the same year that Buchanan and Wagner (1977, p. 89) asserted that the Phillips curve depicted the policy possibilities, that it was a political matter to determine policy preference, and that this way of looking at it was 'initiated' by Samuelson and Solow.

In later work, the accusation against Samuelson and Solow became much clearer. Feldstein (1981) noted that Samuelson and Solow did point to instability, but emphasized their role in making the Phillips curve a 'basic tool of policy analysis in the 1960's', with the result that 'many economists and politicians concluded that it made good sense to accept a permanently higher inflation rate' (p. 160). Bordo and Schwartz (1983, p. 68) similarly claimed that their work led to inflationary policy but in two other respects went further than most, saying

> Phillips (1958), Samuelson and Solow (1960), and Lipsey (1960) reported evidence of a stable inverse relationship for the U.K., the U.S., and other countries...

The inclusion of 'other countries' seems to be unique, but the emphasis on finding a stable relation is interesting because it is the exact opposite of so many earlier readings, and yet became something greatly emphasized about the work of Samuelson and Solow. Plenty of others from around this period see them as presenting a stable or exploitable curve.[11]

By the time of Humphrey (1985) the idea that Samuelson and Solow's paper was the origin of Phillips curve inflationism must have been fairly well established, because he noted what he took to be the importance of

> the Samuelson-Solow interpretation of Phillips' curve as a menu of policy from which the authorities could select the best (or least undesirable) inflation-unemployment combination and then use their policy instruments to attain it. (Humphrey 1985, p. 24)

Similarly, Haberler (1985) discussed Samuelson and Solow's paper, including their notes of caution, but nevertheless said,

> I think enough has been said to justify the conclusion that the paper by Samuelson and Solow illustrates my point that Keynesian economics is characterized by unconcern about the dangers of inflation and neglect of inflationary expectations. (p. 31)

There are plenty of other examples of this kind of thing being confidently assumed.[12]

Another development that becomes visible a little later is that whereas the first to say that Samuelson and Solow believed in an exploitable Phillips curve were advocates of the vertical Phillips curve view, in due course post-Keynesians adopted this view. Harcourt (1992, p. 7) said American Keynesians in the 1960s were grossly overconfident and 'It was Samuelson and Solow who said society could dine a la carte on any combination of inflation and unemployment they wished to choose.' (His main point is that the Phillips curve is not to be found in Keynes' *General Theory*.) Corry (1995, p. 367) said they popularized it 'as a trade-off curve'. Best and Widmaier (2006) said that Samuelson and Solow thought the Phillips relationship exploitable and clearly thought they played some role in diverting thinking from proper post-Keynesian lines.

While this view was developing, it should be noted there were also plenty who continued to see Samuelson and Solow as pointing to the existence of a dilemma, or as noting the instability of the curve, or as describing various causes of inflation, or some variation, accurate or inaccurate, on one of these ideas. As a consequence, what they said tended to be unexceptionable. Laidler (2003) is specifically and pointedly critical of Sargent (1999), noting the ineffectiveness of his footnoted equivocations to the passage quoted above in Section 2.1.[13] Backhouse (1985, p. 340), showing much more appreciation of their intent than most, says Samuelson and Solow examined the implications of the Phillips curve for *anti*-inflationary policy. There are plenty of other examples of later comments on the paper which, through being accurate, are unexciting.[14] Others make a variety of miscellaneous remarks about it with no bearing at all on the issue of the tradeoff or inflationary policy.[15] And, again like the earlier period, there is a collection of confused and incorrect claims about the paper, some of which are more like tomfoolery than anything else.[16]

A couple of new themes stand out in the later period as worthy of comment. One is that there are those who have evidently noticed that Samuelson and Solow did not propound a stable Phillips curve, yet were persuaded that the economists of the 1960s had treated them as if they did. Thus Haldane and Quah (1999, p. 1) note Samuelson and Solow's caution over their results, but nevertheless convey the point, without much discussion, that others took an inflationist message from them. Ormerod (1994, p. 120) similarly feels they concluded there was a stable relation, but notes their caution and gives more emphasis to their effect on others' thinking.

And there are also, in perhaps an unexpected way, those who do indeed see in Samuelson and Solow's paper the origins of the idea of a stable tradeoff, but who approve. They are not the mainstream economists of the 1960s, as yet unenlightened by Friedman and Phelps. They are of the 1990s and after, and are specifically denying that the Phillips curve is vertical because, as they would have it, the data rejects that proposition. They look to Samuelson and Solow not quite as those who taught them this message, but as distant precursors of their own work. Thus Colombo and Weinrich (2003, p. 1) say that Samuelson and Solow 'essentially confirmed' Phillips' findings for the USA and although they obviously believe that Phillips thought the curve exploitable, they offer an argument to the effect that he might have been correct. Lundborg and Sacklen (2006) and Graham and Snower (2008) are arguing for the possibility of a long-run tradeoff and so give Samuelson and Solow *credit* for believing the same.

But, as time went on, in the part of the literature which had come to see Samuelson and Solow as the source of damaging, inflationist policy proposals, that view came to be stated more briefly, with the confidence of routine, and sometimes in more exaggerated forms. So James Galbraith (1997, p. 96) remarked that in 1968 mainstream economists were committed to 'Samuelson and Solow's version' of the Phillips curve. He says nothing about what that was—presumably because he thought it apparent—and this claim is simply adopted by Snowdon and Vane (1999, p. 31), who show no recognition of the possibility that Samuelson and Solow might be anything but inflationists, and immediately move to try to acquit Phillips of the same error. Jossa and Musella (1998) seek specifically to consider the evolution of debate on the Phillips curve, but clearly make Samuelson and Solow the origin of Phillips curve tradeoffism (p. 21). (They also say (p. 19) that Samuelson and Solow were the first to suggest that the Phillips curve could throw light on the relation between inflation and unemployment, which is strange because Phillips (1958) had already done that.) Kirshner (2001, p. 43) said, 'In the early 1960s, most Keynesian economists argued that governments could reduce unemployment indefinitely if they were willing to tolerate a higher rate of inflation', citing Samuelson and Solow as the only reference in support of this claim. Nelson (2004, p. 135) said, without further justification, 'In his academic work, Paul Samuelson was jointly responsible for the proposition that there was a permanent trade-off between unemployment and inflation in the US (Samuelson and Solow, 1960).' Barnett (2004/2007, p. 145), quoting the New School for Social Research website with approval, claimed the paper to be justly famous for presenting the Phillips curve 'to the world', which apart from anything else, seems rather to belittle *Economica*.

Even Jonas Fisher (2008)—writing a New Palgrave entry on the Phillips curve—said that Samuelson and Solow 'were bold enough to posit a stable

and exploitable structural relationship between unemployment and inflation'. And one final step, perhaps due to the growth in confidence of
this view, is that one group of papers—by Cogley and Sargent (2005a),
Cogley, Colacito, and Sargent (2007), and Sargent (2008)—simply use 'the
Samuelson–Solow model' as a tag for an exploitable Phillips curve, with,
one might feel, no more concern for historical authenticity than Samuelson
and Solow themselves had in their use of the expression 'Phillips curve'.

2.6 CONCLUSION

So Samuelson and Solow's role in this story is not quite what has been supposed. They did not say the curve was stable, and they did not really advocate inflationary policy; but if they did, it flowed from the instability, not
the stability, of the curve. They appreciated that the interesting thing about
Phillips' paper was the length of the time period he considered, but their
own findings have no resemblance to that: their analysis owes nothing to
his, and their use of the expression 'Fundamental Phillips schedule' finds
no motivation in the paper—they have some casually assembled data, and
a serious point of concern, but no argument that the curve is fundamental.

Most remarkable, surely, is the point that although some have tried to
paint things otherwise, Samuelson and Solow certainly did not convince
anyone else of the desirability of inflationary policy on the basis of a stable
Phillips curve, because before about 1970 there was no one who took such
a lesson from them. It is not, as might have been supposed, that although
they did not advocate inflation, they were misread as having done so, and
others followed what they thought was their lead. On the contrary, whatever it was that they were advocating, no one both thought they took an
inflationist view and agreed with them. The economists Samuelson and
Solow are supposed to have influenced saw in their paper the possibility
or actuality of cost-push inflation, the instability, or non-existence of the
American Phillips curve, or learned from them a list of reasons to expect
it to move; or if they thought Samuelson and Solow treated the curve as
exploitable, they simply rejected their argument.

It is later—well into the 1970s, when the idea of an exploitable relation
had been raised and widely rejected—that things change. But it is still not
the case that anyone takes an inflationist message from Samuelson and
Solow. It is just that they come to believe that others previously had. It
would have been hard to anticipate such a twist, but this famous paper by
Samuelson and Solow is a substantial part of the Phillips curve story *only*
because it is part of the Phillips curve myth.

CHAPTER 3

The Phillips Curve Literature before Friedman's Presidential Address

In the conventional story of the Phillips curve, the period before Friedman (1968a)—his Presidential Address to the American Economic Association—saw a profession not alert to the importance of price change (or expected price change) in wage bargaining, and therefore convinced that there were substantial issues to be explored in the questions of the shape and location of the inflation-unemployment tradeoff, and the optimal point on it. Nothing of the kind happened. One key to appreciating the point, considered in Section 3.1, is to see what the 'Phillips curve' literature was really about—that is, understanding wage change. In the course of that, it incidentally becomes apparent how little that literature owed to Phillips, confirming his lack of impact on contemporary thinking. A second point, considered in Section 3.2 is that despite attempts to argue to the contrary, it is not even true that price change was neglected. Section 3.3 then identifies such inflationism as there was, and Section 3.4 considers what sorts of rates of inflation were involved. There was some inflationism and, as Section 3.5 explains, in the thinking of the times it was perfectly well justified, in a way that is resilient to the expectations argument. Again, the weight of evidence, particularly in Sections 3.1 and 3.5, is important in making the case that Phillips curve inflationism really was as limited and, such as it was, as well justified as I say.

3.1 THE ORIGINS OF THE ECONOMETRIC PHILLIPS CURVE LITERATURE

Surely one of the things that makes it so easy to believe that econometric studies of the Phillips curve in the 1960s were basically inflationist in their intent is the difficulty in seeing what else they might have been about. If we take the most highly regarded and certainly most noted of the surveys from the scores of 'Phillips curve' papers—Santomero and Seater (1978)— they give no indication of anything else having been at stake. Certainly, their repute owes something to their analysis of econometric methods, but they set their objectives much more widely than that, saying they aim to

> outline the development of the Phillips curve literature from its inception in 1958 to the present,

and to lead the reader through

> the maze of evidence and the manifold advances in the state of knowledge. (p. 500)

In the end they consider about two hundred papers in this 'Phillips curve literature', but by the time they have discussed only the work of Phillips (1958) and Lipsey (1960), they say,

> It seemed established that there was a negative relation between wage inflation and unemployment. The policy implications of this finding were both important and clear. If such a negative relation exists then there is a trade-off between infla- tion and unemployment. If a social welfare function could be chosen, then it would be possible to choose and attain an optimal point on the Phillips curve. (p. 502)

It is on that basis that they proceed, but it is already clear that, for them, there is hardly even a single stride between the existence of a curve and the case for inflation. The same obviously held true for Friedman (1977), as quoted in the Introduction, and there does not appear to be any survey of the literature which presents an alternative vision to this.

One crucial aspect of many such stories is that they suppose the intellec- tual source of the problem to be an inadequate treatment of price change— the recrudescence of the age-old confusion of the real and nominal, as Friedman had it; in Santomero and Seater the failure to understand the importance of expectations.

The real story of the early Phillips curve literature is nothing like this. It is true enough that there are changes in the literature after Friedman (1968a), and even if they are not quite the ones of the usual story, the signs of Friedman's influence are fairly clear. But starting with the literature before then, or just after but uninfluenced by him, three crucial things stand out.

First, there is hardly any interest in calculating an optimal point on a tradeoff relation. For another, the treatment of price change was, most of the time, perfectly adequate to the authors' actual objectives; and amongst the more weighty papers this was almost always the case. But the first mistake in the conventional story, its biggest mistake, and surely the one from which the others flow, is this fixed and unreflective idea that the 'Phillips curve literature' begins—has its inception—with Phillips.

Rather, when the econometric studies of wage change proliferated as they did, coincidentally in about 1958, they drew their inspiration from the ideas about wage bargaining of the 1950s, discussed in Section 1.4. Their aim was to bring econometric treatment to those ideas, and their central objective was the same as that literature—to understand wage determination. That was the scientific question which they addressed.

The importance of profits in wage setting—a staple of that literature—was confirmed by Levinson (1960) in cross-sectional analysis; and he also noted the role of 'wage rounds' whereby bargains agreed in some industries influenced those in others. Eckstein and Wilson (1962) picked up these ideas and developed the idea that certain key bargains influenced others, potentially resulting in general inflation. They came to the conclusion (p. 388) that wage change could not be understood without an appreciation of the role of key groups and wage rounds; and then argued that unemployment and profit had important roles in determining wages for the key group. As noted in Section 1.4, the ideas of 'key bargains' and 'wage rounds' themselves came from earlier work by Dunlop and Ross. There was then further controversy about the 'key bargain' hypothesis itself, which could be said to be loosely connected to the Phillips curve literature.[1]

Also very widely noted—perhaps even more so than Eckstein and Wilson—were Perry (1964) and (1966). The former was something of a trailer for the latter, which was itself a delayed publication of a 1961 thesis with updated data (and which reprinted much of the substance of the analysis of the 1964 piece). These were much more like 'Phillips curves' in that unemployment was given a principal role in wage change, and Perry gave little consideration to 'key bargains'. But he did include profit as an explanatory variable, saying—with very little in the way of explanation—that it

seemed 'conceptually preferable' (p. 287) to do so (and that the econometrics seemed to bear this out). The fact that it needed no more explanation
clearly shows he thought the point well established, and this assumption
ties him to the earlier literature.

Behman (1964) found that the quit rate was more correlated with wage
change than was unemployment. She developed a view of wage setting
which suggested that when demand grows in some sectors, the initial effect
is that laid-off workers are rehired with no increase in wages. If demand
grows further, new hirings are associated with wage increases, and that
has the effect of increasing the quit rate in other sectors. Consequently,
wages would have to rise in those sectors and the result would be a relation
between the quit rate and wage increase.

The same sort of motivation in digging deeper into the operation of the
labour market can be seen in the work of Simler and Tella (1968); they
suggested in particular that Perry's analysis could be improved by noting
that the size of the labour force varied with the state of demand, and that
by taking account of that, one could derive a better measure of the state of
the labour market than unemployment. Kuh (1967) treated the inclusion
of profit as standard practice, and suggested that productivity would fill its
role better (and rejected a role for unemployment).

Eckstein (1968) 'revisited' the question of wage determination in the
United States in the light of these and other contributions, and although
he found wages harder to explain in the later wage rounds (which were
also less distinct), and included more explanatory variables, his general
approach and attitude remained unchanged. Notably, he insisted (p. 141)
that almost all explanations of wage change that had appeared in the preceding years included variables reflecting both the state of the labour market and the state of the product market. The one exception he noted was
that of Behman (1964)—who considered only labour market variables—
and even she had specifically rejected unemployment as a measure of the
state of the labour market. The point for present purposes should be clear,
although Eckstein was not emphasizing it: the idea from Phillips was that
only the labour market was relevant. Even in 1968 Eckstein was convinced
that that was a fundamental mistake.

Strikingly, none of these authors showed much interest in the work of
Phillips. Levinson did not mention him; Eckstein and Wilson in due course
asked whether there was a Phillips curve in America, and in less than half
a page (p. 406, top) concluded in the negative. Perry (1966) said (errone-
ously) that Phillips was the initiator of the approach he was using, but commented that his work was marred by 'inattention to other variables' (p. 7)
beyond the labour market. Perry also noted, quite correctly, that Phillips

had observed that his relationship remained unaltered over the whole of a very long period, and that this

> suggests that the institutional characteristics of the wage-determining process, which have changed so completely over the course of Phillips' time period, are of little significance compared with the fundamental economic variables. (pp. 5–6)

That remark was obviously intended to foreshadow Perry's later observation that,

> In contrast to the view sometimes held, the present results specifically reject the notion that the wage equation has remained unchanged through time. (p. 121)

Just that point which was truly novel in Phillips' work was, therefore, rejected. Behman, too, did not regard Phillips as a particularly important figure, but merely as having initiated 'one line of investigation' (p. 253) into wage change. (A wrong one, as she thought.) Kuh described (p. 334) his own equation as an 'alternative' to the Phillips curve, and Weintraub (1968), summarizing recent developments, saw the importance of Kuh's work in doubting the effect of unemployment on wages. In his 1968 piece Eckstein used the expression 'Phillips curve' quite freely, but did not cite Phillips' paper and said nothing specifically about his work. Furthermore, his idea of the paradigmatic 'Phillips curve' was, as it was for Kuh (following Perry), a relation including profit.

There were plenty of other studies in the general area. Bowen (1960b) provided a theoretical study of 'the wage-price issue' and another volume—(Bowen 1960c)—was its empirical companion. The latter is not really econometric but it is quite intensively statistical, and should perhaps be regarded as part of the econometric Phillips curve literature (although the author made no mention of Phillips) because it identifies the existence and extent of the effect of unemployment on wages as crucial questions. It must be said though that Bowen's success in either finding or dismissing such a relation was limited, and as the book developed a great deal of emphasis was placed on considerations of market power—again contrary to the implications of Phillips' work. France (1962), much more succinctly, considered American wage change since 1890. He made extensive reference to the pre- and post-war literature, both econometric and non-econometric, and although his conclusions, like Bowen's, were none too decisive, the intent to bring all the learning of the older literature to bear on the issues is plain. France's work was the starting point for McCaffree (1963), who hardly mentioned Phillips but came to the conclusion that, in

America, unionization slowed down wage adjustment. Snodgrass (1963) investigated inter-industry relative wage change using cross-sectional and case-study approaches comparing three views of wage bargaining—what he called the 'market forces', 'union power', and 'pattern bargaining' theories. In discussing 'market forces' he referred once to Phillips but the idea he pursued was that the 'market forces' idea would be tested by using, as he put it,

> some factor which in some general way is related to market demand—rate of productivity increase, profit rate, employment change, or output change. (p. 173)

Earlier authors would have been far from unanimous in regarding these as representing 'market forces' as distinct from bargaining considerations, but taken together his list of hypotheses is notable for giving no role to the level of unemployment. He noted the possibility of following Phillips in using unemployment in this test, but simply put that aside and moved on. A different step, and an unusual one for the time, was taken by Scott and McKean (1964), who estimated a 'Phillips curve' as a relation between *price* change and unemployment. They are not tied to the earlier wage-determination literature and do briefly discuss the question of inflation-unemployment tradeoffs, but their main objective was to assess the relationship of growth and inflation. Levy (1966) was, like Samuelson and Solow, interested in discovering how serious the problems around inflation and unemployment were. Stekler (1968) also estimated a price-change Phillips curve, but rejected it in favour of an equation with the change in, but not the level of, unemployment.

Bodkin (1966) was another book-length, delayed publication of a lightly revised doctoral thesis, although the thesis itself had been previously available in the form of Bodkin (1962). Like Bowen (1960b)—or Samuelson and Solow (1960)—the author's objective was to understand the policy problem of achieving full employment and price stability, rather than seeking to understand wage change per se.

Throop (1968), too, came from a thesis. He argued that the union wage markup had been in disequilibrium in the 1950s, so that unions raised their wages, thereby generating cost-push inflation. By the 1960s the system was, he believed, back in equilibrium so that inflation would disappear. His measurement of the equilibrium union wage differential might be questioned, but the roots of his work were clearly in the older literature, and neither Phillips nor Lipsey were mentioned except in the sense that Throop adopted the expression 'Phillips curve'. He said that the curve indicated the 'inflationary bias' (p. 81) of the post-war economy, which was not exactly what Phillips had in mind, but certainly does not indicate that Throop thought the curve was some sort of inducement to inflationary policy. It was a depiction of a problem.

In the latter part of the 1960s there also emerged groups of papers which, in one way or another, seem to lack the grand vision of some of the earlier papers. One group used American wage equations to test for the effects of presidential urgings of wage restraint ('the Guideposts' as they were called in 1960s America). Perry (1967) was the inspiration here. He noted that the equation from his earlier work overpredicted inflation after 1962, when the Guidepost policy began, and suggested that this might show the benefit of the policy. This work was both enlarged upon by others, and doubted.[2]

There were a number of sub-national wage equations. Frederick Bell (1967) was much more elaborate than most—he constructed a whole macroeconometric system for Massachusetts, in the course of which he concluded that, for that area, 'the Phillips hypothesis must be rejected' (p. 115). Although others, using simpler analysis, could persuade themselves to the contrary, on the whole the results were not favourable to the Phillips curve.[3]

There was a small further assortment of works that might be called part of the 'Phillips curve literature' but which are also not notable for their lasting impact.[4] One that perhaps does deserve a special mention is Liebling and Cluff (1969). They discussed several of the post-Phillips studies and suggested there was no convincing reason to prefer any of them to the simplicity of using unemployment as the sole explanatory variable. They went on to argue that the American tradeoff had improved after 1962, making several suggestions (Liebling and Cluff 1969, pp. 246–8) as to why, including, notably, that expected inflation had declined. In virtue of the exclusion of other variables, there is a sense in which Liebling and Cluff are closer to Phillips than the others, but they can hardly be said to be missing the important points about nominal and real variables.

Amongst the British studies, most hardly owe more to Phillips. There is Lipsey (1960), of course, which was directly inspired by him. So was Lipsey and Steuer (1961), which was a rebuttal of the suggestion of Kaldor (1959a)—a non-econometric paper—that profit rather than unemployment would be the better predictor of wage change. But beyond that, for a few years, there is not much. Klein and Ball (1959) and Dicks-Mireaux and Dow (1959) are post-1958 studies which give emphasis to unemployment in the explanation of wage change, although they also feature discussions of variations in union aggressiveness which differentiate them from Phillips. In any case, their genesis is, as their authors explain, to be found in Klein and Goldberger (1955) and Dow (1956), respectively, which shows that they needed no inspiration from Phillips. In a line of thought that was to have enduring repercussions, Hines (1964) suggested wage change was principally influenced by union militancy rather than unemployment, and in Hines (1969) confirmed that theory in an industry-level study. Furthermore, in Hines (1968) he also found that unemployment had been a major influence on wage change in the nineteenth century, and hence that it was easy to suggest that institutional or policy change accounted for the difference between the periods. Hines, then, rejected unemployment as a principal determinant of post-war inflation, thought institutional change essential in understanding it, and found the major problem in cost-push factors—three things that put him in opposition to Phillips' work, although, in due course, this all became part of what was called 'the Phillips curve literature'. Lomax (1966), meanwhile, estimated equations along the lines of Phillips and Lipsey but drew negative conclusions, suggesting that unemployment had little effect on wage change at the national level and less in explaining local deviations of payments from nationally agreed rates.

Perhaps more strikingly still, when Ball (1962) set out to compare the predictive performance of the Klein/Ball and Dicks-Mireaux/Dow studies, Phillips was mentioned only as having made a start at non-linear estimation and as giving too much emphasis to unemployment as the crucial determinant of wage change. The predicative performance of his equation did not, apparently, warrant consideration. That was true when Pencavel (1971) did the same sort of thing, comparing Lipsey (1960), Dicks-Mireaux (1961), and Hines (1964). In that case, it might be said that Lipsey was a close substitute for Phillips—but then that draws attention to the point that Ball did not include Lipsey's paper either. Similarly, Klein et al. (1961) discussed a macroeconometric model of the UK economy but barely mentioned Phillips, and Lipsey not at all. It was, then, Klein et al. (1961) that Sargan (1964)—in his landmark of econometric methodology (cf. Hendry and Wallis (1984) and Qin (2011))—took as his starting point. He gave no special position to Phillips (although at one point he used his name as a label). Gillion (1968)—which the author describes as written 'some time' earlier than that date—was clearly written with Sargan, not Phillips, in mind and suggested that capacity utilization offered a better explanation of wage change than did unemployment.

It is, notably, only in the second half of the 1960s that we find more authors really looking to Phillips as the origin of their lines of thinking. In these cases, whatever significant merits their papers have, they, like the corresponding American studies, cannot be said to be addressing broad problems. One group of whom this is true are a string of papers by Cowling and Metcalf on Phillips curves for parts or sectors of the United

Kingdom;[5] and there were a few papers like Jefferson, Sams, and Swann (1968) in this period seeking to assess the effect of British incomes policy.[6]

The next most studied country was Canada, and one of the things that distinguishes the work on this subject is that it shows a much more consistent influence by Phillips and Lipsey in so far as unemployment is put at the centre of the explanation of wage change. The first fully published work was Kaliski (1964), followed by Reuber (1964), which was a published version of work done for the (Canadian) Royal Commission on Banking and Finance, originally appearing as Reuber (1962). Vanderkamp (1966b) and Zaidi (1969) both came from doctoral thesis, the former, as that author explains, supervised by Phillips and Lipsey. Bodkin et al. (1967) contained a long discussion of previous work, some of which was re-estimated, as well as new 'Phillips curve' estimates for Canada.

A similar centrality of unemployment in explaining wage change is also visible in the scattered work on other countries, although most of these also appear rather later in the period than might be guessed. Klein and Bodkin (1964) made rather rough and ready estimates for seven countries, as well as reporting results for the United States. They (like Scott and McKean) were considering growth, employment, and inflation, rather than just the last two; while they can hardly be said to have settled much, unemployment was central to their treatment. Watanabe (1966) estimated such a relation for Japan—so did Tatemoto, Uchida, and Watanabe (1967) as part of a complete macroeconomic model—and Harris (1967) estimated one for India as part of a larger study. There were others,[7] but these three, like Kaliski, are perhaps interesting for actually using the expression 'Phillips–Lipsey hypothesis' as a label for the idea. But Klein and Shinkai (1963)—another Japanese macroeconometric model—perhaps understandably with Klein involved, gave Phillips and Lipsey no priority.

Right at the beginning of the 1970s, there are then quite a number of papers which give no indication of any influence of Friedman (1968a) and appear to be stragglers from the earlier period which happened to be published only when the leading papers of the literature had taken a different direction. In comparison to what had gone before, they brought very little to the literature, for the most part being concerned with the question of whether some particular sector or country might have a Phillips curve.[8] Attention to such things as the quality of their data, theoretical rationales for the modelling choices they make, and even whether the question they are asking might reveal anything of importance receive strikingly less attention than in the earlier work. This is so true of some that they are not so much stragglers as perhaps the dying gasp of a literature in final decline.[9]

Here then is 'the Phillips curve literature' as it was before Friedman (1968a)—just over ninety works, including stragglers. Whether it is quite appropriate to describe all these as 'Phillips curve' papers might well be questioned, but there is nothing there out of character with the work surveyed by Santomero and Seater (1978).[10] On the other hand, whatever we make of the terminology, it is clear that Phillips' influence was much less than might have been guessed.

A small extra twist on that point is that Phillips' influence is much more visible amongst the later work in the period. If there is an explosion of work that really puts unemployment at the centre of wage determination, it starts in about 1966. Associated with that point is the further one that much of the work influenced by him is of lesser quality. That is by no means a universal characteristic and—for example—the string of Canadian Phillips curves would be amongst those not included. Nevertheless, for a good part of this later work it is not necessary to assess the technical aspects of the econometrics to see that it contains papers with unashamedly little engagement with such things as the quality or suitability of their data, the various lags that might be considered, or commentary on the relation of their work with the pre-existing literature. Even specific comment on the limitations of their own work (as opposed to a general declaration that much more needs to be done) is far more limited. Those things are even truer of the stragglers, where surely the weakest papers are to be found. Of this part of the literature, we may suppose, if we choose, that the econometrics itself is admirable, but still a good part of the work most clearly inspired by Phillips (or Lipsey, in fact), would be no more than a second-class literature, and some of it would not even be that.

On the other hand, in the earlier part of the period there is much less work that could be described in those sorts of terms, and Phillips had much less influence on it. Some, like Behman (1964) or Hines (1964), although perhaps forgotten, brought commitment of purpose and imaginative theoretical insight to the issue—as well as a rejection of the Phillips curve. That would also be true of Kuh (1967), slightly later. Even Bowen (1960b) is supremely thorough. The analysis of the American labour market is at its most in-depth in this period in Eckstein and Wilson (1962), and the British in Dicks-Mireaux and Dow (1959); while the development of the technique of macroeconometric modelling begins with Phillips' precursors, and continues with Klein et al. (1961). None of those owed anything to Phillips, except that in some cases his view was the one they were rejecting. Perry (1966) was a late publication of earlier work. He declared the influence of Phillips on his work, but there was no real basis for that and he found an important role for profit in determining wages, which was very much contrary to Phillips' idea. Of the high-quality work of the earlier part of the period, none but Lipsey's really flows from Phillips, and none of the rest flows from Lipsey.

3.2 THE QUESTION OF PRICES

Despite claims to the contrary, by Friedman (1977) and others, it should be no surprise that the literature of the early 1960s, with the genealogy it had, recognized the importance of price change to wage setting. The labour economists of the 1940s and 1950s had known about that, and those who followed them knew about it too. Price change is, accordingly, almost always included in these wage equations.

That, though, is only really half the story. It is not just the inclusion of price change that strikes the reader, but also the emphasis sometimes given to the point. For example, Dow (1956) had actually treated price change as the principal determinant of wage change. He assumed,

> full compensation for price increases is something which trade unions aim at and which both sides to wage negotiations accept as a standard of reference; and that variations of wage earning about this norm can be treated as a variable affected by employers' demand for labour or the strength or pushfulness of trade unions. (p. 268)

Dicks-Mireaux and Dow (1959) started *there*, seeking to improve that analysis by incorporating consideration of unemployment as well. They said,

> The general impression left by previous studies (in particular Brown, 1955, diagrams 14 and 17) was that before 1939 the rate of change of wage-rates was associated with the level of unemployment; but that since the war the relation has been less obvious, and the rate of change of wage-rates has been more closely related to that of prices. It seemed possible, therefore, that the relation between wage-changes and unemployment had been masked by the relation between wage- and price-changes; and that an attempt to take both into account at the same time would reveal that a relationship of the former type persisted. (p. 7)

Klein and Ball (1959) also convey the importance of the point, saying,

> Actual bargaining over wage-rates takes place in terms of monetary units, but this is not to say that a 'money illusion' is involved. Both sides are only too aware of the 'real' nature of economic affairs. Movements in the cost of living are

prominent facts at the bargaining table. Instead of saying that dynamic movements in real wage-rates are functionally related to unemployment, we take the
somewhat more general and more realistic view that the time rate of change in
money wage-rates is a function of the level of unemployment and the time rate
of change of the price level. (p. 466)

Lomax (1966), denying the existence of a Phillips curve, said, 'By far the
dominant influence on the rate of change of wage-rates is the price change
effect' (p. 6). France (1962)—working on American data—noted that
his statistical analysis did not reveal a role for small price changes, but
expressed his doubts about the significance of this, saying

a continuing period of such changes may have an influence. After two or three
years of increases in the cost of living...both parties may begin to expect continued price increases. (p. 190)

Perry (1966) considered the possibility of constraining the coefficient on
price change to be 1, but said 'one of the most interesting questions in this
area is the degree to which living costs directly affect wages' (pp. 22–3).
Gillion (1968), following Sargan (1964), preferred the approach of estimating real wages as adjusting towards equilibrium to that of including
a price-change variable in the wage equation 'on a priori grounds since
it implies that real wages do not fall during a period of sustained price
increases' (Gillion 1968, p. 65). (He also found it resulted in a better fit.)

Other studies do not make so much of prices. Many quietly include
them, and some exclude them. In some of those cases, the exclusion is
explained by the authors—adequately or inadequately.[11] A number of others are not truly 'Phillips curves' at all—they are not equations estimating wage change as a function of unemployment. Consequently, whether
prices need to be included depends on what theoretical idea is motivating
them.[12] In a small number of other cases, any explanation of their exclusion, if there is one, might have to be more speculative. But even in these
cases, it is perfectly clear that the authors concerned had understood the
point.[13] Taking the literature as a whole, there would be a few—very few
in fact—of which it could be said that the research is seriously flawed by
the failure to consider price change. But later understanding, exemplified
in Friedman (1977), is that there was a general confusion afoot. The truth
is that except perhaps for one or two of the stragglers and the dying-gasp
papers, there is not a single case amongst the work referred to earlier in
this chapter where even the evidence which is internal to this literature

taken alone suggests an author had failed to understand that there was an issue about price change affecting wages.

The suggestion that somehow crept into Friedman's Nobel lecture—that this literature is generally characterized by a confusion of nominal and real variables—is, therefore, simply false, and the fact that it is widely believed is extraordinary. But the discussion of the question most demanding attention is that of Santomero and Seater (1978), for they, with extensive analysis, insist so firmly that the literature before Friedman (1968a) was thoroughly senseless.

First they say that most authors find price change significant, but they complain that,

> the reasons given for including it are usually vague or nonexistent. (p. 509)

and go on to adopt a point they attribute to Archibald (1969) and Archibald, Kemmis, and Perkins (1974) as follows,

> If anticipated trends are ignored, supply and demand provide an exhaustive list of the factors determining the price of any good. Any factors that shift demand or supply cause changes in price through changes in excess demand. In a Phillips-type wage equation, the unemployment rate is a proxy for excess demand. Therefore, changes in variables that affect supply or demand should be captured entirely by changes in the unemployment rate, and the other variables themselves should not be entered separately in the wage equation. (Santomero and Seater 1978, p. 509)

Whether that is a correct interpretation of Archibald et al, is not the issue, nor is the question whether these authors are making a good point.[14] If it is a correct interpretation, it is notable that all concerned are revealing themselves as being far removed from an appreciation of the wage-bargaining literature of the 1950s. Had they had just Hicks (1955) in mind ('It has never been the general rule that wage-rates have been determined simply and solely by supply and demand' (p. 390)), it would have given them pause.

But the immediate point is that Santomero and Seater go on to suggest there are three possible justifications for including price change. The first is that 'it improves the use of the unemployment rate as a proxy for excess demand' (p. 510). This is dismissed on the basis that none of the authors gives that reason. The second is that

> the Phillips curve is misspecified if it is written in terms of nominal wages. Employers and employees bargain over real wages. (p. 510)

They discuss that idea, and introduce the third in a laboured passage, as follows,

> However, if price change is not perceived or anticipated, it will be ignored, and nominal wage change will be determined solely by excess demand. Thus unless price change is perceived or anticipated, it does not belong in the Phillips curve equation. If price change is anticipated, then the expected rate of price change should appear in the equation, which brings us to the third reason for including the actual rate of price change. If actual inflation is used as a proxy for expected inflation, then it is justifiable to have actual inflation in the wage equation. In this case, nominal wages could change even if excess demand were zero. The fact is, however, that virtually none of the early authors used expectations as a reason for including price change as an explanatory variable. (p. 510)

And they go on from there to assert again the importance of Friedman (1968a) and Phelps (1967) and to say, in what would surely be a non sequitur, even were it true, that their work led to the use of actual inflation as a proxy for expected inflation being called into doubt.

Apart from the point that they wish to reach the conclusion that the treatment of price change had been inadequate, it is not clear even what the objectives of this argument are. It is almost as if they are arguing that the problem is that the authors under scrutiny did not *explain* that inflation was included as a proxy for expected inflation. Whatever else it might be, that could not be a complaint about the estimated equations themselves, and the constant stress they put on the superiority of Friedman and Phelps' approach seems to show they have more than this in mind.

In any case, even that idea only arises because of the mysterious disappearance of 'perceived', never to re-emerge, after it is so strongly emphasized in the first few lines of the quotation. If one puts the matter in the terms of Santomero and Seater's argument, surely the truth is that the authors in question included price change in their equations because they thought it was 'perceived' by the wage bargainers—why should it not be? That is a good enough explanation, and one can only speculate as to why Santomero and Seater cannot see it.[15] No doubt, then, the reason they find explanations of the inclusion of prices so elusive, if that is what they are,[16] is that there is so little to explain.

A different point—quite different—is that one might argue that, as a matter of economic theory, it is preferable to explain wages by reference to expected, rather than observed, inflation. Although the difficulties in making the distinction precise are not to be dismissed, Santomero and Seater's attempt to disparage the literature over this point is unreasonable.

Apart from difficulties in making out their own argument, there is the point that the literature on which they were commenting was aiming at a realistic understanding of bargaining and it is very much more natural to think of wage bargainers reacting to actual, than to forecasted, price changes. Infatuation with rational expectations sometimes seems to know no bounds but surely it is not to be disputed that the *appearance* of wage bargaining is that it reacts to recent price change rather than any forecast. It was that appearance that was being modelled.

Most importantly, though, for both current purposes and Santomero and Seater's, the point they are raising cannot explain why anyone would be led to believe in a stable, exploitable tradeoff. If it is an error to consider price change rather than expected price change, so be it, but that is very far short of confusing nominal and real variables. Nor is it just a matter of understanding, since the change makes no fundamental difference to the analysis either. The long-run consequences of adjustment to price change are just the same as those of adjustment to expected price change.

Something that could establish the existence of a problem, although, again, there will be difficulties along the way, is the point that the studies concerned very rarely found the coefficient on price change to be anywhere near 1. That does mean that considering the matter in strictly ceteris paribus terms, price change (or expected price change, if we relabel it) was less than fully incorporated into wages, so that, apparently, a balanced inflation having no other effects could lower the real wage. It might be argued that theory prohibits this. In that case, the appropriate complaint to make about the literature is that researchers did not *constrain* the coefficient on price change to be equal to 1. If theory demands it be 1, then the econometrician must set it to 1. That, clearly, is not Santomero and Seater's complaint (nor Friedman's)—they are not complaining that the econometricians failed when they *tested* the value of that coefficient. What they are doing, in various ways, is suggesting that there was no appreciation of the relevance of price change to the enquiry. That is simply not correct.

Moving away from the way Santomero and Seater make the argument, there is the question of whether that constraint should have been imposed. Clearly, nearly all the authors considered here have proceeded on the basis that the range of reasonable outcomes includes those where the coefficient on price change is less than 1. In considering the significance, and reasonableness of this, three points should then be made.

First, there is the all-important point—very much hidden from view by idea that these sorts of enquiries began in 1958—that the theory of wages as it was understood by so many of these authors was not what Santomero and Seater are presuming. Certainly, if one supposes there is a unique equilibrium wage, one would expect it to be defined in real terms. That is most plainly true of the marginal productivity theory of wages—if the wage is equal to the marginal product of labour, then inflation raises money wages. It would be that simple. But what if the wage is not equal to marginal product, and not determined exclusively by 'economic' forces, and not impersonally driven to some unique equilibrium? The established theory of the time—or a good portion of it—did not presume there was a unique equilibrium wage. None of that meant that real wages might move without limit, but it did mean that, within bounds that could not be precisely known, changes in the relation of the real wage and productivity were possible. For authors taking this view it would be senseless as well as a violation of scientific practice, to constrain the coefficient on price change to be 1. The point that the value of the coefficient was an empirical matter is perfectly apparent in Dicks-Mireaux and Dow (1959, pp. 7–8), who said that, in the course of the work, it 'appeared necessary to relax the assumption' of full compensation for price increases. Evidently it was the econometrics persuaded them to take that step.

Second, it is a mistake to think of these authors either as imagining themselves as discovering anything with a pretence to being a law of economics, or as imagining themselves modelling the effects of continuous, steady inflation. They are in the business of seeing what happened over recent years, forming an impression as to what might be to follow, and perhaps, considering how policy in their times could best serve the needs of their times. It may be a habit of thought from later times to suppose that the generalization of economic relationships is always the highest goal of the analyst. There is something of that in Phillips, of course, and perhaps Lipsey. And there certainly is in Friedman (1968a), whose ideas of the natural rate of unemployment and the expectations augmented Phillips curve are obviously meant to encompass all cases (or point in a direction which would). But all that shows is, again, the misperception that arises from supposing Phillips (1958) is a typical product of this literature. If we look to Eckstein and Wilson, we find they were concerned with bargaining practice. They knew perfectly well that they were dealing with a phenomenon of their times. Remarks by Dicks-Mireaux and Dow quoted earlier in this chapter reveal the same—'since the war the relation has been less obvious...' (1959, p. 7). They make no motion towards generalizing their explanation of the post-war period to the earlier period, but are happy that each be explained in its own terms. They knew, therefore, that they were investigating the character of the economic system in which they lived. For the modern reader to appreciate this work it is necessary altogether to shake off the idea that anyone thought of a wage equation as one component of an implicit general equilibrium model. The economists under consideration thought of it as a way of seeing what was going on with wages at about the time they wrote. Nor in the 1950s or even the 1960s was it necessary to suppose that the inflation which had occurred was not an exceptional instance. After another half-century of continuous price increase it became natural to think of inflation as a normal outcome, but that was not the natural reaction when this literature was written. With these things in mind, it is much less surprising such models were constructed in ways which give no priority to tying down long-run equilibrium relations, even in so far as they might be thought to exist.

The third point is that few of the equations in question—and fewer still of the more sophisticated ones—expressed wage change as a function of unemployment and price change alone. To take one example, profits were also frequently included; another would be simply that there was a constant term. The consequence is that for these studies, the ceteris paribus thought experiment considered earlier in this chapter would not, considered as a proposition about the actual operation of the economy, be a reasonable one. The situation in which the inflation arose would inevitably also have an impact on these other variables and therefore the whole effect of inflation on wages was not measured by the coefficient on price change. Wages would also be affected 'indirectly' through the connection of inflation to the other variables. Consequently, it is not even correct to say that these authors were effectively committed to a view that ongoing inflation would lower the wage without limit, even if—as it should not be—it is supposed that they were treating their equations as eternal truths which would prevail despite all changes in policy or environment.

This point, as it happens, is discussed right at the beginning of the period, by Dicks-Mireaux and Dow (1959, pp. 170–1). They noted that there was a question as to whether the fact that their coefficient on price change turned out to be about 0.5 meant that 'workers ordinarily receive much less than full compensation for price increases', but went on to observe that they also had a constant term in their wage-change equation which kept wages and prices more or less in alignment over the period as a whole, and said,

> It is perhaps not contrary to common impression to say that workers obtain rather less than full compensation for price increases when prices rise more rapidly than usual, and rather more than full compensation when the price-rise is unusually small.

This line of thinking, I have no doubt, is vulnerable to comments to the effect that if that is what the authors were thinking, their econometric technique was deficient. (Indeed, compare Sargan, 1964.) In later periods, better ways of modelling the whole picture would become feasible. But that is merely to say that the econometric possibilities for these authors were limited. Indeed, this may be what Dicks-Mireaux and Dow are getting at themselves when, immediately after the remark just quoted, they say,

> This way of putting it, however, destroys the apparent simplicity of our hypothesis; and there must be other formulations, little more complicated, which are equally valid. (1959, p. 171)

Perhaps so. But the limitations of their econometric technique do not make their appreciation of economic theory inadequate.

So, what nearly all those economists had in the back of their minds was—I am suggesting—that, just as Dicks-Mireaux and Dow say, the whole process saw wages evolve in a reasonable way, although not necessarily in accordance with the marginal productivity theory and the like. And what they had in the front of their minds was that they were seeking to understand the various questions about wage determination that were current at the time.

On the other hand, if we start as Santomero and Seater did, with the idea that the primary concern of this literature was the location of an optimal tradeoff point, things look very different. Indeed, if the question they were addressing was what level of inflation would be required to maintain a specified level of unemployment, then the thought processes I am describing would be subject to much more question. But most of the literature gave no attention at all to that question. For the most part, as I have argued in Section 3.1, the authors were concerned with such issues as whether unemployment should be accorded a primary role in wage determination; what the relation between profit and bargaining strength was; how to gauge the effects of unionization; and, generally, the determination of wages.

So, if it is clear that the 'Phillips curve literature' owed rather little to Phillips, it should be clearer still that it hardly had the limitations that have been thought to have been exposed by Friedman (1968a). The significant papers of the first decade after Phillips are not, on the whole, papers which lack theoretical rational for the form of the equation, and are not critically flawed—or in most cases flawed at all—in their treatment of the difference between nominal and real variables. There are a couple of exceptions, but they are not the most noted papers, and certainly do nothing to substantiate the idea that the whole project of the literature was misconceived.

3.3 INFLATIONISM

On this basis, the case that the Phillips curve literature had a basically inflationist intent is perhaps not off to the best of starts, but there is more to come. First, another consequence of the point that many of the equations estimated are not relations between wage change (or inflation) and unemployment means no issue tradeoff interpretation arises. Hines (1964) thought union militancy explained inflation; so did Throop (1968) in a slightly different way. That leads to policy proposals, but no tradeoff one might contemplate exploiting. Equally, I am not sure how one would extract a tradeoff conclusion from the model of Eckstein and Wilson (1962), where 'key groups' play a central role, and the authors certainly make no such attempt. There are others for whom the idea of generating inflation is more or less excluded by their findings—Scott and McKean (1964, p. 6) list as the fourth of six conclusions that the Phillips curve exists, but the fifth was that either growth reduces inflation or inflation reduces growth. Take your pick, I suppose, but either way there is hardly a case for inflationary policy. The search for a tradeoff interpretation must therefore be limited to those studies which do give a prominent role to unemployment, which, although an extensive group, is by no means the whole 'Phillips curve literature'.

Extensive though it is, that group does, as I have observed, include a high proportion of the pedestrian studies. They are the ones which do not greatly explore the consequences of their own findings. Many of the authors do not seem to be interested in policy at all. Indeed, it is astonishing how many regard the calculation of their equation as more or less the natural place to end their paper. A few others move on from there to say—with only limited reason, I fear—how important it is that more work be done on the subject. These are, as one might say, pure scientists. The authors' objective is to find out whether there is a Phillips curve for a country or region, and to estimate the parameter values, but that being done, the project is complete. Others have what might be called narrow purpose Phillips curves where the objective is to answer some particular question—in this period, most commonly, whether incomes policy works. These authors are, of course, interested in that issue, but again most of the time their conclusions stop with their findings.

There are those with broader questions, or a broader approach to answering them, but who still keep themselves within the bounds they have set. France and McCaffree, each addressing the question of whether unionization matters, are in this category, which is not to say that it was not a central question of American political economy in the era of Lewis

(1963). Snodgrass was, in a sense, pursuing a variation on that theme. These authors were addressed important questions, but really that is all the more reason to doubt that their interest was in a tradeoff curve. In any case they show no such interest. Simler and Tella were much closer to the inflation-unemployment issue, adding to Perry's analysis a measure of labour market slack attributable to temporary withdrawals of the unemployed from the labour force. That led to the conclusion that the American economy was less inflation prone in the late 1960s than before—they made no motion at all towards suggesting this called for more inflationary policy.

These authors simply say nothing about the consequences of their work for optimal inflation, but in the cases where Phillips curves are estimated there might seem to be a temptation to suppose there is an inflationist subtext. Might it not be that the silence of the authors invites inflationist conclusions as much as it does anything else? If incomes policy is found to work, particularly when, nevertheless, inflation has not been zero, might there not be a suggestion that since incomes policy lessens the pain, inflation is acceptable?

That sort of view would have a great deal more going for it if it were true that the general intellectual environment was one of the acceptance of inflation, but if we look to other studies, where something more is said about policy, that is not the direction they point. Rather, where something is said about policy or about inflation, or something is clearly implied, it nearly always carries the implication that inflation is to be avoided. Kaliski drew a diagram where 'equilibrium' is defined as the point of zero inflation—he cannot have had it in mind that there was a menu available. Sargan considered the effect of a permanent increase in unemployment (it would bring a temporary reduction in inflation), but the idea of a permanent increase in inflation does not seem to have occurred to him. He also said (Sargan 1964, p. 305) that the objective of stabilizing prices looked feasible, which suggests that he thought that was a goal. Watanabe (1966, p. 31) said inflation was a 'headache'. He calculated the level of unemployment required to stop it. That was a fairly common move—Phillips did that. Lipsey was extravagantly cautious about what conclusions should be drawn, insisting on how much more research was required, but those comments arose (1960 pp. 30–1) in connection with—and only in connection with—the question of estimating the price-stability level of unemployment. There is no sign that he was thinking of any other policy.

Levy (1966) is not itself an important paper, but it reveals a good deal about the ideas at work. His title was 'Full employment and inflation: A "trade-off" analysis'. He said, from a policy point of view, it is crucial to establish the 'trade-off' region where small additional reductions in the unemployment rate can be bought only at the price of considerable inflation. (p. 21)

Clearly, if one starts from the position that inflationism based on the Phillips curve was commonplace, this will sound like such an instance. But he goes on to say,

In this region, *structural* measures will have to become dominant, while monetary and fiscal expansion gives way either to 'neutrality' or—ultimately—to restraint. (p. 21)

That is typical—the view that a 'tradeoff', or even a stable tradeoff, exists, is far from leading to a presumption that inflationary policy is indicated.

Liebling and Cluff are much more open about the existence of a 'tradeoff' than some and said that its terms had improved, so one might expect an inflationist conclusion. But on the contrary, their conclusion was,

it would appear that for many reasons not yet definitely known the outlook for price stability at lower rates of unemployment holds more promise than had been thought previously. (1969, p. 248)

It is plainly price stability which has priority. A similar point is available from Dicks-Mireaux and Dow (1959). They drew attention to the point that, owing to non-linearities, it would be unsafe to draw conclusions about what would happen if unemployment went outside the range of experience, and emphasized,

Our results therefore provide no basis for calculating what level of demand would have been required to stop wages or prices rising. (p. 171)

So they specifically decline to make the calculations, but they plainly assume, and expect their readers to be assuming, that the point of such a calculation, if it were made, would be to find out how to *stop* inflation. Klein and Ball (1959) clearly thought inflation was the problem and they were trying to understand the solution. Klein et al. (1961), of course, are no more inflationist than other macroeconometric modellers, but one striking feature of this book is that the authors devote a chapter to 'Two special problems in the light of the model'. One of these is the question of estimating trade elasticities, where they take issue on a number of points with Orcutt (1950)—a key paper suggesting that pessimism about the possibility of correcting current account deficits with devaluation was overstated. The other is the problem of distinguishing between cost and demand inflation in Britain. So here we have authors, to whom others could be added,[17] constructing a model for policymaking purposes, and then devoting space specifically to considering what they regard as crucial issues, and yet there is not a mention of the shape or location of a tradeoff frontier, much less an intimation of which would be its optimal point.

These studies are obviously not inflationist. That must affect the view one takes of those where the authors give less indication of their policy presumptions. If it were true that the general outlook favoured inflation, there might be a case for supposing that at least some of those who say nothing about it shared that outlook. In fact, the general outlook gives no such indication, and indeed the opposite seems to be the case.

It is not quite one-way traffic—there are more inflationist contributions. Some of the dying-gasp papers invite the interpretation of being inflationist,[18] but it is hard to believe anyone is going to argue they are representative of the literature. More importantly, Klein and Bodkin (1964) seem to contemplate the possibility, at least, of such tradeoffs. They said (p. 367) they wanted to explore the compatibility or otherwise of the various goals and to find out 'how much' of one had to be given up to achieve another. To that extent, their motivations are much more like what is supposed to be typical. Even in their case, that point can be taken only a certain distance because, in the end, they found their own arguments inconclusive and they did not give clear statements of any alternative policies. It is far from obvious what final position they might have taken and a forensic analysis would be lengthy—it is a long paper, written to be read by a wide range of those interested in policy, and with some informality of expression. Other works by the two authors took divergent views, so there may have been elements of compromise about it. All in all, the authors seem to have set themselves to raise possibilities rather than to resolve anything. Right at the end they suggest that to decrease inflation, increased household saving could be made compulsory. It would be a fairly drastic measure if the authors were, in fact, happy to accept inflation. Perhaps they are inflationists, but if so, they are hesitant ones.

Another case would be that of Bowen (1960c). The 'dilemma model' of the theoretical work of Bowen (1960b) suggested there was a difficulty about achieving full employment and price stability. There, he sought to provide a comprehensive list of the issues in wage bargaining, price determination, and, to a lesser extent, policy responses when inflation emerges below full employment. As Rees (1961, p. 206) observed, at each fork in the road the author sought to follow both paths. Realistically, this could lead him nowhere except to the conclusion with which he began: to the effect that the issues were intricate and that a detailed understanding at the micro level was far distant. It was an ambitious project and Phelps Brown (1961) noted the author's inconsistency as to what it was possible to determine and what was not. It is clear, however, that Bowen thought the dilemma existed, and that he was prepared to contemplate some inflation.

In the second, empirical, volume, he set out most methodically his objectives (Bowen 1960c, pp. 6–7). They were to determine whether unemployment affects wage change, if so, how loose that relation is; whether there has been any trend in it; and what other things affect wage change. That, clearly enough, does not include the location of an optimal tradeoff point. In execution, the work lacked a clear destination, being very much conceived as an exploration, in the same way that the much longer theoretical volume did, with, apparently, every idea needing to be tested. When it came to the influence of price change on wages, he reached the conclusion that it would be hard to deny some effect (Bowen 1960c, p. 53), gave some consideration to the question of how important it was likely to be, and decided that more detailed analysis might help. It is like that all the way through, so it is no surprise that there are inflationist aspects to his conclusions. On the one hand he said that he could not be expected to provide a 'definitive statement of the right mix of anti-inflation policies' (p. 92); various policies though, could certainly affect conditions in the labour market; but there was a clear suggestion of a 'dilemma' in that inflation continues at less than full employment. Various aspects of that were summarized but (p. 97) he argues it would be appropriate to 'frankly recognize' that 'traditional tools' would be unable to solve the dilemma, but 'the probable margin of failure' was not so great as to cause alarm. His final words were,

> At this juncture it is probably wisest to adjust monetary and fiscal policies to the realities of the day as best we can. What is needed is neither pious expressions of faith in the ability of our economy to solve all problems nor counsels of total despair, but rather a tough-minded and continuing effort to find the best possible balance between our conflicting objectives.

He did not suggest what that balance might be—I suppose he hardly could after so many complications and uncertainties had been raised and left unresolved. But if it would be hard to argue that all this meant he was resolved on the importance of strict price stability, it can hardly be said that this is clear-sighted, unequivocal inflationism either.

There is also some inclination to accept inflation in Perry (1966). He says that policy faces the problem of 'deciding what combination of unemployment and inflation to aim at and then adjusting aggregate demand to reach this point' (p. 3), and 'it is important to understand the nature of choices open to policy' (p. 107). On page 59 he says that the best guess as to what is possible is that with 3 per cent productivity growth and profits at their 1947–60 average, price stability would require 6.4 per cent unemployment. Making profit lower would improve that but, he clearly feels, not enough. He continues,

> Although *complete* price stability imposes excessive costs in terms of unemployment, it appears that reasonably low unemployment rates could be maintained without leading to *exceptional* rates of inflation (p. 61)

with the details, of course, depending on what is assumed about profit. (In Perry (1964, pp. 297–8) the same discussion can be found.) In neither work does he indicate that exclusive priority should be given to price stability, so it is clear that he is prepared to contemplate that policy might allow inflation.

On the other hand, he also stresses (pp. 114–23) various ideas for improving the situation—that is, the point of his stress on his rejection of Phillips' view that the relation is immutable. Various tax changes would affect profits, competition could be improved, and trade restrictions reduced. He also suggested that macroeconomic stability would reduce the variability of profit and hence reduce wage increases during booms, and that with more stable outcomes the required rate of return on capital might fall, resulting in lower profits in the long run. He also, of course, supported with optimism the idea that presidential leadership could reduce wage increases. If only because of the insistence on the possibilities of structural improvement, Perry's acceptance of inflation cannot be said to be clear-cut, but there is more suggestion of it here than in the vast majority of the econometric literature.

Then there is Bodkin (1966), who estimates tradeoff relations and gives no indication that he feels they would shift if inflation were tolerated. So, summing up his empirical work, he says:

> The author believes that it may safely be said that with American institutional conditions, the goals of reasonably full employment and price level stability are incompatible—unless 'reasonably' is given an unreasonable interpretation. (p. 120)

Much later, having estimated that price-level stability would require unemployment in the region of 13 million (18.8%), he says,

> One can generalize these results to some extent and obtain, from the model, an estimate of the amount of inflation associated with any level of unemployment. (p. 277)

He does not quite say so, but it is pretty clear that he does not think price stability worth 18.8 per cent unemployment, so he can be presumed to be committed to accepting inflation.

Beyond these few, there are a few more. Reuber (1962) propounded a stable relationship and considered the costs and benefits of various choices, and much the same work was published as Reuber (1964). Others would be Vanderkamp (1966b), who found the price-stability level of unemployment in Canada to be 8 per cent but concluded that the government should not allow unemployment to rise above 5 per cent; and Zaidi (1969), who was less daring about drawing conclusions for the same issue, but tabulated the rates of inflation associated with different rates of unemployment and productivity and so must have had it in mind that policymakers had a choice to make.

Most notable of all, however, is Bodkin et al. (1967)—a special study for the Economic Council of Canada. It is another supremely thorough work, and it is full of both tradeoff estimates, and doubts about the reliability of the results. Price change is of course included in the estimations. They also offer, as Kotowitz (1971) noted, a fine and thorough treatment of the previous literature up to that time. Indeed, it surpasses any other work of the time in coverage and reaches the highest standards in coherent presentation and attention to the variations in variables treated and assumptions made. Almost at the end (p. 280) in a long footnote—could it be an afterthought?—they consider the possibility of there being a unique equilibrium level of unemployment and the tradeoff being vertical there. They say that they believe consistent theory on those lines could be constructed but that they are 'somewhat sceptical' about its applicability. But, despite all that, in the end they calculate what they call 'steady state equations' and clearly believe there are choices for the policymaker to make. This work, then, is the best there is when it comes to giving econometric flesh to the myth of the Phillips curve.

So there is Phillips curve inflationism. There is not much of it, but it is there. As Laidler (1997) noted, the first such inflationist was not Phillips (1958), nor Samuelson and Solow (1960), but Reuber (1962). Laidler could have gone further in noting how little followed. Amongst the British work, there is nothing; amongst the American, there is a very small amount. Laidler winked at his readers and pretended to a coy pride in the finding that, through Reuber, this was a Canadian contribution to economics. In what is certainly a point that raises a further question, it could also be said that *all* the unhesitant, most clear-cut, and least equivocal cases of well-considered Phillips curve inflationism of the 1960s were Canadian.

3.4 THE EXTENT OF INFLATIONISM

So there are inflationists—and *how*! Having found it would take 18.8 per cent unemployment to stabilize prices, Bodkin (1966) worked out (p. 279) that 3 per cent unemployment would be associated with 1.76 per cent inflation (or lower in variations on the calculation). He then moved immediately to discuss other measures that could allow for better inflation control, so he was actually settling for 1.76 per cent. When Perry said that low unemployment could be maintained without exceptional inflation, he followed with calculations of various possibilities, and said that one that had 'perhaps some central interest' (p. 299) (because it was the official employment target at the time), was that 4 per cent unemployment would be associated with 2 per cent inflation. Then he noted that higher rates of productivity growth would reduce this inflation rate. There was no such clear indication of a preference in Perry (1966), but he presented a table of possibilities relating unemployment, the profit rate, and inflation (p. 109). His calculations went up to 6 per cent unemployment—well over 4 per cent—so presumably that was meant to be a sufficient range for all tastes. The calculations for inflation went as far as 3 per cent. There was no indication that higher rates of inflation might be considered.

Amongst the Canadians, Bodkin et al. (1967) did not really indicate a target, because they thought policy should be set in relation to American policy, but when they made illustrative calculations (pp. 283–5) they were on the basis that an inflation rate of 1.5 per cent would be acceptable. Vanderkamp's suggestion that unemployment should be kept to 5 per cent was associated with an inflation rate of 0.6 per cent (or higher with rising import prices). Zaidi's table was something like Perry's, also taking inflation up to 3 per cent. Reuber is the most specific, as well as the most inflationist, and said that freed of a fixed exchange rate he believed the best option would be 2.5 per cent unemployment and 3.75 per cent inflation. So, amongst the estimators of Phillips curves there is a little inflationism. There is not much—indeed, it is a real rarity. And it does not, I think I am

right in saying, contemplate anything that would later be regarded as a terribly shocking rate.

3.5 EXPLAINING INFLATIONISM

Still, inflationism is there, and the issue must arise as to what they thought
its long-term effect would be. The conventional story of the Philips curve
says, in effect, that until Friedman (1968a) economists had no ideas about
this at all, and simply presumed the estimated equations would be invariant to policy changes. As we shall see at the beginning of Chapter 4, there is
a major problem with that story, but before leaping to the conclusion that
even this minority of 1960s econometricians were so foolish, it should be
noted that there is a much better explanation of their attitude.

That explanation is that there was a widely understood argument that
high levels of employment were likely to be associated with gentle inflation without there being a general excess demand. This argument was later
associated with Tobin (1972b), but the best-known earlier statements
were those of Schultze (1959, 1960). The core of the argument is that when
demand shifts from one sector to another, with labour (and other factors)
only imperfectly mobile between sectors, prices or wages rise more readily
in the expanding sector than they fall in the contracting one. Operating
on prices, this will generate inflation, and operating on wages it will do so
if the asymmetry of wage adjustment and the size of the demand shifts
are great enough to make average wage increases greater than productivity
growth. In either case, inflation comes about without aggregate demand
being excessive. The inflation could be stopped by running lower demand
but that would make for a slower adjustment and lost output. On the
other hand, the inflation, by overcoming these rigidities, brings a quicker
adjustment.

Persistent inflation from this source, like any other, would obviously
become incorporated into expectations, but, as Tobin noted, that point
does not change the essential story. The force of the argument does not
arise from misperceptions, and so that point, in itself, leads nowhere. It
could be that a persistent inflation would convert the downward nominal
rigidity of wages into a downward real rigidity, and that would reinstate the
full force of the expectations argument. That is a rational point, but one
needs to tread carefully. One point would be that since the downward rigidity of nominal wages probably does not arise from strictly rational behaviour itself, it would be perverse to insist that the duration over which that
behaviour would survive must be rationally determined. There are, after

all, numerous explanations of wage stickiness, many of which, as it happens, are not far removed from the kind of thinking about wages which was prevalent in the 1950s, even if they were brought together later. Many of them are in the family of those considered by Bewley (1999). He pointed to Solow (1979b) and Akerlof (1982) as theoretical sources, but his conclusions might be summed up by the idea that pay cuts damage morale, and that, of course, is thoroughly in tune with the earlier labour economics literature. Other explanations which might focus more precisely on the question of fairness were certainly not more foreign to the times, and would also find a later expression in the likes of Kahneman, Knetsch, and Thaler (1986), perhaps combined with Akerlof and Yellen (1990). So it is very easy to argue such things in the light of the theory of wage bargaining from the 1950s, and only slightly harder, from a realistic outlook, at any other time.

Even if it is said that in the long run there must be downward flexibility, the argument still has force. Its point is not that adjustment is impossible without inflation, but that it is a lengthy and costly process. Since it is different sectors which are expanding and contracting at different times, the fact that in each there must be 'long-run' adjustment does not mean that there is some period of time after which no further adjustment will be required. At any point in history there will be some sectors needing to adjust, and that adjustment can be aided by inflation; therefore, there is a permanent role for inflation and the expectations argument deals no death blow here.

A further point, which can be made much more powerfully than Schultze or Tobin could have made it, is that, as a matter of fact, after decades of more-or-less uninterrupted inflation, it seems that there is still a specifically *nominal* downward rigidity.[19] That can hardly be because the labour market has not yet recognized the fact of inflation, so it is presumably because it does not, in the particular respect of the importance of avoiding specifically nominal wage cuts, adjust to it.

In considering the very low rates of inflation being contemplated, this argument is clearly important. But a crucial point about it is not that it was merely available, but that it was so widely appreciated. The frequency of reference to the argument is astonishing. Schultze's 1959 paper itself was enormously highly regarded, and for a time, frequently cited. It appeared as the lead paper amongst those prepared for Congressional Hearings. The whole package received very wide attention. Soule (1960) did not single out Schultze for comment, but thought such works might eventually rank with the *Federalist Papers* in historical interest. Romney Robinson (1960, p. 1004) particularly noted that all the 'important' papers in the Staff Report relied on the Schultze study paper, and that his name had already become associated with the argument under discussion, although he went on to express some doubts about the argument itself. Minsky (1961), reviewing the Report, may not have been greatly impressed by the argument, but explained it (without naming Schultze), and, interestingly, Minsky (1968) seems to have accepted the argument, and attributed it to Schultze (1959) and Lipsey (1960). Wonnacott (1960)—another reviewer—commented on Schultze's contribution at some length (pp. 561–4). The argument also featured in Eckstein (1959)—'The Eckstein Report' as it is sometimes called—which naturally drew extensively on the papers by Schultze and others. The basic problem is stated on page 394, with attribution to Schultze, and on page 403 it is clearly said that stopping that kind of inflation would generate unemployment.

Other explanations of Schultze's work rapidly appeared—Warren Smith (1960), who had been a contributor to the same volume, gave a brief explanation of the argument, attributing it to Schultze. Ackley (1961) outlined a version of the argument (pp. 445–6), citing Schultze's 'excellent study'. It was also considered and explained by Bronfenbrenner and Holzman (1963). There were plenty of others citing Schultze, some widely read, some little read, some laudatory, some sceptical. But there were plenty of them, and one striking measure is that—to judge by Google Scholar—in the first five years after each was published, Schultze (1959) was cited slightly more than Phillips (1958). The Schultze paper is much longer, of course (although most of those citing it do so in connection with the argument in question). On the other hand, unless, improbably, one counts Carlos Meyer (1964) using the expression 'efecto Schultze-Olivera' (p. 636) as equivalent, Schultze had no Samuelson and Solow to eponymize his work—and nor, unlike Phillips', were many of those citing his paper doing so to criticize him.

That alone is an impressive impact, but Carlos Meyer's nomenclature points in another important direction, which is that its statement by Schultze was only one source of the argument. Olivera (1960) is representative of another major pre-existing strand, which was the application of the argument by the 'structuralist' analysts of Latin American inflations. Seers (1962, pp. 181–2) was another, and Olivera (1964) was obviously intended to bring structuralism—including the argument later adopted by Tobin—to a wider audience. According to the recollection of Ito (1996), the same point was made in Japan in the 1950s and 1960s. That argument was, therefore, an aspect of what might be regarded as a whole school of thought—and not by any means one unknown to the mainstream. In any case the argument itself was deployed in policy discussion in relation to the United States in the Report of the Council of

Economic Advisers (CEA 1968), and in the United Kingdom rather earlier by the Council on Prices, Productivity and Incomes (1958b), although they thought it might be possible to overcome the problem by promoting downward price flexibility. Machlup (1960) took the same sort of view of it. Others again made it plain how commonplace the argument was, with Thirlwall (1969) citing Schultze as a popularizer of it. The argument, in various versions, appeared fairly frequently in textbooks of the period—including in Reynolds (1966, p. 596) where he presented it as an explanation of 'the Phillips curve'. It is notable that by that date, and on that basis, Reynolds was prepared to adopt that terminology. Samuelson (1961a) and Lipsey (1966) both mentioned the argument in textbooks, as did Snider and Irwin (1971), this time bringing an international dimension to it.

None of that is to suggest that the argument originated with Schultze or the structuralists. There is a full appreciation of it in Hart (1942, p. 92), and Rees (1950, p. 260) presented it in a book review. That surely forces one to the conclusion that he thought it nothing special. It is in Clark (1951, pp. 20–1) and Worswick (1952, p. 25)—analysing the post-war development of the British economy—and was presented by Lerner (1958) in Congressional Hearings.

Rees (1970) gave it another outing in a piece which was, like Tobin (1972b) explicitly a response to the argument by Friedman (1968a). He said,

> A gently rising price level will lubricate relative price changes... This lubricating effect will help prevent the generation of excess unemployment in industries or areas where relative prices are too high... So long as the pricing behaviour of firms is asymmetrical for price cuts and price increases, moderate inflation generates higher output and employment than price stability, even when it is fully anticipated. (Rees 1970, pp. 236–7)

This 'lubrication' argument, then, was frequently stated—it is easy to present another dozen instances, prior to 1968, each of them perfectly clear in itself, or citing a source which is.[20]

This therefore provides a clear explanation for why it would have seemed reasonable to contemplate accepting low rates of inflation and why an approximate tradeoff would have seemed calculable. Since the argument was so widely stated it can be presumed, absent any contrary indication, that it was understood by those discussing inflation and unemployment, and therefore provides a good explanation of what those few Phillips curve inflationists had in mind.

As it happens, the one significant case of there being such a contrary indication happens to be Canadian in that James Coyne, Governor of the Bank of Canada from 1955 to 1961, persistently and vehemently denied the existence of any tradeoff. This was not (or not merely) a piece of early Friedmanite wisdom, since the point was to deny what would later be called the short-run tradeoff—he simply denied that his anti-inflationary monetary policy was responsible for the high unemployment being experienced. That brought him into conflict with a group of economists,[21] eventually leading to his removal from his post. It is easy to see Coyne's attitude as a provocation to put a numerical value on the tradeoff that, because of the lubrication argument, almost everyone accepted was there.

With that one exception then, there can be no doubt that this was understood by anyone thinking about the problems of inflation and unemployment, and therefore there is no sense in denying that it was in the minds of those contemplating acceptance of a gentle inflation. And it makes very clear sense out of the arguments of those who thought they were estimating a stable exploitable relation, because none of them contemplated high rates of inflation.

3.6 CONCLUSION

On conventional accounts, before Friedman (1968a) there developed a large body of work derived from Phillips, with far too little understanding of the importance of price change, and far too much inclination to pursue inflation as a means of lowering unemployment. In the five sections above I hope I have shown that the reality is that we have rather little of any note derived from Phillips; a fine understanding of the role of price change; far more authors presuming price stability to be an essential than were inflationist; amongst the minority, usually only a very mild inflationism; and finally a good argument that there should have been much more of it.

CHAPTER 4

The Post-1968 Literature

In the usual story of the Phillips curve, the literature after 1968 is distinguished by the necessity of confronting the new idea brought by Friedman and perhaps Phelps (1967) about inflation expectations. The idea that this was a new insight from about that time needs to be laid to rest, and Section 4.1 seeks to do this. That raises the question of what the econometric Phillips curve literature of the 1970s was all about. In Section 4.2 I argue that a large part of the American literature was concerned simply with explaining why inflation and unemployment were both so high. Section 4.3 considers the British literature, which was perhaps less closely tied to that question, but raised various others. And Section 4.4 treats that of other countries and some multi-country studies. Section 4.5 then considers that part of the literature—not a large part—which was concerned with arguing specifically about the adjustment of expectations. As will become apparent in Chapter 7 particularly, that part has special significance, not for expressing the central concerns of the 1970s, which it does not do, but for the role it seems to play in the development of the Phillips curve myth.

4.1 THE ORIGINS OF THE EXPECTATIONS ARGUMENT

Whilst it must be clear that in the Phillips curve literature of the 1960s there was no confusion of nominal and real variables, and consequently Friedman's influence on its later development cannot have been what is usually thought, there is another clear demonstration of the same point available. That is, that even the expectations argument—'the Friedman/ Phelps expectations argument'—as it might conventionally be called, was nothing new when stated by either of them, and its common acceptance long pre-dates Friedman (1968a).

The point, it might be added, is nothing whatever to do with the slight frisson one sometimes detects between those who seem to want to emphasize Phelps (1967) as the originator of the argument, getting there before Friedman (1968a), or then again those who find Friedman (1966a) in the lead. Nor is the point that there are one or two uninfluential or unnoticed earlier statements of the argument. Indeed, that has been occasionally said, but what is important is precisely that the argument was widely known, and that has—since about 1970—hardly been appreciated at all.[1] Although it is hard to explain how there could be so many unrecalled and unnoticed earlier statements, in Forder (2010b) I had no difficulty at all in showing it to be the case.

There, one of the prize exhibits was Haberler (1960). He made the argument in other places too but really he added nothing to several earlier authors when he said,

> as creeping inflation continues, more and more people will expect a further rise in prices and will take steps to protect themselves…labor unions will ask for high wage increases in order to secure real improvement…(p. 51)

And that inflation could permanently reduce unemployment only

> if unions, and everybody else, could be fooled indefinitely to regard, despite rising prices, exactly balancing increases in money incomes as representing increases in real income. (p. 52)

Like most of those I quoted, Haberler showed little sign of thinking his point was original when he made it. No wonder: Leudicke (1957/1957) made the point in a newspaper; Bronfenbrenner (1963) made it slightly later, but correctly noted it had already been made by Morton (1950). I also quoted Vickrey (1955), Scitovsky (1940–1), and Simons (1936), amongst others. I had to stop somewhere, but there were plenty more I could have quoted.

One such would have been Polanyi (1944)—although far from an orthodox work of economics, and it is unclear whether his attribution of understanding to 'the masses' is well founded, there is no doubt that the author himself understood the point, saying, of the 1920s and 1930s,

> Under a modern money economy nobody could fail to experience daily the shrinking or expanding of the financial yardstick; populations became currency-conscious; the effect of inflation on real income was discounted in advance by the masses. (p. 24)

Apart from the point that expectations must adjust to reality, another aspect of the argument is that it is specifically misperceptions that allow inflation initially to reduce unemployment. Explicit recognition of that was also very common before Friedman, and it was put specifically that way by some of those I quoted before, and also by Lerner (1949, p. 194), who, like Stein (1958, p. 665), actually argued—just like Friedman (1968a)—that inflation is bad because it fools people into doing things they would not otherwise do.

Or one could go back to Mill (1844/1974) who noted that a boom occurs when prices rise, and said,

> For, the calculations of producers and traders being of necessity imperfect, there are always some commodities which are more or less in excess, as there are always some which are in deficiency. If, therefore, the whole truth were known there would always be some classes of producers contracting, not extending, their operations. If *all* are endeavouring to extend them, it is a certain proof that some general delusion is afloat. The commonest cause of such delusion is some general, or very extensive, rise of prices (whether caused by speculation or by the currency) which persuades all dealers that they are growing rich. And hence, an increase of production really takes place during the progress of depreciation, as long as the existence of depreciation is not suspected; and it is this which gives to the fallacies of the currency school, principally represented by Mr Attwood, all the little plausibility they possess. But when the delusion vanishes and the truth is disclosed, those whose commodities are relatively in excess must diminish their production or be ruined. (p. 67)

An early statement from the post-war period would be that of Reder (1948) who thought about it like this:

> assume that each of the various unions wants a given real wage rate for its own members and bargains for money-wage rates on the basis of the product price level existing at the moment of bargaining... Suppose that each union secures its money demands, but that the employers of its members thereafter raise their selling prices...

> ...if this process were to go on for a considerable length of time, the unions might insist on bargaining in terms of expected increases in the price level...(p. 52)

There are plenty more like that. The (British) Council on Prices Productivity and Incomes (1958a, para. 98) contemplated responding to the injustices of slow inflation by a deliberate generalized indexation of incomes, and said that if the inflation was not stopped, such arrangements would probably develop in any case. But, they said, this would be undesirable because 'they would be cumbrous and inefficient' and, they said, 'the most important result' of such a system would likely be

> that the upward movement of prices would cease to be slow. At present the groups which are in a strong strategic position derive gains corresponding to the losses of the weaker groups. As the losses were diminished, the attempt to preserve the gains would tend to speed up the whole inflationary process.

This clearly discloses an appreciation of the argument, and it comes from the heart of British policy discussion.

That statement was referred to with approval by Karmel (1959) who—calling the argument 'traditional'—said,

> if wage-earners are continually seeking increases in real wages greater than productivity, the consequent price rises may merely induce bigger and bigger wage demands. (p. 353)

He also pointed to the equivalent argument in Meade (1958, pp. 6–10). Weintraub (1959) was a theoretical monograph arguing against the quantity theory. On page 71 we find

> In equation (7.4) the wage is a function of immediate past unemployment, U_{t-1}, the immediate past real wage which affects labor bargaining attitudes, and the expected price level (P^*) which also conditions bargaining decisions.

Stein (1962) pushed the case for price stability, saying that because of the adjustment of expectations, high employment with no inflation was the only objective 'at which we can logically and consistently aim' (p. 25). As noted in Chapter 3, France (1962, p. 190) made the point that behaviour would adjust to ongoing inflation. And Pitchford (1963, p. 88), noted that unions would be naïve to bargain for money wages without regard to prices, citing Hicks (1955) as making the same point. Dow (1964), which is the classic study of British policy in the early post-war period, said, more or less as an aside, and clearly not thinking it a great insight,

> The pace of inflation is dependent (it was suggested) on customs and habitual expectations. (p. 398)

Again, understanding of the point is perfectly clear. There are yet others, but perhaps the best argument that this idea was not original when Friedman stated it in 1966 or 1968 is the fact that Friedman himself had stated it earlier. It is in Friedman (1958) as a response to the lubrication argument—Friedman argued that that effect would disappear as expectations adjusted, and he stated the importance of expectations in 1963. He did not then mention the possibility that anyone might think inflation lowered unemployment—that is a noteworthy omission in itself—but he did feel that some thought that inflation redistributed income or wealth in a desirable way. So, of inflation he said,

> If it is done deliberately, many people will know about it and will act so as to prevent the redistribution from taking place. If you announce to the public that you are going to adopt the deliberate policy of increasing prices at the rate of 3 per cent a year everybody will adjust to that announcement. In order to have the redistributive effects favorable to development, you will have to increase prices at the rate of, say, 6 percent a year. Once people adjust to that rate, you would have to go to a still higher rate and there is no stopping place. (1963/1968, p. 35)

And the point was linked directly to wages because he said,

> Such a steady inflation will soon be widely anticipated. The public at large will come to expect prices to rise at more or less the average rate. As a result, all sorts of economic arrangements will take into account the expected future price rises. Wage contracts will be drawn up so as to allow for periodic rises or so as to be linked to a cost of living index number... (pp. 46–7)

It might seem, I suppose, that the later treatments are superior to this sort of thing in virtue of offering a more complete theory. No one uses the expression 'natural rate of unemployment' before Friedman (1966a); few put the point they are making specifically in terms of 'expectations' (or 'anticipations', which was the word Friedman preferred). Plainly, they have no theory approaching the sophistication of Phelps (1967). But in terms of assessing the Phillips curve literature of the 1960s or 1970s such points are, despite occasional attempts to fan them into life,[2] entirely empty.

The earlier arguments clearly have—and are understood and intended to have—the implication that nominal changes have no enduring effect on employment. The claim conventionally made is that before Friedman and Phelps this was not understood.

In this connection, a point particularly deserving clarification is that of what is meant by 'expectations' (or 'anticipations'). We can—and should—distinguish various ways in which the point about adjustment to ongoing inflation could be theorized. One such distinction would be along the lines of the debate between 'rational' and 'adaptive' expectations. In the former, agents are in a position to compute future values of relevant variables from an extensive knowledge of the structure of the economy. In the latter, they form expectations by some formulaic processing of recent experience. In either case it might be said that the theory is that they act 'as if' these things are the case, but the natural way of discussing the ideas supposes that behaviour is determined by actual appreciations of the future. It is in that sense that behaviour would then properly and clearly be said to be affected by *expectations*. However they are formed, one might say there are conscious cognitions of the future.

A different possibility arises when behaviour simply adapts to the surrounding reality without the kind of understanding suggested by the idea of expectations. The theoretical extreme would make adjustment tropistic—done with no more understanding than that of a flower which turns towards the sun. Although, of course, not literally tropistic, the adjustment of institutions could be thought of in this way. So, for example, ongoing inflation might result in a shortening of conventional wage contract periods, or the introduction of indexation clauses to them. Equally, one can imagine that if there were a steady inflation, it might just be that habits would adjust to raise wages in parallel. Here, there is no conscious cognition, but merely an adaptation to the environment.

In some contexts, the difference between these views could be crucial,[3] and it is certainly open to question which of them offers the best account of behaviour—or which of them applies in which circumstances. It could even be questioned which of them it was that Friedman (1968a) had principally in mind.[4] These sorts of issues make it apparent that it is not altogether easy either to separate conceptually the possibilities and the various mixed cases that might be considered, nor to devise appropriate tests to distinguish the cases. But if the question is simply about whether there is a long-run tradeoff, they all lead to the same conclusion. In considering that question there is no reason at all to be fussy about the exact mechanism, and most of the time there is no reason to be fussy about whether the discussion is put in terms of changing 'expectations', although there is room for confusion on that point. One temptation might be to say that Friedman and Phelps were innovative in putting the argument clearly in terms of expectations, strictly understood as conscious cognitions about the future. Even that would not be correct, but more importantly in the context of the discussion of the shape of the Phillips curve, it would be to say they introduced nothing new, but *narrowed* the scope of the argument.

So the idea has malleability as well as antiquity, but the most important thing is its currency: all through the Phillips curve period it was no dark and mysterious idea reserved to the highest ranks of intellectual, but an obvious piece of common sense. Consequently, I doubt anyone would seriously argue that, despite all this, economists generally remained unaware of the argument—or even that anyone serious would argue it at all. It is not just the number of statements of the argument, nor the prominence of so many of the authors and the outlets in which they were published, but additionally the fact that the argument is an obvious one that intelligent people, thinking about wage determination, can hardly fail to recognize, however poorly read they may be. But in any case, there are other sorts of evidence as well.

One simple point would be that there was wide discussion of 'escalator' agreements whereby wage bargains contained agreements about indexation. These were highlighted by Jacoby (1957) and Soffer (1959) and so well recognized in America that the *Monthly Labor Review* ran annual accounts of their operation all through the 1960s. In any case it would be incredible if a union leader could keep his job whilst missing the opportunity of pressing a wage claim on the basis that prices had risen, and it is no surprise that Woytinsky (1949) found that 84 per cent of unions said the cost of living was the most important criterion in wage bargaining. Surely this must have got through to the minds of the public, economists, and econometricians.

Another consideration is that a number of authors discussing the argument immediately after it was put by Friedman and Phelps use language which clearly shows they knew it was not original. Donner (1972) recognized the argument as an old one and said that its 'most recent articulate supporters' (p. 17, n. 4) were Phelps, Friedman, and Cagan (1968). Rees (1970) described Phelps and Friedman as the 'strongest proponents' of the argument, although he named no others. Lucas and Rapping (1969a) tested the hypothesis, noted Friedman had advanced it, but also made it clear that it was not original to him. Brechling (1969) said in stating the argument, that Phelps (1969) was 'Following a long tradition in macroeconomics' (Brechling 1969, p. 161)—not a tradition starting in 1966, presumably.

Indeed, Phelps himself clearly recognized many earlier statements of the idea. In his 1968 paper, he attributed (p. 682) it to von Mises, Fellner, and

Wallich, also citing Lerner. In Phelps (1970c, pp. 129–30) he did so again. He clearly saw no originality in the idea himself and so there is no reason for others to insist on attributing originality to him. Indeed, it could be said that none of the authors quoted above give any indication of thinking the point original. According to the conventional story, any one of them has scooped one of the great insights of post-war macroeconomics. Yet not a single one makes play of that—none emphasizes their own originality, none makes the argument the centrepiece of their paper, and none alleges that there is a reigning error on the point. They all just write it down as if it is one of the points one makes in that kind of discussion—and indeed some of them specifically say that is what it is.

A further warning that the argument was neither exciting nor properly attributable to Friedman and Phelps at least comes from Mittra (1971). It is a book of readings for students and, as explained in his preface, includes three categories of article: those reprinted in full; those which could not be because of space limitations, but which were summarized; and others that were too long or too hard to summarize and which are listed as further reading. In the chapter on 'Prices, inflation and monetary policy', Friedman (1968a) made it into the second category—being, therefore, less important than Brunner (1968), Mundell (1963), Johnson (1968), and Horwich and Hendershott (1969), which were reprinted in full. So, Friedman's supposedly revolutionary paper merited only a four-paragraph summary—and that did not even mention the expectations argument. Of course not—that was not a novel and interesting aspect of the paper. (Phillips (1958), by the way, did not make it even to a summary.)

In the same sort of way, one of the authors who makes nothing of the originality of the argument is Friedman. Neither in Friedman (1958) nor Friedman (1963/1968), nor when deploying it in *Newsweek* in Friedman (1966c) did he indicate the argument was new. But the starkest demonstration of the same point comes from Friedman (1966a). Later work has persistently quoted this piece as his first statement of the argument and as bringing revolutionary insight to the issue, and indeed, it might be said that he was—later on—not altogether unwilling to accept this view. But the original statement does not have such an appearance. Much like many of the earlier authors, he seems to be repeating what he takes to be a truth of the human condition, as if he is warning that the love of money is the root of all evil or, more likely for Friedman, that a stitch in time saves nine, saying,

> By speeding up the rate of monetary expansion and aggregate demand, you can unquestionably increase output and employment temporarily. You *can* cut the

level of unemployment down, but at what price? At the price of postponing the adjustment. What happens is that, as people get adapted to any given rate of price rise, as they come to anticipate a continuation of the price rise, the unemployment rate will creep up. Say you cut unemployment down to 3 per cent. Then, at the same rate of price rise, it will creep up. If you then try to hold it down by stepping up the rate of inflation from 3 per cent to 4 per cent or 5 per cent, you will again be able to cut down unemployment, but, again, only temporarily—only until people adjust their anticipations. (p. 59)

What is more, these remarks come in Friedman's comments on the presentation made by Solow (1966b) in the course of a debate at a conference. Where are the signs that close attention is demanded? Where is the fanfare that should be accompanying an argument that will change macroeconomics? Did Friedman really save up a revolutionary idea, not even for his main presentation in a debate, but for his comments on his adversary's? Excuses can be made, of course—it was a deep play by a master rhetorician to deploy the argument quietly at the end of the debate. But that is the kind of idea that arises from the fact that the conclusion has the benefit of being constantly repeated. If we do not start with the idea that this is a revolutionary idea, there is nothing to make it seem so.

Anyway, if he did intend some such dramatic purpose, it was rather a misjudgment because two reviewers of the publication—Lekachman (1967) and Kendrick (1967)—despite discussing the debate between Friedman and Solow, made no reference at all to the expectations argument; the introduction to the volume—Shultz and Aliber (1966)—also failed to mention Friedman's argument; and when the *Monthly Labor Review* selected three of the papers from the conference for publication in June 1966, Friedman's was not among them. Stranger still, though, is this: when his main contribution to the debate—Friedman (1966b)—was reprinted in Friedman (1968b), these final comments were not. So even Friedman, apparently, did not think them novel and exciting—or anyway, he did not think them worth reprinting. If there were even a shred of truth in the story that in his comments on Solow's paper Friedman had transformed macroeconomics, that would make *five* astonishing omissions.

4.2 EXPLAINING THE DETERIORATION OF THE TRADEOFF

It should be no surprise, in the light of this, that the idea of expectational adjustment did not by any means have the transformative effect on the Phillips curve literature that is sometimes suggested. The literature was transformed, but when we consider it free of the presumption that it becomes all about testing this new idea, it is possible to see what else happened.

One thing, which is just a terminological one but turns out to be important, is that the expression 'Phillips curve' was, after 1968, freely applied in both the econometric and the wider literature to price-change as well as to wage-change relations. That may follow in part from Friedman and Phelps, who both used it that way, but in the 1960s generally that usage had been very unusual. Another notable change was that the decline in the quality of the literature that was so clear towards the end of the 1960s is immediately reversed—or more than reversed—in about 1970. One reason for that may just be that 1970 happens to be the year that the *Brookings Papers on Economic Activity* appear, and they contain a large number of the most serious treatments of the Phillips curve. Another point, no doubt, is just that it is at about that time that inflation became a serious problem and in particular that high rates of inflation persisted at higher levels of unemployment—it was, in other words, the time when what became known as 'the breakdown of the Phillips curve' first became apparent in America. Explaining the new combination of high inflation and high unemployment was a major objective of the literature and attracted serious work.

Those explanations, though, did not by any means necessarily focus on expectations. A good part of this work proceeded on bases linked to the earlier discussions of wage change but sought to incorporate the consequences of continuous high inflation. One example of this approach comes from Wachter (1970), who reiterated the observation that there was a range of wages paid for equivalent labour and that some firms were persistently high, and others low-wage firms. This meant that whereas the low-wage firms were operating more or less in competitive conditions, the high-wage firms—confronted with a 'queue' of would-be workers—could increase their labour force without raising wages. This meant that in significant sections of the economy, there could be long lags between changes in demand and changes in wages. In Wachter (1976b) he explored the determination of these lags. He argued that they would depend on the formal and informal institutional arrangements for the setting of wages and so would depend upon the variability and recent level of inflation. Then, his explanation for the shift of the Phillips curve was that during the 1960s—when inflation had been low and stable—the lags lengthened, so that when demand was too high at the end of the 1960s the long lags continued to hold down inflation at the beginning of the 1970s. The importance of price change in wage bargaining is a clear feature of this argument, but there was no need for a new story about expectations—understood as conscious cognitions of the future—rather that some other form of adjustment.

Wachter's attitude to inflation and the shifting Phillips curve is also enlightening. He said,

> if the full-employment unemployment rate was between 4 and 4.5 percent during the 1950s, then it is approximately 5.5 percent today. (p. 116)

The point of the 'full-employment' rate must be that there is a single rate of unemployment which is of special interest. That was, in his paper, given by price stability, and his expression clearly suggests he was not thinking about there being a continuous 'menu'. He should also be read carefully in his discussion of the disappearance of the old Phillips relation, when he said that wage inflation was moving in the direction his model suggested but that,

> it has not, since 1957, moved rapidly. This slow response is probably the immediate cause of the concern that the Phillips curve is becoming flatter. (p. 156)

Concern? A 'flat' Phillips curve is one where a small rise in inflation is associated with a large fall in unemployment. Wachter was referring to the fact that contractionary demand seemed on the face of it to have lost its power to reduce inflation, but of course anyone wishing to 'exploit the Phillips curve' would yearn for it to be flat. It is when it is seen as determining the costs of inflation control that this is a concern.

Hall (1974), like Hall (1970), shared with Wachter the objective of modelling firm-level wage setting and hiring, and the idea that accelerationist properties of the Phillips curve arose from the fact that wages responded to the conditions prevailing in the labour market. There was again no properly expectational element in his hypothesized behaviour. Rather, firms set wage scales so as to recruit the labour they needed. In tight labour markets unemployed workers would tend to find higher paying jobs than their previous ones, and in slack markets the opposite—hence the Phillips curve. He estimated tradeoff relations over a 25-year horizon, suggesting the United States might end up with either 13.3 per cent wage inflation at 4 per cent unemployment; or 2.6 per cent at 5.8 per cent. He said himself that it was 'statistically entirely plausible' (Hall 1974, p. 366) that he was understating the power of the accelerationist position, so it can hardly be that these very long-range estimates are to be taken entirely seriously. Other than that the point most firmly emphasized (pp. 377–8) was that maintaining unemployment was an effective means of reducing inflation. In that, any 'stability' of the Phillips curve meant that unemployment continued to have the power to reduce inflation.

Hall (1976) was of a different character. There, for the purposes of the argument, he accepted the existence of the natural rate and considered—in the manner of Phelps (1967) and Phelps (1972b, part III)—the question of the approach to the natural rate, noting that the benefits of temporary reductions in unemployment might make permanent inflation a price worth paying. That might well be an inflationist argument, but it has nothing to do with a naïve idea of the curve. Others similarly considered wage bargaining in this kind of detail.[5]

Perhaps the line of thinking which ended up being of most lasting importance started with Perry (1970). That paper is also a fine example of the character of this strand of the literature. It turned on developing the idea, previously seen, for example, in Simler and Tella (1968), that unemployment was an inadequate measure of labour market pressure. Perry presented a carefully constructed series for 'adjusted unemployment' and the dispersion of unemployment. The former allowed for different labour supply by members of different demographic groups and for wage differentials between them; the latter for imperfect substitutability between groups of workers. A particular finding was that the very low rate of prime-age male unemployment made adjusted unemployment low despite the entry of women and younger workers into the labour force seeming to make overall unemployment higher. That explained the apparent deterioration of the tradeoff without needing to invoke expectations and Perry spent only about a page on that issue, naming neither Friedman nor Phelps, and saying that although he had not really tested the idea, the indications of his work were against it.

Perry (1973) adopted a similar position with less econometrics and more discussion, reaffirming the existence of 'a stable long-run tradeoff between inflation and labor market tightness' (p. 577), and also offering (pp. 581–3) a fairly detailed rationale for rejecting the vertical Phillips curve. This included a statement (p. 582) of the lubrication argument and a discussion of Perry's doubts about the value of the models of search unemployment of the kind exemplified by Phelps (1968) and Mortensen (1970).

In other work, Perry adopted the same general position, but also offered more discussion of expectations and in particular the relation between expectations and what he called 'inflation inertia'. Clearly that draws the distinction between what I called 'conscious cognition', or 'expectations' strictly defined, and 'adaptation'. In Perry (1971) he said that he believed inflation was continuing despite low aggregate demand because of 'high "habitual" rates of wage and price increase' (p. 446). In Perry (1978) he put this sort of idea in terms of inflation being 'firmly entrenched' (p. 259) and on page 268 discussed the difference between the cases where inertia in inflation arises from 'a purely backward-looking process' so that 'wage setting would be influenced by wage changes that have already occurred', with the consequence that 'The prospect that inflation would accelerate or decelerate in the future' would not affect the process, and the case where the process is 'purely forward looking' so that 'only expectations of future inflation would matter'. He noted two important things about this distinction. One is that time series analysis found it difficult to distinguish them, not least because expected inflation was often modelled as being determined by past inflation. The other was that the difference between the two nevertheless has policy significance since it affects what kind of measures might be effective in slowing inflation. He noted that Fellner (1976b) had suggested that making manifest a commitment to control inflation, whatever the cost, would change expectations, but Perry thought that such things as tax-based incomes policy could reduce inertia. He developed this line of thinking slightly in Perry (1980) where he described the possibility of 'wage norms' being something like the habitual rate of wage increase. In a comment on the paper, Duesenberry (1980, p. 258) suggested thinking of the norm as the wage increase a personnel manager would want to give if the firm had no special needs. These kinds of ideas clearly lead to the possibility of inflation inertia without introducing properly forward-looking behaviour.

The specifically historical interest in the distinction comes from this. Perry was disputing the importance of 'expectations' in the Phillips curve—he was denying that they should feature in econometric estimates. He was not, though, arguing that a record of inflation would make no difference to wage bargaining or inflation. In 1970 he had been able to explain the data without any version of expectations, but later in the decade, with inflation long-standing and high, he showed no resistance at all to the view that it mattered—in *that* sense, they could be categorized as accepting the 'expectations' argument, but he was not thinking about conscious cognitions of the future.

Another possibility was raised by Eckstein and Brinner (1972). They suggested a non-linear response of wages to price change. That could come in various forms but their analysis allowed for a negative relationship between wage change and unemployment while inflation was below 2.5 per cent, but above that level the curve would be vertical. Such analysis obviously had the potential to reconcile the older findings of a less-than-full adjustment to prices with a clear sense of the idea that the labour market could not ignore higher rates of inflation—indeed that is exactly how those authors saw it, as did others who incorporated similar ideas.[6] Their conclusion—also not so far different from the sort of things said before 1968—was that an unemployment rate of about 4 per cent was as low as was achievable without explosive inflation. Brinner (1977), commenting on Eckstein and Brinner's finding of a threshold effect at 2.5 per cent, labelled that 'severe' inflation. Several others considered inflation expectations with various objectives that were not closely related to agreeing or disagreeing with Friedman.[7]

Other studies—particularly *Brookings* studies—were focused on the question of the best policy to be pursued at the time of writing. One such was Modigliani and Papademos (1975), who considered the appropriate recovery path from recession. They described themselves as holding an 'intermediate' position on the shape of the Phillips curve, meaning that it was flat at high rates of unemployment but nearly vertical or even backward bending at low rates of unemployment, but they also clearly invoked the lubrication argument.

All these studies share the characteristics of having sophisticated arguments about economic behaviour combined with serious attempts to make use of econometrics to reveal their value. It would be ridiculous to suggest that any of them is basically an estimation of a tradeoff function, whether presumptively stable or not. As to their response to the expectations argument, they are all attempts to understand much more subtle matters than that. Most of them make some reference to Friedman or the expectations argument, but none is principally concerned with putting Friedman's argument to the test, and certainly not with trying to defend the idea of a stable, exploitable Phillips curve against him. Just as it is not the case that the 1960s literature revolves around estimates of the tradeoff, so it is that in the 1970s it does not revolve around assessing Friedman's argument, whether it be thought new or old.

4.3 THE BRITISH LITERATURE

Another development of 1970 and after was the emergence of a British Phillips curve literature which was in certain respects substantially independent of the American. It is a curiosity, perhaps little noticed, that in the earlier period there were the Phillips precursors and Phillips competitors, like Klein and Ball or Dicks-Mireaux and Dow; there were the out-and-out Phillips critics; and there were those who sought to present alternatives to his work, but, except for Lipsey's, there are no important British works that were truly part of the Phillips curve literature. When it came, though, the reimportation of the idea to the United Kingdom was dramatic, and between 1970 and 1976 an enormous number of estimates of British Phillips curves (or similar relations) were made. Part, but only part, of the explanation was that the Phillips curve was a popular device in a series of six books called 'studies in inflation', appearing between 1972 and 1976 under the general editorship of Michael Parkin and David Laidler,[8] who were, of course, also the authors of a major survey of inflation—Laidler and Parkin (1975). There were also numerous other Phillips curves estimated for various reasons, many closely concerned with policy. But again, it is quite mistaken to suppose that arises from any willingness to accept inflation. Indeed, such an idea could hardly be further from the truth.

Some of the British papers more or less fit the American pattern of being responses to the 'disappearance' of the curve, which in the British case was usually dated to 1966 or 1967. Bowers, Cheshire, and Webb (1970), for example, suggested that vacancies provided a measure of excess demand for labour which exhibited a stable relationship with wage change through the 1960s, and that therefore the breakdown of the Phillips relation amounted to a change in the vacancies-unemployment relation, which they suggested might be explained by a combination of factors prevailing at the time. Romanis Braun (1971) thought its disappearance due to special factors, but also, perhaps following an idea from Phelps Brown (1968), expressed (pp. 168–70) doubt as to its stability on the basis that it arose because unions timed wage bids to coincide with low unemployment, but if a higher level of unemployment were targeted, similar average wage increases would occur at a higher average level unemployment.

Alternatively Henry, Sawyer, and Smith (1976) suggested that a modified version of Sargan's (1964) model both performed well and suggested an important role for unions in wage determination so that their relation was a 'cost-push' one. They found that higher unemployment did not lower wage increases. A marked characteristic of their attitude is that they firmly treated this as showing that there had never been a 'Phillips curve' whereas others, finding they could estimate a relation, seemed more or less content to pass over that issue. Others pursued similar or related lines, and different parallels in the American literature could be found for yet others, none of which are of much lasting independent importance.[9]

A more distinctively British aspect of the literature—still owing nothing to Friedman—arose as a result of the debate over Hines' argument that union militancy determined wage increases, and the clearly evident case for incomes policy it suggested. Such militancy appeared to be a more and more serious problem late in the 1960s and in the 1970s, so the argument he had first made in Hines (1964) and Hines (1968) was, naturally enough, a source of interest. Hines' approach, however, proved controversial, and a sometimes bad-tempered argument went on for some time,[10] until Mulvey and Gregory (1977) ended it, at least for the time being, by arguing that Hines inadequately distinguished the effect of changes in unionization from changes in the union wage premium.

A quite different argument about incomes policy followed from the innovative approach of Lipsey and Parkin (1970). Rather than including a dummy variable for such policy in the manner of Perry (1967) or Jefferson, Sams, and Swann (1968), they sought to estimate separate Phillips curves for 'policy on' periods when incomes policy operated, and 'policy off' periods when it did not. Their conclusion was that policy had the effect of 'flattening' the curve, and they argued that since policy tended to be 'on' in periods of contractionary policy the outcome was higher inflation than would have been achieved with the same contraction and incomes policy 'off'. There was a considerable debate over this paper which, unusually, led to each of the authors accepting that it was econometrically flawed. In that sense, this line of argument was also productive of more literature than insight, but, interestingly, the Lipsey–Parkin paper continued to be an occasional point of reference in subsequent discussion.[11]

Thirdly, there was a debate over 'regional policy', which became a major policy issue, particularly after 1967.[12] A number of authors used Phillips curves in seeking to make their cases. The argument was readily connected to the idea of Lipsey (1960), to the effect that the non-linearity of the Phillips curve meant that if unemployment rates differed between sectors (or geographical regions), the aggregate curve would lie above sectoral curves. Archibald (1969) found that both regional and sectoral dispersion had the effect suggested by Lipsey, although later, in Archibald, Kemmis, and Perkins (1974), seemed to doubt that. Both of these were wide-ranging papers and the discussion of regional policy is only one aspect of them. Metcalf (1971) looked at regionally disaggregated data and was unusual in denying the existence of the curve—unemployment had no effect on wages. He thought that the change in unemployment did have such an effect, and policy should be directed to controlling that. Others treated regional matters in various ways, with some version of the Phillips curve performing a role.[13]

An important reason that these papers are significant, despite any doubts about their lasting contribution, is that, taken as a group, they go a long way to explaining the impression that the Phillips curve was at the heart of policy debate in the United Kingdom. Indeed, in a sense it was, although the debate was not about the effects of inflationary policy, or the optimal tradeoff point, or anything of that kind. Indeed, in none of the cases was the stability of the curve even a central issue. A few of the authors commented on that issue in passing, but it was not relevant to the questions they were asking, which were about the effectiveness of incomes policy and regional policy.

It is, of course, easy to imagine that what is meant by, for example, an 'effective' incomes policy is one that lowers the whole Phillips curve so as to provide an improved 'menu', and hence that the implication is then that there is a choice to be made, and a more favourable one than there would be without the policy. Indeed, in some non-econometric discussions, ideas like that can—occasionally—be found, but they are absent here. The focus of the authors on the immediate scientific questions is remarkable. The question at stake in the debate over incomes policies was whether they lowered wage settlements and hence inflation. The advocates said that it did, the opponents that it did not (or occasionally that the other costs were greater than such benefits). That issue neither turns on the attitude one takes to accelerationism, nor leads to any conclusion on the desirability of inflation, so it is clear that the question was about the control of inflation, not the improvement of a menu. Just the same kind of point can be made about regional policy.

4.4 OTHER COUNTRIES, MULTI-COUNTRY STUDIES, AND MACROECONOMETRIC MODELS

If we stick with studies that did not have testing the expectations argument as a principal objective, there are Phillips curves for a few more countries, some multi-country studies, and the curves estimated as parts of macro-econometric models to consider. Still, there is not much hint of an attempt to discover an optimal point on a tradeoff.

Reuber (1970) considered the matter of key bargains in relation to the Canadian economy, and thought there was nothing much in it, but this time refrained from any inflationist conclusions; there were some other Canadian studies with more of a methodological aspect.[14] There were also a couple of estimates for Italy. One, by Modigliani and Tarantelli (1973), was inflationist on the basis that a high level of demand would improve the quality of the labour force, so that the location of the curve could be improved by a period of inflation. They specifically said that for their purposes they did not need to decide the issue of whether the curve was ever vertical, but clearly had no resistance to the idea that it was. And there was Spinelli (1976) who considered cost-push inflation arising from union militancy at length, but rejected the idea in favour of an expectations Phillips

curve and found it to be vertical. V. B. Hall (1976) offered rather monetarist conclusions on New Zealand. Toyoda (1972) found a kind of Japanese
Phillips curve with the bizarre conclusion that the price stability level of
unemployment was lower in the long run than in the short run—but in
any case it was price stability that interested him. Unusually for such a late
work, Marczewski (1978) did not engage with the issue of expectations,
but he did think the control of inflation essential for France.

Jacobsson and Lindbeck (1969) estimated a Phillips curve for Sweden
for the purpose of discovering whether incomes policy is necessary to the
simultaneous achievement of full employment and price stability, and followed up in Jacobsson and Lindbeck (1971). They accepted that high rates
of inflation would affect wage change, but doubted it for lower rates. The
earlier paper earned criticism from Isachsen (1977) over the treatment
of prices, even though the authors discussed the effect of expectations
(pp. 87–8). Their idea was that as a matter of the realistic psychology of
wage bargaining there is more to it than strict calculation of real wages,
and there is no question of their not having understood the point. Even
here there is no suggestion of exploiting a tradeoff and the policy questions
raised are about the control of inflation. Clearly, their introduction of the
possibility of even limited money illusion makes their presumption that
price stability is the goal more striking.

The only country for which there were a good number of Phillips curves
estimated in the 1970s but not in the 1960s was Australia. Before then,
there was the abortive Phillips (1959/2000), which was only fully published
when it became a matter of historical interest, and Hancock's (1966a) hybrid
relation in which the deviation of wage payments from the then-existing
highly centralized administered rates was estimated as a function of unemployment. Perhaps one should also mention Pitchford (1968) which was
an econometric study of changes in the price level. That paper shows no
sign of inflationism but rather followed from Pitchford (1963) which was a
theoretical work giving an unusually thorough taxonomy of inflation types
along the cost-push/demand-pull axis. Like so much of the literature of the
1960s, the later paper is simply concerned with understanding the sources
of inflation and gives no indication of thinking in terms of there being a
tradeoff.

From the 1970s, there are other cases to be mentioned shortly, but one
who was mildly inflationist was Nevile (1970). He estimated price change in
terms of wages and unemployment and except for a comment on his views
on fiscal policy, he did not mention Friedman, nor Phelps, nor expectation,
nor, for that matter, Phillips. Still, the book is concerned with policy. It
presumes the relation between inflation and unemployment is exploitable

and that the levels of unemployment associated with price stability are unacceptable, and (p. 21) Nevile seems to accept that a case could be made for steady inflation of up to 6 per cent. Whilst there are certainly hints that the lubrication argument lies behind his thinking, he does not offer a clear response to anything like the expectations argument. This is not an altogether authentic example of the kind of view supposed to be common because it is so clear that prices are presumed to be driven by wages, so that inflation is cost-push, but it is, nevertheless, quite close, and clearly contemplates higher levels of inflation than others.

There is also discussion of wage equations as components of large macroeconometric models. In these there is routinely less than full adjustment to price change so that in that sense they embody a stable, non-vertical Phillips curve. Since they are, fairly obviously, concerned with policymaking, that might seem to indicate that policymaking also was based on such a view. But any further consideration reveals that such inferences are inappropriate. For one thing, the models originate in the 1960s and were developed gradually, so that the specification they had at any particular time always reflected work in progress. That work, of course, must have responded to whatever appeared to be the most pressing issues at the time. So, for example, Suits (1962) described a model with a wage-change equation without price change. It seems much more reasonable to suppose that was the outcome of effort being spent on other aspects of the model at a time when price changes were small, rather than that it grew from a considered view that wages were set independently of the price level. The position is not satisfactory, but nor is the world perfect. Sometimes this is even noted, as it was by Ando and Modigliani (1969)—who considered the Federal Reserve–MIT model. They felt that their wage-change equation was 'much too crude' (pp. 310–11). One aspect they highlighted was that the wage mechanism was not an equilibrium process so the model would allow errors to accumulate and consequently 'we cannot count on our simulation tracking the historical path closely for more than, say, two or three years' (p. 312). There is a further point, perhaps also suggested by what Ando and Modigliani say. That is these models were, after all, short-run forecasting models. It should not be too surprising if they embody short-run relations, and inferring what is generally believed about the long run might therefore be difficult.

Nevertheless, for what it is worth, there are a number of discussions of these models, many of which embody non-vertical Phillips curves. In some cases, like de Menil and Enzler (1972)—again discussing what was by then called the FR–MIT–Penn model—there is a clear explanation of their attitude in that they referred to Rees (1970), who stated the lubrication argument amongst others. That rationalizes their econometric findings against the vertical Phillips curve. In other cases, nothing is said about it, but there is scarcely ever a hint of inflationist conclusions. The closest to inflationism, perhaps, comes in Fromm and Taubman (1968), in their discussion of the Brookings model. They do say that policy should be aimed at the optimal point on a properly specified Phillips curve, but they are much more concerned with analysing the difficulties of finding that specification than making policy proposals. Griliches (1968) gave a reasoned account of his view that the price equations will 'turn out' to be unsatisfactory, but clearly recognized that more work on the model is required. Hirsch (1972) reported that the Office of Business Economics model generated a stable 4 per cent rate of inflation at 4 per cent unemployment. He noted the expectations argument, but is unusual in feeling it worthwhile in using the model to offer a 20-year forecast. At the other extreme, perhaps, are Evans and Klein (1968) discussing the Wharton model. They say, 'changes in wage rates have become increasingly dependent on changes in the consumer price index, until presently there is almost a marginal one-to-one correspondence between percentage changes in these two indices' (p. 35). There are various other papers, but none offer great surprises.[15]

4.5 RESPONDING TO FRIEDMAN

All that, I hope, shows there was a great deal to the post-1968 Phillips curve literature which was nothing to do with Friedman or Phelps. That is not to say that none of the literature was more directly aimed at responding to Friedman or testing the expectations hypothesis. One of those responses, which is a telling one in the light of the misperception of the 1960s literature that was to develop, was simply to relabel 'price change' as 'expected inflation', and carry on. Bent Hansen (1970, p. 5) noted that including current inflation as an explanatory variable was a simple and reasonable way of introducing expectations into the equation. Lipsey and Parkin (1970) interestingly say,

> in common with previous studies, we enter the rate of change of prices in the wage equation as a proxy for the *anticipated* rate of change of prices. (p. 117)

The point about 'previous studies' suggests they were putting this interpretation on the price-change variable in the pre-1968 work, and presumably all the way back to Lipsey (1960). There might well be a bit of rewriting of history in that, since very few of those authors had shown any sign of thinking that way, but even so, the thought that their work could be so reinterpreted is perfectly reasonable. In practical terms, in the circumstances of 1970, or perhaps at any time, there might be no better way of measuring currently expected inflation than by currently experienced inflation. Others made the same move with no more fuss.[16]

In the light of that response, it could have been said that there was nothing in 'Friedman's hypothesis' that required new and separate testing since price change had always been routinely included in the earlier studies. That is in itself an important point, but it also means it is no surprise that when authors do set out to test the expectations idea more specifically, they have something further to say about the measurement of expectations. Particularly amongst the earliest of these studies it is possible to see quite serious attempts to develop thinking in this area.

Solow (1968) and the similar, better-known, Solow (1969) were two early responses of this kind. First of all, expected inflation was modelled as a distributed lag of past rates of inflation. That resulted in a rejection of the vertical Phillips curve. He also tried (1969, pp. 15ff) a version where the coefficient on expected inflation increased as inflation did so as to reach 1 when inflation was 8.5 per cent. That was an attempt to accommodate the common sense of the expectations idea whilst the data rejected the literal version. Even that was obviously not final, as Marin (1970) noted, calling the results 'stimulating and suggestive, rather than conclusive'. Lucas and Rapping (1969a) adopted a version of a formula for expectations of a kind suggested by Jorgenson (1966), noting its theoretical superiority to a simple distributed lag. Their results were mixed. Turnovsky and Wachter (1972) used survey data for expectations and found that had some predictive power but a coefficient of 0.35, which they noted was not far from others' estimates. Their conclusion was that the 'stringent' version of the hypothesis (that the coefficient is 1) should be rejected, but that price and wage expectations are significant in explaining actual wage change. They also said, doubting whether they reached the bottom of the matter,

> although the long-run Phillips curve may be vertical, no dynamic wage equation has yet been developed to express the underlying labor market mechanism. (p. 52)

Nordhaus (1972b) noted that average wage growth in seven industrial countries had increased sharply in 1968 and suggested that there should be a common explanation. He had a number of candidate explanations and sought to test five of them. Two of them were a Phillips-type explanation with and without expectations. He ended up concluding that for the United States and Canada one or other Phillips curve explanation was to be preferred, and that their inflation was communicated to the other countries by the operation of the exchange rate system, but he offered no policy conclusions.

The point that all these had more to offer than merely being a response to Friedman is even truer of a string of papers based on rational expectations—of which Lucas (1973) is widely noted—and the various methodological points made around them by, particularly, Sargent (1971), Lucas (1972b), and Phelps (1972b, pp. 49–52). They tended to point towards a vertical curve. There were various other studies of the issue, probably of less note, or less noted.[17]

In this sub-literature, however, the work of Gordon demands special attention first of all because, in his earliest papers—Gordon (1970) and Gordon (1971a) notable amongst them—he offered some of the firmest rejections of the vertical Phillips curve, and drew mildly inflationist conclusions. But then, in later papers, he gradually changed his view and in Gordon (1977) accepted Friedman's position.

In Gordon (1970, p. 11) he clearly stated the goal of testing the idea of a vertical Phillips curve as a 'major purpose' and had no difficulty accepting the sense of the idea, since he said,

> Today's labor force is forward-looking and influenced by the expected level of consumer prices in relation to current nominal wages

and a few lines later

> in my research, as in all previous research on price expectations, changes in the expected price level are assumed to be a function of past price changes. (p. 16)

As did others, he gave considerable attention to the measurement of expected inflation, considering three approaches—various arrangements of geometrically declining weights on past inflation; a weighting scheme estimated as part of the process of estimating the model; and a weighting scheme deduced from the interest rate on bonds. This last presumed that the numerical value of the bond rate reflected expected inflation, and made it possible to deduce econometrically what weights should be applied to past inflation so as to give rise to that observed expectation. This way of looking at it also suggests that he was thinking of actual assessments of the future, rather than simply habitual adjustment, and trying to work out a way to determine what was anticipated about the future.

He did, though, come to the conclusion that there was a non-vertical curve and explicitly offered (p. 33) policy alternatives—some with more inflation, others with less—and clearly accepted that policymakers faced alternatives. He stopped short of proposing inflationary policy but he clearly thought it a reasonable possibility, saying that if it were thought important to maintain low unemployment,

> inflation will at least be steady rather than accelerating, even though it may be substantial. (p. 11)

The associated calculations reported on page 31 and the following pages show that what he meant by 'substantial' was something under 4 per cent. Gordon (1971a) is, in the respects being emphasized here, rather similar. This time incorporating Perry's measure of unemployment dispersion amongst demographic groups, he described the objectives of that paper as being to pursue various forecasting goals relating to alternative recovery paths and said that he calculated 'the short- and long-run tradeoffs between inflation and unemployment' (p. 106). He said that as in 'most previous econometric research' (p. 107) he presumed the rate of change of wages to be determined by the excess demand for labour and the expected rate of increase in prices and wages. (He too was presumably treating the pre-1968 literature as having this aspect through actual price change measuring expected price change.) He again took the problem of measuring or estimating expectations seriously (pp. 110ff), but this time, he specifically said that 'by definition' (p. 136) expectations were correct in equilibrium. That makes it clear that he was interested in how the economy behaved when expectations were satisfied, and there is in the findings of non-vertical Phillips curves no presumption that expectations do not adjust to inflation, but rather that fully perceived inflation has real effects. In these papers he does not describe the lubrication argument, but his awareness of it is very clear from its appearance in Gordon (1973b).

It could also be said that there are a couple of notes of nervousness in his conclusion that

> The 'accelerationist' hypothesis can be statistically rejected but by a narrower margin than in most previous research. (p. 143)

Nevertheless, narrow though the margin is, and statistical as the desiderata may be, the rejection is still present, and indeed he even drew a long-run tradeoff (p. 138), noting that it was steeper than suggested in his 1970 paper, but saying (p. 144) that policymakers would have to choose the combination of inflation and unemployment they preferred, although in this the emphasis was on the question of whether it was worth raising unemployment to lower inflation. (Gordon (1971c) and Gordon (1971b), which do not themselves present econometrics show fairly clearly that Gordon's view was that it was not.)

Gordon (1972a) was principally concerned with assessing the effectiveness of wage and price controls. It is probably safe to describe his forensic comparison of Gordon (1971a), Perry (1970), and Eckstein and Brinner (1972) as a remarkable testament to his seriousness of purpose in understanding the mechanisms concerned, but in the end he came to conclusions much like those of his previous papers, although this time without actually suggesting alternative stable rates of inflation. He also experimented with a 'variable coefficient' approach to the expectations issue. There, expectations were determined in the same sort of way as in previous papers, but their coefficient was allowed to increase as expected inflation did (reaching its maximum of 1 at an inflation rate of about 7 per cent (Gordon 1972a, p. 406). This, he noted, had some resemblance to the 'inflation threshold' formulation used by Eckstein and Brinner (he could have listed Solow and others too) and had the advantage of reconciling the theoretical appeal of the expectations hypothesis with its empirical rejection. Gordon (1973a) and Gordon (1975a) are probably less significant papers; the first revisits but adds little to the 1972 paper, the second shifts attention to product prices rather than wage change and dismisses the view that anticipated policy has no effect on output, but does not discuss long-run tradeoffs.

Gordon (1977), however, reaches very different conclusions. There he performed further estimations using officially revised data and the result was the contradiction of his earlier findings. 'Ironically', he said,

> the 'natural rate hypothesis' in the form of a coefficient of unity on price inflation, is vindicated by the revisions in the official data. (p. 265)

That it was only incorrect data that ever led him astray is surely a memorable finding but again his seriousness in trying to get to the bottom of the matter is palpable and his willingness to change his conclusions when that seemed appropriate only strengthens the impression created by his evident commitment to scrutinizing the data; considering as wide a range of hypotheses as possible; seeking out tests of them; and applying an intensity in his analysis which matches any of the Phillips curve literature of the time. That impression is that work embodied in these papers is not to be dismissed—even if it rejects the expectations hypothesis—as foolish or ill-considered.

Some Canadian studies also tested Friedman's view. Vanderkamp (1972) incorporated productivity and expectations formed in a backward-looking way, finding no tradeoff in the long run, and not much of one in the short run. He may have been thinking of the earlier, inflationist Canadian studies when he said his results

> do not provide as much of a menu for policy choice as the traditional Phillips curve. (p. 68)

Kaliski (1972, p. 91) accepted the expectations argument using new data, although he saw room for doubt; and Riddell (1979), following a careful argument about the issues at stake in the expectations argument, and using survey data on expected inflation, also accepted it.

The Australian literature took its own turn with Parkin (1973). He was certainly testing the question of whether the Phillips curve there was vertical, but his presentation has a couple of extra aspects which have interesting historical significance. One is that he labelled the idea of complete adjustment the 'Lipsey–Phelps–Friedman model' (p. 128), although Lipsey (1960) did not find a vertical Phillips curve. It contrasts, though, with the fact that Laidler and Parkin (1975 p. 755) specifically identify Lipsey as the author of the theory under attack by Friedman and Phelps. The second point is that in making a number of comments on the earlier Australian studies, he calculated the 'long run trade-offs implicit' (p. 133) in them. The original authors had not done that and there is an obvious danger of making them seem more inflationist in their conclusions than in fact they were.[18] As noted in Chapter 3 the author who estimates a wage-change equation with a view to determining the level of unemployment which stabilizes prices is not led astray by a failure to consider the hypothetical question of what would happen if policy targeted a positive inflation rate. There would be no presumption that such an author would have any belief that there was a long-run tradeoff implicit in the calculation.

Parkin's paper was criticized—although not for that reason—by McDonald (1975), Challen and Hagger (1975), and Nevile (1975). There was overlap between the three although McDonald's was perhaps the most comprehensive—he criticized Parkin's mathematics, assumptions, theory, terminology, and the consistency and compatibility of his data (and rejected his conclusions). Challen and Hagger recalculated various conclusions on different and—as they thought—better assumptions. Indeed, they ended up making illustrative calculations of the reduction in wage growth achieved by a one-point increase in unemployment in various cases. Parkin (1975b) responded to Nevile, saying in the process and very firmly that the relevant expectation was the expected rate of wage increase, and Parkin (1976) replied to the other two, accepting much of what they said, but sticking to his conclusion about the trade-off. Jonson, Mahar, and Thompson (1974) was primarily concerned with understanding the determination of 'award' wages in the Australian arbitration system, but treated the question of expectations sympathetically, trying various measures. They found there was no long-run trade-off; as indeed did Nevile (1977), although he continued to insist on the superiority of his approach over either of Parkin's. Like the American literature, the Australian moved towards accepting the vertical Phillips curve, although it perhaps showed slightly more inclination to accept inflation—and certainly in Parkin's treatment it was made to seem much more as if inflationism was at its heart.

4.6 CONCLUSION

Again then, sustenance for the conventional Phillips curve story is very thin, whereas there is a great deal that flatly contradicts it. Friedman and Phelps cannot possibly have revolutionized the understanding of the long-term effects of inflation. Phelps even said it was an old idea, and Friedman as good as did the same by the way he presented it. Most of the literature, though, was not about responding to that idea at all, but about addressing the actual problems of the time—including analysing the consequences of sustained inflation. And again, as in the 1960s, whatever the limitations of the econometrics itself, the economic thought was, most of the time, quite reasonable. Where there was testing of the expectations idea, much of the attention was on the problem of measuring expectations; and where it was rejected, the lubrication argument was easily visible. In the end it is probably fair to say that there is more overt or nearly overt acceptance of inflation in this period than in the 1960s. But it is difficult to see how that fits in with the usual story of inflationism having been a great mistake of the 1960s, corrected in the following decade.

CHAPTER 5

Attitudes to Inflation

Econometrics—dare I say it?—is not everything. Nor, I hope it is now clear, is the Phillips curve. Having given a sense of the orientation and objectives of the econometric literature and established some key points about which the usual Phillips curve story is simply wrong, I turn to considering attitudes to inflation more broadly, and then see how the remainder of the Phillips curve literature fits in. The first point, considered in Section 5.1 is that the whole period was characterized by a very notable anti-inflationism. Inflation was a problem, not a tool for achieving other objectives. That is a matter of the attitude of the times, rather than the understanding, but it accords with the general picture of Chapter 3 and stands in sharp contrast to conventional wisdom. Section 5.2 considers the various ideas of cost-push inflation. They are sometimes seen as closely related to ideas of exploiting the Phillips curve, as well as perhaps manifestations in themselves of the foolishness of the period. But it becomes apparent that this is anything but accurate, and certainly cost-push inflation made no case for inflationary policy. The issue of the relationship between cost-push inflation and 'the tradeoff' is, however, an important one. Whether the possibility of a relation between *growth* and inflation might be seen as making such a case is a more difficult issue and is considered in Section 5.3. To the extent that belief in such a tradeoff is detectable, it throws the absence of the corresponding one concerning employment into yet sharper relief. In Section 5.4, drawing on the understanding of Sections 5.2 and 5.3, I consider various explanations of slow inflation which were current in the 1960s and earlier and which have the general effect of suggesting that, though it was a problem, it was a minor one. With all these things in mind, in Section 5.5 I try to offer a rounded view of academic attitudes to the problem of inflation in the light of its relation to other objectives. In all that, there is little to say about 'the Phillips curve', so in Section 5.6 I look at what, and how much, was said about it, first in the 1960s and then in the 1970s. There is reason to note that information for its own sake, but in due course it also throws further light on the development of the conventional story.

5.1 ATTITUDES TO PRICE STABILITY

One of the things most completely obscured by the conventional story of the Phillips curve is the extent, firmness, and durability of the commitment to price stability. It is not altogether easy to establish what attitudes were typical since there are both more and less inflationist authors from any period who can be quoted or ignored so as to give a different impression, but taking the literature as a whole, there is great continuity in economists' aversion to inflation. Certainly there is no difficulty in finding anti-inflationist views from a range of outlooks. Marget (1962) was as anti-Keynesian as any, fearing its inflationist tendencies; Galbraith (1960), as unconventional as any, except when considering inflation. He said, 'To do nothing is not a tolerable choice' (p. 67). Burns (1957) was later a policymaker, and certainly inflation averse. But rather than quote a collection of such individuals, perhaps a picture of consensus views might come from the succession of international reports on the inflation problem.

Clark et al. (1949)—a report for the United Nations, already quoted in Chapter 1—said that full employment policy enhanced a government's responsibility for price stability and

> It is essential, therefore, that effective and continuing action to preserve general price stability should be undertaken by governments. (para. 173)

Fellner et al. (1961), writing with more experience of full employment policy, saw the threat of inflation, saying,

> The prospect of continuing inflation is indeed a new one which has arisen from the fact that governments are determined to act forcefully to maintain high employment. We entirely support this determination; but we think it inevitably implies that the danger of rising prices was not a passing phase of postwar developments and that it will be constantly with us in the years ahead. (pp. 10–11)

But they continue with at least equal clarity, saying,

> First of all, we wish to state our positive belief that stability of the level of prices
> should be one of the basic objectives of economic policy. We believe that it is a
> feasible objective. (p. 11)

Since that remark was in the context of their support of full employment
policy they were obviously not adopting a Phillips-type view. Later they say,

> rising prices are not compatible with steady growth. (p. 75)

Surely that makes their position clear? It certainly did to Smithies (1962)—
one of the authors of the 1949 report—who remarked, approvingly, on the
'striking feature' that 'a representative group of economists regards it as a
self-evident truth that price stability should be a major objective of policy'
(p. 538).

OECD (1970) drew attention to the need for anti-inflationary action to
be concerted between countries and called for further work on the problem. Then, OECD (1971), said,

> It is fully agreed that the present situation calls for action in all Member coun-
> tries...this means that all countries should pursue and, where necessary, inten-
> sify, their anti-inflationary policies. (para. 27)

Slightly later, and well into the period when inflation had become a serious
problem, came McCracken et al. (1977)—often known as 'The McCracken
Report'. This was perhaps the most discussed of the collection. They considered the idea—very controversial itself—that some form of social conflict lay at the root of the inflation problem, and said,

> In our view the biggest single constraint in achieving reasonable rates of growth
> in the future—and the greatest barrier to a rapid return to full employment—is
> the increased tendency towards inflation, both domestically and internationally,
> which has emerged over the last few years. (para. 269)

Rather in contrast to the earlier ones, this report was criticized from various sides. Keohane (1978) lambasted it for failing to explain the sociological roots of wage pressure. Laidler (1978), arguing from a monetarist
perspective, and feeling it had insufficient to say about the economics, as
distinct from the politics of the problem, thought it worthy of the same
marks as a camel at a horse show. Others thought more of it, of course, but

one thing it was not, is inflationist. Inflation was 'the greatest barrier'. And in the next paragraph we find,

> But, before going further, we should make it clear that in putting forward our suggestions we have definitely rejected the view that inflation might offer a way of resolving the underlying conflicts which produced the inflation in the first place. (McCraken et al. 1977, para. 270)

That, again, is perfectly clear.

It may be that these sorts of groups are sometimes suspected of seeking out a consensus so that they cannot be relied on to present the range of views that exists. Certainly in the last case, the fact that The McCracken Report was so criticized from both sociological and monetarist positions shows that they satisfied neither, and might suggest a search for consensus where none existed. But in the current context, that does not weaken the impact. If there was a compromise of views to be made, and if there were any truth in the usual story of the Phillips curve, one would expect to read that inflation is not such a bad thing, and brings certain benefits. But no, four times out of four, these groups clearly stated price stability as an essential. The 1961 report was called *The Problem of Rising Prices*, not 'the advantages of rising prices', as the Phillips curve story would suggest; and the McCracken Report was officially called *Towards Full Employment and Price Stability*. In 1977, both those outcomes were still objectives.

There is one consideration, though, which might seem to promote a different view. It is that quite often, when authors are being cautious, the objective in question is stated as being the achievement of 'reasonable price stability', or something of that kind. Equally, a close reading of some of the texts makes it clear that the objective of 'price stability' is regarded as having been met when inflation was low enough. That would be true, for example, in OECD (1970), when a distinction is drawn between

> the 1–2 per cent rise in GNP deflators which is sometimes regarded as an inevitable and acceptable price to pay for high employment and rapid growth (p. 7),

and rates like 5 per cent, which they thought much more serious. In the case of McCracken et al. also, after a discussion (1977, p. 179) about the costs of inflation, they accepted (p. 180) that some inflation was harmless and said that it should be kept below the level at which it tended to accelerate and not be so high or variable as to impair the role of money as a standard of value.

As with the traces of inflationism in the econometric Phillips curve literature of the 1960s, one notable point is that only such low rates were considered. But it also appears that those rates were not so much accepted, as disregarded. That impression was powerfully conveyed by Saulnier (1963), who had been Eisenhower's Chairman of the Council of Economic Advisers. His attitude to the importance of price stability is perfectly clear when he says,

> there is no alternative to an anti-inflationary policy. Anti-inflationism is the first imperative of economic policy. No other policy will work. No other policy is viable. It is not possible for governmental policy to favor inflation. Whatever the reaction to price increases that are inadvertent, the reaction to an explicitly inflationary strategy of policy can spell nothing but disruption and a setback for the economy's growth. (pp. 27–8)

But then that attitude must carry over to the words immediately following:

> This is why a quite explicit and sincerely intended acceptance of reasonable price-level stability as an economic objective is an inescapable requirement of economic policy.

There is no sense of there being a menu of choice. Rather, the picture from all these discussions confirms that of the econometric literature. What is said suggests that there is a *de minimis* inflation which is, as it were, not really inflation at all. It was as if, rather in the way that 'full employment' did not mean that everyone had a job, so 'price stability' did not quite mean what it says. But still the anti-inflationist commitment is clear.

5.2 COST-PUSH INFLATION AND ITS FAMILY

There is, then, no basis for saying inflation—*real inflation*—was thought not to be a problem. It was seen as a problem throughout the period and indeed there was a great deal of discussion as to what should be done about it. But to appreciate either the content or the character of that discussion it is essential to recognize the key distinction that was made between demand-pull and cost-push inflation. As observed in the Introduction and Chapter 1, a basic distinction can easily be made. Demand-pull inflation is inflation that results from excess aggregate demand; cost-push inflation results from cost increases which occur despite the fact that aggregate demand is not excessive. Two issues, however, need amplification. One concerns the variety of further complications that emerged, showing that simple distinction offered only limited insight. But first, there is another point which is that it was—and is—sometimes said that cost-push inflation is impossible, and that the idea of it arises only from confusion or poor theory.

One such argument was raised by Friedman (1966b) who said that the idea rested on a simple mistake, because whereas unions or monopolies might cause prices to be high, they could not cause them to rise continuously. Inflation might be caused by an increase in market power, but that could hardly be a continuous process, so there could be no ongoing cost-push inflation.

The difficulty with this is that the idea of cost-push inflation was not that an isolated union could cause inflation—it was that groups of unions, along with labour market forces tending to maintain constant differentials, might do so. If, starting from full employment equilibrium, such forces could raise the general level of wages, then the resultant increase in prices would restore the situation in which there was market power so that a further increase in wages would be possible. A response to that—and a second argument on the impossibility of cost-push inflation—would be that a restriction of demand can always stop inflation, so that if it continues the policymaker must be complicit in allowing too much nominal demand. One rejoinder was put forward by Machlup (1960, pp. 126–7) amongst others. That was that cost increases might lead to the banking system creating extra purchasing power. A more pertinent response, though, is that the problem of cost-push inflation was precisely a problem of achieving full employment and price stability simultaneously. The primary issue was not whether it was possible for the policymaker to stop the inflation, but whether it is possible for the cost-push forces to exist so as to create for the policymaker the choice between inflation and unemployment.

Understandably then, neither of these responses to the problem of cost-push inflation had much impact on the concerns of the 1960s, and indeed they were hardly raised. Rather, interest in this topic focused more on the various elaborations of the idea of cost-push inflation and possible responses to it. The simplest response, as noted in Chapter 1, was to hope that market power would not be exercised. That was not only simple, but probably recognized as naïve at an early stage. But other developments did not make the problem any easier.

One group of issues concerned the distinction between cost-push and demand-pull inflation. At the practical level, since there was no sure way to determine when 'full employment' was reached, there was no sure way to determine when aggregate demand was excessive. Consequently, at high levels of employment, there might always be an argument as to whether prices were rising because of cost-push or demand-pull inflation. Furthermore, on a theoretical level, it was apparent, for example from Pitchford (1957), that the two might interact in various ways so that a pure case of either one would be unlikely. And even conceptually, they were not completely separate, since if there were shortages in particular areas prices might rise in one area without prices elsewhere falling—so there was 'bottleneck inflation' as it was sometimes called. Such inflation is demand-pull in the sense that the rising prices are rising because of excess demand, but there need not be excess aggregate demand; and the fact that inflation results could be said to be because of the failure of other prices to fall, which suggested an absence of perfect competition in those markets, rather in the manner of cost-push inflation. Arguments like that of Schultze (1959)—the lubrication argument of Chapter 3—were an elaborate version of that idea.

Another complication arose from consideration of additional varieties of cost-push inflation. The idea that industrial monopolies might be the source of inflation was, at an abstract level, not much different from tracing it to unions, although the distinction could certainly generate political heat. Thus, the importance of profit-seeking behaviour as a source of inflation, and the inappropriateness of labelling it 'cost-push', were both emphasized by Barkin (1958). In the United States, much emphasis was put on steel prices—for example by Galbraith (1957) and Eckstein and Fromm (1959)—as being oligopolistically determined, as well as crucial in the costs of other industries. If they rose, there would be the potential for ongoing inflation, if unemployment was not permitted. More generally, Means (1935) had described 'administered prices' because of which, he said, prices in concentrated industries did not fall in the Depression. In later work, including Means (1959), he converted this to those industries generating price increases without excess demand. Galbraith (1952/1956) developed the idea in a different way, with perhaps a suggestion that concentrated industries and large unions were almost in conspiracy to raise wages and prices. Scitovsky (1978) similarly split blame between firms and unions, but saw them each as exercising power in different markets, so that there was a continuous tendency for the price level to drift upwards.

Late in the 1960s, further lines of thinking about wage-push inflation were described. One saw workers desiring an ongoing increase in real wages. Ashenfelter and George Johnson (1969) used that, together with a model where union leaders have political interests which are not identical to the economic interests of their members. This was used to explain strike activity, but the link to cost-push inflation is clear enough. Another strand developed the idea that inflation—and cost-push inflation particularly—could be seen as an outcome of the incompatibility of various social groups' aspirations as to income. That idea can be seen in Turvey (1951) and Bronfenbrenner (1955), but became much more prominent in the 1970s with Phelps Brown (1971), Harrod (1972), Wiles (1973), and Hicks (1974) all arguing along those lines. Wiles in particular noted the growing unreasonableness of wage demands and went on to condemn conventional economics for being unable to appreciate the nature of the problem. In a relatively calm passage (Wiles 1973, p. 382) he said that successful econometrics would require the quantification of mood—clearly not something he expected to see. Deep down, Rowthorn (1977) had the same kind of idea as these authors but he changed the argument's character by putting it in mathematical terms. He even described what he called a 'Phillips curve'—a cost-push Phillips curve, in effect—the location of which was determined by the gap between the aggregate income aspirations of various sectors and the value of potential output. That gave the argument a more conventional appearance, but it did also bring it a step closer to being seen as a mechanical process of the market – and therefore took it a step away from the outlook on the theory of wages described in Section 1.4. Blackaby (1978b), like others, also saw the period as being characterized by a growing intensity of cost-push factors and perhaps a more calculating approach by unions. And the 1970s also brought a further source of inflation in the form of commodity price booms. Whether that was cost-push or demand-pull would certainly depend on the explanation of the boom, but even if it appeared as cost-push, it was a different kind of problem to control it.

There was also sometimes the question—visible in some of the work already mentioned—as to whether it would even be possible to control cost-push inflation by the restriction of demand. That concern can be found early in the post-war period in Lindblom (1948) and Hart (1952). The latter thought that higher levels of unemployment might raise public sympathy for unions and thereby strengthen their bargaining position, and Moulton (1958) simply asserted the impossibility of controlling cost inflation with conventional, demand, tools. Later, the issue was given a more theoretical feel by Turner and Wilkinson (1971), and more fully by them in Jackson, Turner, and Wilkinson (1975). They started with the idea of rising aspirations and added to it the point that those aspirations related to after-tax real income (including the benefit of publicly provided goods). In that case, contractionary policy would, by reducing those incomes, intensify cost-push pressures. And there was also the broader thought, clearly visible in Goldthorpe (1978), that wage-push arose as a consequence of perceptions of social injustice, and policies aimed at creating large amounts of unemployment would surely intensify those feelings. Nell (1977) had a different view, but also one pointing in the same direction, when he suggested that contractionary policy led oligopolies to raise prices so as to maintain revenue.

The idea that there was an aspect to the inflation problem which was a matter of momentum was another case. As discussed in Section 4.2, there was a variety of specific arguments which are not always distinguished from simple matters of changing expectations, but they all point to the idea that once inflation started, wage bargaining and perhaps price setting might give it an aspect of self-perpetuation. Inflation with that kind of momentum thus shared with cost-push the characteristics that it could persist at levels of demand that were not excessive, and that more than narrowly conceived economic forces might affect it.

All these arguments—although there is a great variety of them—shared descent from what, in Chapter 1, I described as 'volitional' rather than 'mechanical' theories of wage setting of the 1940s and 1950s—and most of them are quite naturally regarded as 'bargaining theories' in the sense in which the expression was used before game theory ruled that roost. Perhaps in the most sociologically minded accounts, there was an occasional hint of the forces of historical inevitability playing a hand, but they are still not the neoclassical forces of optimization. If there is nothing volitional about expectations formation, there still might be something psychological, so it is not simply a matter of market forces. Certainly, the idea of 'fairness' which was so important in the earlier literature was still visible in some form—even if organized labour took a more assertive attitude to what would count as 'fair' or perhaps even pursued something more naturally described as class interest. And to recall a crucial point: it is not that analysis drifted into normative territory by extolling fair wages. It is that the authors believed that, as a matter of scientific truth, ideas of such things were causally important.

The relation between the idea of cost-push inflation and the inflation-unemployment tradeoff certainly deserves comment. In the purest theoretical form of cost-push inflation there would be a (reverse) L-shaped aggregate supply curve with inflation determined by cost-push factors, independently of demand (except above full employment). Demand policy would therefore be ineffective in controlling inflation and there would be no tradeoff. Alternatively, ideas of cost-push might be interpreted along the lines of a statistical Phillips curve so as to give rise to the 'dilemma' of Bowen (1960b) and others. Then, demand policy might be effective and there could be, in that sense, a choice to be made.

However, there was, on the basis of the arguments and evidence of the 1960s, every reason to believe that there were other ways of stopping or preventing cost-push inflation. If so, they were definitely to be preferred because they could operate without a loss of output. Fellner et al. (1961) put it in exactly this way. They say that to base anti-inflation policy on Phillips-type relations

> and to rely only on influencing the level of demand, would be to ignore the fact that it may often be more appropriate to bring governmental pressure to bear on the factors other than demand which are treated as constants in these studies. (p. 49)

Here, demand policy is recognized as an inefficient way of stopping an inflation which is due to cost-push factors.

In stark contrast, in a pure demand-pull inflation there might be an inflation-unemployment tradeoff (albeit only temporarily). That kind of inflation would be stopped by reducing demand—realistically, that would be the only way, since in that case price control would amount to an attempt to overrule market forces. And in this case, since demand was in any case excessive, its long-term maintenance would be impossible, and the policy of reducing demand is therefore not wasteful.

So the diagnosis of inflation is a crucial aspect of understanding the character of any possible tradeoff and it is not the case that the Phillips curve will serve equally well as a depiction of either cost-push or demand-pull inflation. In the case of cost-push, it might be—or it might not be—that demand restriction could stop inflation, but there were certainly other, better, ways to tackle it. Full employment and price stability could both be targets. In that sense, no tradeoff was perceived.

5.3 GROWTH AND INFLATION

The question of the possibility of a relation between growth, rather than the level of employment, and inflation, however, raises quite different points. The issue has perhaps become a specialist interest rather than a centrepiece of introductory economics, or else is treated, as it is by Temple (2000), as principally a matter of identifying ways in which inflation impedes growth. But Hamilton (1929) suggested that inflation could speed growth; and that idea was quickly taken up by Keynes (1930a, ch. 30), and then later brought to prominence again by Hamilton (1952). There, he suggested that in several historical periods from the sixteenth century onwards, very slow rates of inflation over long periods had been associated with wages and rents lagging behind prices, thereby raising profit. This, he said, had allowed the accumulation of wealth and finance for increased investment and hence promoted growth; and he clearly had it in mind that the same effect might be possible in post-war America. Here, of course, there is an issue about the adjustment of expectations, but there is no point in anyone arguing it, at least in relation to the history, since Hamilton was—he believed—looking at decades of data showing that wages did lag behind prices.

After that, further theoretical arguments emerged, notably from Tobin (1965) and Sidrauski (1967). Tobin's argument arose from the idea that an expected depreciation of money would encourage substitution into real assets, including investment goods. That had been a subsidiary point made by Hamilton, but Tobin's argument was widely noted for some time afterwards. Sidrauski pursued what is in some respects a similar line, although beginning with explicit utility maximization. Those ideas were part of the broad family of arguments instantiated earlier in Mundell (1963), who said,

> Foreseeable fluctuations in the rate of inflation can thus have very real effects on economic activity. When prices are expected to rise, the money rate of interest rises by less than the rate of inflation giving impetus to an investment boom and an acceleration of growth. (p. 283)

By now it will be no surprise that in 1963 Mundell had plainly grasped the importance of making the point about *foreseeable* inflation, but the point is that this is a genuine argument about a tradeoff, and such points continued to be made, with first Dornbusch and Frenkel (1973) and then Turnovsky (1978) seeking to synthesize the various approaches.

There was also a considerable amount of empirical work done on the question. Wallich (1969c) stands out as clearly finding that inflation reduced growth; others like Allais (1969) and Paldam (1973) saw the results as inconclusive; and Glezakos (1978) thought inflation had little if any effect, whilst also suggesting that it was its variability that was damaging. But others—like Barton and Thirlwall (1971)—clearly thought that moderate inflation might speed growth.

Perhaps because so many results were inconclusive, interest in the matter petered out, although rather later it had something of a revival, with Hineline (2010) and Funk and Kromen (2010) dissenting from the more usual view that inflation damages growth. But, more importantly, it is clear that for a time the issue attracted distinguished authors. And the importance it had in the academic thought of their time must be clear from the fact that it was one of seven topics considered by Barro and Stanley Fisher (1976) in their survey 'Recent developments in monetary theory'.

Similarly, there is no denying that it was a feature of policy thinking (if not policymaking) particularly in the United States. The Joint Economic Committee (1960) report *Employment, growth and price levels*; the Staff Report on the same issue—'the Eckstein Report' (Eckstein (1959)—and the Report of the Commission on Money and Credit, were all, in their time, much more significant than the limited attention they have received from historians of economics would suggest,[1] and they all considered the issue carefully. Something of the same could be said of the United Kingdom where the matter was addressed by the Radcliffe Committee and the Council on Prices, Productivity and Incomes (1961, p. 14). Although the balance of views in these sources was against the existence of a relation ship there was clearly consideration of the possibility of a tradeoff. The Commission on Money and Credit in particular saw the point in just those terms—there were two desirable goals, and an issue as to whether both would be achievable.

Other arguments might be considered relatives of these. One was over 'high-pressure economics', advocated particularly by Hansen (1957). The idea in essence was that maintaining a high pressure of demand would encourage investment and incentivize labour-saving, both of which would promote growth. He clearly accepted that this might lead to some increase in the price level, so there was a tradeoff of sorts at work.

Kaldor (1959b) made a point to the same general effect, perhaps with more panache but certainly less finesse, when he told the Radcliffe Committee that the British economy was so lacking dynamism it was necessary to keep 'doping it with inflation'. The point was controversial, but perhaps not as lacking merit as some suggest.[2] He later offered another variation based on 'Verdoorn's Law', derived from Verdoorn (1949), but so named by Colin Clark (1962, p. 5, n. 2). His idea—presented in Kaldor (1967)—was that because of economies of scale, an increase in output would in due course promote productivity growth. Consequently, there was scope for the idea that high levels of production would tend to lower the price level, even if moving to those higher levels initially involved some inflation.

None of these lines of thinking went without controversy. One point was that it was apparently not universally agreed that speeding growth would even make a case for accepting inflation—Eckstein (1958) used the expression 'even if the growth of economy were considered a more important objective than price level stability' (p. 371) in discussing anti-inflationary policy options. On the question of whether a growth-inflation relation existed, there were certainly those who expressed a conviction, often without feeling the need to explain it, that only through price stability was there any hope for growth. Fellner et al. (1961) were quoted to that effect, but theirs was an older view—a traditional one, really. More specifically, on the arguments considered earlier in this chapter, Felix (1956) gave meticulous, critical attention to Hamilton's work while Kessel and Alchian (1960) attacked hypothesis that wages lagged behind prices; Williams (1945) thought high employment impeded growth and Wallich (1958) preferred low-pressure economics to Hansen's proposal. And the debate over Verdoorn's Law went on and on—at least up to Rowthorn (1975) or even Thirlwall (1980).

What is interesting, however, is not the outcomes of these debates, but that they occurred at all and were perfectly serious. And their relation to the issue of the Phillips curve should be clear: there was none. Yet it is here, if one were looking, that there would be good case for saying that there was a genuine debate about a tradeoff involving inflation.

5.4 EXPLANATIONS OF SLOW INFLATION

In Section 3.5, I noted the prevalence of the 'demand-shift' or lubrication argument from Schultze (1959) and others. That was an important argument in that it had special relevance to 'Phillips curve' calculations like those of the 1960s econometric literature because it suggested there might be a relation between employment and inflation that could be estimated reasonably well. So an appreciation of it is, I suggested, essential to understanding the motives of the econometric work. But when it came to more general discussions of the inflation problem, there were, in addition, other arguments that suggested slow increases in the price index were nothing much to worry about.

One is simply that if there were to be an insistence on strict price stability (or any specific target rate), it would be necessary to decide which index was to be targeted—it might not always be possible to achieve strict stability in, for example, both retail and wholesale prices. In a world sufficiently near to being ideal that there were no larger issues to worry about, reasons for preferring one to the other might be devised, but, in a realistic setting, to say that what we want is 'reasonable price stability' avoids the problem. Another consideration would be that the business cycle had long been associated with something of a cycle in prices—that was certainly apparent from Wesley Mitchell (1951). That data arose from a period when there was much less economic management of any kind than in the post-war period, and clearly raises the question of whether that management, when introduced, should be seeking to prevent such price variability. Again, detailed responses could be devised, but in practical terms what was wanted was a policy that would prevent such price increases getting out of hand. There is the further point that if policy succeeded in preventing severe downturns, it might well be reasonable to expect a long-term upward drift of prices, and again, it is not immediately obvious what profile of changes would be ideal. That sort of argument was a relative of the idea that the price level at full employment would be higher than at lesser levels because of diminishing marginal productivity—then there would be a one-time price rise in the approach to full employment, as often suggested. One might add the pragmatic point mentioned by Reuber (1968), but presumably recognized earlier, that inflation might make for a convenient way of reducing the real value of certain fixed claims, such as minimum wages, which would otherwise be difficult to reduce, and in that way provide a benefit, including, in that case, a lower level of unemployment.

A point with perhaps a slightly more sophisticated feel is that it was believed that, because of measurement difficulties and statistical issues, there was an upward bias in the price index. Perhaps this idea is sometimes casually misdated to the report of the Boskin Committee (Boskin et al. (1996)). In fact, it is much older than that, being well understood in the 1940s, and despite objections to it on the part of Milton Gilbert (1961) it came to prominence in the 1960s with Stigler et al. (1961), amongst others.[3] The magnitude and sometimes even the existence of the problem were debated, with Bodkin (1966) being one who expressed some doubt about it. But most thought there was some upward bias, and Jacoby (1967a, pp. 72–3)—certainly a sound money man by usual standards, and a member of Eisenhower's Council of Economic Advisers—accepted 1.5 per cent measured inflation as price stability on this basis.

Another idea, perhaps more specific to the outlook on wage determination of the time, would be that if rates of productivity growth differ between sectors, and wages in the fastest growing sectors rise at the same rate as productivity, other wages will tend to rise faster than productivity, owing to the 'orbits of comparison' and 'contours' of wage theory of the time, and that may generate a slight inflation. The international application of this idea, which makes for a higher price level in high-productivity countries, has later been commonly attributed to Balassa (1964) and Samuelson (1964b), although Viner (1937, p. 315) and Harrod (1939, p. 70) stated it. But in any case, the argument was certainly known as an explanation of inflation in a single country in the 1960s—Saulnier evidently recognized it, being reported (by Anthony Lewis (1959)) in the *New York Times* of 26 August as calling for price cuts in fast growth areas so that the overall price level could be stabilized. And both OECD (1970) and McCracken et al. (1977) explained their acceptance of mild inflation using this argument.

The idea of cost-push inflation, and consideration of what might cause it, gave rise to more arguments. One point was that unions bargain individually, so that an aspect of the problem is that each benefits from a wage rise without materially contributing to inflation. That means the unions face a prisoner's dilemma, although of course it was not put that way at the time. Lerner (1949) was one of those who made this argument, saying,

> No degree of understanding of the problem by responsible trade union leaders can help very much since each trade union owes it to its members to make sure that it is not left behind in the general rush. (p. 198)

The same thought is at work when it is said—as by Holzman (1959, p. 327)—that breaking up large unions into small ones may speed inflation since each of the smaller ones recognizes the absence of macroeconomic consequences of their actions. This sort of argument is perhaps not made as frequently as some of the others, such as the lubrication and expectations arguments, but it is noted often enough to be presumed widely known. It is, as with those two arguments, notable that when it is made, those making it did not seem to feel they had discovered it.[4] A further point is that with inflation diagnosed in this way, there need be no continuous accelerationist tendency. In Lerner's terms, at some positive rate of inflation— 'the rush'—is fast enough that, in keeping up with it, the union discharges its duty to the members, and deeper theory to the same effect could be devised.[5]

A spreading awareness of these kinds of points would blunt the edge of the case for setting policy to achieve strict price stability. It might still be said that the problem with gentle inflation was that by imposing a cost on the holding of money it might provoke a flight from currency, and an accelerating inflation. The idea of inflation acceleration from that source might well underlie the insistence on the importance of strict price stability that was sometimes expressed. But this idea was tested and rejected by Brown (1955) and Lipsey (1961), and in any case, as time went on, experience showed that it was not of practical relevance at the rates of inflation under contemplation.

Whilst all that seems to make quite a good case for accepting some inflation, one aspect of the character of the case should be noted. Individual economists might take particular attitudes to some of the foregoing arguments—they might build a model even. But from the point of view of later understanding it is better to treat them as a collection of lines of argument which are not wholly distinct, but all point in the same direction. It might be that inflation was a characteristic of the growth process, or one of the determinants of growth; or it might be that wage bargaining and perhaps price setting could not reasonably be kept on such a tight leash as to prevent it. Or it might be that the inevitable frictions of adjustment to changing conditions brought more price rises than falls. Anyone could appreciate all these ideas. Any of them could be analysed in isolation, but in a broader view they were in the character of details, indicating imperfections of mainline models. So there might be no point in trying to be too precise. The point would be that, without necessarily specifying a particular reason, almost anyone could accept that this family of arguments gave reason to be relaxed about mild inflation.

The ordinariness of the arguments, as well as their interrelatedness is worth emphasizing. I have already commented on the absence of claims of originality when some of them are presented, versions of many of them (along with the expectations argument) are in Dale (1957)—a newspaper article. Robertson (1955/1966) was not one who approved of this way of thinking, and complained that price stability had been redefined to mean 2 or 3 per cent inflation, but that too shows the ordinariness of it. And Thorp and Quandt (1959) is a particularly useful barometer. Those authors set out to make a popular presentation derived from a conference on inflation. It is an unashamedly consensus-minded work intended to display the ideas and the difficulties in sorting them out. Versions of the arguments considered earlier in this chapter and perhaps some others are considered. Nothing, except the problems, is particularly highlighted, but the picture of their being a whole collection of issues, not distinctly separated, is the clearest thing to emerge. And there is nothing very much the matter with that outcome, since it is how things were.

We have, therefore, an outlook in which it is accepted that strict price stability—continuous zero inflation—is not a sensible objective. The absurdity of such a target—in the particular context of the issue of the index bias—was caustically highlighted by Rees (1958) who mused (p. 656) that if zero-measured inflation were the objective it would be better to spend money constructing a more accurate index, than to raise unemployment to hold down the existing one. But more than this, it is also apparent that there was neither a practical way to determine what would be an ideal outcome, nor any particular importance attached to achieving the ideal, whatever it might be. Hence, the objective was well expressed as the achievement of 'reasonable price stability'. And it is when we dispense with the idea that the Phillips curve was always central to discussions of inflation, and see the range of issues actually in the minds of economists of the time, that it becomes clear beyond doubt that there was nothing in that attitude to suggest attempts to 'exploit the tradeoff' or any such thing.

5.5 INFLATIONISM, WITH AND WITHOUT THE PHILLIPS CURVE

All this makes it possible—I hope—to achieve a balanced consideration of the significance of remarks made about inflation policy, and to do so without the preconceptions engendered by the Phillips curve story. It is certainly impossible to consider more than a sample of the work, but what follows is illustrative of the more inflationist things that were said. Those from the 1960s might give some appearance of accepting inflation. But it is remarkable how rarely that is more than a weak impression, and even more remarkable how even that fades away when the context of the views discussed in the last four sections is recognized.

Interestingly, perhaps more effort has been made to establish the inflationist attitudes of figures before the 1960s, than of that decade. One of them—Sumner Slichter—was often regarded as the outstanding inflationist of the 1950s. Leeson (1997c) considered his work along with that of Alvin Hansen, describing them both as 'self-conscious revolutionaries' who went 'down to the political marketplace in search of influence' (Leeson 1997c, p. 448). He seems to want to say that their work, even before the Phillips curve, was somehow the origin of the inflationist sentiments he believes to have centred on the curve. This, however, is a poor representation of their work. As already noted, Hansen (1957) advocated high-pressure economics, and he also took a robust view of that, questioning whether it was even proper to use the word 'inflation' to describe the sorts of price increases that had been experienced in America. He went on to say,

> I suggest that at no time in our history, nor indeed in that of any other country, can it be shown that price increases have injured the economy and the general welfare if in the period in question the increase in the aggregate output has exceeded percentage wise the increase in prices. (p. 43)

He even contemplates that it might be appropriate to pursue even faster growth in special circumstances, suggesting such a case had existed in 1946 because of the urgency of increasing non-military output. It is clear that what is being proposed is refraining from stopping an expansion just because prices have started to rise—while the expansion continues, the price rise is acceptable. The point of this, though, is that if contractionary policy was to be implemented in order to prevent any rise in the price level, then it would begin when inflation was due to bottlenecks and therefore would be cutting recovery short prematurely. Hansen feared, as he put it, that policymakers would make,

> a fetish of rigid price stability. This fetish could easily become a serious obstacle to optimum growth and expansion. (pp. 42–3)

But there was in this no proposal for ongoing inflation. Rather, it is a question of what happens during the process of adjustment to a high level of employment. So, despite the attempt of Leeson (1997c) to argue otherwise,[6] it is hard to see Hansen as a great prophet of the Phillips curve.

In the case of Slichter it is fair to say that, by later standards he would not be thought a great theorist. He was widely respected as the outstanding expert on industrial relations and he also wrote extensively and optimistically on growth, emphasizing, for example in his last and posthumous work (Slichter (1961)), as he had in earlier works, the possibilities for investment and the entrepreneurialism of American business. Optimistic as he was about that, he was, in earlier writings, pessimistic about stopping inflation and concluded that, up to a point, it should be allowed. In doing so he drew on many of the arguments considered earlier in this chapter, often without presenting them in theoretical terms, and indeed, often making the arguments in a journalistic outlets. His view of the cause of inflation was mostly fully worked out in Slichter (1954). It was that it was to be found in the wage-bargaining arrangements of unionized industry. The same idea was put clearly in a more popular outlet, while he also made a case for accepting some inflation. Thus, in Slichter (1952a), he said,

> At some point short of full employment the bargaining power of most unions becomes so great that they are able to push up money wages faster than the engineers and managers can increase output per man hour. (p. 54)

The inflation he was considering was therefore clearly of the cost-push variety. Furthermore, later on he doubted whether there was any reliable way to stop wage inflation with higher unemployment, saying in Slichter (1957) that there were too many influences on wage bargaining for such a policy to deliver consistent results (and, on p. 30, also noting the lubrication argument). In Slichter (1952a, p. 55) he made the point about individual unions not having an incentive to act to stabilize the price level and agreements between them to do so being hard to enforce. In this connection he even noted said that Swedish unions, recognizing that they faced this problem had been seeking ways to increase management resistance to their own wage demands. In Slichter (1959/1961) he questioned whether breaking up large unions would diminish wage pressure, noting that the resulting unions would be rivals, each desiring 'to make a good showing' (p. 144). These ideas are all of the family of ideas considered earlier in this chapter.

Much of Slichter's motivation also arose from his views on growth. In Slichter (1957, p. 30), as in Slichter (1959), the case for allowing inflation arose more from the avoidance of policy which prevented growth than it did on the wastefulness of stopping it with unemployment. There is really no theory there, but rather the general idea that buoyant demand spurs innovation, and perhaps that a general tightness of the labour market makes for labour-saving improvements as well. But that view is consistent with much of what was often said about growth and inflation. In Slichter (1952a, p. 54) he said, 'In a vigorous and dynamic economy' prices rise much of the time, but that process is interrupted by occasional recessions, and asks 'should the community stand aside and let the recession develop without restraint?' He says that would be bad policy and that an American recession would dangerously disrupt the economies of other countries (thereby aiding Communism). He then noted 'the policy of keeping recessions as mild as possible is incompatible with the ideal of long-run stability of the price level' (p. 54). All that thinking clearly also arises from the kinds of ideas considered earlier in this chapter.

Perhaps the range of arguments deployed, but certainly the frequency with which he put them and his willingness to call a spade 'inflation' rather than 'reasonable price stability', make him seem exceptionally inflationist. Yet the rates of inflation he proposed accepting—2 or 3 per cent in Slichter (1952a)—and no higher in other writings,[7] is actually barely more than others were willing to tolerate. So attempts to make him more of an inflationist than that are unavailing.[8]

Considering authors who were actually writing after Phillips (1958), a good example of the importance of putting aside the preconceptions of the usual story can be found in remarks by Ackley (1966b) during a lecture. Commenting on the success of the Kennedy policy of lowering unemployment up to then, he said that further reductions

> will necessarily involve a somewhat greater cost in terms of the price level than did earlier reductions. Those who value price stability more highly relative to employment will advise more restrictive policies than those with another set of values. (p. 174)

Perhaps that had the appearance of a piece of Phillips curve inflationism, but the next paragraph is not really consistent with a view that inflation was acceptable. Saying that knowledge was so limited that perfect policy was not reliably attainable, Ackley said

> We would all like the economy to tread the narrow path of a balanced, parallel growth of demand and capacity—at as high a level of capacity utilization as is consistent with reasonable price stability, and without creating imbalances that would make continuing advance unsustainable. (p. 174)

That seems fair enough in any period. Johnson (1963a) took the step of actually describing the 'Phillips curve' as a tradeoff relation—but he also referred to Schultze (1959), thereby invoking the lubrication argument, so it is clear enough what he had in mind. Later, Okun (1970, p. 4) discussed the same theme, although he put it in more specific terms. He defined inflation as 'a condition of *significantly* or *substantially* rising prices' and went on to explain that rates of price increase below 1.75 per cent were not really inflation whereas rates of 2.75 per cent certainly were. His basically anti-inflationist position could equally well be seen even in Okun (1965a), although there he clearly said that the policy problem is to find the optimal tradeoff. He too, though, points at Schultze, and he says it is necessary to achieve 'reasonable price stability'. That expression is not defined, but he did say that 3 per cent inflation was clearly unacceptable.

Farrell (1965) did take an inflationist position—in an Institute of Economic Affairs paper, what is more. But it was overtly based on the lubrication argument, which he saw as making a powerful case that flexibility would be improved by inflation. He is not specific, but he does seem to have thought the benefits would exist at higher rates of inflation than most contemplated.

Something else that sometimes encourages the thought that a stable Phillips curve was at the heart of inflationist thinking is the appearance of a diagram with such a curve tangent to an indifference curve in inflation-unemployment space, with the obvious implication that the point of tangency is an optimum. Such diagrams were used for various purposes, but one case was that of advocating 'manpower policy' (government-sponsored retraining schemes and other devices for lowering frictional unemployment). So, R. A. Gordon (1967, p. 71) drew such a diagram and on page 177 even made it explicit that he is prepared to sacrifice strict price stability for high employment, suggesting that 1.5 per cent inflation and 4 per cent unemployment would be achievable and have public support, but 3.5 per cent inflation and 3 per cent unemployment would not. Then, on page 178, he said the point of manpower policy was to improve the possibilities, and the whole book is really about advocating manpower policy so as to reduce unemployment. The same diagram was used by others with equally little inflationist intent, despite contrary remarks sometimes made.[9]

Manpower policy was also put in terms of the Phillips curve by others,[10] but the great exponent of it in those terms was Charles Holt, with Holt (1970a, 1970b) both appearing in Phelps (1970a). In Holt (1970a), after surveying the econometric literature on the American Phillips curve, including that by some sceptics, he concluded, 'We are beyond the point of asking whether the relation exists—it does' (p. 119). In the context of the advocacy of manpower policy, that did not mean that an exploitable trade-off had been found and should be exploited. It meant that it needed to be accepted that macroeconomic policy could not achieve all its goals. It was, as he thought, beyond doubt that more policy tools were needed.

Again, the absence of an inflationist understanding of the curve can be seen rather clearly in the author's other works. In Holt (1969) he argued for a stable Phillips curve (on the unimpressive basis that frictions might be such as to prevent workers seeking full compensation for inflation), but he took this as a warning that the inflation-reducing benefits of unemployment would be temporary and said,

> The likelihood that there is a stable Phillips curve...persuades the author that economists—and indeed national policy-makers should devote serious attention to the issue of how the Phillips curve might be shifted to the left. (p. 141)

Even the *stable* Phillips curve did not make a case for inflationary policy.

The discussion of incomes policy in the 1970s also started to be conducted in terms of the Phillips curve rather more than it had before, but the same sort of picture emerges as in relation to manpower policy. Sometimes these discussions give an impression of suggesting the existence of a stable exploitable Phillips curve, but on further inspection, there turns out to be nothing much there. Galenson (1973) used the expression 'presumptively stable Phillips curve' (p. 83), but the point is expositional, not programmatic. His 'Phillips curve' arose from a relation between strike activity and unemployment (p. 80)—another expansion in the application of the term—and hence a relation which is basically cost-push in nature. Ulman and Flanagan (1971) referred to a 'stubborn' (p. 3) Phillips curve—meaning one that made it impossible to achieve full employment and price stability together—and said that incomes policy was a mechanism for shifting it downwards. Like so many others, they give little in the way of real theoretical explanation, but it is clear that the idea is to restrain price-setting power, not limit the effect of excess demand. Brittan and Lilley (1977) also referred to Phillips curves in this context, although their objective was to deny the effectiveness of incomes policy.

Another issue arose from the increase in inflation at the end of the 1960s. This led to some consideration of whether it would be better to stabilize it at the level it had reached, rather than bear the costs of reducing it. Gordon (1971b) took the view that it would, and Breit and Ransom (1981) quote Samuelson (1973), saying that maintaining a rate of 6 per cent inflation, with expectations adjusted to it, would be acceptable. These might be presented as instances of Phillips curve inflationism, as Breit and Ransom (and Leeson (1997c), quoting them) seem to have intended. But the truth is more likely to be the opposite. Gordon made it clear that it was precisely the adjustment of expectations which rendered the inflation harmless, and meant by that that there was no point in bearing the costs of reducing it. Read in context, that was also clearly the point being made by Samuelson when he said

> I would not, by the way, think it disastrous if we went from now until the end of the world at 6-percent inflation with everything adjusted to that—including the plight of the elderly, the real victims of inflation—but I cannot look without concern on the prospect that 6-percent inflation might do what it has done in so many places abroad, become 8 or 9 percent. (Samuelson 1973, p. 324)

It is the acceptance of the expectations argument, making steady inflation harmless, not the exploitable Phillips curve, that induced these comments. What he is concerned about is the possibility of a continuing acceleration. Similarly, Okun (1971) and Fellner (1976c) opposed the idea, doubting the practicability of stabilizing inflation and expected inflation at a high level. The same issue was raised in relation to British policy by Blackaby (1971), although he did not reach such a firm conclusion.

A few authors perhaps deserve specific attention even though they make little of the curve, just because they were, in one way or another, prominent figures. Walter Heller was Chairman of the Council of Economic Advisers from 1961 to 1964. In Heller (1965), discussing the economics of the Kennedy period, he said there had been a good performance in terms of reducing unemployment, but it had not gone far enough to test the '4% full-employment bench mark and its attendant Phillips curve assumptions' (p. 237). That could appear to be a remark about an exploitable tradeoff, but the assumptions in question were that unemployment could be lowered to 4 per cent whilst maintaining 'reasonable price stability'. So he was making a point about what could be done without inflation, not what would happen if there were inflation.

Another case is Lerner (1967). He discussed the inflation-unemployment problem using the Phillips curve. Indeed, in about the first half of the paper, Lerner could be said to give a superficial impression of believing a tradeoff is available and he wrote of the possibility of accepting some inflation to reduce unemployment, saying that the Phillips curve was a refinement of his idea of a distinction between 'low' and 'high' full employment and that,

> Since it is marginal equivalence which gives us an optimum, we should strive for the point between low and high full employment where the harm from additional inflation is just equal to the good from the accompanying increase in employment. (p. 3)

He went on to argue that, over plausible ranges of inflation, the marginal costs of inflation are much lower than those of unemployment, so that if it is necessary to make a choice policy should be much more inclined to accept inflation than he believed it was. He also mentioned the possibility of inflation accelerating but said that he was less inclined to fear it than he had been in the past since there had been observations of steady inflation. His conclusion was that a high level of unemployment was too great a price to pay for the avoidance of the danger of acceleration.

Two points to note are that, first, after this he immediately went on to say that the choice was not necessary since a well-designed incomes policy could prevent inflation. Making that case was what he called his 'primary purpose' (p. 7). The second point is that the allusion to his earlier views on acceleration was no retrospective pretence at insight. In Lerner (1951, p. 196) he had given a very clear statement of the expectations argument. He said the control of inflation 'would permit us to reach the high level of full employment' (p. 195). That was all—not that it would permit it painlessly. So the implication is that the control of inflation is a constraint. Then he said of 'overfull' employment that it

> cannot be maintained. Wages and prices will rise. They may at first rise quite moderately... (p. 196)

and then explained the expectations argument. Again, that was 'cannot be maintained', not 'cannot be maintained without other disadvantages'.

The difference in his view in 1967 was, therefore, not that avoiding an accelerating inflation was not a priority, but that he had come to doubt that acceleration was inevitable. There is nothing in the 1967 paper to suggest that if inflation did accelerate, that would be acceptable, and it is impossible to interpret it as being written by someone who has not understood the expectations argument. So Lerner offers something to the idea that there was thought to be a possibility of reducing unemployment by accepting inflation, but not very much—he has too much understanding of the range of issues to be a naïve character from the usual story. He offers nothing at all to the idea that economists were ignorant of the issue of expectations. But he does offer an ideal example of what I have argued was the attitude to incomes policy—it was to stop inflation.

Finally we might consider Paul Samuelson's work in greater detail. In Samuelson (1956) he said that the preceding years had seen high employment together with stable prices but anticipated that would not last, and said that in responding to the resulting 'dilemma', 'social welfare functions and not scientific economic principles must play the decisive role' (p. 373). In Samuelson (1961b) he gave a fuller account, saying he doubted that, despite recent price stability, full employment would no longer bring inflation. He described the problem as 'a price creep', which, he said, had to be distinguished from inflation due to excess demand, and continued,

> the goal of high employment and effective real growth cannot be abandoned because of the problematical fear that reattaining of prosperity in America may bring with it some difficulties; if recovery means a reopening of the cost-push problem, then we have no choice but to move closer to the day when that problem has to be successfully grappled with. (p. 1482)

He is not advocating inflation, but he is admitting that it might happen. That could be said of Samuelson and Solow (1960). In Samuelson (1960 and 1963) he referred to Samuelson and Solow (1960), in both cases presenting the curve as depicting a problem of cost-push inflation. That is how he described the curve in his textbook as well, starting with Samuelson (1961a). In the 1960 paper he said it indicated the existence of a 'dilemma' (p. 265) and that consequently it was not clear that a policy of price stability was best; he also said that he would like to see the Federal Reserve consider that question. In the 1963 paper, Samuelson and Solow (1960) are described as having 'dramatized' the idea of cost-push with 'the convenient Phillips curve' (Samuelson 1963, p. 3).

In the textbook slightly more is said—only slightly—but it does give a much better idea of Samuelson's idea of the Phillips curve. As Pearce and Hoover (1995, pp. 205–7) say, discussing Samuelson (1961a), he certainly appreciated that, as they put it, 'if the economy were always near full employment there would be something like Friedman's natural rate of unemployment'; and that different countries would have different Phillips curves, 'depending on their institutional pattern and psychological out-looks'. They also recognized that he saw a policy problem in the fact that there is an important question concerning how a society can 'give itself a Phillips Curve in which closer approaches to high employment can be made without engineering a considerable price creep?' (Samuelson 1961b, p. 384). The striking thing about his idea is how very far from Phillips' it is—despite his use of the Phillips curve label. Here, the curve is a cost-push relation; far from indicating a law of economics, it is not even a presump-tively regular bargaining relation, and the role it is given is that of depicting a problem to be wrestled with, not indicating the level of unemployment that would stop inflation. He is clearly not proposing inflation as a means of lowering unemployment.

Another observation about these views might offer something to the overall picture. That is, that contemporary commentary does not seem to have seen inflationism on the rise. Tobin (1966)—discussing the period up to 1962—said that opinion against inflation hardened; Ross (1966b) said that there was 'no objective definition of price stability' and that some conservatives interpreted the phrase literally, and some romantics wanted a falling price level. He went on to say,

> During the 'creeping inflation' debate of the 1950s, Sumner Slichter and like-minded economists were thinking in terms of 2 or 3 percent annually. A popular rule of thumb today is that 2 percent isn't too bad, but 3 percent would be unac-ceptable. (pp. 99–100)

Similarly, Jacoby (1967a), although he cited only Slichter (1957), said,

> A subtle change in attitudes has taken place during the last decade. Few econ-omists defend creeping inflation today, whereas many did during the Fifties. (Jacoby 1967a, p. 56, n. 4)

The fact that these authors have only the example of Shlicter between them relating to the 1950s does not suggest there was much inflationism then, although it might be possible to find others. But, more importantly, these figures from the period of the flood of the Phillips curve tide see a decline in inflationism.

Another indication of the same sort of thing comes from comparing comments in Samuelson's textbook. It is difficult to know whether his own views were changing or he was moving in the same direction as the major-ity opinion, but whereas Samuelson (1948, p. 282) said 5 per cent steady inflation is not too serious; in Samuelson (1955, p. 250), in an almost identical discussion, puts the crucial figure at 3 per cent; and in Samuelson (1961a, p. 305) it is 2 per cent!

There is another thing about these sorts of presentations, which is not immediately obvious but which nevertheless seems to be an interesting characteristic. That is, that there is a preponderance of them in popular writings, lectures, and sources very closely tied to policy discussion. Ackley (1966b) was a lecture. MacDougall (1959) and Phillips (1962) could be added as two other inflation-accepting lectures. Samuelson and Solow (1960) were not far from the same thing. Kaldor (1959b) and Samuelson (1973) were giving evidence to policymakers; Farrell (1965) was policy advocacy; Okun (1970) was popular writing; Hansen (1957) was a text-book; and five out of nine of the Slichter citations were lectures, or were in newspapers or magazines; one more was Congressional testimony, and one was a fairly popular book. My selection of presentations is not by any means a full summary, but the suggestion is that a large number of the most inflationist pieces were in less formal work.

What might we learn from that? Certainly that the idea that economists were busying themselves with refining the tradeoff and computing optimal points on it is yet further from the truth than it might have seemed. Where tolerance of inflation is expressed, it is often in much less formal terms. But it is also easy to see much of what was said as being in the character of public education, or spreading the word amongst economists, at least. Just as Hansen deprecated the 'fetish' of price stability, Slichter (1952a) described (in *Harper's Magazine*) an 'uncritical and almost hysterical fear' of inflation 'in a large part of the community' (p. 53). His was not advocacy of inflation at all, it was a counsel of calm—an acceptance that not every-thing could be perfect, and that policy, therefore, should not be set to react to every drift of the price index as if it were the only priority. The idea that it should was a fetish, born of hysterical fear.

5.6 THE NON-ECONOMETRIC 'PHILLIPS CURVE' IN THE 1960S AND 1970S

If there is practically nothing to be said for the idea that the Phillips curve motivated inflationism, there remains a little to be said about its role in other discussions. But as regards the 1960s, the most important of those things is just to say how little was said. The Phillips curve is very far indeed from dominating thinking. One clue to the lack of attention it initially received is that it is absent from Johnson (1962). That is significant not only because he was acclaimed for his breadth of appreciation of the literature and the quality of his syntheses by Tobin (1978) and Laidler (1984) and that the 1962 piece was a survey and itself particularly noted for its excellence by Tobin. It is also because in that survey Johnson specifically bemoaned the lack of quantification of the terms of any inflation-unemployment tradeoff. One explanation might be that he did not regard the curve as representing a tradeoff. But when, in Johnson (1963a), he did first advert to it, he presented it as an inflation-unemployment relation and discussed it in terms of its implications as a policy tradeoff function, clearly supposing that it gave policymakers options (he also presented the lubrication argument). Whilst that is an instance of the curve being treated as promoting inflationist policy, it also suggests that its absence from the 1962 paper is explained by Johnson simply not having heard of it—and that is a powerful point against the usual story.

More broadly, in the 1960s when the curve was supposedly so important, there are not nearly so many references to it as might be expected. As of April 2014, there are 268 JStor hits for 'Phillips curve' between 1960 and 1969. Of these, 110 are tables of contents, lists of dissertations, society news items, and the like. Of the 158 remaining, 96 were published in 1968 or 1969. As with the econometric literature, it seems the take-off in references to the idea starts in 1968, and is simultaneous with, or perhaps even a response to, Friedman (1968a).

Even of the 62 cases before 1968, more than a third were book reviews, often, curiously, of books which did not themselves contain the expression 'Phillips curve'.[11] So, ignoring these, in JStor articles there are about five mentions per year before 1968. And these are uses of the expression 'Phillips curve', not citations of Phillips' paper. And furthermore, a few of them are included only because they cite papers with that expression in their title, so that the expression only appears in the list of references. Amongst the remainder there is a miscellany of unimportant remarks and minor discussions. There is one isolated remark in each of Gallaway (1963), Raimon (1964), and Clower (1964); a thoroughly sceptical discussion in Gilpatrick (1966); Waterman (1966) treats the curve as a constraint on policy and could be said to be treating it as stable, but draws no inflationist conclusions (and considers a curve shifting with inflation on p. 463). Haberler (1966a) referred to Samuelson's (1965) use of it. And then, at the end of the decade, perhaps inspired by Perry (1967), it sometimes features in discussions of incomes policy; or, a little earlier, inspired by Lipsey it features in theoretical arguments about the inflation-unemployment relation,[12] or other theoretical points that have since faded from view.[13] But, as it was in the econometric literature, if the issue arises at all, the discussion is about the reduction and control of inflation, not about how any of the arguments made might change the choice of optimal point on the trade-off.[14] A few other sources use the expression simply as a label;[15] or say that they doubt the existence of the curve;[16] or suggest methods of shifting it;[17] or other ideas about it generally,[18] and there are some real oddities.[19] Most of this is trivia, but that is the point—there was not much discussion, and most of it was as inconsequential as it comes.

That is of course not true of the line of thinking initiated by Phelps (1967) and Lucas and Rapping (1969b) focusing on microeconomic behaviour giving rise to aggregate outcomes for inflation and unemployment, with—just as the 1970s begin—the volume edited by Phelps (1970a) containing key early contributions. That was the beginning of very important developments of theory, but a further valuable point about the history of the Phillips curve arises from considering the objective of this book. It was not, as might be thought, to demonstrate that as a matter of theory, the long-run Phillips curve should be vertical. It would hardly take a book of over 400 pages to do that. Rather, it was addressing the relation of microeconomics and macroeconomics in the determination of prices—the lack of attention to which was called a 'major scandal' by Arrow (1967, p. 734). More than this, though, Phelps' (1970b) introduction to the volume, explains the first issue as being to consider why changes in demand result in changes in employment at all—in the neoclassical labour market there would be no unemployment to be reduced—or, if there is frictional unemployment, why inflation (or surprise inflation) should reduce that. If the answer is to be in terms of 'wage stickiness', then the next question would be why there should be such stickiness, particularly when ascribed to sophisticated economic units such as firms and unions rather than individuals. Phelps explains that 'The papers here offer new reasons why money wage rates are "sticky" in the face of price-level movements' (p. 3). Having reached this point he notes that many of these models generate a Phillips-type relation and that it dissipates as expectations change. Then, having noted the antiquity of the argument that, in the long run, the employment-raising effects of inflation will dissipate, he says, 'The novelty of the work here in this connection is its development of the microeconomic underpinning' (p. 4, n. 5) of this outcome. To that end, in particular, Alchian (1970) focuses most directly on the consequences of workers' incomplete information about existing opportunities; Mortensen (1970) considered wage setting by firms aiming to optimize recruitment; Phelps (1970c) (a reprint of Phelps (1968)) emphasized issues concerning the quit rate—all three of them with extensive reference to the earlier literature. And in discussing the intellectual context of own paper, Phelps said,

> Recently, Friedman and I have sought to reconcile the Phillips hypothesis with the aforementioned axiom of anticipated inflation theory. (p. 130)

There, then, is an authentic view of the 'revolution' brought by Friedman and Phelps. It was not that the Phillips curve was established in thought, and the revolutionaries needed to show that money was neutral in the long run. It was that long-run neutrality was the established view, and what was sought was a way to incorporate the Phillips curve into that established thinking. It is not even right to think that the direction of thinking was to diminish the role of the Phillips curve—rather, Phelps' work, and in his view, also Friedman's was a defence of the curve, not an attack on it.

In any case, in the 1970s, and the dramatic increase in the use of the expression 'Phillips curve' seen in 1968 and 1969 continues apace. There are vastly more sources mentioning it in the latter decade than the former.[20] One important reason for that is simply that in the 1970s it became normal practice—as it did in the econometric literature—to apply the term 'Phillips curve' to inflation relations, but there are important developments in the content of the literature as well.

One, also mirroring the econometric literature, was that there was much discussion of the 'shift' or sometimes 'disappearance' of the Phillips curve. For example, Fleming (1972, p. 151) was simply discussing current macroeconomic developments but put it in the language of the Phillips curve. The same is true of Maynard and van Ryckeghem (1976), although most of their discussion relates to the 1950s and 1960s. There were also those who were more directly addressing the issue of whether there was any future in thinking in terms of the Phillips curve. Kaliski (1971) should be seen as addressing that issue—he doubted (p. 17) that any specific level of unemployment would, if maintained, stop inflation.

There was more purely theoretical work involving what the authors more and more described as concerning 'the Phillips curve'. Phelps' work continued with Phelps (1972a) being a major theoretical work with something of an inflationist orientation. In this and related work, the author clearly thought the case for price stability overstated and none of the reasons for it convincing, and presented a variety of arguments for favouring inflation, all the while accepting that expectations would adjust and basing much of the argument on the presumed existence of the Phillips curve. He saw arguments for non-zero inflation, benefits in accelerating inflation even to lower unemployment temporarily, and he said, furthermore, that he hoped to rapidly influence policy. In Phelps (1971) he even said, 'One can be an inflationist, as I am, without holding out much hope that anyone's "long-run Phillips Curve" is anything but very steep' (p. 31). Here, inflationism is indisputably detectable, but it is hard to argue that it flows from a failure to recognize the expectations argument.

This period also saw the appearance of Rothschild (1971) and Goldstein (1972). The second was a survey of 'the tradeoff' and the first was more of a personal reflection, but had some of the character of a survey. Both clearly contemplated inflation and Goldstein actually calculated tradeoff functions implicit in the work of others, without seeming to wonder why they had not done so themselves. Neither is very clear about why such policy would be reasonable but Goldstein mentioned Schultze (1959) and Rothschild (1974), answering criticism to the effect that the earlier piece had neglected inflation expectations clearly presented the lubrication argument.

There are also a good number of lesser discussions of the Phillips curve of a more or less purely theoretical kind. One branch continued to treat the existence of the curve, or of some detail about it, as raising puzzles, often looking back to Lipsey (1960).[21] The curve also continued to be used, in something of the manner of Lipsey (1965), as a convenient instrument for illustrating some argument or point of theory, without there truly being any commitment to specifics of its shape or durability. For example, Peacock (1972) used the idea of choosing a point on a Phillips curve and shifting the whole curve to illustrate the idea of using policy instruments to achieve targets. That was illustrative of principles, and no policy conclusions followed from it.

What is more important as the story unfolds, though, is that the 1970s also saw the appearance of the Phillips curve in discussion of two policy-related issues that had not been prominent earlier. One concerned the political business cycle. That idea had, as Oppenheimer (1970) observed, been perfectly well understood in practical applications since the British elections of 1955 and 1959, and a range of similar ideas were explored by Downs (1957). But it was Goodhart and Bhansali (1970) who used the Phillips curve in a discussion of vote-maximizing macroeconomic policy in the context of a supposition that voters favour low inflation and low unemployment. Nordhaus (1975) then focused on the idea that manipulations of policy could generate a political business cycle. He assumed the existence of a short-run and a steeper, but non-vertical, long-run curve, and argued that on plausible views about voter preferences, there would be an incentive for policymakers to lower unemployment before elections. Hibbs (1977) treated the evidence for the existence of the curve as conclusive and suggested that observed outcomes were consistent with the idea that left-wing governments favoured higher inflation and lower unemployment than right-wing ones. In a different line of thinking, although one that has sometimes seemed similar, Kydland and Prescott (1977) put the short-run

curve at the heart of the 'policy credibility' problem. Gordon (1975b) is perhaps not quite part of this literature but it is closely related in considering
the political forces that favour and resist inflation as being, in an important
sense, the place to look for explanations of policy.

Something which was more of a new theoretical departure, but which
was soon considered in terms of the Phillips curve, was the case for
European Monetary Union. This came onto the agenda with the publication of the Werner Report in 1970, setting the date for monetary union
of 1980. Beyond thinking of the question simply as a matter of the desirability of fixed and flexible exchange rates, there was something of a theoretical vacuum. However, the Werner Report's conception of 'monetary
union' was merely the irrevocable fixing of exchange parities, not the
introduction of a common currency leaving the mechanics of policy in
national hands. Since it was a matter of common observation that inflation rates of the countries concerned had in fact been very different, this
raised the issue of whether they really wished to pursue the same monetary policy. Here, the Phillips curve gave economists something to say
about running common policy.

Grubel (1970) suggested that the case for monetary union turned on the
effect of it on income, the stability of income, and 'national economic independence'. The last of those was, in his treatment, characterized by the possibility of choosing rates of inflation and unemployment. He noted (p. 322)
the argument that there was no long-run tradeoff but said that a choice
remained in the short run—Corden (1972) and Balassa (1973) made the
same sort of point, also discussing European integration. Magnifico (1973)
also discussed the Phillips curve in considering monetary union, but was
perhaps more sceptical about the existence even of a short-run relation,
whereas Fleming (1971) gave some credence to the possibility of a tradeoff in the long run. Hamada (1977) was still discussing monetary union
in terms of the possibility of costs arising from different choices about
the Phillips curve (as was de Grauwe (1994), in relation to later political ideas—but by that time, it had even greater theoretical artificiality).
A cost of joining a monetary union, he said, was that the 'attainment of
the nationally desired level of unemployment and prices levels is sacrificed'
(pp. 16–17), and that,

> Since countries differ in their positions of the Phillips curves, in their rates of
> productivity growth, and in their preferences in the choice between unemploy-
> ment and inflation, policy co-ordination does not mean that most of the partici-
> pating counties may not have to sacrifice attainment of their policy objectives.

In all this, a notable fact—and an important one, as I shall argue in Chapter 7—about the treatment of manpower and incomes policy, the political business cycle, and the case for monetary union is that 'the Phillips curve' came to be a label for a relationship between solely inflation and unemployment. This is not merely that it changed from being a wage-change to a price-change equation, but that in these discussions it became common to use the expression for that simple relationship, with none of the other variables that had been included in the econometric studies. Bent Hansen (1970) even *defined* it that way, in relation to wage change, saying,

> The Phillips curve expresses ΔW as a function of *u* alone.(p. 8)

That was something that in the econometric literature it had never been.

A further point that might be noted is that the beginning of the decade saw a little surge of renewed scepticism about the existence of the Phillips curve. As noted in Section 1.1, there were initial responses to Phillips (1958) which were very hostile. During the 1960s there is a little more, but probably nothing of such intensity. The closest might be Rees and Hamilton's (1967) discussion of Bodkin (1966), in which they came to the conclusion '*Apply with extreme care*'. But in the early 1970s, there is much more overt hostility to it. Balogh (1970, pp. 27–8) treated it with contempt. He always did—in Balogh (1982, p. 214, n13) he called it 'hair-raisingly absurd'. Phelps Brown (1971) thought it all wrong, Robinson (1972) ridiculed the curve and in Robinson (1973, p. 8) dismissed it, sarcastically, as the 'late-lamented' Phillips curve. Galbraith (1975/1976) dismissed it much more mildly, but still dismissed it, noting that Phillips' work had been 'considered suspect by more perceptive economists' (p. 242). That group might be said to be 'old Keynesians' expressing the same kind of hostility as arose in 1958, but the early 1970s saw something else as well. Fellner (1971) doubted the econometricians were generating any persuasive results in the area. He noted that different formulations, each of which appeared to support the existence of the curve, were in fact contradicting each other. Laffer and Ranson (1971) said their results 'do not confirm' the Phillips idea. Even Lucas (1973) might be read more as dismissing the idea of the curve outright than of seeking to argue that it was vertical.

5.7 CONCLUSION

Taking a broad view of the matter, attitudes to inflation from the 1960s and 1970s seem to be very reasonable. A wide range of arguments were made. Some were better than others, but the idea of cost-push inflation was a serious attempt to understand the problems of the times; there were many reasons to be unconcerned about low slow inflation, and a few, perhaps, to welcome it. Different people put their views in different ways, but trying to see them all as versions of Phillips curve inflationism is simply hopeless. As to finding anyone actually favouring inflation, as opposed to taking a balanced view of the idea of reasonable price stability, it is a long search. The two best cases are probably Slichter and Phelps. The former is really only distinguished by his speaking the language of inflation rather than reasonable price stability; the latter can hardly be said to have been confused about real and nominal variables.

One key point about the history of the Phillips curve is that there is a clear discontinuity in the discussion between the 1960s and the 1970s. But this is not the one of the conventional story. In the earlier period, when latterly conventional views suppose it was so dominant, it is in fact marginal. In the later, when it is supposed to be under siege, there is very much more discussion, and that discussion is very much more broadly based, and has various possible applications to policy.

A second point, also important for that history, is that, as far as discussions of cost-push inflation, inflation and growth, and arguments about the acceptability or otherwise of minimal rates of inflation are concerned, there is a notable continuity over these years. Where the tenor of discussion changes, it is not primarily because theory changes, but because the world changes—inflation rose, unions appeared more militant, and inflation acquired momentum. To those debates, the sharp change in the Phillips curve literature appears irrelevant. That too is a measure of the unimportance of the Phillips curve.

CHAPTER 6

Policymaking and Histories of Policymaking

So I turn to policymaking and—more importantly—accounts of policymaking. In Section 6.1 I hope it quickly becomes clear that policymaking itself owed nothing to the idea of an exploitable tradeoff. My treatment is brief, because with so little to be said for the story in the academic literature, the task is really only to show that there is nothing strikingly different to be seen in policymaking. A much more interesting observation comes from considering what has been said about policymaking: in Section 6.2 I consider contemporary and near-contemporary accounts of it and, in Section 6.3, slightly later ones where the emergence of the Phillips curve myth can be traced rather clearly and, I believe, dated very precisely. That development is reflected in accounts in other sources, such as textbooks, survey articles, and the like, which are considered in Section 6.4. Section 6.5 then briefly considers some points concerning statements of the Phillips curve myth from the period when it was apparently unquestioningly accepted—they are routine statements of what the authors take to be routine observations. Some of them are statements by economists, others by those working in related fields who have evidently been persuaded of the historical truth of the myth. Taken together, what is notable about all this, I suggest, is not any story of policymaking, which would in any case warrant more detailed treatment, but tracing the appearance and establishment of the Phillips curve story in accounts of policymaking.

6.1 THE GENERAL PICTURE

I suppose it will not be a surprise that there is no acceptance of inflation by the policymakers of the 1960s. The objectives of policy, amongst other things, were full employment and price stability. The British White Paper (1944) *Employment Policy* has long been seen as the great landmark of the official adoption of Keynesian economics. As was immediately apparent— for example to Merry and Bruns (1945)—the Canadian and Australian White Papers were, in the crucial respect of seeking those objectives, very similar. In the United States, the Employment Act of 1946 perhaps had a more colourful gestation—and certainly a more deeply studied one, notably by Bailey (1950)—but there too, the federal government accepted that there should be such a thing as employment policy. None of these documents had much to say about inflation, but there was no reason they should, since it was beyond doubt that price stability was an objective, and as is already apparent from Sections 1.3 and 1.4, the proponents of full employment policy did not see themselves as challenging that.

Again, just as in the academic literature, the simple optimism of the immediate post-war period did not last long, as inflation emerged at levels of unemployment that were regarded as too high to be 'full employment', and the control of inflation, believed to be cost-push in origin, proved to be more than just a matter of asking for responsible behaviour, or even of pointing out that a generally rising price level served no interest. In any case, the distinction between cost-push and demand-pull inflation was blurred, so it was hard to say exactly what policy response was appropriate. But, as argued in Chapter 5, together with these things came also the recognition that low rates of inflation are probably illusory, and in any case all but harmless, and quite possibly, following Schultze (1959), a symptom of a well-run economy. An argument along one of those lines could adequately be made on the basis of the price index being biased, prices tending to rise in recovery or the approach to full employment, or the existence of other bottlenecks. It would even be possibly to blame trade unions, oligopolies, or both, according to taste, for inflation at low rates, whilst at the same time, Slichter-style, arguing that it was not a serious problem.

And that is why the absence of overt acceptance of inflation by policymakers really *should* be a surprise. In this environment, it should have been an easy matter to see the benefits of accepting a gentle inflation, and any of the lines of argument just suggested would have had academic support. Furthermore, if there is any consensus in the econometric literature considered in Chapter 3 it is in the finding of an incompatibility of price stability with full employment. Even more, then, one would expect to see inflation being accepted. And even that leaves aside any idea of there being a professional consensus around the exploitability of this newly discovered 'menu of choice'. If we were to believe that consensus existed, then we could add, to the inevitability and harmlessness of inflation, the idea that the latest science showed it to be beneficial. What would have been more attractive to the elected policymakers of the 1960s?

The most that might be said is that, as regards demand, policy was not usually set with real intent actually to stop inflation. In that limited sense, policymakers might be said to have accepted inflation. But that response is not near to meeting the point—even Friedman (1977, p. 466) conceded that policymakers did not actually announce inflationist policy (although in his case this is difficult to reconcile with the rest of his account). The issue would be why it is that when there were apparently excellent reasons that could have been given for allowing a little inflation, policymakers continued to insist on the importance of price stability, even as they failed to deliver it. If the Phillips curve story is to be kept alive, at a minimum we need some examples of policymakers telling of the benefits of inflation. But where are they to be found? It seems, if anything, that it was not until disinflationary policies were ended in the 1980s, with the price level still slowly rising, that there was overt acceptance of ongoing inflation by policymakers.

The Economic Reports of the President during the 1960s suggest no acceptance of inflation. They are partly political and partly persuasive. If the case for inflation were to be officially made, it would be here. But the acceptance of inflation is not suggested, let alone advocated. The nearest they come is that the Report of 1968 discusses the bias in the price index, suggesting that inflation up to that time may have been exaggerated. In 1969—the Report delivered in the last days of the Johnson administration—there is a Phillips-type scatter chart of data from the 1960s on page 95, and the discussion notes that the relation 'has been neither mechanical nor precise' (p. 94), citing various factors causing it to vary. After a discussion of recent events and about 20 pages on ways of controlling inflation without raising unemployment, some in the character of supply-side reform, some relating to government procurement practices, and some to private-sector voluntary restraint, the conclusion was reached (p. 122) that the task of reconciling price stability and high employment could not be accomplished by government alone, other groups would have to co-operate and this required

> an awareness of the bleakness of the alternatives: either achieving stability by
> sacrificing high employment or realizing high employment by acquiescing in

persistent inflation. We cannot, and need not, accept either of these alternatives. (p. 128)

I suppose the authors might be accused of believing in a menu of choice, although by this time they have noted the danger of an accelerating wage–price spiral. But in any case, the menu, if it is a menu, is presented as offering unacceptable outcomes and the whole discussion was on achieving price stability and high employment. Earlier and later Economic Reports similarly sometimes discuss 'the tradeoff' but the point then is that things must be done to improve its location. In the 1970s, the discussion sometimes concerns transitional targets so that the tradeoff on the path back to price stability is discussed. But there is no inflationism, and before the 1990s the tradeoff is never described as a 'Phillips curve' in connection with current or prospective policy.

In the United Kingdom, budget speeches of Chancellors of the Exchequer have much less economic analysis than the Economic Reports, but what they say points in the same direction. Whatever else they may also contain, they are always anti-inflationary. The political reluctance to accept inflation, even when it was forced on them, is also evident in election manifestos, which seem never to accept it.[1] Indeed, if there is one single preoccupation in this period, it is with the balance of payments. There were devaluations in 1949 and 1967, and the abandonment of fixed exchange rates in 1972. But that is only the tip of an iceberg which is more fully discussed in Forder (2013a)—difficulties with the balance of payments were a major feature of the budgets of 1946–8, 1952, 1961, 1964, 1967, 1968, 1975, and 1976. That leaves actions taken in crisis conditions outside the budget—of which notable examples were the suspension of convertibility in 1947, actions aimed at reducing imports in 1951, bank rate increases in 1954, 1955, 1957, 1959, the export rebate and import surcharge of 1964, and a collection of measures in each of the following years before devaluation, and yet more afterwards to make it effective.

A point to be particularly emphasized about these events concerns the character of the 'stop-go' policy that resulted from these crises and responses to them. Between crises, there were periods of rapid expansion and falling unemployment, and the policy response to the crises tended to result in rising unemployment. If it is to be put in those terms, the tradeoff that faced policymakers was between a balance of payments and a high level of employment. Although inflation would certainly tend to make the balance of payments worse, it does not follow that policy responses to crises were principally aimed at reducing it. On the contrary—increases in interest rates were presumed to attract capital inflows, whereas reductions in government expenditure, restrictions on consumer credit and similar arrangements, and tax increases were expected to reduce imports. Even incomes policy, where it was applied as a response to a crisis—as it was in 1949, 1962, and 1966—could be seen as much as a way of preventing an increase in consumption, and hence imports, as a way of affecting the real exchange rate. In any case, the rates of inflation actually experienced in the period were too low for changes in them to have a quick effect on the balance of payments. The point about the 'tradeoff' between unemployment and the balance of payments, then, was that the level of employment affected the *quantities* in trade, not the prices.

This line of thinking is indeed evident and well illustrated by the discussion offered by James Callaghan, the Labour Chancellor of the Exchequer from October 1964 to November 1967, in the Budget Statement of 1967. Having described the importance of incomes policy in controlling wages, he said of the balance of payments:

> A better trend in our costs and prices improves our competitive position. A lower pressure of demand improves the supply position, ensuring that deliveries are quicker and the urge to export greater...As regards imports, a lower average pressure of demand than we have permitted in the past should also mean that we do not again suffer the kind of upsurge that has so often damaged the balance of payments. (Hansard, col. 980)

So the question of costs and prices—a matter for incomes policy—was separate from the question of the pressure of demand, and the quantity of imports was principally controlled by demand pressure.

The equivalent thought about devaluation, when it came in 1967, was, of course, that a lower value of the pound would make a higher level of employment consistent with a sustainable balance of payments. That is because the imports are a function of the level of employment and the exchange rate. That, as will now be clear, is a very different thing from a higher level of inflation being consistent with that sustainability—a proposition which would in any case be hard to rationalize. If it were to be suggested that the 1967 devaluation was thought of as the first of a series, and that would make possible a continuous inflation, then the response is that there appears to be nothing whatever to be said in support of such a speculation. In any case, a government which wishes to—as it might be put— 'exploit the Phillips curve' would surely prefer a floating exchange rate to repeated crises and devaluations.

The role of incomes policy in the 1960s is also easily understood. Contemporary accounts tell a uniform story. A good number of British discussions are considered in Backhouse and Forder (2013) and, amongst American studies, Sheahan (1967) was perhaps the most noted from the 1960s, and Goodwin (1975) from slightly later, while Ulman and Flanagan (1971) considered western Europe generally. None of them gives any indication that inflation was anything other than a problem, or that incomes policy was expected to control inflation which was understood to be due to excess demand. Where – and only where – cost-push inflation is diagnosed, incomes policy is seen as creating a countervailing force for price stability. Sheahan (1967), for example, discussing the policy of 1962 said,

> The principle underlying the guideposts was that the economy would work more efficiently if discretionary price and wage decisions were brought more in line with the results that would be expected in competitive markets. (p. 14)

As an example from policymaking, we might consider Conservative Chancellor Maudling who, in the budget of 1963 where the plan was announced to achieve a 4 per cent rate of growth in the following years, said,

> The extent to which I can safely stimulate demand now depends upon the movement of other factors that affect costs and prices: by far the greatest of these is the level of personal incomes. (Hansard, col. 475)

And he declared the necessity of an incomes policy. The 'other factors', then, were not matters of demand. The point is perhaps clearer still in the Economic Report of the Council of Economic Advisers (CEA 1964) where it says,

> Adherence to these general guideposts not only would make for over-all price stability but would be generally consistent with the tendencies of competitive labor and product markets. (p. 119)

It was at most, then, an attempt to provide a force to countervail monopoly power, not to hold money wages below their competitive level.

In the 1970s, outcomes in respect of inflation and unemployment both deteriorated, there was much more concern about both, and it would be possible to paint policy as being inconsistent and confused. But a better understanding arises from appreciating the consistency of thinking with the earlier period. Some things were certainly different—most notably the range of possible causes of inflation, which was extended to commodity price shocks, and the high rate of inflation, which brought attention to the question of whether it had a momentum of its own, and if so, what caused or sustained that momentum. Neither of those things, however, required any fundamental change of attitude—they did not, in themselves, show that bargains were not determined by the human interaction of actual bargainers, nor did they mean it was definitely impossible to achieve full employment and price stability.

As it happens, in both Britain and the United States new administrations (the Heath government and the Nixon presidency) were initially committed to a reduction of the role of the state in economic management, but when inflation rose and unemployment seemed to fail to restrain it, incomes policy and reflation were introduced.

In the United States, the Council of Economic Advisers (CEA 1970) (Nixon's first Report), stated the intention gradually to control inflation. The 1971 Report emphasized the importance of full utilization of resources, and the Economic Report of the President, contained within it described (p. 6) the 'full employment budget' submitted by the administration (while expressing the view that inflation would continue to fall). By the time of the 1972 Report, the administration had already launched the 'New Economic Policy', in August 1971. Nixon noted (p. 3) that inflation had fallen, and employment risen but said they had not done so sufficiently, so he had (amongst many other things) imposed a 90-day freeze on prices, wages, and rents. The reason given was the stubbornness of the 'inflationary momentum' (p. 4) that had arisen as a result of previous policy. He also celebrated the effect in raising employment of the 'stimulative tax program' (p. 5) that had been enacted. The emphasis on inflation control continued in the Economic Reports of the President without interruption throughout the 1970s. There is discussion of such things as the optimal rate of inflation reduction and the consequences for unemployment, and of the possibility of reducing inflation and unemployment together; but of a stable 'Phillips curve', by that name or any other, affecting current policy, there is no indication.

In Britain, similarly, the Heath government accepted that unemployment would need to be somewhat higher than it had been, and expected this to control inflation. If the event, unemployment ran beyond the planned level and yet this failed to control inflation so that it could well seem that excess demand was not the cause of inflation. Policy then switched to demand expansion (to reduce unemployment) and a price freeze was introduced in November 1972 (to control what then appeared to be cost-push inflation). It was, by common repute, a badly judged expansionary policy and quickly ran too far, so that a reversal was begun in May 1973. The Labour government which took office in 1974 faced continuous difficulty with crisis—it would be remarkable if anyone really felt they could find anything as pertinacious as targeting a point on the Phillips curve in what they did, but there was a collapse in the value of the pound and an appeal to the IMF which took policy partly out of their hands in any case.

The combination of an attempt to reduce inflation at the same time as adopting an expansionary policy deserves comment. It is easy to see how the idea could appear to be to shift the Phillips curve with incomes policy and simultaneously move round it with demand policy. Not at all. In 1970, the conditions were conditions of unemployment. If the Phillips curve said anything about that, it was that inflation should fall, even if policy was increasing employment. The plan was to reduce unemployment while inflation continued to fall. In the event, inflation did not fall as expected—that was the 'breakdown' of the Phillips curve that later discussions have attributed to 'expectations'. But the contemporary policy view would probably be better characterized as seeing it as being due to 'momentum', and it appeared that incomes policy could contribute to breaking that momentum. (The facts might even be that it was the *falling* unemployment that prevented prices stabilizing. One might take that message from Phillips (1958) and others who emphasized the importance of the rate of change of unemployment, but not from the simple 'Phillips curve' of 1970 vintage.) Alternatively, it was even sometimes said—as it had been by Smith (1966)—that incomes policy could affect expectations and thereby control inflation. That again is something hard to rationalize convincingly if one starts from a view that wage determination follows mechanical laws, and that fact has perhaps obscured the sense of it from later understanding. But when the underlying process is volitional, operating on expectations becomes a possibility.

There is, therefore, nothing in the policy record to suggest that 'the Phillips curve', or 'the tradeoff', or the same thing by any other name, had any role in motivating or influencing policy. It was hardly discussed in a policy context in the 1960s, and when it appears right at the beginning of the 1970s—if it does—it is to describe anti-inflationary policy. After that, what is said about it is not much more than that it had broken down. And that too meant exactly the same as it did in the academic literature—that unemployment seemed to have lost its power to control inflation.

6.2 EARLY COMMENTARY FROM THE 1960s

Whilst it is clear that there is no reason to describe actual policy in terms of the Phillips curve, and certainly not in terms of attempts to exploit it, it is also important that amongst contemporary and near-contemporary commentators, almost no one did. One notable aspect of their work is that the simple weight of evidence is magnified by the uniformity of the picture across different sources.

There was in the United Kingdom a series of books intended to give authoritative accounts of policy and economic developments organized by the National Institute of Economic and Social Research. These were Dow (1964), Blackaby (1978a), and Britton (1991); and one might also consider Beckerman (1972) as an assessment of the Labour government of 1964–70, and Worswick and Ady (1952, 1962) covering the period up to 1959. Writing in each of these last two, Little (1952, 1962) thought there had been periods when fiscal policy kept demand too high had thereby caused-inflation, but the suggestion was that these incidents were due to imperfect control or political imperatives—not, therefore, an idea that sustained excess demand was actually desirable. Dow, who was also the author of one of the Phillips-competitor papers—Dicks-Mireaux and Dow (1959)—contemplated the existence of a tradeoff (Dow 1964, p. 403) but does not seem to have thought policymakers were conscious of it, and expressed his own view that unemployment should be kept higher to maintain price stability. That is as close as anything else in these volumes to suggesting that such an idea motivated policy. (The Phillips curve itself is almost invisible: the Dow volume, of just over 400 pages, has three index entries for Phillips, all in footnotes, two relating to the 1958 paper; Blackaby has three in over 600 pages; Beckerman has one in over 300 pages; the second Worswick and Ady volume, of over 500, has none.)

A different sort of work was not so much concerned with the minutiae of policy, but more with bringing historical perspective to bear on some aspect of developments. Hutchinson (1968) was dealing with the goals of macroeconomic policy, including price stability and high employment in British policymaking. He noted what he regarded as a weakness—that there was a lack of clarity about the relation between policy goals—and said that even at times where there was a precise formulation of objectives, it seldom went as far as a statement about 'how much of one objective is to be sacrificed to attain another' (p. 263). Phillips—or his supposed tradeoff anyway—had obviously not made much impact on that author. Lipton (1968) set out to assess British performance specifically by considering policy aims and the extent to which they had been achieved. Phillips is mentioned on page 11 for providing engineering analogies and on page 240 for the fact that his curve does not tell policymakers what they need to know. Lipton himself clearly thought the problem of inflation per se greatly exaggerated, but said (p. 58) that the balance of payments constraint makes a clear-cut case for controlling it.

Winch (1969/1972) was a history of British policy from the 1920s with some comparison with the United States—'an account of the constant dialogue between economic thought and economic policies, between the intellectual propositions and enquiries of the political economists and the problems of society itself'—as it says on the back cover of the 1972 edition. There is no indication that the Phillips curve had ever been discovered or that policymakers thought there might be benefits to be gained from inflation.

Those are three works offering considered and detailed treatments of policy, all aiming at elucidation of matters that should—if it was at that time seen as having any significance at all—have brought the Phillips curve to the surface. In fact, there is scarcely a reference amongst them. And the dates are significant too, since these are all from what should be the absolute high tide of the Phillips curve—just at the time when Friedman was supposedly correcting the reigning error.

There are fewer systematic treatments of the United States on this kind of scale, but Goodwin (1975)—on the efforts at price control—leaves no room for thinking that inflation at anything more than a *de minimis* level was seen as anything other than a problem; and Stein (1969)—a study of 'the fiscal revolution in America'—does not seem to contemplate that the tax cut of 1964 was framed by those who had it in mind that there would be anything more than *de minimis* inflation. There is again no mention of the Phillips curve itself.

One more nearly contemporary account of policymaking might be considered since it offers a particularly clear contrast to what is said later. That is Tobin (1966). Tobin was a member of the Council of Economic Advisers which presented the Economic Report of 1962, calling for the setting of an interim target level of unemployment of 4 per cent, saying that structural measures would, in due course, allow that figure to be lowered. In about 9,000 words he described what he called the 'intellectual revolution' in macroeconomic policymaking. This revolution, as he saw it, had brought the views of academics with those of 'men of affairs' much closer together, so that there was a much greater consensus than previously that

> a steadily growing fully employed economy is both desirable and attainable; that governmental fiscal and monetary powers can contribute greatly to achieving full employment, steady growth, and price stability; and that these powers should be dedicated to economic objectives rather than to other ends. (p. 2)

He went on to describe the obstacles that had to be overcome to achieve this, including persuading people that the business cycle was not inevitable;

rebutting the view that unemployment was 'structural' rather than due to a deficiency of demand; and a general resistance to increased government spending. Economic arguments by the Council of Economic Advisers were, he said, one of the things which changed opinion on these issues. He noted the value of the specific numerical target of 4 per cent unemployment and said it was an estimate of what could be accomplished by demand policy

> without encountering unacceptable price inflation because of sectoral and regional shortages and bottlenecks. (p. 12)

Slightly later he noted that there was public fear of inflation, that this attitude had hardened during the 1950s, and that, although he thought it exaggerated, the Council of Economic Advisers had been confident

> that a considerable expansion of demand could occur without pulling up prices. (p. 17)

At the time Tobin was writing, it should be remembered that the policy seemed very successful, and according to the usual story the existence of a stable Phillips curve had not been called into question. On neither count did Tobin have any reason to conceal the role of the curve in the events he was describing, and yet it is completely absent. Indeed, beyond the 'shortages and bottlenecks' of the lubrication argument there is no hint of any willingness to accept inflation.

Another group consists of commentators who were hostile to the policy they were discussing specifically because they regarded it as causing or permitting too much inflation. In the light of the widespread recognition of the expectations argument noted in Section 4.1, these authors might be expected to deploy it—if they thought policy was seeking to exploit the Phillips curve. Even if they are, for some reason, inhibited from doing so, they might be expected to challenge the view that inflation was a price worth paying for higher employment—if they thought that view prevalent. But in those respects, they are all dogs that do not bark.

Robbins (1972) actually noted the expectations argument in the form that leads to the view that steady inflation is harmless. Whilst calling for the control of demand to stop inflation, he dismissed it, apparently as not being of practical relevance. Presumably that is because he did not suppose that inflation, if permitted, would be steady. But it can hardly be that he thought others were led to advocate inflation because they had not appreciated that wages would adjust to it, since he would surely have pointed out the error if he had. Robbins (1974) criticized policy for allowing inflation but again made no mention of anyone trying to exploit the Phillips curve, or anything of that kind. Modigliani (1974) reviewed the Economic Report of the President of that year, and thought the inflation situation more serious than the Report suggested, but even in the Report there was no concealing that the fact that inflation was a problem, and he gave no hint of thinking inflation was or had been used to lower unemployment.

The clearest such British case is found in the work of Frank Paish. Always paying close attention to macroeconomic data, he was, from the late 1940s until the beginning of the 1970s, a critic of British policy as tending towards excess demand. In a radio broadcast published as Paish (1948) he said stabilizing prices was essential and specifically emphasized that this would take, in his view, 4 per cent unemployment. In Paish (1958/1966) he argued that British inflation had invariably been demand-pull rather than cost-push, and, therefore, that a reduction of demand would be required to stop it; Paish (1964/1966) criticized incomes policy on the basis that the inflation being observed was due to excess demand, and in Paish (1968/1970), he took the same view, calling for more than 2 per cent unemployment. His estimates had changed, but his attitude had not—inflation prevailed because governments caused or permitted excess demand.

So consistent was he in the character of his arguments, that he was— very much more than Phillips, certainly—the leading and most authentic of the British 'demand-pull' school. As he made clear in Paish (1958/1966, p. 109), he also recognized that his policy might pose a political challenge. What he did not do, however, is give any indication of thinking that policy was seeking to exploit a tradeoff, or the inflation was being consciously pursued. He did not, for example, say that he felt that the wrong point on the tradeoff was being targeted, or that a problem with the policy was that it would lead to acceleration of inflation. His point was a diagnostic one, and every appearance is that he felt policymakers shared his view that inflation was too high but had mistaken the cause. It is difficult to see that after two decades of arguing a consistent line he had failed to understand the basic motivation of policy. So again the evidence is against the Phillips curve story.

Another case is that of Jay (1976)—a re-presentation of arguments which had been first made in articles in *The Times* earlier in the decade. His concern was that British policy had veered between expansion and contraction, with each phase of expansion raising inflation and reducing unemployment, and each phase of contraction doing the opposite, but that at each cycle, both inflation and unemployment rose. He suggested that continued deterioration on this kind of path threatened the stability of democracy.

That has a vague resemblance to a story of exploiting the Phillips curve, but again, any serious attention reveals it is crucially different.

For one thing, at the root of the trouble, as seen by Jay, was irresponsible trade unionism and cost-push inflation. He was, it is true, rightly regarded, by Parsons (1989) amongst others, as sympathetic to monetarism. But the explanation of that is to be found in his view that some way had to be found to stop inflation, not in a rejection of the cost-push diagnosis. There is no doubt about that point since he debated the issue of cost-push inflation with Friedman in Jay (1974). Consequently, he recognized that there could be the possibility of a way out through incomes policy, but in his doom-laden interpretations they were unworkable in practice. Jay (1976, p. 15) mentioned the idea of a stable Phillips curve tradeoff, saying it was believed to exist in a narrow range near to full employment (in other words, as I would put it, in the range where the lubrication argument was applicable). His criticism of policymakers, though, explicitly related to the effects of policy outside this range. The substance of his argument was more that policymakers were reacting—or overreacting—to the immediate problems they faced and lurching from pillar to post, rather than that they are so calculating as to find an optimal point on a curve. So there was, in this view, no stable Phillips curve, no optimizing point, no choices over which there might be reasonable disagreement. Nor was the root of the problem some such thing as a failure by government to understand simple economics— for Jay the root of it was a fundamental breakdown of social consensus that underlay the cost-push inflation.

There is one particular incident which is often presented as showing the importance of the Phillips curve in previous thinking, which was a speech given by Prime Minister Callaghan to the Labour Party Conference in September 1976. He said,

> We used to think that you could just spend your way out of a recession and increase employment by cutting taxes and boosting Government spending. I tell you, in all candour, that that option no longer exists, and that in so far as it ever did exist, it only worked on each occasion since the war by injecting a bigger dose of inflation into the economy followed by higher levels of unemployment as the next step. (Callaghan 1987, p. 426)

When this remark is quoted—as it was by Friedman (1977), telling his famous story about Phillips curve inflationism—it tends to be without much commentary, presumably because it is taken to be self-evident that Callaghan was admitting that the Phillips curve (or something similar) had been motivating policy, and that if he said so, that must be true. It is helpful, therefore, to recall that, as Burk and Cairncross (1992) recount, this speech was made at the time of a very sharp fall in sterling and in the immediate prelude to the application to the IMF, the announcement of which was made the following day. It was rather clearly an attempt, amongst other things, to suggest that there was going to be a much more serious attempt to control inflation with demand policy.

Furthermore, Callaghan's way of putting it matches Jay's account of events much more closely than it matches any Phillips curve story. As it happens, Jay was at the time Callaghan's son-in-law, and it seems to be undisputed that he wrote that section of the speech (Matthijs (2012, p. 100) asserts it particularly clearly). It would seem, therefore, better to suppose that the ideas were Jay's rather than that this is the unique instance of a policymaker admitting to having set policy in the manner of the Phillips curve myth.

The catalogue of commentary from the 1960s which shows no interest in Phillips could certainly be enlarged much more, but it would serve little purpose. Although the decade should be the high point of enthusiasm for the Phillips curve—it is supposed to be the period when there was an excess of confidence in it—more or less nothing is said about this great breakthrough in economic understanding. There is, though, one more author whose comments from the 1960s should be studied most closely.

Friedman (1968a) is the paper that is famous for introducing the idea of the 'natural rate' of unemployment, and deploying the expectations argument—supposedly innovatively—in discussion of the Phillips curve. But, in what will be an important point in the argument of Chapter 7, and contrary to what is sometimes implied, he made no suggestion that the Phillips curve had actually been seen to provide a basis for policy, and nor was the Phillips curve by any means the centrepiece of his presentation. Indeed, the whole discussion of it is contained in two paragraphs and a long footnote. Having put forward the idea of the natural rate of unemployment, and having said it is that level 'ground out by the system of Walrasian general equilibrium equations' (p. 8), Friedman said,

> You will recognize the close similarity between this statement and the celebrated Phillips curve. The similarity is not coincidental. (p. 8)

He went on to say that Phillips' analysis was deservedly celebrated as important and original, but that it is defective in failing to distinguish nominal and real wages so that,

> Implicitly, Phillips wrote his article for a world in which everyone anticipated that nominal prices would be stable and in which that anticipation remained unshaken and immutable whatever happened to actual prices and wages. (p. 8)

That made Friedman's account one that fitted together his theory with the idea of the Phillips curve. He is showing the compatibility of two theoretical thoughts in just the way that Phelps (1970c), discussed in Section 5.6, described. On the other hand, he is not diagnosing any policy error.

The discussion in the long footnote (p. 9) offers more theory and, even more interestingly, more commentary on previous work on the Phillips curve. Here, he says that for alternative stable rates of inflation, the Phillips curve will differ in 'level' but that where inflation is variable, it will not be well defined and

> My impression is that these statements accord reasonably well with the experience of the economists who have explored empirical Phillips Curves.
>
> Restate Phillips' analysis in terms of the rate of change of real wages—and even more precisely, anticipated real wages—and it all falls into place. That is why students of empirical Phillips Curves have found that it helps to include the rate of change of the price level as an independent variable.

Whether Friedman's comments on Phillips himself are fair might be debated, but he was perfectly clear, as well as perfectly correct, that the empirical work on the Phillips curve did not ignore the effect of price change, even if he was suggesting that the theoretical understanding of the relation was limited. Just as notably, nowhere in Friedman (1968a) was it said that the curve or any understanding or misunderstanding of it was thought to offer a menu, or that it in fact guided policy, or was even used by policymakers to describe the results or intentions of their actions. In Friedman's own account from 1968, then, stories about the Phillips curve seeming to make a case for inflation are completely absent.

6.3 THE BEGINNINGS OF THE PHILLIPS CURVE MYTH

Right at the end of the 1960s it is possible to see some movement in the direction of putting the Phillips curve in the role of promoting inflationary policy. Introductory remarks by Lucas and Rapping (1969a) include the claim that estimates of the Phillips curve have led to the conclusion that 'sustained inflation is both necessary and sufficient to the sustained maintenance of low unemployment rates' (p. 342). Fand (1969) saw the Phillips curve as having affected policy not because anyone favoured inflation but because, as he put it, it 'firms up' the willingness 'to take risks with the price level' (p. 556, fn.). That could be true without anything having gone very wrong with their thinking. Wallich (1969b), commenting on

Fand's paper, said 'analysts with a Keynesian bent have made frequent use of the Phillips curve to demonstrate that employment can be bought at the expense of inflation' (p. 595), but he offered no substantiation of this point. In any case, by the time he made that point he had already said that the expectations argument was well known, and had, slightly mysteriously, also declared himself to be a 'right-wing Keynesian with a monetarist bias' (p. 590). Gordon (1970, p. 11) used the expression 'the Phillips curve argument' to describe the idea of a permanent tradeoff. Another case is Johnson (1970). He described the curve as a 'trade-off function' between 'the rate of inflation and the rate of unemployment', and said,

> the policy-makers can either be assumed to choose a point on this function according to their or the community's preferences, or advised to choose a point on it that maximizes social welfare (p. 111)

He cited Reuber (1964) as an example of an author giving that kind of advice—as indeed he did, but there were not many others.

A couple of early cases of statements of the Phillips curve story actually add a small extra twist in that the authors change the presentation of their ideas in an important way. One would be Haberler (1972) who said that that Slichter's idea of permanent harmless inflation had been

> revived, provided with a new, up-to-date econometric foundation, and redecorated with Phillips curve, expectational analyses, and cost-benefit computations and what not. (p. 236)

That is all very well, but Haberler (1960) made no mention of the Phillips curve; in the revised version—Haberler (1966b)—he mentioned it once to deny its existence and in Haberler (1971) discussed it more, but still only in an appendix, without making claims like those in the quotation. So those historical claims were new in 1972.

Something similar might be said of Brittan (1971). Supposing that aggregate demand determines employment, and without specifically mentioning the Phillips curve in the context of policy formation, he said,

> The basic assumption behind most post-war writing on economic policy was that the authorities can, whether by fiscal or monetary policy or both, determine the 'pressure of demand'…A high pressure of demand was associated with more rapidly rising prices than a low one…the authorities had to choose their own compromise. (p. 472)

There is, however, no comparable passage in the previous edition of the work—Brittan (1969)—nor the differently titled edition previous to that—Brittan (1964). The passage from the 1971 version appeared in an additional chapter which the author describes as 'a personal essay on some current problems' (p. 12), and was said to be no use as a summary of the book and likely to date quickly. He also said, of his consideration of demand management,

> my main interest in all editions has been less in the instruments than the way they are used...My real main concern has been, not how to change demand by £xM., but *why* £xM. has been chosen rather than £yM. (pp. 13–14)

So it is remarkable that the earlier editions of the book are not only without a discussion of the vertical Phillips curve, but also without a discussion of a non-vertical one, or any other presumptively stable tradeoff being an aspect of policymaking. He was, then, addressing the question of why the choices were made, but not addressing the idea of an inflation tradeoff. Brittan made later comments on both the substantive issues and his own attitudes to them which further reinforce the view that the remarks from 1971 should not be treated as authoritative.[2]

In the cases of Haberler (1972) and Brittan (1971) then, it appears that the discussion of the Phillips curve seems to be something that was added to the authors' understanding after the events they were describing. Over a longer time scale the same could be said of others, by comparing for example, Stein (1984) with Stein (1969).

A related case that may have been more important just because the later statement seemed so authoritative is that of Tobin (1972a). In complete contrast to the mode of expression of Tobin (1966)—but with content along very similar lines—he described the 'New Economics' of the Kennedy administration, introduced in the Economic Report of the President of 1962. Here, though, he said that the 4 per cent target for unemployment was

> chosen with an eye on the Phillips curve, specifically on the 4% inflation that accompanied 4% unemployment in the mid-1950s (pp. 16–17)

and

> Somehow the impression had been conveyed that the New Economics promised full employment, steady growth, and price stability too. The facts of life pictured in the Phillips curve came as a shock (p. 37)

and even

> Maybe it would be healthy for the country to have an explicit public debate about
> which point on the Phillips trade-off we should aim for. (p. 38)

On the face of it, and certainly if that book is read alone, it seems to make
a powerful case for thinking that the Phillips curve was at the heart of policy. But as Laidler (1997, p. 96) noted, there is nothing whatever in the
Economic Report itself to suggest this story, and as we have already seen
there is nothing in the policy record, academic literature, or other discussions either. And of course, the lubrication argument was clearly stated
in Tobin (1972a) as it was in Tobin (1972b) and Tobin and Leonard Ross
(1971). Tobin (1972a) put the argument like this,

> I agree that we cannot count on sustained money illusion or misperception of
> wage and price trends to preserve a Phillips trade-off in long-run equilibrium.
> But I do not agree with the policy conclusion drawn from this observation. The
> Phillips trade-off is, in my view, essentially a phenomenon of perpetual disequi-
> librium and adjustment in diverse labor and product markets. In this setting a
> trade-off lasts long enough for policymakers, if not indefinitely. (p. 94)

Tobin (1972a) is not, then, any more than Brittan (1971) or Haberler
(1972), a demonstration that the exploitable tradeoff was at the heart of
policymaking. If it is a demonstration of anything, it is that usage of the
expression 'Phillips curve' had changed. But, nevertheless, these sources are
the earliest seemingly authoritative discussions which might be said to put
'the Phillips curve' at the origin of inflationist policy. And perhaps Tobin,
because of the specificity of his treatment, is the most notable of them.

At about that time, it is possible to find a couple more straws in the
wind. One would be Mundell (1972), who in just a sentence, said that 'the
Phillips curve theory' had been very damaging by suggesting that inflation
lowered unemployment and that this belief was the cause of inflationary
policy (p. 49). Another work of interest, although it is not highly cited, is
that of Humphrey (1973). He offered an account intended to familiarize
his readers with this 'widely-used concept' of the Phillips curve and 'to
indicate its changing policy implications' (p. 2). He described the history
of the curve in terms of its being widely accepted, and treated as offering
a menu of choice, such that different policymakers would choose different points, and drew Phillips curves tangent to different 'social disutility contours'. But, he went on to explain that the curve was based on
poor theory in that the importance of expectations was not appreciated

before Friedman. He said that at the time of his writing, no one any longer believed in the 'naïve' Phillips curve but there was a debate as to whether it was strictly vertical.

Although some of his historical claims are incorrect, and it is fairly clear that Humphrey favours the strict accelerationist view, the discussion was balanced in that he did not suggest that anyone was egregiously foolish in what they thought. All in all it seems to be a piece written to elucidate some of the debates around the Nixon administration's policy, with a reconstruction of earlier thought with little firm connection to the facts, but which is by no means dependent on that history for its interest.

Just a little later, though, we find the same sort of view of the history of the curve, combined with much firmer denunciations of the economists of the 1960s who supposedly believed in this stable tradeoff. The sudden and nearly simultaneous arrival of several such treatments is itself remarkable.

Surely an important one, and the first to be actually published, was the Report of the Council of Economic Advisers (CEA 1975). That was the first of the Ford presidency, and of the chairmanship of Alan Greenspan. It declared,

> During the 1960's many economists believed that there was a long-run, negative relation between the unemployment rate and the rate of increase in wages or prices, initially described by the 'Phillips curve' and later by functions involving additional variables and equations. Empirically, simple charts relating the U.S. rate of increase in prices or wages to the unemployment rate did show a downward-sloping relation for the 1960's, although by the 1970's there was clear evidence that the relation was not stable across decades. (p. 94)

When it came to the analysis of policy they did not say that inflation had arisen because of this belief, but nevertheless, their assertion of the error of understanding is perfectly clear.

Next is Friedman (1975a), which is a thoroughly unsympathetic discussion alleging that the economics profession, from Phillips himself onwards, was misled about the nature of the tradeoff, and that policymakers quickly followed them, until the expectations argument was disclosed by Friedman and Phelps.

Gordon (1976a) described the Phillips curve as a tradeoff relation and said,

> It was common in the U.S. for economic advisers to Democratic Presidents to recommend the choice of a point on the curve northwest of the target of Republican advisers. (p. 190)

Much of his discussion is then organized around issues raised by the curve, and even more so his presumption that thinking was revolutionized by Friedman and Phelps, but nothing more is said about the inflationist intent of any policymakers or presidents.

Brunner and Meltzer (1976) said that the Phillips curve 'appeared to fill a gap', that Phillips presented evidence that suggested the relation 'had remained stable in the UK for a century', that the curve was,

> absorbed quickly in econometric models, in policy discussions, and in policy decisions. The notion of a stable and reliable 'trade-off' between inflation and unemployment made the journey from professional literature to the counsels of policy and even the Councils of Economic Advisers more rapidly than most

and that,

> the belief in a stable Phillips curve either encouraged or rationalized policy choices that led to a range of observations on inflation not matched in the peacetime experience of the United States. (p. 1)

None of that happened, but it is clear that Brunner and Meltzer feel a very basic mistake was made because they say that by 1973, 'a growing number' of economists accepted the natural rate hypothesis, which 'reminds economists', as they put it,

> that if all demand and supply equations are homogeneous of zero degree in prices and nominal wealth, inflation cannot bring a permanent reduction in unemployment. (p. 2)

They also suggested that 'Sociologists or historians of science may one day explain why economists and officials accepted the Phillips curve so readily' (p. 2), but such a statement only confirms how completely they had lost touch with their subject matter.

Lucas (1976) said that the idea that 'permanent inflation' would 'induce a permanent economic high' had

> undergone the mysterious transformation from obvious fallacy to cornerstone of the theory of economic policy (p. 19)

and that the earliest embodiment of the tradeoff was in Klein and Goldberger (1955) but that the idea moved to centre stage because of Phillips (1958) and Samuelson and Solow (1960). There is something strange about that because the reasons given in Lucas (1972a, 1976) for rejecting the stable curve are not by any means obvious. But that is a minor point—he has no basis for thinking that Phillips' paper was important in bringing about the change, and, as has been argued, Samuelson and Solow's certainly was not. He gave citations to studies of the 'long-run Phillips curve'—de Menil and Enzler (1972), Hirsch (1972), and Hymans (1972)—all of them from the same volume, and all of them, like Klein and Goldberger, equations esti-mated in complete macroeconometric models. Those were short-run fore-casting models, so Lucas' description hardly captures the intention.

Writing under the title, 'Some current controversies in the theory of inflation' Humphrey (1976) said he was offering 'A careful sorting-out of these issues and a clarification of the rival claims and distinctive features of competing schools of thought' and described the 'once-dominant' view of a 'stable Phillips curve trade off' (p. 8) but could hardly make it clearer—in contrast to Humphrey (1973)—how foolish he believed it all to have been. He described the 'naive Phillips curve hypothesis' as being that 'the rate of money wage increase depends on the excess demand for labour' (p. 9) and wrote an equation with just those variables—so price change was excluded. Another view was 'The expectations-augmented/excess-demand hypoth-esis' which 'introduces the price-expectations variable into the Phillips curve…' (p. 9). No one had ever defended the 'naive' view, so not only was there no current controversy between those two, there had never been one. Humphrey (1978) gave a picture which is very similar in the relevant respects. Only with the introduction of expected inflation does he admit to any price-change aspect featuring in the curves.

And then there is Buchanan and Wagner (1977) who certainly have a clear agenda of arguing that inflationary policy was an essential aspect of Keynesianism. They—specifically concerning themselves only with the United States—said,

> The Phillips curve was alleged to depict the set of possible outcomes; the choice among these possible positions was to be made on the basis of the community's preferred rate of trade-off between the components. Economists diagrammed all of this by introducing a set of community or social indifference curves… (p. 89)

But they only cite Samuelson and Solow (1960) in support of this.

Then, of course, there is Friedman (1977) and Lucas and Sargent (1978), both of which were mentioned in the Introduction, and Santomero and Seater (1978), discussed particularly in Section 3.2, all of which appeared at about the same time.

So it seems clear that Phillips curve myth appeared quite suddenly. There are hints earlier, but clear statements that policy was misled and led in an inflationist direction by the discovery of the Phillips curve are first found in the middle of the 1970s. Friedman (1975a) might be regarded as the origin of it, or alternatively there is a single paragraph in Friedman (1975b) which is slightly earlier still. But it is difficult to see that either of these—publications from speeches in the United Kingdom and Australia—had a rapid influence. Greenspan's Report of the Council of Economic Advisers (CEA 1975) would presumably have been more influential, but it is probably best to regard the whole group up to Friedman (1977) as the common origin. If it is not quite true that all the authors were long-standing anti-Keynesians, there was a predominance of such figures including Brunner and Meltzer, Buchanan and Wagner, and Lucas and Sargent. Their predecessor, who put the Phillips curve at heart of policy, without suggesting a basic error, on the other hand, was Tobin (1972a, 1972b). He was one of the leading Keynesians, so there is a temptation to see him as originating the line of thinking. It is a mischievous temptation, perhaps, but may not be inapt.

6.4 THE PHILLIPS CURVE MYTH IN TEXTBOOKS AND SURVEYS

In any case, after this the myth caught on very quickly, and one interesting aspect of that, discussed in more detail in Forder (2013b), is the speed with which it appeared in textbooks. In the early 1960s—when the Phillips curve supposedly made an immediate impact—it is little noted. In the mid-1960s, there was more discussion of the relation of inflation and unemployment—not necessarily in terms of 'the Phillips curve'—but where any possibility of permitting inflation was considered, some version of the lubrication argument was always explained. In the 1970s, the expectations argument started to be reported. Tendencies, as time went on, to attribute it more and more firmly to Friedman and Phelps and to emphasize the importance of their work are also detectable. One example is Dornbusch and Fischer (1978). That is their first edition, and the story about policy previously having been motivated by the idea of a stable tradeoff appears. In other works, interestingly, that story also appears in post-1978 editions even when earlier editions of the same book gave no indication of it. And when it starts to be claimed that there had been inflationism in the past, the lubrication argument disappears, even when it had been present in earlier editions. That gives the impression that the supposed inflationism had no explanation, except a failure to understand the expectations argument, but it also seems to show those authors as being overly anxious to display errors in the thinking of the past.

Very much the same pattern is found in the scholarly literature of surveys, specialist textbooks on inflation, and like writings. In the first half of the 1960s, there is little sign of Phillips being regarded as special—Hagger (1963a) named Phillips only to say his work was not relevant to the matter under consideration (i.e. the state of the theory of inflation), and Phillips has no special place in Hagger (1964). That is certainly not true of Hagger (1977), which has the 'Phillips–Lipsey studies' giving 'an extraordinarily powerful impetus' (p. 93) to studies of the wage equation. Pitchford (1963) referred to other works of Phillips, but not the 1958 paper. Bronfenbrenner and Holzman (1963, p. 631) said the 'Phillips curve' was the most widely discussed 'methodological innovation' in inflation theory and that it was originally used by Brown (1955) and Bent Hansen (1957). But later, Phillips is given much more prominence—Rothschild (1971) treats him as special, Goldstein (1972) simply begins his survey in 1958, seeming to take it for granted that its beginning was with Phillips. Laidler and Parkin (1975, p. 754)—the successor work to Bronfenbrenner and Holzman—say Phillips made a 'particularly impressive contribution' and the curve could 'predict almost exactly' the relationship between wage change and unemployment—there is some exaggeration there, surely, which suggests the authors were keen to present Phillips as important. As noted in Chapter 3, Santomero and Seater (1978) regarded 1958 as the moment of the 'inception' of the literature.

Then, it is in the mid-1970s that such sources show an increasing tendency to say that the Phillips curve led to inflationary policy. Even the earlier works which might be regarded as inflationist themselves, and contain substantial surveys of the literature—Bodkin et al. (1967), Rothschild (1971), and Goldstein (1972) would all be cases—do not say that common interpretation of the curve had led to inflationary policy: They do not put that interpretation on the history. Neither Bronfenbrenner and Holzman (1963) nor Laidler and Parkin (1975) make any suggestion of there being an inflationist tendency in policy (although the latter say that policy discussion sometimes treated a stable tradeoff as a constraint). Laidler and Parkin actually remark on the absence of a literature on actual policy determination. Parkin (1975a) addressed the question and argued that governments generate inflation because it is in their electoral interests in various ways, but there was no mention of the Phillips curve, nor suggestion of a stable relation of inflation and unemployment being part of anyone's outlook.

On the other hand, Frisch (1977) makes it rather firm, describing (p. 1290) Phillips' work as 'an important innovative contribution to the theory of inflation', and saying,

> The determination of negative correlation between the rate of growth of money wages and the unemployment rate was not new; new was the contention that there was a *stable* relation between the two variables. (p. 1290)

He quickly moves to saying that Samuelson and Solow (1960) were responsible for giving it the menu interpretation—indeed, as noted in Chapter 2, this was just the time when it started to be said that those authors had been the key inflationist interpreters of the curve. (Frisch (1977), it should be added, also includes a long discussion of varieties of the lubrication argument.)

For Ashworth (1981), Phillips' was the 'first substantial contribution' (p. 187) to the question of a predictable relationship between wage change and employment and, because of his work, 'Economic policy had become a matter of choosing the most preferred point on the trade-off' (p. 189). (Friedman and Phelps, however, are only the 'most influential' critics.) Sumner (1984) was much clearer than any previous surveyor about the significance of Phillips' long period of investigation and the immediate responses to his work, but in relation to the expectations argument said, 'The economics profession was slow to appreciate the implications of elementary theory for the Phillips curve. They were first spelt out [by Friedman and Phelps]' (p. 192).

6.5 ROUTINIZATION

In the wider literature, the Phillips curve myth rapidly became a matter of routine. One way in which that can be seen is the unselfconscious way in which so many authors report what they take to be the facts of the case, with no indication of feeling it needs substantiation. Since the point I am making is about leaving important claims unsubstantiated, I can hardly avoid quoting some. The purpose though is not to criticize those individuals who were in most cases giving no suggestion that they have investigated the history. Rather it is to show how completely the story was accepted, and accepted beyond question. The high standing of those authors strengthens the point, so there is no reason to read these comments as seeking to diminish that standing.

Poole (1978) said, with no supporting evidence or citation,

> Belief in a stable tradeoff between inflation and unemployment has had much to
> do with the persistence of excessively expansionary policies since 1965. (p. 210)

The existence of that belief is apparently beyond doubt, even if its connection to inflationary policy is made to seem weaker than some suggested.

The first lines of Feldstein (1979) were, with no citations in support,

> It was not so long ago that most economists regarded the Phillips curve as a stable menu of policy options. A permanent reduction in unemployment appeared to be possible if the nation were willing to pay the price of a permanently higher rate of inflation. Even rather pessimistic estimates of the slope of the Phillips curve suggested that the price was well worth paying. (p. 749)

Apart from anything else, as observed in Chapter 4, a *pessimistic* Phillips curve was a flat one.

Reagan's first Report of Council of Economic Advisers (CEA 1982) said

> Phillips curves jumped quickly from scholarly journals to the policy arena. The speed with which the case made for this tradeoff was accepted as a cornerstone of economic policy contrasts with the slow acceptance of both neoclassical economic theory and the substantial body of evidence which suggests that there is no lasting tradeoff between inflation and unemployment. (p. 49)

Here, the emphasis on the speed with which various ideas were accepted is entirely misleading and is based on what?

Recitals of the myth are by no means the preserve of those overtly hostile to Keynesianism. Akerlof (2002) said,

> The basis of the Phillips curve is supply and demand. Phillips posited that when demand is high and unemployment low, workers can bargain for higher nominal wage increases than when demand is low and unemployment high. Firms' pricing policies translate wage inflation (adjusted for productivity) into price inflation. For policy makers, therefore, a durable trade-off exists between inflation and unemployment.
> In the late 1960s, Friedman (1968) and Phelps (1968) added an important new wrinkle... (p. 418).

And he explained the expectations argument and its importance. Here, one indication of the completeness of his acceptance of the story is that he seems to regard it as natural that the idea attributed to Phillips should have been novel as late as 1958.

Snowdon and Vane (2005), writing a history of macroeconomics, said,

> During the 1960s the Phillips (1958) curve was quickly taken on board as an integral part of the then-dominant orthodox Keynesian paradigm, not least because it was interpreted by many orthodox Keynesians as implying a stable long-run trade-off which provided the authorities a menu of possible inflation-unemployment combinations for policy choice. Within academia the textbook interpretation of the Phillips curve came to be presented as a proposition that *permanently* low levels of unemployment could be realistically achieved by tolerating *permanently* high levels of inflation. (p. 140)

They explain this rapid acceptance by the fact that without the Phillips curve, there was an equation missing from prevailing theory. Later (pp. 174–5) they say that Friedman and Phelps challenged the idea of a stable Phillips curve by pointing to the importance of expectations. The only citations from the 1960s supporting any of that are the Friedman and Phelps' papers on expectations.

And Krugman (2007) wrote,

> In 1958 the New Zealand-born economist A. W. Phillips pointed out that there was a historical correlation between unemployment and inflation, with high inflation associated with low unemployment and vice versa. For a time, economists treated this correlation as if it were a reliable and stable relationship. This led to serious discussion about which point on the 'Phillips curve' the government should choose.

And he goes on to explain how Friedman and Phelps innovatively argued that the tradeoff was temporary.

The same sort of thing, although concerning the history of thought more than policy, can be seen in Gordon (2011), who started by saying the history of the Phillips curve before 1975 is well understood and straightforward, and then said,

> The initial discovery of the negative inflation-unemployment relation by Phillips, popularized by Samuelson and Solow, was followed by a brief period in which policy-makers assumed that they could exploit the trade-off to reduce unemployment at a small cost of additional inflation. Then the natural rate revolution of Friedman, Phelps and Lucas overturned the policy-exploitable trade-off in favour of long-run monetary neutrality. Those who had implemented the econometric version of the trade-off PC in the 1960s reeled in disbelief when Sargent demonstrated the logical failure of their test of neutrality, and finally were condemned to the 'wreckage' of Keynesian economics by Lucas and Sargent following the

twist of the inflation-unemployment correlation from negative in the 1960s to positive in the 1970s. (p. 1)

And, of course, this myth continues to feature in textbook accounts of the development of economist thinking. Mankiw and Mark Taylor (2011, pp. 783–9) tell a story of Phillips discovering a previously unknown relation between inflation and wage change, Samuelson and Solow regarding it as offering a menu of choice, and Friedman and Phelps making a 'bold forecast' (p. 791) about the adaptation of expectations.

When it comes to more serious historical discussions of policy, the same sort of picture is visible, although in more cautious terms. Discussing policymaking in the United States, DeLong (1997) cites Samuelson and Solow and their 'menu' as part of the 'background' that led to inflation, although he places no emphasis on specific claims about the stability of the curve, rather seeming to think that the problem was an excess of optimism about how low unemployment could be driven. Commenting on that paper, John Taylor (1997) said that the development of the 'new economics' deserves 'credit, or blame' for the inflation, saying that

> The ideas were intellectually exciting, carefully explained, and widely disseminated; and the timing was just about perfect to explain events. (p. 278)

Mayer (1997) illustrates how deeply the myth had penetrated since he saw it as absurd, but did not question it, saying, 'It may seem hard to believe now, but at least until about 1968 the simple Phillips curve without a price expectations terms seems to have been considered adequate' (p. 82). Perhaps Maloney (2011) should also be seen as principally substantiating the depth of penetration of the myth. Using archival sources he established that there was a debate as to whether the Phillips curve was vertical in the Treasury in the 1970s. He seems to regard that as supporting the usual story, but it might be suggested that the more interesting debate he discovered was over the question of whether reduced demand would even be effective in reducing inflation. When it is seen that that was the central issue, the idea of exploiting a tradeoff disappears. There is something of that in Romer and Romer (2002). They discuss policymaking in the 1950s with approval, but believe that for some reason the good understanding of that decade was replaced by an inferior model in the next decade.

Then there are those who take the exploitable Phillips curve and its rebuttal by Friedman and Phelps as axiomatic in treating of subsequent events. They may make no pretence of exploring the story of the Phillips curve and are entitled to feel duped by those who do, but still their contributions mark the routine nature the Phillips curve story acquired. McNamara (1998) is such a study of the origins of European Monetary Union in the 1980s. Much of the argument concerns the power of ideas of the vertical Phillips curve and related theory. But she bases the beginning of the story on the suggestion that the idea of an exploitable Phillips curve was abandoned in the 1970s: and that is clearly a flaw. Matthijs (2012) is about the politics of economic crisis in Britain, and accepts a version of the Phillips curve story. Stedman Jones (2012), charting the triumph of neoliberalism with much skill said that Phillips had been the first to 'posit a curve' indicating 'an inverse correlation between unemployment and inflation', and that, in what followed, the 'acceptance of inflation was characteristic of Keynesian policy in Britain and the United States in the 1950s and 1960s' (p. 188). His interest, though, is in what followed, so no real damage is done by this misperception.

To these, perhaps one could add sources which do give some citation, but without thereby carrying much conviction. The citing of Samuelson and Solow (1960) to demonstrate the prevalence of inflationism, or to give weight to the claim that it became prevalent is by far the most notable of such cases. The merits of it were considered in Chapter 2. There are smaller numbers of citations of the Council of Economic Advisers (CEA 1969) which are similarly intended to illustrate the prevalence of Phillips curve inflationism. I argued earlier in this chapter that it does not contain a case for inflation, and does not suppose the tradeoff exploitable. Nevertheless, it is sometimes cited for those things, as well as for containing a Phillips curve diagram.[3] Similarly, the Callaghan speech to the Labour Party conference of 1976, also considered earlier in this chapter, was cited with that objective by Friedman (1977), Leeson (1996b), and Arndt (1998).

Where there is more suggestion of the history of the matter really being investigated, the failure to locate actual instances of the Phillips curve being discussed by policymakers strikingly suggests that there are no such instances to be found. Leeson (1996a) said the goal of his paper was to analyse 'the process by which the Phillips curve trade-off became influential in British policy-making circles' (p. 232), but he assumes that to have happened, so the problem of demonstrating it is never properly addressed. Rather, there are numerous assertions of it, but nothing that is convincing evidence. So, for example, Leeson says that there were disputes between two factions in the Treasury and their various allies, and 'Both sources of advice located themselves on the Phillips curve' (p. 232) (no citations). On the same page he says that

Prime Minster Wilson at one stage adopted a deflationary policy, and reported,

> he was regarded as having 'adopted the [Phillips–]Paish theory with a courage denied his Tory predecessors' (Brittan 1969, 218; Tobin 1974, 33 n17; Opie 1968, 66).

This time there appear to be plenty of citations, but Tobin merely says that the Labour government defended sterling longer than the Conservatives would have done; and the nearest the Opie comes to being relevant is that he says Paish thought price stability required some unemployment. The quotation actually comes from Brittan, but he says 'the Paish theory'. That theory was discussed earlier in this chapter and concerned the diagnosis and treatment of inflation. Indeed, at the time in question, Wilson could be understood as planning to reduce inflation by allowing higher unemployment. But the policy was nothing to do with Phillips, nor was it said to be by Brittan; it was nothing to do with belief in an exploitable tradeoff; and it was not inflationist, so it establishes nothing of value to Leeson's argument. Making what I suppose is the same point again, this time relating to Chancellor of the Exchequer Callaghan, Leeson (1996a) said,

> in 1967, Callaghan invoked the names of Phillips and Paish in order to justify his Budget projections. (p. 238)

That time he gave no citation and did not say when the invocation occurred. In other places, Leeson and others made similar remarks about Callaghan in 1967, but again without passable substantiation.[4]

And, furthermore, concerning those involved in policy formation, Leeson said,

> The basic assumption of nearly all participants was that demand management could locate the macroeconomy along a point on the Phillips curve. Political considerations, or the point of tangency with a community indifference curve would determine the point chosen. The Phillips curve became part of the tool kit of economic advisers and could be used, it was thought, to facilitate the pursuit of full employment (Goodhart and Bhansali 1970; Chossudovsky 1972; Opie 1968, 81; Stewart 1977, 2–4). (Leeson, p. 232)

Here it is not clear what the citations are intended to establish. Goodhart and Bhansali, as discussed in Chapter 5, were investigating ideas in the family of the political business cycle. The authors suppose governments choose a point on the Phillips curve in order to win popularity. That is not using the curve to facilitate full employment. Choussudovsky's is a deeply theoretical treatment of the problem of working out community preferences. Opie says that economic advisers were confident, but since he does not mention the Phillips curve, that avails nothing, and there is no text on those pages of the Stewart.

In the section of Leeson's paper, which is headed 'Politicians, Policy-Makers and the Phillips Curve' the word 'Phillips' appears three times. First, Leeson speculates that civil servants telling policymakers what they were thought to want to hear could have been 'a factor in the propagation of the Phillips curve trade-off' (Leeson 1996a, p. 239). Apart from that being entirely speculation, it is a poor one since there is no basis at all for saying that politicians wanted to be told anything other than that they could have high employment and price stability. Second, it appears in the claim about the use of Phillips' name by Callaghan, considered earlier in this section. Thirdly, it appears in a quotation from Tobin about America— Tobin's remarks have already been considered, and Leeson's article is about British policy. So again, they establish nothing pertinent.

Amongst all these, it should also be noted that there are authors who understand the position very well. The history of the period is sometimes written without any undue discussion of the Phillips curve. The idea that the curve had a role in policymaking does not seem to have occurred to Cairncross (1992) studying British policy, for example. At other times more is said, but the curve is put in an entirely proper perspective, as it is by Perry (1976, 1978), studying American policy generally, or Ulman (1998) specifically in relation to the Kennedy period and the Guideposts. Very occasionally there is an actual rebuttal of the some part of the usual story. Nelson (2005b, p. 9) recognized that American monetary policy was not seeking to lower unemployment by raising inflation and Nelson (2009) similarly noted the absence of Phillips curve inflationism in Britain. Nelson's discussions of policy, and the outlook of policymakers, are closely argued and, without being limited to that topic, contribute far more to the question of the role of the Phillips curve than any of the preceding literature. He gives much less attention to the views of academic economists, although in Nelson (2005a) he says that those of the 1960s generally believed in an exploitable tradeoff, identifying Samuelson and Solow (1960) as the origin of that viewpoint. Beggs (2010) even more clearly, although only in relation to Australia, described the supposed influence of the Phillips tradeoff as 'between caricature and myth' (p. 223). But such authors are very much the exceptions.

6.6 CONCLUSION

So, there is nothing in policymaking to substantiate the myth and early accounts of policymaking make no mention of it. But, rather precisely between 1975 and 1977, it suddenly emerges, and then it is in the textbooks by 1978. After that, it quickly became routine, but without being substantiated. Quite a bit later still, there are occasional attempts to substantiate it, but they are so flimsy that fact itself emphasizes that the argument is wanting. Just as notable, though, is the fact that these statements seem to have gone almost completely unchallenged.

CHAPTER 7

Explaining the Emergence of the Myth

The question that remains, then, is how it could be that a fiction, so suddenly introduced, could become established so quickly, with scarcely any protest being made. Clearly there has been a failure of historical understanding and there must be something to be said about how that came about.

It is difficult to see how one could be absolutely sure how such a general delusion arose, but drawing on the large amount of material that has fallen under consideration, I can make some suggestions and there would seem to be several factors contributing in various ways. In Section 7.1 I note that the most well-known papers in the Phillips curve literature are not typical of it, so that a reading of those alone would give a false impression; in Section 7.2 that the question of what is meant by 'Phillips curve', first mentioned in the Introduction, has created room for particular and pertinent confusions; in Section 7.3 I show that certain arguments have come to be casually but conventionally misdated and these create a misleading impression of where the landmarks lie in the story. To these things, I would add the manner in which his opponents responded to the arguments put in Friedman (1968a). They were, in certain ways, poor responses. So, in Section 7.4, I argue that Friedman's opponents conceded points unnecessarily and created a false impression about the essentials of the argument. In Section 7.5 I try to put all this together with considerations of the circumstances of the times to give an account of how the Phillips curve myth could emerge and become routine with so little said to challenge it.

7.1 THE FAMOUS PAPERS

One benefit of studying a large part of the Phillips curve literature is that it becomes apparent that famous papers are not at all typical of it. If we take Phillips (1958), Samuelson and Solow (1960), Phelps (1967), and Friedman (1968a) as being the papers most commonly thought to have shaped the literature, and the ones must likely to be appreciated by later authors, then it is apparent that they are atypical in crucial ways—in precisely ways that relate to the Phillips curve myth. Phillips and Samuelson and Solow stand out as not systematically considering price change in their curves—although for the former it was because the period under study had not had consistent inflation, and in the latter because they were considering the 'years immediately ahead'. But in any case, virtually every other study did include price change. Samuelson and Solow, Phelps, and Friedman all used the expression 'Phillips curve' to describe a price-change relation—but that was very rare in the 1960s. Samuelson and Solow went as far as using the expression 'menu of choice' even if they did not mean quite what later authors have said, but again, that sort of idea was very rarely applied to the Phillips curve in the 1960s. And Friedman and Phelps did write about expectations, and did treat the point as refining a theoretical idea, even if not as being an original thought at that time. If a fifth work were to be added, it would be Lipsey (1960). His does not share all the characteristics of the others, but is also atypical since it is more or less the only early paper that can properly be regarded either as inspired by Phillips or as refining his relation.

The usual story does not quite fit even these papers, and perhaps to some extent they are the famous papers because they appear roughly consistent with the story, and this causes them to come to attention. But in any case, amongst them, the Phillips curve myth is just about discernable. One might imagine that a later reader of just these, who has the story from Friedman (1977) already in mind, might feel they seemed to confirm it. That would perhaps be particularly true if Lipsey, with his treatment of price change, were excluded. One thing, then, contributing to the acceptance of the myth may just be that the famous papers reveal so little about the character of the literature.

7.2 THE MEANING OF 'THE PHILLIPS CURVE'

I noted in the Introduction that the question of whether the Phillips curve was a demand-pull or cost-push relation has been confused at least since

Samuelson (1961a). There was an occasional protest about that kind of thing, including from Lipsey (1981), then based in Canada, who said, 'the Phillips curve was persistently misunderstood on this side of the Atlantic as a cost-push phenomenon' (p. 556). In addition to clear cases, like Samuelson's usage, there were also less clear, or mixed cases, such as the 'Phillips curves' including profit like that of Perry (1964). But there is more confusion than that since, as I noted in Chapter 3, the expression came to apply to econometric relations with a wider and wider range of explanatory variables, some of which were nothing like Phillips–Lipsey relations, but were actually intended as rivals to them. Then, as seen in Chapter 4, in the 1970s usage spread even further, to include price-change equations, again with an elastic range of explanatory variables. As a result, the expression was applied in a whole host of ways so that it had, in common usage, no very specific meaning at all. 'The Phillips curve' became a generonym, with, like 'Hoover' or 'Kleenex', no special link to the original.

The resulting situation was probably confusing enough, but there is more to it than that because, in Chapter 5, it became apparent that something else happened. That is, that the expression 'Phillips curve' started to be used in general discussions to mean just the relation of inflation and unemployment, with other variables ignored, so the 'Phillips curve' was also the simplest of relations. There is, of course, that aspect in Samuelson and Solow, but *none* of the econometric relations of either the 1960s or 1970s were of that kind. Nearly all of them had a variable reflecting price change, and they all had something beyond unemployment—as indeed was recognized by Friedman (1968a). Yet, when the idea of 'the Phillips curve' appeared in non-econometric discussion occasionally later in the 1960s, and very much more frequently in the 1970s, it routinely took this simple form.

One aspect of the situation is that there was an unnoticed divide between the econometric and the non-econometric literature. In the former, Phillips curves were a whole range of different, often rather sophisticated, relations. In the 1960s they mainly reflected thinking about wage bargaining, and the 1970s certainly the best of them reflected up-to-the-minute thinking about inflation momentum or the problem of measuring expectations. Meanwhile, in the non-econometric discussions, there was none of that—it was the most basic possible relation. The questions asked there, using that kind of Phillips curve, were different, but there was nothing naïve about them—they were questions about what had gone wrong, or what the consequences of monetary union would be, or how governments might manipulate policy to secure re-election. But in these, 'the Phillips curve' was still an altogether different creature.

One result is that there was simply room for confusion over what was meant—or, more importantly, perhaps—what previous authors had meant by a 'Phillips curve'. Another aspect, though, is that it made for the appearance of a great consensus. Almost anyone could find a 'Phillips curve' that they thought offered a useful account of something and almost everyone would find some theory they were content to regard as rationalizing it. So the appearance was that everyone believed in 'the Phillips curve'. That consensus was, though, entirely artificial.

The next twist comes from the adoption of the terminology of the 'short-run', 'naïve', or 'simple' Phillips curve. The 'short-run Phillips curve' ought to pose no difficulties. It is a theoretical construction describing—depending on the exact formulation—something like the relation of unemployment to increased or surprise inflation. That idea has a clear theoretical role, analytical utility, and occasional relevance to policy. The expression is not in Friedman (1968a) and was perhaps first used by Leijonhufvud (1968), and shortly after by Akerlof (1969), who was responding to Friedman by suggesting the possibility of a permanent tradeoff, and by Lucas and Rapping (1969a) in a close discussion of the conditions that would permit the existence of short- and long-run tradeoffs. In this usage, the 'short-run Phillips curve' is contrasted with a 'long-run' curve and the difference between the two arises from the theoretical timeframe.[1]

Other cases leave more room for confusion. One such might be in Wachter (1976a), who said,

> Until recently most of the empirical literature focused almost exclusively on estimating the short-run Phillips curve. This functional relationship, however, proved itself an unstable tool for stabilization policy. The most widely accepted explanation for this instability is found in the various accelerationist models. (p. 65)

What can this mean? If 'short run' means the curve that makes no allowance for expectations changing, then it must also be one making no allowance for price change, since the equation could be the same one. But that makes the first sentence incorrect. The last sentence raises the equivalent difficulty since an equation incorporating actual price change, as the 1960s equations did, will exhibit inflation acceleration. Somehow the contrast between 'short run' and 'long run' has become confused with that between those excluding or including *expectations* specifically, with only those including them being labelled 'accelerationist'.

As matter of theory, a 'naïve' Phillips curve is, of course, just the same thing as a 'short-run' curve. But again, that might not be the impression formed from some things that were said. Johnson (1970), for example, described the expectations argument, noted that the empirical work of Solow (1968)—the first paper really to take issue with Friedman over the shape of the Phillips curve—gave a coefficient on expected inflation that was less than one, and concluded

> The outcome is a 'sophisticated' Phillips curve…which still offers a trade-off to the policymakers, though its slope is steeper than that implied by the 'naïve' Phillips curve. (Johnson 1970, p. 112)

That might be defended on the basis that the 'naïve' curve is a theoretical construct, but the appearance is surely that it describes the relations preceding Solow's. But that is not correct. Solow's expectations Phillips curve was steeper than a version of the same thing from which the expected inflation term was removed. But Solow did not estimate such a thing, and earlier studies had a price-change variable with about the same coefficient as on Solow's expectations variable. So it is not true that Solow's curve was steeper than *those*.

Nordhaus (1972b) said,

> One of the most popular orthodox explanations of wage behaviour is the so-called 'naïve' Phillips curve. This explanation simply relates the rate of increase of money wage rates or earnings to some measure of labor market tightness…(p. 441)

He continued,

> For obvious reasons most econometricians have preferred the more sophisticated versions of the Phillips curve (p. 443)

noting that these included price-change variables amongst others, and said,

> The most carefully studied version, sometimes called the expectations hypothesis, includes a proxy measure of the expected rate of inflation.

The claim about popularity may be careless expression, but it certainly creates a very false impression. As should be clear from Section 3.2, there was, even in the 1960s, almost no one estimating such a relation. On the other hand, in the non-econometric discussions 'the Phillips curve' was used that way. But there it was not offering an explanation of inflation at all but—on the contrary—often expressing the point that it was difficult to explain.

So, in Nordhaus' presentation, again without it quite being said, the naïve curve appears as one without a price-change variable, *and* as one that some people thought was a proper specification.

Similar things can be said of discussions of the 'simple' Phillips curve. That expression is sometimes used to contrast with a complex curve, so that, for example, a curve including profit would not be 'simple'. It was sometimes used as a substitute for 'naïve'—as it was by Perry (1975) and Teigen (1975) discussing Nordhaus' work. But the expression 'simple Phillips curve analysis' is used by Laidler (1971) to mean analysis with a curve without expected inflation, and associated with a diagram of wage change against unemployment. He discussed Lipsey's (1960) theory of the curve without mentioning price change and said (p. 78) that he thought that nothing of fundamental importance was added to the contributions of Phillips and Lipsey up to the mid-1960s. Then (p. 79), he said that the curve embodied a hypothesis about money wages, whereas relevant theory was about real wages and that to connect the two, expected inflation must be introduced. This led to a discussion of the shape of the long-run curve and he said that whether it is vertical is not fundamental, and stated that, from the point of view of anti-inflationary policy, the important thing is that during an inflation

the trade-off becomes steeper with the passage of time...(p. 81)

Nowhere does he say that the 1960s curves excluded price change, but again, a later reader might easily form that impression.

There is, it should be clear, no suggestion that any of these authors were attempting to mislead their reader. Wachter was continuing his entirely serious and sophisticated efforts to understand wage determination; and Nordhaus testing a collection of possible explanations of what had happened. (In Nordhaus (1972a, n. 12) he clearly recognized that at least some of the pre-1968 work addressed the issue of price change.) He might have excluded the simple Phillips curve from his discussion, but he chose to include it. The points Laidler was making about policy are unimpaired by the way he discussed the two types of curve: from a didactic point of view, his way of putting it may be best; and very probably it did not occur to him in 1971 that readers needed to be told that price change was included in the earlier equations. Rather, the point is that it is the autonomous development of the terminology, amongst other things, which has led to the statements like these appearing later to report inadequacies of the 1960s literature which were not in fact present.

It was then 'simple' and 'short run' that Friedman (1977) used, apparently interchangeably ('naïve' also appears in Friedman (1975a)). His graph of inflation and unemployment, which he said showed the relation widely taken to offer a tradeoff, was captioned 'Simple Phillips curve', but even in his abstract he claimed that one stage of the development of thinking on the matter had been

the introduction of inflation expectations, as a variable shifting the short-run Phillips curve...(Friedman 1977, p. 451)

Had he said, 'the introduction of inflation expectations as an alternative to price change', there would be no complaint, but, as he put it, the inference must be that the previous approach had no price-change variable—it is only then that expectations will *shift* the curve. In the body of the paper he said,

A few still cling to the original Phillips curve; more recognize the difference between short-run and long-run curves but regard even the long-run curve as negatively sloped, though more steeply so than the short-run curves...(p. 459)

If the 'original' Phillips curve means the one in Phillips (1958) the contrast between short and long run might just be said to be appropriate, but no one had ever clung to that. If the original curve is the kind of wage change equation that was estimated before 1968, then the implication that many had believed that the relation excluding price change (the 'short-run' curve) was empirically useful is clear and false. Those who resisted Friedman's position were resisting accelerationist arguments based on expectations strictly understood as perceptions of the future, not the idea that ongoing price change mattered.

In due course there would also be a 'Keynesian-Phillips' model—in Branson (1975)—then a 'New Keynesian Phillips curve' as well. This is usually traced to Calvo (1983), although he did not use the expression. Like some of the other cases, it is a retrospective piece of labelling, this time apparently following on from Roberts (1995)—no doubt there is scope for yet more confusion to arise there.

But there is one more terminological issue which warrants attention because of its importance in the 1960s and 1970s—that is, the idea of a 'stable Phillips curve'. Phillips (1958) did not describe the relation with that word. Lipsey (1960) used the word several times, but not to suggest an exploitable tradeoff saying, for example, that Phillips concluded that 'the form of the relationship has been remarkably stable over a period of almost one hundred years' (p. 1). He also used the word in 'Can there be a valid theory of wages?' (Lipsey, 1962) which I quoted in Section 1.2 saying the,

> question about the possibility of finding stable, hence predictable patterns of human behaviour in the economic sphere must be sought from empirical data ...

Here, a 'stable' relation is simply one that can be discovered, or is susceptible of estimation, and in the particular context one that was impervious to institutional change. It is nothing to do with a possibility of using inflation to reduce unemployment, or of the curve's invariance in conditions of inflation.

However, in the early 1970s, the label 'stable Phillips curve' started to be used to describe a curve that did not change with inflation. Holt (1969, p. 139) said that the only stable Phillips curve in equilibrium would be a vertical line; Rothschild (1971) used the expression when specifically rejecting the idea that the curve was strictly vertical. Rowley and Wilton (1974) used it to say that Friedman and Phelps denied the existence of a stable curve, and Corden (1976), just discussing possibilities, said 'if one believed in a stable Phillips curve ...' (p. 374). Again, the terminology might be said to be incautious, but the points being made were perfectly understandable.

But again, the abstract of Friedman (1977) says that the idea of a stable tradeoff was accepted, and he says of Phillips' relation that it was

> widely interpreted as a causal relation that offered a stable trade-off to policy-makers. (p. 454)

If, as one supposes it must, that means the relation was taken to be invariant to inflation, then of course the statements are false. The interesting point here is that Friedman in particular might have been expected to grasp the issue over stability since, in his famous discussion of the stability of the demand for money in Friedman (1956), he faced the same issue, and he said,

> The quantity theorist accepts the empirical hypothesis that the demand for money is highly stable ... This hypothesis needs to be hedged ... he does not, for example, regard it as a contradiction to the stability of the demand for money that the velocity of circulation of money rises drastically during hyperinflations. For the stability he expects is in the functional relation between the quantity of money demanded and the variables that determine it, and the sharp rise in

the velocity of circulation of money during hyperinflations is entirely consistent with a stable functional relation. (p. 16)

But Friedman apparently did not see that point at the time of his Nobel lecture. The Quantity Theorist *did* regard it as a contradiction of the stability of the Phillips curve that the relation would change in conditions of inflation.

It starts to become clear, I suggest, how easy it was for confusion to arise—particularly in the minds of later readers—from the way 'the Phillips curve' was discussed. It would be very easy to form the impression that the econometric Phillips curves of the 1970s were distinguished by their inclusion of expected inflation; and that the 1960s equations did not include it. Then, considering the non-econometric discussions of the 1970s, it appears that a 'simple Phillips curve' is just an inflation-unemployment relation, so that if it was 'simple' curves that were estimated in the 1960s, they were 'naïve' in lacking any treatment of price change. And they were believed to be 'stable' as well. If—following the trail of the famous papers—any of those later readers should happen to consult Phillips (1958), as the font of it all, or Samuelson and Solow (1960), they would find that price change was not properly treated. And Samuelson and Solow with their label 'fundamental Phillips schedule' might seem to be saying it had a status in thinking that it did not. Those later readers could easily come to believe that the literature could be properly criticized over the matter of price change, and certainly there would be nothing in Friedman (1977) to disabuse them.

7.3 THREE CRUCIAL MISDATINGS

So we have a trap in looking only to the famous papers, and a mass of terminological confusion, but this is only the background. A different dimension comes from its becoming routine to misdate three crucial theoretical ideas, each of which is a vital part of the story. I take it that enough was said in Chapter 1 to show that there was nothing remotely original about the idea of a negative relation between wage change and unemployment in 1958; enough in Chapter 3 to show that the 'lubrication argument' was commonplace since the 1950s at the latest; and enough in Chapter 4 (and Forder (2010b)) to show that the expectations argument was similarly part of the economist's ordinary understanding when stated by Friedman and

Phelps. But there is another question about the perceptions of the early 1970s of these things.

7.3.1 The Phillips Curve

I noted in Section 3.1 that Phillips' actual influence on 'the Phillips curve literature' was much less than might be supposed, but his work did come to be seen as its inspiration. In the 1960s there were some gentle indications of Phillips being treated as an innovator in devising the negative relation of wage change and unemployment. One is that whereas the earliest studies tended to regard his work as just as one of a group of related studies,[2] a little later—in the middle of the 1960s—he or his work is frequently described as 'pioneering'.[3] It was also at about that time, or perhaps a little later, that his name was routinely paired with Lipsey's to make the 'Phillips–Lipsey curve' or 'Phillips–Lipsey theory'.[4] Since Lipsey was plainly inspired by Phillips, that usage serves to emphasize Phillips' supposed priority even as it suggests the superior quality of Lipsey's work. And in Section 6.4 I noted that Phillips was given more and more prominence in retrospective treatments as time went on.

In the early 1970s, though, there is a much more powerful indication that he was widely seen as the discoverer of the relation. That indication comes from the string of strident denials of his priority that appeared almost simultaneously. Amid-Hozour, Dick, and Lucier (1971) pointed to Sultan (1957)—a textbook—as presenting the theoretical relation, saying he had concluded that full employment, price stability, and free collective bargaining were not simultaneously attainable, and said,

> We suggest that Phillips' work was an independent empirical verification of the hypothetical relations which, unknown to him, had been earlier postulated explicitly by Sultan. (Amid-Hozour, Dick, and Lucier 1971, p. 320)

So impressed were they that they compared Sultan's achievement with Harrod's discovery of the marginal revenue curve before Robinson. Then, in successive pages of the next volume of the same journal, Donner and McCollum (1972) noted that Fisher (1926) had more theoretical discussion than Sultan and also did empirical work; and Thirlwall (1972) said,

> As a matter of historical fact, A J Brown's *The Great Inflation*, published in 1955, antedates both Sultan and Phillips,

and

> I have often thought that the 'Phillips' Curve ought to be called the 'Brown'
> Curve—unless, of course, Brown himself had precursors. (p. 325)

Brothwell (1972) similarly noted Brown's priority over Phillips. Then Bacon (1973) responded to Thirlwall by identifying Tinbergen (1951) as particularly interesting whilst noting earlier works by that author. Meanwhile, the *Journal of Political Economy* actually reprinted Fisher's article (as Fisher (1973)), with an introduction by the editors proclaiming his priority, despite the fact that he, like Sultan, actually presented a price-change relation. They obviously thought that it was inflation that was Phillips' primary concern.

The coincidence of timing of these things presumably reflects both the sudden appearance of the Phillips curve in policy discussions of the early 1970s, and the fact that some of these authors are responding to others. Two important points to note, though, are these. First, all these authors evidently felt that Phillips was generally believed to be the first to describe the relationship. That is an important point because theirs is an authentic reaction from the period in question—it really makes it seem as if that was believed, even as early as 1972 or so. And second, they themselves all thought some particular individual should be substituted in that role. That shows they have no inkling of its being a commonplace idea, and they give no indication of appreciating that as far as economists' general awareness is concerned, the idea was not new around about 1958. The view that the ordinariness of the idea was not recognized, even by those who realised it was not original to Phillips is substantially confirmed by Donald Gordon (1976, p. 69) who himself recognizes how ordinary the idea was—'an ancient empirical generalization' is what he called it. But he was making that point to rebut what he thought to be the clear conviction that it was a special idea of the 1960s.

It is hard to see what explanation of this there can be if it is not simply that the fact that the label 'Phillips curve' was applied to the relation led people to believe that he was the originator of the idea, and therefore that it was new in 1958. Then, the fact that there was such muddle over what kind of relation a Phillips curve was also readily explains the suggestion that Sultan or Fisher might have priority, even though their relations, describing price change, were in fact something different from Phillips'.

7.3.2 The Expectations Argument

In the course of arguing that the expectations argument was not new in 1968, I pointed to some early responses to Friedman and Phelps which in one way or another hinted that there were earlier statements. Brechling (1969), saying Phelps was following a long tradition, was one of them. That practice did not carry on for very long, and even while it did, an emphasis was sometimes put on Friedman and Phelps particularly. For example, Gordon (1970) commented on 'the accelerationist hypothesis, associated in the professional economics literature with the names of Milton Friedman and Edmund Phelps' (p. 11)—and indicated that Wallich had also advanced it. I suppose Gordon might have had it in mind that outside that literature it had different sources, but by singling out Wallich he probably creates an impression of the argument being more or less new. As time went on, there were stronger and stronger impressions of either Friedman or Phelps being the originators of the idea, or of their contributions being the important ones. In Rothschild (1971, p. 263), it was 'above all' Friedman and Phelps who challenged the stability of the curve; and in Goldstein (1972, p. 665) it was these authors who, 'most notably', raised the point. S. R. Johnson (1973) said 'Milton Friedman and E S Phelps have suggested that . . . [the curve will shift if inflation persists]' (p. 86). Even more clearly, Hall (1974) said, 'The Acceleration Theorem, discovered and advocated by Friedman and Phelps' (p. 360). But in Gordon (1976a) there is said to be a pre-existing puzzle over the relation of the Phillips curve and the presumption of money neutrality, which was 'independently resolved' (p. 191) by Friedman and Phelps. For Frisch (1977, p. 1294), they were 'the first'.

As to how this happened, there are several points to be made. One is that although the expectations argument was old news—not even news, it was just old—it is true that Friedman and Phelps were almost the first to put any version of it together with the 'Phillips curve' – using that expression. On a point of detail, Samuelson (1965) put it in those terms in a newspaper article, and Wallich (1966) did so in congressional testimony a couple of months before Friedman (1966a). But even if it was really only in their use of language, Friedman and Phelps might still reasonably appear to be almost original in that narrow respect.

Secondly, there may be some lack of clarity about what it was that was 'Friedman's idea'. If it was merely something along the lines of the proposition that behaviour wage bargaining will adapt to ongoing inflation, there was nothing new in it. If it was to emphasize a strictly expectational, forward-looking interpretation of that idea, then there would be more to it that was new. But another possibility, perhaps not to be dismissed, is that the issue was whether the adjustment of expectations would be such as to remove the lubricating effect of gentle price increases. That would amount to saying that continuous inflation would convert nominal downward rigidity into real downward rigidity. That would not have been such a routine point and would have been worth testing. The idea that this was Friedman's point obviously also coheres with my suggestions that his opponents took the econometric rejection of the vertical Phillips curve to be explained by the lubrication argument and to amout to a rejection of 'Friedman's' hypothesis. That might explain why it seemed natural to call the vertical Phillips curve 'Friedman's' hypothesis, and—with the disappearance from view of the lubrication argument—how a mistake about what was meant could emerge, with Friedman seeming to be credited with originality that was not his.

Finally, and in any case, it can also be seen that there was reason to see Friedman as the inspiration of the econometric work which sought to test the expectations issue. The immediate stimulus to Solow, or Gordon was his presentation. But still, the impression that the idea about expectations mattering, or affecting wage bargaining was a new one at the end of the 1960s is quite wrong and wholly misleading.

7.3.3 Lubrication

A third case concerns the dating of the lubrication argument which, after 1972, was quickly attributed to Tobin. In this case, Tobin himself may have given some impression that his statement of it was original. No doubt from his point of view the argument from Schultze seemed so well known that there was no need to attribute it to him, but he did say he was building on ideas from Lipsey (1960), and elaborated by Archibald (1970) and Holt (1970a, 1970b). And he did also introduce the argument in a rather florid way saying,

> The Phillips curve has been an empirical finding in search of a theory, like Pirandello characters in search of an author. One rationalization might be termed a theory of stochastic macro-equilibrium ... (Tobin, p. 9)

Quite apart from its dubious critical appreciation, the remark was ill-judged in suggesting that there was no respectable theory of the Phillips curve available.[5] That may well have suggested the theory Tobin put was new, and certainly his later readers can be forgiven for thinking that was the suggestion. In fact the process did not take long. Hall (1974, p. 384, n. 6) said 'Parts of Tobin's theory were anticipated' by Lipsey (1960) and Archibald (1969) and continued,

> Although Tobin does not seem to have written on the subject before 1971, his theory became an important part of the oral macroeconomic tradition at the Cowles Foundation many years earlier.

Even if that suggests a better dating, it clearly labels the idea as 'Tobin's theory' and suggests that recognition of it was limited. (In fact, Tobin (1967) stated the central aspect of the argument and quoted himself in Tobin (1968a).)

Similarly, Wachter (1976a, p. 67) said 'nonvertical long-run trade-offs appear in James Tobin' (and Stephen Ross and Wachter (1973)) but gives no indication that the idea might arise earlier. For Malcolm Fisher (1976), 'a point made by Tobin' (p. 312) was that inflation and involuntary unemployment can coexist; Fellner (1976a) said Tobin stressed the asymmetry of adjustment in expanding and contracting sectors resulting in inflation bias. Gordon (1976b) said, 'Tobin's Presidential Address *assumes* an asymmetrical upward flexibility and downward rigidity of wages...' (p. 100). Again, Tobin seems to have priority.

Perhaps rather more than in the other cases, here there continue to be authors who understand the position perfectly—both in the 1970s and later. So Shupp (1976) refers to the hypothesis advanced by Schultze and Tobin; Barry (1985) cited Schultze; and Akerlof, Dickens, and Perry (1996) attributed the argument to Schultze while also noting that it was well known in the 1960s. But even then, in the discussion of their paper by Mankiw (1996), it is described as 'an old argument of Tobin' and 'Tobin's idea' (p. 66).

Apart from the character of Tobin's own presentation, the explanation of the conventional attribution of the argument to him probably owes something to his exposition being punchier than Schultze's very long and thorough analysis of data, and something to its greater accessibility, being published in a journal rather than congressional papers. No doubt it also owes something to the fact that, being presented in the same forum as Friedman (1968a) and clearly intended as a response to him made it appear that the argument was devised to fill that role. But it also, surely, again owes something to the terminology. Except for Rees (1970), Tobin was in the same position as Friedman and Phelps in being the first to present his argument as an account of 'the Phillips curve'.

7.3.4 Consequences of Misdatings

A forensic study of these sources would reveal that some take on more of a mantle of knowledge of the past than others, but none is by any means primarily concerned with reporting history. They are all getting on with their theoretical or empirical work and are motivating it by reference to the then-current state of thinking, adopting convenient labels as they did. Certainly none of them is in any way meaning to mislead. 'Friedman's hypothesis' or 'Tobin's argument' would easily have been understood by contemporaries, and even 'Phillips curve'—despite the multiple meanings it had—would surely have been understood in any of the contexts where it was used. Despite occasional assertions about history, the question of where any of these ideas came from was not the real point under discussion in those scientific enquiries. And the adoption of these labels is all the easier to understand with the idea in mind that, as previous chapters have argued, none of these arguments in fact has a clear origin—there is no *other* name by which they should be known by, since they all had the nature of folk wisdom.

Nevertheless, it seems safe to infer that even by 1975 the true origins of these arguments had faded far from the consciousness of those engaged in debates around the Phillips curve. And as it happens, each of these misdatings builds a crucial part of the myth. Were it not that the Phillips curve was believed to be a discovery of the late 1950s, and the expectations argument to come some time later, it would be impossible to present the curve as sparking a new industry of research into the terms of a tradeoff, or as 'filling a gap' in Keynesian theory, or as inspiring anyone's views on inflationary policy in the 1960s; and similarly, there could not be a revolution in thinking at the end of that decade unless the expectations argument was new at that time. And if 'Tobin's argument' was called 'Schultze's argument' and dated to the end of the 1950s, it would certainly show the discussions of the relation between inflation and unemployment in the 1960s in a different light. It is hard to see how the myth could be sustained if these ideas were correctly dated by common understanding.

But as things went, by 1975, it is easy to imagine that those new to the field, setting about reading the latest scientific work, would find themselves swamped in discussions of 'the Phillips curve', and no reason to date it other than to Phillips (1958); and 'Friedman's argument' on which there was much comment, and on the specifics of it, much debate; and 'Tobin's argument', which had every appearance of being an argument in favour of an exploitable 'Phillips curve', and therefore linked to the earlier literature, and a response to Friedman, and a new argument, and therefore a retrospective justification of something that had gone before. And if it was justifying what had gone before, it would seem that the foregoing idea was a simple, naïve Phillips curve of just that kind that sources said had been so common. In any case, the fact that terminology failed to reveal that the 1960s Phillips curves were about wage change, not inflation at all, but suggested that they were 'simple' or 'naïve', could only reinforce this kind of view. And, again, the fact that Phillips (1958) is taken to be the origin might lead to his paper being read, but there is nothing there, nor in Friedman (1968a), to suggest a correcting of the datings.

7.4. POOR RESPONSES TO FRIEDMAN

A focus on the famous papers, terminological confusion, mistaken dating—important as they surely are these seem to make it all just a matter of the way things were talked about, and not at all of what was said. That might be enough to cause any amount of confusion, but there is more to say. First, Friedman's opponents also responded poorly to the substance of his arguments.

7.4.1 Presenting the Lubrication Argument

Tobin's presentation of the lubrication argument in such a way as to conceal the antiquity of the idea could be seen in this way. But there is more to it than that because Tobin and Leonard Ross (1971) also presented the argument—or a version of it—in the *New York Review of Books*. They criticized the expectations argument—'Friedman's argument' as they called it—on the basis that it

> rests on an appealing but unverified assumption: that you can't fool all of the
> people all of the time

and claimed that existing evidence was against the argument (as it was at that time). Clearly, the reader could very easily be forgiven for thinking they based their policy on the presumed effectiveness of a permanent deception. Tullock (1972) evidently did believe that, which gave Tobin and Leonard Ross (1972) a chance to clarify the point and state the lubrication argument properly. That put their intention beyond doubt, but probably did little to change the impression the original statement created. That impression can hardly have been that Friedman's opponents were adopting a reasonable position, and indeed, Haberler (1972, p. 136) cited the *Times* piece, saying that Tobin admitted that his case for inflation relied on the proposition that it was possible to fool all the people all the time.

7.4.2 Cost-Push Inflation and Incomes Policy

As noted in Section 5.2, Friedman's position was that cost-push inflation was all but non-existent. As I argued at the end of that section the relation of cost-push inflation to the idea of an inflation-unemployment trade-off is quite different from that of demand-pull inflation. For that reason, the possibility of cost-push inflation is crucial to the development of the understanding of the period. If it is impossible, then for practical purposes observed inflation (outside the limits of the lubrication argument, etc.) must be due to excess demand. If that is the case, the policymaker who does not tackle it by reducing demand almost must be presumed to be adopting a short-term, inflationary policy. By the same token, the utility of incomes policy in tackling inflation depends on the possibility of cost-push inflation.

The case for cost-push inflation is, perhaps naturally, put in common sensical terms, but it should have been possible, when necessary, to put it more theoretically. A notable feature of the discussion of both cost-push inflation and incomes policy, when they were challenged, was that this did not occur. Consider, for example, the point that in debate with Solow, Friedman (1966b) overtly threw down the gauntlet over both cost-push inflation and incomes policy, saying,

> One thing that always impresses me about this argument is how briefly it is alluded to *when* it is alluded to—at all. In paper after paper in the discussion of guideposts and cost-push inflation, or of market power as a source of inflation, you discover that there is but a sentence of two and then the author goes on to other things. (p. 57)

and continued with his claim that no worthwhile theoretical account was available. Since this was part of a debate where each participant made a second contribution, Solow (1966a) might have been expected to respond. The nearest he came was to say he was concerned about 'the degree of tightness' in the economy at the point when prices started to rise. Supposing that the 'degree of tightness' is to be determined by comparison between actual employment and full employment, that was in effect the point at issue—how tight *is* the economy when prices start to rise? Has it gone beyond full employment? If so, it was demand-pull inflation. Solow therefore offered no response to Friedman's challenge.

Ackley (1966a), in the final contribution to the conference at which Friedman and Solow spoke, moved towards repairing the damage, saying,

> Since Friedman asked for the theoretical underpinnings of this idea, I will give it. (p. 71)

But continued by saying that, in an upturn, oligopolists would find

> Although their ideal monopoly price may be no higher, their ability to realize it will strengthen as excess capacity is reduced. Thus as the economy expands, producers in these industries attempt to raise their margins over cost by lifting their prices.

What is an economist to make of the idea of an 'ideal price' that cannot be 'realized'? Ackley gave no indication.

Slightly later, Solow (1968) perhaps took the matter somewhat more seriously. He clearly acknowledged the force of the point about monopolists setting high rather than rising prices. He suggested that particular inflations with which he was concerned (such as that of 1955–8) might be explained by one-off price increases. But again, when he moved to an explanation of the case for cost-push inflation, his argument became vague, and although this time presented somewhat more in the language of theory, still lacks a coherent statement. He says that 'a situation becomes more cost-pushy, so to speak, when the curve relating price-change to excess demand shifts adversely' (p. 5). It should have been easy to do better.[6]

These, though, if anything, are amongst the statements which come closest to addressing the issue. Far more often, it is simply asserted that union power or oligopoly can raise prices and thereby cause inflation; or even just that incomes policy is necessary for inflation control. On this point, Friedman was certainly right: accounts of cost-push inflation, when there was anything at all, were inadequate.

Just the same point applies to the case for incomes policy. Solow (1966b)—in the same debate as that just quoted—put it like this:

> The problem is that modern mixed capitalist economies tend to generate unacceptably fast increases in money wages and prices while there is not general excess demand. No particular view of the economic process or of the determinants of demand need be implied by this observation. (pp. 41–2)

And later,

> The logic of the guidepost policy is, I suppose, something like this. In our imper-
> fect world, there are important areas where market power is sufficiently con-
> centrated that price and wage decisions are made with a significant amount of
> discretion. When times are reasonably good, that discretion may be exercised in
> ways that contribute to premature inflation. (p. 44)

And, indicating how they were supposed to work,

> People and institutions with market power may, in our culture, be fairly sensitive
> to public opinion. To the extent that they are, an educated and mobilized public
> opinion may exert some restraining pressure to forestall or limit premature infla-
> tion. (p. 44)

That is correct, but it is hardly designed to appeal to the economic theorist.
With the depth of vision behind this made clear by an appreciation of the
outlook described in Chapter 5, the force of the mechanism as well as the
idea of 'premature inflation' are clear. But without that, it does create an
impression of a theoretical vacuum in contrast to Friedman's clear account
based on simple theoretical principles.

7.4.3 The Expectations Argument

The third issue concerns the way authors reacted to the apparent refutation
of the expectations arugment. The notable point is that despite again and
again declaring the plausibility of the argument, when their econometrics
rejected it, those responding to Friedman gave so little indication of what
they believed the explanation to be.

Consider Solow (1968)—the first response to Friedman (1968a)—again.
He noted that there appeared to be a tradeoff and indicated that it arose as
a consequence of 'the structure of labor and commodity markets' (Solow
1968, p. 6), but did not elaborate on that. He discussed Phillips curve
equations (pp. 8–9), noting that they included price change, but said that
the coefficient on it turned out to be less than 1, and then moved to price
expectations, referring to Friedman's argument and explaining (pp. 10–11)
the theoretical idea that only unanticipated price change should have real
effects, and that these will therefore be temporary. He then said (p. 11) that
it is a plausible argument but its practical value depends on the period of
adjustment, then presented econometric work, and reached the conclusion:

If these estimates are in the ball park at all, they suggest that there is, in the not-so-short-run, a trade-off locus between inflation and real output; and that its position is such that high employment and price stability may be incompatible. (p. 16)

He then repeated the plausibility of the long-run neutrality view, saying his opinion was based on the 'general principle that you can't fool all of the people all the time' (p. 17), and that he wondered whether the 'not-so-short-run' and 'very-long-run' results could be reconciled, bearing in mind the point that the short run tradeoff relation would itself be subject to change. The nearest he came to explaining the failure of the expectations hypothesis in his results was the allusion to the structure of markets, and the implication that people can be fooled for short periods.

His line of econometric thinking was perhaps more fully developed in Solow (1969). The general picture he paints is similar to that in his earlier paper: he again refered to Friedman (1968a), and asserted the plausibility of the expectations argument. Again he presented econometrics seeming to reject the hypothesis, concluding that his estimates 'offer no support whatever' (p. 14) for the idea of strict adjustment. He then said,

> One is driven to ask: How can it be? How can so simple a consequence of economic rationality fail? (p. 15)

The answer he suggests is:

> the expectations hypothesis asks more of economic rationality than it can deliver. I can believe that a 10% annual rate of inflation, maintained steadily, will eventually become built into expectations just as the hypothesis describes. But it is not clear that this requires me to believe that a sequence of mostly small, irregularly varying, rates of inflation is fed into the economic system's memory in the same way to produce an expected rate of inflation. (p. 15)

Then he returned to econometrics and there is no further discussion of the kind of economic behaviour or structure that would give rise to his result.

Similarly, Gordon clearly understood the full significance of the expectations argument from the beginning of his researches on the Phillips curve, since in Gordon (1970) he said,

> Today's labor force is forward-looking and influenced by the expected level of consumer prices in relation to current nominal wages. (p. 16)

Similarly, in Gordon (1971a), he asserted the importance of expected inflation, saying,

> Workers do not evaluate wage offers by employers in a vacuum, however, but measure them against . . . the expected price level of the goods they will be able to buy with them. (p. 107)

In this paper, though, he goes beyond that, saying,

> the rate of expected inflation is set equal to the actual rate of inflation (since by definition in the long-run equilibrium the actual and expected rates of inflation are equal) . . . (p. 136)

That perhaps makes it even more notable that he does not seek to explain the failure of the hypothesis, and indeed very clearly does not, since in on pages 142–4, he discusses 'four important questions' (p. 142) to which he says his work gives rise—but explaining why the expectations hypothesis is rejected is not one of them, and, to confuse the matter more, he actually said that his results 'confirm the Phillips curve argument' that there was a non-vertical relation. The same sort of thing is true, I think, of *all* the principal rejections of the expectations hypothesis from the first half of the 1970s.[7] They all allow the econometrics to speak for itself in showing Friedman to be wrong, giving no explanation of what economic behaviour might underlie such a result.

The natural explanation is—of course—an argument along the lines of Schultze and Tobin or one of the other arguments considered in Section 5.4. Those arguments make the case that inflation can be associated with lower unemployment without inducing misperceptions. That is presumably what Solow was getting at with his reference to the structure of markets, while the fact that Gordon (1973b) presented the argument in a different context puts his awareness of it beyond doubt. The fact that they do not explain it seems surprising but it needs to be recalled how well known the argument was—it presumably did not seem to be necessary to explain it. It may even be that the fact that there was a variety of related arguments available creates something of a motive for not being specific—it does not matter exactly what the explanation is, and competent economists would be expected to appreciate the range of ideas that would lead to the same conclusion. Later, once those arguments faded from awareness, the impression created is the very strange one: a view apparently being held that people did not adjust their behaviour to their expectations.

7.4.4 The natural rate of unemployment

A further point relates less precisely to the history of the Phillips curve but still bears on those issues. It concerns the way Friedman (1968a) described the process of disturbance and return to equilibrium, and again, the absence of an appropriate response from his oppopents. The natural rate of unemployment was described by Friedman (1968a) as being determined by,

> the actual structural characteristics of the labor and commodity markets, includ-
> ing market imperfections, stochastic variability in demands and supplies, the
> cost of gathering information about job vacancies and labor availability, the costs
> of mobility, and so on. (p. 8)

Except for 'stochastic variability in demands and supplies', which would presumably have only temporary effects, that made no allowance for the level of demand. Then, when Friedman offered his analysis of the effect of monetary expansion he started his analysis at a time when prices had been stable and unemployment was 'higher than 3%' (p. 9), but, it is implied, at the natural rate. In that case, inflation lowers unemployment temporarily. But if indeed he is starting the analysis at the natural rate, then there is no unemployment due to demand deficiency and so, of course, inflation results. He did not consider the situation where there would have been a case for expansionary policy—namely one where there was demand defi-cient unemployment.

It is amazing how rarely this point has been noted. It is stated explicitly in Hahn (1982, pp. 74–5) and de Vroey (1998), who both saw the point and expressed surprise at how few others had. But these are much later. The extraordinary thing is that none of the immediate responses to Friedman seem to have noted this point. Yet precisely the point the American tax cut of 1964 as well as measures in numerous British budgets was that an increase in demand would lower unemployment *without* inflation. Friedman's argument about inflation being at first unanticipated then gradually incorporated into the wage bargain fails even before its first step, since there is no inflation to anticipate.

But the responses to Friedman, considered in Section 4.5, ignored the issue of demand deficiency and attacked the issue of the adjustment of expectations. Although they initially seemed to refute Friedman's claims on that point, later, when the econometrics confirmed that inflation had no lasting effect on employment, there seemed to be no suggestion that anything else might have, and those early responses seemed to be an econo-metric charge to he Light Brigade—attacking an impregnable position, instead of defending the one that mattered. The supposed refutation of Keynesianism, so often said to follow from the vertical Phillips curve, actually depends on the idea that inflationary policy is the *only* way demand policy can lower unemployment. And in response to Friedman (1968a), at least, that was never questioned.

7.4.5 Consequences

The arguments being put in these kinds of ways could certainly help the myth develop. With the expectations argument seeming to have been new in 1968, and with it seeming to have been tested and often rejected, it would be easy to make a mistake about what had really been at issue. If one starts with the idea that the literature of the 1960s was inflationist and foolish, and that Friedman, in 1968, challenged its presumptions and this led to a great contest, a later reader would surely feel that Friedman won. If any idea of cost-push inflation featured, it would seem to be based on a rejection of elementary propositions of theory. Incomes policy, if considered, would then naturally seem to be an attempt to overrule market forces—neither of those things suggest a revision of the idea that the period was beset with foolishness. But, more than this, it might appear that Friedman's opponents had the idea that permanent deception could lower unemployment, and—since they gave no other explanation, either of the existence of a long-run, non-vertical Phillips curve, or of any other mechanism allowing policy to be effective—that they thought their econometrics confirmed that view. And again, with the whole literature labelled with Phillips' name, readers of his paper would learn nothing to put them on the correct path to understanding the attitude of the later literature to price change.

7.5 THE CIRCUMSTANCES IN WHICH THE MYTH DEVELOPED

To muddled terminology, mistaken history, and poor rhetoric, we must add the circumstances which developed, and the aspects of what happened which have, in certain respects, some similarity to what developed into the Phillips curve myth.

Amongst the circumstances is the fact that inflation rose. It has often enough been said that this had the effect of making Friedman seem prescient. Perhaps so, but there is an aspect of misdating about this as well, since Friedman (1968a) did not forecast a rise in inflation. His discussion of policy seeking to lower unemployment was hypothetical—he did not say that it was being done. More important, the higher rate of inflation took it beyond the level at which anyone (except perhaps Farrell (1965)) thought the lubrication argument was relevant, and consequently it ceased to be relevant to policy discussion, and ceased to be discussed.

Likewise, cost-push inflation, as a truly distinct problem, disappeared from discussion. That may be partly as a consequence of the way the argument was conducted—especially by Rowthorn (1977) translating the argument into mathematical, seemingly mechanical terms. In any case, after 1968 at the latest, it was apparent that the Vietnam War (or its method of financing) was generating excess demand, so that the inflation being experienced was certainly demand-pull. No doubt it was also partly because, when incomes policy was seen simply to fail, demand reduction became the only option. In these circumstances, the significance of the cost-push/demand-pull distinction evaporated and the issue of inflation 'types' seemed otiose. Then, with inflation outside the range that could reasonably be explained by the lubrication and like arguments those sorts of arguments would also have faded from attention.

With those arguments out of mind, and as I have already argued, poorly presented in the 1970s, it must have been harder to appreciate that they had ever been a feature of the economics of the 1960s—or ever been a serious feature of discussion. Without a better rationale than it was given, I suppose cost-push inflation and the inflation-types debate came to seem to be an artefact of primitive thinking. That left some versions of the idea of a Phillips curve high and dry—there was no Bowen-type dilemma in a world where wages and prices reacted exclusively to the balance of supply and demand (and expected inflation). So discussion which had in fact been motivated by a desire to solve (or just measure) that dilemma, might seem to have no real rationale. That leaves the idea that it was about finding a point on a tradeoff curve as seeming the only plausible motivation.

Then, of course, are the facts that policy in the 1960s had sought to maintain a very low level of unemployment, particularly in the United Kingdom, and after 1964 in the United States. It was perfectly understandable if it appeared this had in fact led to inflation—demand-pull inflation, of course. In the 1970s, 'the Phillips curve' was propelled to the centre of policy discussion—not to promote inflation, but to understand how to reduce it. And when it was said that 'the Phillips curve' had been greatly studied in the 1960s that was true, even though it was wage determination that was usually being studied, not inflation at all. One of the aspects of the situation might even be that the 1960s econometricians had so little interest in explaining exactly what they were doing, and the 1970s ones had no interest in finding out. The field was left vacant and confusion occupied it.

To all this one more point should be added. That is, that because of the sudden emergence of the myth, authors who had been writing only a year or two earlier had no idea that it was about to be said. In particular they had no reason to expect that what was about to be claimed that they did not appreciate the significance of real variables and related matters. Solow (1968), Gordon (1970), and Tobin (1972b) can all just about be read in ways which *seem* to be consistent with the myth. Certainly, what they do not contain is assertions of understanding the difference between nominal and real variables; or denials of having been busy with trying to refine Phillips' equation to discover the true menu of choices. Those authors had no reason to suppose that it was ever going to be suggested that they had been so foolish—they were all written before 1975.

Consider in particular Tobin (1972a)—his popular discussion of 'the new economics'. As my rather extensive enquiries have, I hope, revealed, he was using the terminology which was current in 1972, and 'the Phillips curve' of that vintage was nothing like the Phillips curve of 1958 or even 1968. It was merely a label for a general idea of a connection between inflation and unemployment. Yes, no doubt the Council of Economic Advisers of 1962 did have an 'eye on the Phillips curve' (Tobin 1972a), as Tobin put it, in the sense that their estimate of the sustainable level of employment was framed with regard to maintaining reasonable price stability. That is many miles from seeking to exploit a stable tradeoff.

Tobin clearly does indulge in some loose talk about the role of 'the Phillips curve' in the thinking of the Council of Economic Advisers in 1962. But this is why the suddenness of the emergence of the myth, and the fact that is not contained in Friedman (1968a), are important—Tobin was writing in 1972, before Friedman (1975a) or Dornbusch and Fischer (1978). Tobin used the expression 'Phillips curve' in the way it was used in 1972 to mean any relation between inflation and unemployment, not in the way it had been used in 1962, strictly as a wage equation. Having an eye on the Phillips curve meant they were choosing a level consistent with price stability (or reasonable price stability). In 1982, or 1977, it might mean 'selecting an optimal point on a presumptively stable tradeoff' And he had no reason to defend himself against the allegations of having made foolish errors, because they are contained in a story which is a fiction, and in any case, had not then been told.

It is in just this sort of way that all the pieces I have suggested come together. By 1975 ideas of 'the Phillips curve' were so varied that in looking back one can find all kinds of things were said about it. On the other hand, there was little sense of there being confusion about the labelling. The various arguments that had gone on, over expectations, or the inclusion of profit in the wage-change equation, or whatever it may be, had emerged in one context, but when inflation rose they were considered in a different light entirely. The datings of various ideas that had become conventional seemed to provide a framework for understanding the history but in fact did no such thing.

And finally, there is surely relevance in the point that dismissing earlier work is often easier than studying it. Johnson (1971b, p. 5) said Keynesianism was just difficult enough since it allowed the young to leave their elders behind without having to read what they had written. Here it may even be that it is relevant that the econometric work at the beginning of the 1970s was undertaken almost exclusively by a new cast of characters. Lipsey's last contribution was Lipsey and Parkin (1970); Hines wrote no significant pieces in the 1970s; Eckstein and Girola (1978) was Eckstein's only one. On the other hand, Gordon wrote nothing before 1970—the same is true of Hall and Wachter. Perry is the only person to make a substantial contribution to both parts of the literature, and as noted on page 169 he stands out as giving later accounts of the history which cannot be faulted.

7.6 CONCLUSION

Step by step, then, perhaps one can see the emergence of the myth as an understandable development. The atypicality of the famous papers; terminological confusion; a laziness, even if perhaps an understandable one, about dating of major insights, and casual inference therefrom; and some arguments constructed in a particular context which turned out to be presentationally quite inappropriate to the intellectual environment that was about to emerge. That is quite a collection of contributory factors, although they are all readily visible in the details of the record. Beyond them, perhaps the fact that as things turned out, they came together as they did, is just happenstance.

CHAPTER 8

Conclusions

8.1 A NEW STORY OF THE PHILLIPS CURVE

So here is a new story of the Phillips curve. In 1958, traditional wage theory held that wages were bargained with the fairness of the settlement baulking large in the outcome. Enquiries into wage determination therefore focused on such things as employer profits, price change, productivity, and the wages of comparable groups of workers. More purely economic forces were not disregarded, and nor was there anything surprising or mysterious about the idea of a relationship between wage change and unemployment. In that, Phillips (1958) had near and distant precursors and there were certainly superior contemporary presentations of the idea. But in the study of wage bargaining these were not the things emphasized, and no very regular relations were expected. For that reason, there appeared to be no definite impediment to the achievement of full employment and price stability.

The same outlook opened the door for the possibility of cost-push inflation in a context where the policymaker was committed to maintaining a high level of employment. Since wages were not determined by purely economic forces, unions might exercise pressure and achieve higher wages in the absence of excess demand for labour. They would be stepping outside the bounds of fairness if they did, but it was a recognized possibility that they might. If that were widespread, the maintenance of full employment with price stability would become impossible.

In this environment 'the Phillips curve'—to use the expression in the all-encompassing way it later was—could play any of three separate roles. One was that intended by Phillips—to question the traditional wage theory by suggesting that, usually, the only things determining wage increases were unemployment and its rate of change. That finding, if accepted, had profound consequences for the conception of labour economics and industrial relations. It would also have a particular consequence for the achievement of price stability—namely that unemployment would have to be at the appropriate level.

Secondly, 'the Phillips curve' could be a vehicle for the econometricization of the older theories of wage determination. It just so happens that computing capabilities opened up possibilities for econometric testing just at the time Phillips wrote. These studies were, naturally, concerned with the question of what determines wages. That was the same question as Phillips', although such studies grew out of a literature based on quite different presumptions and to that extent were on the other side of the great divide over whether it was strictly 'economic' or 'bargaining' considerations that were pre-eminent. It may be that Phillips had some influence in promoting the introduction of unemployment to these equations as a variable determining wages, although of course he was far from unique in finding some role for it—Klein, and Dicks-Mireaux and Dow, offering more highly regarded work with that characteristic, from a similar time. That a wide range of studies that did not place much emphasis on unemployment were ever called 'Phillips curves' has caused confusion. The authors of the work did not, for the most part, so describe their work—that is later labelling, and labelling which flies in the face of what Phillips was thinking. But that is how the expression came to be used.

Thirdly, again around 1958, serious questions started to be raised about the practicability of achieving full employment and price stability. In itself, this concern could arise just from an observation of what was happening, rather than presuming any particular theory. It gave rise to enquiries into the existence or otherwise of a 'dilemma' in which Bowen (1960b) and Bodkin (1966) are landmarks. They both mentioned Phillips but neither truly owed anything to him. Similarly, Samuelson and Solow (1960) were primarily investigating the existence of such a dilemma, although they showed more interest in Phillips' findings, and for better or worse, adopted his name as a label. All these authors first and foremost wanted to know whether there could be full employment and price stability, and if not, how bad the problem was.

Later, but still in this vein, a fourth role for 'the Phillips curve' developed. That was its use as a presumed relation to test for the effectiveness of various policy proposals. Most important was the idea, starting with Perry (1966), that it could be used, in a rough and ready way, to try to detect the effect of incomes policy; but the benefits of regional policy were also considered slightly later. In a similar way, though without quite the same relation to policy, such things as the effect of trade unions on wage bargaining would also be tested. Here, as in certain other cases, the existence of the basic relation was not being tested at all—it was being assumed, so that there could be consideration of how other things affected it.

So there were several different scientific enquiries, all in full flood at the same time, and any of which might draw on the same—or very similar—econometrics. No doubt some of the econometrics was good and some of it was bad. Some of the studies hardly deserve to be so labelled at all—Samuelson and Solow (1960) is usually not; Bowen (1960c) has no real claim; and surely one should question whether Phillips (1958) deserves to be so described since on that score it stands no comparison with contemporary work. I suppose his was not the only study that was limited by the shortcuts their authors took in the light of computational difficulties; the econometric technique they used was the technique of their time, which may not have been very good; and there is no point in trying to defend the position that nothing foolish was ever said about economic theory. But there is every point in insisting that all branches of this literature were entirely serious enquiries into the character of economic relations of modern society. There is nothing about it which is juvenile, or naïve, or to be dismissed by a flick of the professor's wrist. On the other hand, it is also an essential that, even here, 'the Phillips curve' had no particular identity—the use of the expression could import very different presumptions, depending on what exactly was under discussion.

In the 1970s, the scene was rather different but 'the Phillips curve' was again at the confluence of a number of rather different streams of thinking. Inflation had risen, and the combinations of inflation and unemployment that had been achieved seemed no longer attainable. At this time, there was no hesitation in using the expression 'Phillips curve' much more freely than before, and just as a piece of terminology it was convenient to say 'the Phillips curve had shifted'. In that observation about the facts of the time, there is no issue about exploiting a tradeoff, then or in the past. It was a way of talking about things, of describing the fact that things were worse than they had been. There was a question about why that had happened, and that inspired more econometrics—so more 'Phillips curves' were estimated to elucidate that. One of the possibilities was that it was because inflation expectations had changed, but that was one of the things being tested. The issue of how to measure expectations also arose and inspired more econometrics, much of it again, rather than testing the issue, took its sense from the presumption that some form of Phillips curve existed.

Meanwhile, various theoretical enquiries found a central role for a specific connection between inflation and unemployment. Some of these were enquiries into the question of why there should be such a relation at all. Tobin (1972b) addressed that in one way, presenting the lubrication argument in the guise of a theory of 'the Phillips curve'. The search theories like Phelps (1970c) were also in this category. They were not, as later accounts often presumed, designed to show the impossibility of a tradeoff in the long run, but, as Phelps himself said, to explain why there might be a relation in the short run. Rowthorn (1977) was more concerned with wider macroeconomic issues, but still he theorized a 'Phillips curve' in otherwise authentically cost-push terms. One consequence was that although these theoretical approaches were all quite different, the combination of them meant that almost everyone could find some satisfactory rationale and have a 'Phillips curve' as a part of their outlook. There appeared, more and more, to be a consensus on the existence of 'the' Phillips curve.

Other theoretical enquiries—such as the work around the political business cycle and development of thinking about optimal currency areas—put a Phillips curve at the centre of the enquiry. Here there was no issue about rationalizing it. Rather, it was again its presumed existence which was, one way or another, the basis for the rest of the enquiry. Again, the seeming ubiquity of the curve is notable. And again just because the analysis in question and its intellectual animus must presume the existence of the curve, it acquires a sheen of being part of a consensus.

In this second period some of the enquires in which the Phillips curve featured made relevant the distinction between its 'short-run' and 'long-run' versions, and accordingly, that distinction started to be drawn. Amongst these were the study of the adjustment of expectations, some of the theoretical rationales for its existence, non-expectational explanations of the deterioration of outcomes in the 1970s, and some of the abstract policy issues.

That could have been the end of the story. If it had been, there would have been a confusion of tongues worthy of Genesis 11, but nothing else to report. Demand-pull, cost-push, either, or both could be described by a 'Phillips curve'. There were naïve, simple, and short-run, augmented, and I suppose by implication, unaugmented versions in any role. It might be theoretical or statistical, with unemployment as its principal argument, or unemployment alone, or perhaps something else emphasized. It might be wage change or price change that was investigated, theoretically or empirically. Or it might not be investigated, but just assumed. All of those would have been part of 'the Phillips curve literature', but no harm would have been done. There was nothing about most of its interpretations that was either 'Keynesian', or 'anti-Keynesian'. It would be necessary—as it is—to recognize that there is really no such thing as 'the' Phillips curve. There is no sense in supposing that a discussion of 'the' Phillips curve, or 'the' theory of the Phillips curve, or, for that matter, the history of 'the' Phillips curve can be conducted without a much fuller specification of what is at issue. But, where there were issues of interest, that could perfectly well be done.

However, that is not the end of the story, because part of the Phillips curve story must also be the development of the myth. Quite how that happened can perhaps not be absolutely settled, but it can be said that in the mid-1970s authors who shared a hostility to the reigning orthodoxy started to say that the idea of an exploitable tradeoff had been central to policy and that high inflation resulted from that. They started to say, in effect, that what was then known as the 'short-run' curve had featured as if it were a 'long-run' curve in the earlier period. They presented an analysis of how policy which was based on the presumption of a stable 'short-run' curve would lead to accelerating inflation, and that—as a piece of theory— proved, quite understandably, to be widely appealing. Friedman (1977) was not the first statement of the idea that policy had in fact proceeded on that mistaken basis, but of the early ones, his is the most thoroughgoing in its condemnation of the supposed erstwhile consensus, and it is hard to doubt that his was the statement that had the galvanic effect on understanding. Certainly, the essentials of the historical picture he presented appeared very rapidly in textbooks and surveys, and, thereafter, there was neither any questioning of it, nor much in the way of attention to the actual litera- ture he had supposedly summarized. 'The Phillips curve' came to be seen as quite a well-defined idea—still with a variety of possible theoretical expla- nations—but one-dimensional in being a tool for analysing the effects of demand policy in the short and long run.

8.2 THE OLD STORY AND THE NEW

That story is not *like* the conventional one. It is not the conventional story with corrections made, and it is not intended to be. I hope my first six chap- ters have provided enough detail on the particular failings of the conven- tional story and that Chapter 7 has offered some reassurance that the facts as they were could be converted into the story as it became. In doing so perhaps it points out where there are just enough glimpses of historical verisimilitude to make the conventional story inviting, whilst also showing they are far too slight to make it retrievable.

Still, there are possible responses to my argument which should be answered. One, I suppose, might be that in my emphasis on the lubrication and related arguments I have conceded that there *was* an idea of a policy choice. The answer to that, of course, is that one might disagree with the lubrication argument for one reason or another, but it would be an extreme position to regard it as unreasonable, and an extraordinary one to regard it as equivalent to the kind of mistakes alleged in the usual Phillips curve story. Consequently, it would have to be accepted that all the conventional story amounts to is the claim that economists of the 1960s and 1970s took a reasonable view of the costs of achieving strict price stability, and there would be nothing over which to criticize them. Since the lubrication argument originated before 1958, there would be no claim that in respect of the existence of a tradeoff Phillips brought a new idea; the point that the 1960s literature failed to appreciate the importance of price change would be abandoned; there would be no point in attempting to argue that Friedman and Phelps revolutionized the literature. The whole story would simply fade away. Furthermore, a crucial point would be that only very low rates of inflation were under consideration, so it would then be agreed that the 1960s were no more inflationist than, say, the European Central Bank which actually does, just in the way that annoyed Robertson (1955/1966), *define* price stability as 'inflation below, but close to, 2%' (ECB 2003, p. 5). This, says the ECB website 'Definition of Price Stability' is 'low enough for the economy to fully reap the benefits of price stability'. And indeed, whatever criticism were made of the economists of the 1960s for their inflationism would also need to be made of Draghi (2013), who stated a version of the lubrication argument in a press statement for the ECB. It can hardly be that the story is to be summed up by saying that the weakness of the macroeconomics of the 1960s was that it was just as inflationist as the European Central Bank.

In practical terms, I suspect more resistance to my conclusions would come from a combination of the feeling that the conventional view is so well established, the events themselves apparently being remembered by some, and the story even being in textbooks, and going so long unchallenged, that there must be something in it; the point that, try as I might, I cannot read everything, and there could be more inflationism to be found; and an idea that, in any case, there was perhaps some substratum of inflationist feeling which only rarely or imperfectly made it to the printed word, but was nevertheless influential. And all this takes support from the notable fact that the components of the conventional story do hang together very well—there is an unfolding story there, a consistency of historical narrative, which has appeal, and might seem to have plausibility.

It only needs to be stated to be clear that constant repetition is itself not worth anything, and the fact that the story appears in textbooks is nothing unless it is also correct, all the more so when it is appreciated in what strange circumstances it found its way into those books. Similarly, people's memories might be tested against the written record, but it would be a strange thing to perform the test the other way round. And the point about the conventional story having gone unchallenged certainly leads nowhere. The most it could mean is that intellectual vacuums sometimes persist longer than might have been guessed.

On that point, though, there is more to it, because—as has been pointed out—it is not exactly true that it has gone unchallenged. Phillips' primacy in discovering the negative relation has been challenged; as has his inflationism. Moderately informed opinion probably accepts neither of these things. The fact that Samuelson and Solow did not advocate inflation has also been noticed, even if the point that almost no one thought they did, and those few disagreed with them, has gone unnoticed. And there have been several comments on presentations of the expectations argument before Friedman and Phelps. But when parts of the story have been challenged, or particular early cases of statements of ideas have been noticed, they have not been seen as challenging the whole story. It has, for some reason, a greater resilience than that. There is, it could almost seem, a reluctance to abandon it.

As to the general appeal and plausibility of a story in which the components seem naturally to gel, it must be remembered that it comes at the cost of an extreme implausibility in other ways. It is my story which, by avoiding the claim that the ordinary and the great minds of the 1960s fell into an elementary error, has plausibility. The expectations argument is no more than common sense, and it is an absurdity that anyone contemplating a policy of ongoing inflation would not consider it. Or, back in 1958, what is the plausible basis on which it might be claimed that the idea of a non-linear relationship between wage change and unemployment would have been a great innovation—filling a gap, indeed, in a theory that was by then more than two decades old? And Friedman's claim that in the environment of the time it was natural to think in nominal rather than real prices is extraordinary since the 1960s were a period of intense concern about inflation.

As to the point that the conventional story takes strength from its narrative consistency, there are several things to say. One is that the elements of my account have the same consilience as that story, and also take strength from each other. The fact that the idea of a negative relation between inflation and unemployment was nothing like a new idea in 1958 must make it easier to accept that Phillips had no special role in inspiring the later lit-erature. The fact that the sources of the ideas of the econometric literature can easily be found in labour economics of the earlier period makes it eas-ier to see that no inspiration from Phillips was needed. The near-complete absence of inflationism in the 1960s and the attention given to price change as a determinant of wage change make it easier to appreciate that Friedman's presentation of the expectations argument did not bring the transformation that has been supposed. And so it goes on.

A further point, though, is that the internal consistency of the conven-tional story is a double-edged consideration, since the weakening of one part detracts from the others. I hope I have said sufficient about each part to be convincing, but there are further points which, even if they seem small details of the historical record, are very hard to explain on the basis of the usual story. For one, if the economists of the 1960s were treating the Phillips curve as exploitable, why does Friedman (1968a) not say so? It is all very well treating that as the key statement of the expectations argu-ment, but the way it is put should fit with other aspects of the story—and it does not. Similarly, why is it that the claim that Samuelson and Solow were the inspiration of inflationism not to be found in the 1960s? It is to be remembered that—supposedly—the inflationist policy was not only being followed but appeared to be successful. So why are Samuelson and Solow not *lauded* for discovering it? Why does Tobin (1966), at the height of the success of the New Economics, not praise them? Why does he not proclaim that the key to ongoing prosperity has been found in a policy of inflation? Remembering this view was supposedly unchallenged, then if it were believed, the discovery would certainly be a source of pride.

The fragility of the conventional story is most evident, though, in con-sidering the relationship between the expectations argument and the idea that there might be substratum of inflationism I have failed to discover. It might seem to be that I have shown the argument was known, but I have not shown that the early proponents of the expectations argument were themselves widely cited for the argument. Indeed, I do not think they were—there would be no point in citing them for something so routine. So it might seem it could be argued that there were, in effect, numerous isolated cases of recognition of the argument, but each of them wholly uninfluential, and remaining unnoticed. It does not sound likely, but still, someone might say, where are the citations? The fatal difficulty there is that what would have to be argued is that all these eminent authors were ignored in a context where, simultaneously, there was a great substratum of inflationism—undetectable to me, but, ex hypothesis, known to everyone of the period. How could that be? Those authors, well known as they were, would have to have failed to put their message across; anti-inflationary interests would have to be incompetent in the discovery and propagation of the arguments. It seems there would have to have been a perfect seques-tration of the Phillips curve authors and the supposed inflationists follow-ing them, from this other, wiser group. That would indeed be a story.

We must return to reality. Once the wide appreciation of the expecta-tions argument is accepted, it becomes impossible to believe there was inflationism that went unanswered. Then, the Phillips curve literature of the 1960s cannot be interpreted as aiming to discover an optimal tradeoff; there is no reason to suppose anyone was confused about real and nominal variables. And likewise, there is then no reason to suppose the existence of a substratum of inflationism of which there are only in any case, only second-hand reports from the mid-1970s. The self-supporting aspect of the conventional story is all very well, but the idea that no one had thought of the expectations argument is its keystone. When we take that away, the roof falls in.

8.3 HISTORICAL FAILURE

The result is that in so far as the history of post-war macroeconomic thought has been developed through stories of the Phillips curve, it would be best to throw that history away altogether and start again. There has been, one might say, an historical failure on a grand scale, and there is no point in setting about sorting through the rubble, because there is no rea-son to believe there is anything of value there. The Phillips curve story is a *Just So* story—'How the Phillips curve became vertical'. And it is nothing more.

In case that point needs more emphasis, it might be said that what has gone wrong is not the development of a foggy uncertainty like not being quite sure whether Rutherford Hayes came before Chester Arthur, or for that matter, Turnham Green before Stamford Brook. The story is far too central to later understanding for that. Nor is it just piece of ignorance which, nevertheless, serves to add colour to the story, like thinking that flat-earthers were common when Columbus sailed. It is more like the mis-take reported by Susan Jacoby (2008), of thinking that the Vietnam War was started by an attack on Pearl Harbor. The importance of it is the con-sequent impossibility of piecing together any worthwhile history in the area. If we start with propositions such as that it was natural for those economists, wrestling with inflation though they were, to think in nominal terms, and that it took Milton Friedman late in the 1960s even to point in the right direction, and another decade to win the argument, then we might as well try describing constitutional history on the assumption that Appomattox came before Yorktown.

There is no chance, in other words, of understanding macroeconomics in the period whilst the Phillips curve myth is accepted as even a characterization of what happened. With that as the starting place, it will be impossible to understand the operation of demand management, full employment policy, incomes policy, the response to stagflation; or even make any headway with the practicalities of the rules and discretion debate, the argument over fixed exchange rates, or the case for central bank independence as it grew out of experience and interpretations of experience, or some aspects of the genesis of European Monetary Union—to suggest only some of the things which are, in fact, often discussed, and often related fairly directly, to the Phillips curve.

Discarding the specifics of the Phillips curve myth is one important step but there is more to achieving historical understanding than that. One crucial point concerns the general character of the literature. One point is that it has, by later standards, an informality. But, it is very much a mistake to regard that as a lack of clarity. No one wrote down p-dot-e, to represent expected price change, but that does not mean they failed to understand that it could matter, much less that anyone thought the effects of a surprise inflation would be as lasting as the inflation rather than just the surprise. The broad lesson about the economics of the 1960s is that it was far wiser than has been supposed; the narrower one about the appreciation of economics is that the discovery of an idea should not be dated to its first rigorous presentation, much less its first mathematical one.

A further point is that in the 1960s, and to some extent the 1970s, there was very much less concern over specifying the conditions of long-run equilibrium, or—a different matter, although not always seen as one—of analysing behaviour in terms of strict rationality. Later work has tended to take it as a methodological postulate that all theorizing should be about long-run equilibria, or equilibrium paths, generated by strictly rational behaviour. That is one way of looking at things, although the insight generated by the approach might be exaggerated. More importantly, the attempt to assess arguments asking other questions on the basis of this postulate is deeply flawed. A wage equation which serves to explain developments of its own period may well leave larger questions unanswered. But it is not therefore useless, nor misleading, nor evidence of a defective outlook, nor necessarily primitive or vague. If someone else condemns it for failing to be a reasonable characterization of long-run equilibrium it is not the author of the equation who has lost touch with basic aspects of reality.

Accompanying the informality and tendency to analyse in terms of less than perfect rationality, there is an acute concern with understanding what seemed to be the realities of the situations under discussion. There is a connection between the two, of course, since formal, rational-actor theorizing does not always generate results directly applicable to the problems of the day. The literature of the 1960s is full of economic theory offering acute observation on the economic problems of the times.

The dismissal of those ideas, apparently for no better reason than that they are tainted by being merely attempts to patch up the Phillips curve without recognizing the importance of real variables is itself an historical failure. Amongst these ideas are the various points remarked on in Section 5.4, about the imprecision of the idea of price stability, many of which are still more or less features of careful treatments of that question. But there were also ideas like the value of including in the wage-change equation such things as measures of profit, the rate of change of unemployment, and union aggressiveness. The rate of change of unemployment features in Phillips (1958) but it features in plenty of other sources as well—Dicks-Mireaux and Dow (1959), Gillion (1968), and Kuh (1967) are just three. The inclusion of profit became a standard feature of American Phillips curves, following Perry (1966). In British work, on the other hand, union aggressiveness—variously understood—frequently featured. Hines (1964) had a particular treatment, but it was in Klein and Ball (1959), and Dicks-Mireaux and Dow (1959) again, and in different ways in much of the literature of the 1970s. And from the 1970s there would be the subtleties of understanding the mechanisms by which inflation might come to be incorporated in the wage bargain—all of which were later encompassed in the term 'expectations'. These things substantially disappeared from view, and an historical treatment should recognize the real place they once had in economic thought.

8.4 PHILLIPS

From all this, the work and influence of two individuals stands out as wanting further attention. Indeed, the historical position of Phillips (1958), and the idea that his inspiration in any way generated interest in the curve in any of its manifestations, needs as complete a reassessment as anything. Objectively speaking, it was a negligible paper. It is not even the case that it inspired ideas which turned out to be wrong-headed. On the contrary, it inspired very little. Many later authors have supposed that there was something special or impressive about it, and some have obsessed about it. But in so far as he had a unique idea—that the wage-change equation was invariant to institutional change—it was wrong, and not much better than meritless. The vaguer idea of unemployment affecting wages went back two hundred years and surprised no one; and his statistical analysis, if it bears scrutiny at all, made Phillips very definitely, as Keynes (1946/1972) said of Newton, the last of the Babylonians. The first of the moderns was Tinbergen, 25 years earlier.

It is not even the case that, whatever fate it deserved, the curve made the impact so often supposed. Except for its role in the myth, the paper itself had very little impact. As was clear in Chapter 3 and Section 5.6, discussion of the curve, and certainly applause for it, were initially rarities. Its absence from Johnson (1962) was, I suggested, very notable, but it was not anomalous—when one looks to the record, rather than later reports, it is clear the curve was mentioned rather rarely at that time. It is after Friedman (1968a) that mentions become frequent. Simply counting instances reveals that. But there is also the evidence of the widespread application of Phillips' name to an inflation relation, combined with the sudden interest (noted in Section 2.5) in the fact that Samuelson and Solow were the first to do that. And then there is the string of notes all pointing to—supposedly interesting—precursors of Phillips, which all appear in 1971 or 1972. Sexual intercourse may have been invented, as Larkin (1974) said, in 1963, but 'the Phillips curve' came five years after that.

Another point that falls easily into place is the question of why it was that Phillips did not object to the use of the curve as a tradeoff relation. Leeson (1994, n. 20) has about 200 words on it, asserting that Lipsey was puzzled by the same thing, and it is part of Chapple's (1996) argument that Phillips in fact did believe in an exploitable tradeoff. The answer is perfectly simple. Phillips died in February 1975. At that time the myth had not emerged and he had nothing to complain about.

One can also easily see the answer to Santomero and Seater's (1978) question, quoted in Section 1.1, about why it was Phillips in particular who became famous for the curve. It is, first of all, because it happened to be his name that was attached to the idea; and, second, because, that having happened, the label was used extremely flexibly. This is not so much Genesis 11 as Corinthians 9:20–2. The curve of Phillips was an empirical, demand-pull relation which had persisted over a remarkably long period. But to those who saw cost-push inflation, the Phillips curve became cost-push; to those who saw a measure of the effect of incomes policy, it became a measure of the effect of incomes policy; to those who saw a tradeoff, it became a tradeoff function; to those who needed a vehicle for discussing the effects of monetary union, the Phillips curve was that vehicle. There is nothing in Phillips (1958) to explain that, it is just that 'the Phillips curve', like St Paul, became all things to all men. In all this, Phillips himself is nothing but an innocent bystander.

The confusion that has resulted has been immense and is certainly no credit to those who dismiss the importance of the careful use of terminology. But sticking with the question of Phillips' position in twentieth-century economics, there is another unfortunate aspect to this. Studies of his work that take a patristical attitude to the 1958 paper, to Phillips (1962)—his inaugural lecture—and the 'Australian Phillips curve' paper he never bothered to fully publish, Phillips (1959/2000), create no opportunity for his contribution to be recognized. If he deserves fame, it would be, I venture, for Phillips (1954) and Phillips (1957)—his papers on the mathematics of stabilization policy. It would take a particular combination of talents to achieve it, but it is there that credit might be given; not in poring over his worst paper and least analytic remarks.

8.5 FRIEDMAN

The import of Friedman (1968a) also warrants careful attention. It obviously is not the paper that drew attention to the adjustment of wages to ongoing inflation—that was a routine matter in the understanding of the time. Nor can it possibly be the paper that first presented the idea of the natural rate of unemployment. That terminology was new, but the idea of a unique equilibrium level of employment certainly was not—or else what was it that Keynes (1936) thought he was attacking?

A somewhat better possibility is that Friedman brought a particular understanding of the mechanism of expectational adjustment. As I have argued in Section 4.1, there is a variety of ways in which the idea of expectations adjusting to inflation could be understood. Friedman is usually interpreted as having both insisted on behaviour being rational in the sense of being free of money illusion, and on the relevant notion of real wages being a prospective one, based on foreseen future developments. If he did have that idea, it is difficult to see why he would have supposed (see Friedman (1968a, p. 11), that the adjustment of expectations would take decades. Perhaps he had it in mind that what was at issue was more like a slow institutional and habit-based adjustment of the kind I called 'tropistic'. In later work certainly, he clearly favoured the interpretation based on more straightforwardly forward-looking behaviour. But since we know that his attitude to the Phillips curve generally changed in later work, this shows nothing.

It may be this issue also relates to whether one might think that, in presenting the expectations argument, Friedman was not merely pointing to a general tendency of behaviour to adapt to reality, but suggesting that it would eventually unpick the lubrication argument as well. That would certainly explain why the effect takes decades, and if not really original, would certainly have been distinctive. It would also have been a serious piece of commentary on policy attitudes of the time. And I have already suggested that some of those who were seeking to test his claim should be seen as rejecting it because they favoured that argument. If that is right, one consequence would be that Friedman's victory in the matter would be very much open to question—the lubrication argument is still widely accepted. But whether it is right would turn on a detailed interpretation of Friedman's work over a long period.

In any case, it might be said that Friedman was either immediately or very soon taken to have been arguing for a very thorough kind of rationality. That is a point of some interest because it is so much in contrast to the attitudes of ten years earlier and yet has attracted little comment. Perhaps those most averse to it were least inclined to engage with Friedman at all. But still, it is suggestive of a substantive change of attitude amongst economists. Ten years earlier—in the world of the presumptions discussed in Sections 1.3 and 1.4—the idea of wage bargains being set to such strict principles of rationality would have seemed very strange, and being set according to actual forecasts of the future, completely incongruous. The growing acceptability of that strictly rational interpretation, later culminating in its almost hegemonic dominance, is one aspect of the development of economics between 1958 and 1968, as well as being one of the things making it hard to assess the 1960s literature on its own terms. Friedman may be part of the cause of that development, but in terms of the esteem in which various economists are held, he is surely one of the principal beneficiaries.

Meanwhile, there is another point concerning the short-run Phillips curve as an analytical tool. Before 1968 there was no such idea. It was not—*pace* the myth—that what was later called a short-run curve was treated as a long-run curve. It is that policy analysis did not make that distinction. The idea that there was a 'short-run Phillips curve' *anywhere* in conventional analysis is an illusion created by the Phillips curve myth. There was a problem with achieving price stability and full employment and there were arguments for ignoring low inflation but neither of those require the distinction of short and long run to be made. There was also interest in understanding wage bargaining, but in that area there was no interest in the idea that inflationary policy be pursued. If the research was related to inflation at all it was concerned with understanding how to prevent it. Nowhere, then, was this distinction a matter of concern. And sure enough, the idea of the 'short-run' Phillips curve makes no appearance at all until after Friedman (1968a). It is a peculiar consequence, but whereas Friedman (and Phelps) are believed to have killed off the idea of a long-run exploitable relationship, it is nearer to the truth to say they invented the idea of a short-run exploitable relationship. Since that idea is so central in so much economics, it is a notable consequence of their work.

8.6 POPPERIANISM AND THE PHILLIPS CURVE

It is perhaps interesting to return to the question of the character of economic enquiry itself—not to make any general pronouncements, but to consider how it is exemplified in this single case. As I argued, following De Marchi and others, Phillips (1958) arrived at a time when Lipsey and his colleagues were thinking of the methodology of economics in particular ways, roughly characterized as 'Popperian', or anyway, 'falsificationist', and that this gave them particular ideas about scientific conduct and scientific progress. Lipsey (1962) was, I suggested, a key response to Robbins (1932/1984). Certainly, a good case can be made that Lipsey (1960) and perhaps Lipsey (1966) took seriously the issue of subjecting the existence of the Phillips curve to a crucial test. That idea is visible in other places as well. To identify only one case amongst the investigators of the Phillips curve, much of Gordon's work on expectations formation could well be seen as coming up to this standard. Friedman (1977) did not pick up that idea by name, but his account was specifically framed as one of scientific progress by the consideration, rejection, and development of alternative hypotheses, and he did say (p. 452), following one of the more 'Popperian' thoughts from Friedman (1953/1966), that hypotheses could never be proved, but only fail to be rejected, and that confidence in them depended on their breadth of application and survival of attempts at refutation.

Quite apart from the details of the story of the Phillips curve, it is remarkable how poorly the development of thinking fits even a diluted version of this Popperian ideal. Of those three suggested determinants of wage change considered in Section 8.3—profit, the rate of change of unemployment, and union aggressiveness—none was decisively rejected. There is no clear-cut, unqualified demonstration that they should not feature in the wage-change equation. On the other hand, to expect such a thing would be to set a very high standard and it is not easy to envisage how that might realistically be achieved. But there could be lesser standards in the same spirit—a body of studies, conducted on different data sets, or with different methodologies, reaching similar conclusions. Or there might be a powerfully convincing explanation of wage change which, excluding them, strongly suggested their irrelevance. Or there might be a careful study aimed specifically at dismissing them which was able to establish and then meet standards for doing so. Or, leaving the empirical aspect of the problem aside, there might be a persuasive argument that they ought to be excluded.

It could be said that the arguments of Hines on union militancy were treated this way. That was one particular treatment of aggressiveness, so they cannot be convincing rejections of the underlying idea. Perhaps it would also be said that there was a strong appearance during the 1980s of union aggressiveness ceasing to be a material consideration. The inclusion of profit was specifically addressed, and rejected, by Lipsey and Steuer (1961). The broadly Popperian spirit of that enquiry is beyond dispute, but it did not end the matter—subsequent studies continued to find a role for profit. There are other scattered cases of those finding no role for the rate of change of unemployment. But the possibility of pointing to isolated 'refutations' of ideas does not confirm the Popperian credentials of the process. The fact that a particular equation survives statistical testing and reveals no effect of a certain variable is not a crucial test falsifying a hypothesis—it is just a statistical result. What would be required as a minimum is an account of why those particular studies are rightly treated as decisive in the face of so much work pointing in the opposite direction. In practical terms, what is much more important than occasional rejections is the fact that, in all these cases, the variable in question is later ignored—it is excluded from studies *ab initio*—far more often than its importance is tested and rejected. Certainly, in the case of unemployment change and profit, there are more studies finding them important than there are addressing the issue and finding the opposite. That would be true of 'union aggressiveness' too, given a broad view of the meaning of that expression so as not to confine the matter to Hines' particular proxy for aggressiveness.

Something very similar can be said about the various interpretations of expectations and inflation momentum that were considered in the 1970s. Gordon treated a variety of hypotheses seriously, and others treated individual ideas in that way. If the issue had actually been whether behaviour adjusts to reality, it would be reasonable to say that it was settled. But in that case, what was 'settled' was something that had not been disputed before it was subjected to econometric testing—amongst all the discussions of the expectations argument before 1968, none suggest doubt about the view that high inflation will affect wage bargains, and few question the idea that any inflation will. In any case, that was not the principal issue in dispute in the 1970s. Rather, the issue was first whether the hypothesis of changing expectations was necessary to the explanation of outcomes, and slightly later, whether it was specifically change in expectations (rather than actual price change operating by some other route) that was the causal factor, with those, like Wachter (1976b), considering alternative ways of generating momentum. Again, the idea that there was momentum other than from genuinely forward-looking behaviour was never decisively rejected. What happened is that when the problem of controlling inflation came to dominate thinking, and it was accepted that demand reduction would be necessary, the question of the source of momentum ceased to matter, and largely ceased to be investigated.

When the Phillips curve literature restarted in the 1970s, with the problem of inflation manifest, and issue about expectations and momentum to the fore, the older questions arising from the study of wage bargaining were simply ignored. The role of profit, and the rate of change of wages ceased to feature in Phillips curves, not because they had been shown to have no role, but because interest had moved on. The role of trade union militancy perhaps survived better, although largely outside the econometric Phillips curve literature. Similarly, in the mid-1970s, when it became clear that inflation had some kind of momentum and controlling it was seen as a major problem, it ceased to matter whether that momentum was attributable to expectations narrowly understood, or some other form of adaptive behaviour, and that question too ceased to be asked. Nowhere was it demonstrated that it was specifically expectations that mattered, and certainly there is no clear rejection of other hypotheses. It is simply a fact of history that attention shifted to other things and it became conventional to use the language of expectations without giving attention to the underlying processes. Not only is the general development of the literature is anything but Popperian. It is hard to see that what of any substantive was really learned by any criteria. The old ideas just lapsed away, they were abandoned, like toys left on the floor at bedtime.

8.7 THE SURVIVAL OF THE PHILLIPS CURVE

In juxtaposition to the disappearance of these unfalsified ideas we find the survival of the Phillips curve. The point here is not merely that the long-run vertical Phillips curve goes almost unchallenged. There are indeed few dissenters from that but Hughes Hallett (2000) and Karanassou, Sala, and Snower (2008) could be listed as examples. These works are both elaborations of the lubrication argument, and to that extent, not out of character with older ideas. But generally, and beyond the limits of lubrication, the idea that inflation brings no lasting benefit in lower unemployment is accepted as, naturally, one would expect.

Rather, the point is that the Phillips curve is routinely taken to be a central or the central relation in macroeconomic policy. As a reasonably, but not extravagantly, broad idea of what has been meant by 'the Phillips curve' since 1970, we might consider something like 'the relation between the level of unemployment (appropriately adjusted and measured) and the rate of change of prices (appropriately adjusted and measured)'. Then it could be said that it is not merely the Phillips curve's existence that is accepted, but that its *centrality* to macroeconomics is a routine presumption. In this guise, just as in the idea of inflation bringing no lasting benefit, it seems almost unquestioned. But here is a crucial question: Do we know that at any point in time, if demand policy causes or permits a fall in unemployment, it must thereby cause or permit the price level to rise more rapidly, to some determinate extent, than it otherwise would have? Here is another, to make a specific point as well. Do we know that the Phillips curve, rather than the rate of change of unemployment—the speed of demand expansion—is, over a wide range of employment level, the crucial constraint on policy? Where has that been shown?

Here again it is possible to find doubters—but not many. Freedman, Harcourt, and Kriesler (2004) described what they called a 'horizontal' Phillips curve. What that amounts to is that there is no Phillips curve at all, of course. That makes their adoption of the conventional terminology all the more notable—it is almost as if it cannot be said that there is no such thing, even when that is the finding. It can, though, and in a poignant development of the story it is said by Carlaw and Lipsey (2012). In a paper that described the 'evolutionary vision' of economics, contrasting it equally with 'New Classical' and 'New Keynesian', the authors concluded by rejecting the existence of a well-defined short-run, negatively sloped Phillips curve, a non-accelerating inflation rate of unemployment, a unique general equilibrium, and the neutrality of money, amongst other things. Storm and Naastepad (2012) is another exceptional case of a broad-fronted questioning of the consensus which surely deserves attention. But far more often, the existence of the Phillips curve could almost be ranked with heliocentrism as a part of the intellectual framework beyond doubt and questioning.

In this, I take it Laurence Ball and Mankiw (2002) were not too far from capturing the professional mood when they said of those denying the existence of a short-run Phillips curve,

Even Samuelson and Solow's (1960) classic discussion of the Phillips curve suggested that the short-run menu of inflation-unemployment combinations would likely shift over time. Skeptics are sometimes tempted to use the shifting Phillips curve as evidence to deny the existence of a short-run tradeoff. This is pure sophistry. It would be like observing that the United States has more consumption and investment than does India to deny that society faces a tradeoff between consumption and investment. The situation is not hard to understand and, in fact, arises frequently in economics. At any point in time, society faces a tradeoff, but the tradeoff changes over time. The next question is what factors cause the tradeoff to shift. (p. 117)

Their target was those who thought the curve vertical in the short run, but that probably underlines the point that the possibility that it might simply not exist is not even contemplated, even as sophistry. Furthermore their confidence in the existence of the Phillips curve is even more emphasized their analogy with a definitional identity which puts its unrebuttable status, in their eyes at least, in a clear light.

If we ask the source of this confidence, then it is not that the proposition has survived a battery of sincere attempts to falsify it. There are attempts to falsify it—they include Eckstein and Wilson (1962), Kuh (1967) and Hines (1968)—and they have the appearance of *succeeding*. Perry (1966) used the terminology of the Phillips curve, but his emphasis on profit calls into question whether he should not be regarded as rejecting what was called a 'Phillips curve' in the 1970s. Certainly if the role of profit, rate of change of unemployment, and union aggressiveness have been 'rejected', then so has the curve. Nor, in this case, is progress made by abandoning the falsificationist ideal—neither in the 1960s, nor the 1970s, nor later has consensus formed around an empirical Phillips curve. There is no reliable, stable—that is, estimatable—Phillips curve, resilient to the passage of time, arising as a predictable relationship of a reasonably small number of variables. Given half a century of trying—rather more than that, if we start the clock, as we should with Fisher or Tinbergen—there is no reliable Phillips curve, nor even a reliable measure of the price-stability level of unemployment. That point was made by James Galbraith (1997), but the extra years since then have made no difference beyond the elapse of time. If it is a fact that the Phillips curve—in some extended, modified, and augmented form—is sufficiently viable to hold its place at the centre of macroeconomic policy analysis, then it really should be possible to find out more about it. It is just what Robbins (1932/1984) anticipated for Blank. Indeed, if one were looking for econometric failure on a grand scale, the evident intractability of this easily understood and vital problem would surely be it.

Rather, I suppose, the source of confidence in the Phillips curve—the idea that we really do know that some such relation is of central importance in macroeconomics—is in large part an adventitious product of the same process that generated the Phillips curve myth. The truth is that, at the end of the 1960s, the Phillips curve literature was derelict. The leading papers on wage determination in the couple of years before 1968 were those that did *not* give a pre-eminent role to unemployment. For the most part the papers that were really Phillips curve papers—those giving an exclusive or leading role to unemployment—were either the simple, mechanical works, or those twilight papers which really had nothing to offer by way of serious analysis. That was no high tide of the Phillips curve, but even that was before the stagflationary outcomes of the early 1970s, usually said to have done so much damage to the old idea of the Phillips curve.

Three things can perhaps be suggested to explain the survival of the idea of the Phillips curve. One is that it has become very hard to show that it does not exist. One thing that happened in the 1970s is that introduction of the idea of 'expectations', along with any number of ways of measuring them, together with 'adjusted unemployment', with any number of ways of adjusting it, made for an explosion in the variety of Phillips curves that might be estimated—but did so without moving away from a rather basic idea of the curve as a relation between unanticipated inflation and unemployment. In this way, the inflation of the 1970s, by spurring these developments, created the epicycles of the theory that made the existence Phillips curve proof against refutation.

Meanwhile, the development of the Phillips curve myth helped to suppress any interest there might have been in older ideas about wage determination. In the light of what came to be believed about the older literature—that it was concerned with 'patching up' a relation which in fact was flawed by the failure to distinguish nominal from real variables—it is understandable if seemed that enquiring into the details would be as scientifically productive as a study of the *Literatura Runica*. That left the idea that the key relationship concerned inflation and unemployment without nearby challengers.

Thirdly, though, there is another aspect to the Phillips curve myth, the aspect which more than any other makes it appropriate to describe it as a 'myth'. In part perhaps it is a reflection of some of the same forces promoting the acceptance of central bank independence that I considered in Forder (2005). In this view the conventional story of the Phillips curve is not just a story, it is also an account of the creation of a community – a body of economists, *modern* economists, who have thrown off the false gods of the past. The 1970s saw a great war of truth against falsehood;

our society against the primitives; or reason, logic, and rationality against superstition, ad hocery, and the denial of market forces. And the result was that superstition in the form of indeterminacy, the L-shaped supply curve, and cost-push inflation gave way to the true gods of equilibrium, model consistent expectations, and zero degree homogeneity. Thus we escaped the horrors of these intellectual blunders. And furthermore, this story is told, as Friedman (1977) intended and claimed, as a demonstration of scientific credentials. Every student learns this foundation myth—and it is more or less the only piece of the history of economic thought that they do; and every teacher teaches it. It is a story of how the errors that led to policy failure have been put behind us, and how the dissent for which economists were once so notorious was ended. It is the story of how economics became the science it is today. That whole story revolves around the Phillips curve. Of course it goes unchallenged.

8.8 CONCLUSION

So this is the story of Phillips' unjustly famous curve. It was born in ridicule, was quickly rejected by others, and was thereafter more or less ignored by its originator. Perhaps as a result of the label 'Phillips curve' being applied to relations that were nothing to do with Phillips—first by Samuelson and Solow, later by Friedman—it led a ghostly life, disembodied from its real form, but seemingly ubiquitous in many other shapes. It became too the centre of a story of abject failure followed by scientific progress that everyone believed. To say that the United States emerged in revolution is a claim scarcely more ordinary than to say that macroeconomists moved from error to truth through their developing understanding of real variables in connection with the Phillips curve. Yet those mistakes certainly never happened, and most of the supposed progress needs to be seen in a wholly different light from that of the Phillips curve story.

So I would like to think that I have killed the old Phillips curve story, although I appreciate that it may be that it takes a myth to kill a myth and that history only bores the fantasist. A response to that, however, is that I hope my study of these developments is not only of historical interest. Economists should not be telling themselves that the progress of their understanding exhibits the best and most powerful aspects of the scientific approach, they also should not be telling themselves that their modern understanding was forged in professional humiliation. The great failure to understand economic behaviour which supposedly blights our history did not occur. That is the history part. But it may be, as I have also hinted, the substance of many of the ideas of the past has much more merit than has been guessed and that even the centrality of the Phillips curve in macroeconomic analysis might be challenged. What the historical record offers as an alternative to a long-run vertical Phillips curve is not an exploitable curve, but doubts about the connection of inflation and unemployment. That is a point that goes to the heart of modern scientific understanding.

NOTES

CHAPTER 1

1. Humphrey (1985) discussed the contributions of a number of notable economists who had this idea before Phillips, including Thornton (1802) and Attwood (1831–2), and others from the twentieth century. Leeson (1997b) made no mention of Humphrey and omitted Attwood but listed several others, including, in addition to those already mentioned, Martineau (1832/2004), Bellerby (1923), Fuss (1926), and Pigou (1944). Others pointed to particular levels of unemployment at which they said wages were stable. That would add Hansen (1954), the three or four more authors considered by Ascheim (1955), as well as, presumably, Ascheim himself, and Schmidt (1957), who put the magic figure nearer to 5 per cent for the United States. Leeson also mentioned 'Marxian analysis' as having a Phillips-like idea, but it was Marx (1867/2003, p. 596) himself who put it so nicely, saying, 'Taking them as a whole, the general movements of wages are exclusively regulated by the expansion and contraction of the industrial reserve army, and these again correspond to the periodic changes of the industrial cycle.' Some might also be inclined to include the unpublished paper of one R. J. Pounce referred to by Dicks-Mireaux and Dow (1959, p. 7), or the *Fackföreningsrörelsen och den fulla sysselsättningens* of 1951 cited by Meidner (1969). Then there is Lerner (1951), who put it in a different way, describing 'low full employment' and 'high full employment', with wages, and hence prices, starting to rise in the former state and doing so gradually more quickly as the latter was approached; Christ (1951), who obviously had the idea; Valavanis-Vail (1955) who has been scarcely noticed at all; and Bent Hansen and Rehn (1956) who suggested—rather cautiously—that a substantial part of wage change in Sweden might be accounted for by excess demand for labour. Based on their archival work, Goodwin and Herren (1975, p. 92) thought the idea well known in 1945; Baumol (1978) would add Cantillon (1755/1959). It was a very ordinary idea.

2. Desai's theory developed from Desai (1973), itself building on Richard Goodwin (1967). From Phillips' point of view, this was all in the future—*and* he worked it all out on a wet weekend? If that was what he had in mind he would have made some indication of it. Instead, his identification of the level of unemployment that would stabilize prices strongly gives the impression he thought what he had written was complete. There is also the point that the recollection of Lipsey (2000) is that he had no idea, and Phillips gave him no indication, that his interpretation was not correct, and yet he was working on his two 'Phillips curve' papers—Lipsey (1960) and Lipsey and Steuer (1961)—at the LSE, with Phillips as a colleague. It would also be hard to explain why Phillips did not adopt the same approach—if it

was really so innovative—when he worked out his 'Australian Phillips curve', presented in Phillips (1959/2000). Nevertheless, Desai (1984) made a further case for his point of view, and in Desai (1995, p. 347) seemed to assume that it described 'Phillips' own model'; Corry (2002) was favourably disposed to it, and Cross, Harold Hutchinson, and Yeoward (1990) seem to have seen some merit in it, but there is no basis for attributing such ideas to Phillips. Desai (2000, p. 356) seems to abandon the specifics of his approach.

3. Leeson (1998a, p. 85) said almost all of the early responses to Phillips were hostile. In that he is not far wrong. He seems to intend to provide a catalogue of what he describes as 'early doubts about the Phillips curve trade-off' but he casts the net far too wide for the work to be considered a systematic commentary on the reception of Phillips' 1958 paper. As Leeson said, many of those he quoted were writing before Phillips. But he also seems to treat any discussion of inflation and unemployment as a discussion of a tradeoff between them, and hence of the 'Phillips curve'. Indeed, sometimes a discussion of either inflation or unemployment appears to be sufficient to bring a work within his purview. For example on page 93 he quotes Haberler (1961) saying that excessive wage increases will ultimately lead to a devaluation of the dollar, and counts that, apparently, as an 'early doubt' about the 'tradeoff'. But who ever doubted that point and what has it to do with the relationship between inflation and unemployment? Others are just people who feel the need to disencumber themselves of an hostility to inflation generally; and some are drawn from even further afield: Kalachek and Westebbe (1961) are cited on pages 93–4 to the effect that international comparisons were shown to be dangerous, presumably to reinforce the impression of widespread doubt about the Phillips curve, but their study was about comparing the method of measurement of unemployment in Britain and the United States and is very far removed from any policy recommendation, certainly any one involving inflation, a tradeoff, or Phillips. Even on the basis that any 'tradeoff' is as good as another for these purposes—and we are not looking for doubts about Phillips specifically—one must wonder why Dicks-Mireaux and Dow (1959) warrant mention by Leeson (on pp. 87–8) for their 'doubt', in that they 'noted that their linear coefficient differed from that obtained by Phillips' (Dicks-Mireaux and Dow 1959, p. 170). They are just one example of 'doubters' who are in fact authors of their own Phillips-type relations. The overall effect is that Leeson provides a barrage of 'doubters'—few of them located in a reliable context—no sense of what it is that really concerned them, and an altogether misleading impression of how much attention there was not just on the Phillips curve, but more importantly on the proposition that a policy of inflation could lower unemployment. And Leeson himself denies that Phillips adopted a tradeoff view of the curve, which makes his motivation even more baffling.

4. Sumner (1984) considered the 'history and significance of the Phillips curve', dwelling on the 'loops' and clearly presuming Phillips started it all. In a vitriolic debate constituted by Chapple (1996, 1998, 1999) and Leeson (1998b and 1999) the idea that Phillips was not the key initiator of the literature seems to be unconsidered. Jossa and Musella (1998) treat Phillips (1958) as the first important contribution and for Schwarzer (2012), the presumption that Phillips was special motivates the whole argument.

5. Popper's 1963 book is perhaps more accessible than his 1959 one. Hutchinson (1938) is widely regarded as an early Popperian in economics and Blaug (1980) another. Boland (1992) critically considers the view of his approach presented by the contributors to de Marchi's book. Magee (1973) presents an integrated account

of the various strands of Popper's, and Newton-Smith (1981, ch. 3) is a recommended source on the interpretation of his methodology of science in particular.

6. Lipsey (1963, pp. 158–61) took aim directly at Robbins' argument, quoting him at length and saying that his position amounts to saying that the presumption that there are no stable relationships is so strong that it is not even worth looking for them. Lipsey (1997, n. 8) dismissed the suggestion (which originates in de Marchi, 1988b, p. 147) that he was 'itching to get into combat with Robbins and other old-line liberals' (De Marchi, 1988b, p. 147) but nevertheless agreed that proselytizing his approach to methodology was an objective in writing the textbook, and (p. xxi) said that in that book he was a 'naive falsificationist'—presumably, therefore, not a sophisticated Popperian. The general sense of Popper being seen as an important figure by Lipsey and his circle is also attested by Hendry and Mizon (2000, pp. 355–6). Lipsey (2009) also attributes his interest in Popper to the latter's work seeming to offer a means of wriggling free from Robbins' ideas.

7. Before anyone else points these things out: the serialization of *Great Expectations* (Charles Dickens, 1861) actually began in December 1860, before its publication as a book, and Harold Macmillan, said 'Let us be frank about it: most of our people have never had it so good' as reported by *The Times* on 22 July 1957. The dating of Michaux's invention of the bicycle turns out to be slightly controversial but Beeley (1992, p. 22) says he produced two velocipedes in 1861.

8. An early twenty-first-century equivalent might be that of the relationship between surprise changes in interest rates and currency values. Surely all economists appreciate the point made by Dornbusch (1976) that the interest differential and expected depreciation exactly offset each other, and many treat that as a working, simple basis for thinking about exchange rate dynamics. But equally, I suppose, that no one believes it is the full and literal truth of the matter. What would we say to some future historian telling future students that we all believed there was a 'strict relation' of this kind?

9. Indeed, the terminology of the 'L-shaped' curve is more or less a later invention. Kaldor (1957) is an exception—he used the expression 'reverse L-shaped supply function' whilst noting that it offered a simplification and that in fact there would be a zone in which increases in demand were reflected in both price and output changes (he was therefore yet another 'precursor of Phillips', if you like). Friedman (1951/1966, p. 118) described the then-popular 'full employment policy' as being based on a view which neglected price changes below full employment. The origin of that view could certainly be found in Keynes (1940), and there is something with a close resemblance in Keynes' 1936, pp. 295–6), although there is overtly a simplification. But neither of these authors uses the expression 'L-shaped' or anything like it.

The expression 'L-shaped curve' in this context probably only comes into the everyday vocabulary when Lipsey (1966) used it in the second edition of his textbook. His treatment put the idea squarely in the role of being an inferior alternative to the Phillips curve, and it is notable that it does not appear in Lipsey (1963)—the first edition, which was written when the Phillips curve was much less well known. The work of Allen (1967)—another textbook—does it better, saying (p. 147) that one view of inflation makes it due to wages which are exogenous and subject to autonomous shifts and that this is easily incorporated into the 'Keynesian framework'. That is the point: wages (and hence prices) were more or less independent of unemployment, not that they were fixed.

10. Most of this work would later be classified as 'industrial relations' rather than eco-
    nomics, and Kaufman (1993) discusses the process by which that came about. He
    also, through his 1988 work, provides a sympathetic retrospective of much of the
    work I am briefly describing, and which I have treated at more than slightly greater
    length in Forder (2013c). In addition to Richard Lester and John Dunlop, the work
    of Lloyd Reynolds and Clark Kerr formed the core of the literature.
11. Hicks' emphasis on the point that both sides to a bargain might well share a
    feeling for what is fair is an important point in the overall view. It is also plainly
    true that in some cases different people will have different ideas, and that ideas
    of fairness, in wages or anything else, can change. Making allowance for the
    possibility that modern economists' ideas of fairness are, in many cases at least,
    partly shaped around the marginal productivity theory, I doubt that anyone who
    has been involved in negotiating a wage—their own or anyone else's—is in any
    doubt that achieving what is regarded as a fair result is an essential of a satisfac-
    tory bargain. This view is reinforced by Rees (1993, p. 243)—a Chicago man by
    his PhD—who, writing late in his life, said of his textbook (first edition, 1962),
    'The neoclassical theory of wage determination, which I taught for 30 years and
    have tried to explain in my textbook...has nothing to say about fairness', but
    continued by saying that once he served in a variety of roles as director, provost,
    foundation president, and trustee he found 'in none of these roles did I find
    the theory that I had been teaching so long to be the slightest help...The one
    factor that seemed to be of overwhelming importance in all these real-world
    situations was fairness.' Rees is quoted at length on this point by Akerlof and
    Shiller (2009) who are on the side of the angels in that they are anxious to see
    the importance of fairness properly recognized in modern economics, but sadly
    they take from Rees the idea that it has been systematically neglected, saying
    that consideration of fairness 'has been continually pushed into a back chan-
    nel in economic thinking' (p. 20). Not so. Rees carefully specified *neoclassical*
    theory neglected fairness. Richard Lester and his school would not be included.
    Mainstream work on wages of the 1950s and 1960s was perfectly alive to the
    importance of fairness, even if Rees was not. (Actually Rees (1973, p. 226) does,
    just, touch on the point in relation to the question of why wages are not cut in
    recessions.)

CHAPTER 2

1. Leeson (1997b, p. 143) quotes them as follows ('...' in the original Leeson):

    > Our own view will by now have become evident. When we translate the Phillips'
    > diagram showing the American pattern of wage increases against degrees of
    > unemployment into a related diagram showing the different levels of unemploy-
    > ment that would be 'needed' for each degree of price level change...this shows
    > the menu of choice between different degrees of unemployment and price sta-
    > bility as roughly estimated from the last twenty-five years of American data.

    The impression that 'our own view' is principally about the existence of a tradeoff
    is clear. The words replaced by '...' are those quoted on pages 35–6 of this book
    about the possibilities for the years immediately ahead, and are from page 192 of
    Samuelson and Solow 1960. Leeson's continuation 'this shows...' is in fact not part
    of the text of Samuelson and Solow at all but the caption to their chart (and it
    should be 'This shows...').

Even before he gets this far, though, Leeson has said that Samuelson and Solow used the Phillips curve

> to demonstrate that an annual inflation of only 4 or 5% 'would seem to be the necessary cost of high employment and production in the years immediately ahead'. (p. 129)

The 'only' is, of course, Leeson's. Samuelson and Solow (p. 192) said 'as much as 4 or 5 per cent per year'. When precisely what is at issue is what attitude the authors took to inflation: the difference between 'only' and 'as much as' is interesting and important.

In a related paper—Leeson (1997a)—he avoided 'only' but said that Samuelson and Solow suggested 4 or 5 per cent inflation would be the cost of high employment, and then said 'Using aggregate demand to stabilize the price level, they argued, may have a "certain self-defeating aspect"' (Leeson 1997a, p. 161). That was one of the suggestions they made, but Leeson makes no acknowledgement of their balancing suggestions pointing in the opposite direction.

2. The quotation is used by Leeson (1997b) in his summary. That was the first time in that work that he referred to Solow (1979a). He gave no indication that it was Phillips' work under discussion, and moved rapidly to the remark quoted at the beginning of this chapter asserting that Samuelson and Solow believed they had discovered a stable tradeoff. Bell (1980) quoted the same passage (without the last five words) in a footnote supporting the claim, 'Phillips's study had been a "straight empirical one. But the theoretical implications for public policy and Keynesian economics were worked out in 1960 by Paul Samuelson and Robert M. Solow"' (p. 67). Exactly the same words were used by Bell (1982, p. 69) who also quoted at length from Solow (1979a) and clearly regarded it as authoritative history, although he did not quote the passage referred to in the text and used by Leeson. Bell went on to quote the 'menu of choice' caption from Samuelson and Solow's 1960 paper and to say that this meant it seemed possible to manage the economy 'even more decisively'. He gave no hint as to the sophistication of the account of Samuelson and Solow, and for that matter, no actual sources for the quotations. Breit and Ransom (1981, p. 28) quoted the passage from Bell (1980), also presenting it as an authoritative statement to the effect that the Phillips curve was taken as offering a menu of choice. Wulwick (1987, pp. 841–2) quoted from Bell, incorrectly giving Solow (1978) as the original. She did briefly note that there were qualifications and doubts expressed by the authors but nevertheless strongly implied that their paper led to the existence of a stable curve being accepted. Rather later, Thomas Hall (2003, p. 25) quoted the passage without the last five words, citing Leeson. He interpolated '[of inflation and unemployment]' after 'diagrams'. Had he realised it was Phillips' diagrams he would presumably have said '[of wage change and unemployment]', so he must have formed this false impression from Leeson. He went on to say 'The critical misinterpretation that Samuelson, Solow, and many others made about the Phillips curve was that it presented a stable, exploitable tradeoff between inflation and unemployment.'

Thomas Hall and William Hart's 2012 article is ostensibly a paper about the consequences of Samuelson and Solow hand-drawing their curve rather than estimating it, but the authors lean very heavily on Leeson, whose work they obviously admire. They too quote from Solow (1979a), although they say they are drawing their information from Leeson (1997b) whilst adding (incorrectly) that Leeson said the quotation comes from an interview by Samuelson and Solow from the mid-1960s. Their ostensible point is that Samuelson and Solow's hand-drawn curve looks nothing like a properly estimated one using their data. In Forder (2014), I argue that amongst other things, Hall and Hart's estimated equation is inappropriate to the question they have set themselves.

Whereas Solow originally wrote 'those diagrams', Leeson (and Hall) made it 'these diagrams', Bell 'the diagrams', and Wulwick 'the diagram', although what the significance of that is, I am not sure.

3. The fact that Samuelson made no reference to the paper in the 1960s editions of his textbook—Samuelson (1961b, 1964a, 1967)—ought to be enough in itself to call into question the view that the paper was important in shaping opinion. He made only a few, brief references (which are considered in Chapter 5.5) anywhere else.

4. The expansionist inclinations of the authors ought not to be in doubt, and in any case it should also be clear that forensic analysis of the particular paper in question is no way to go about discovering them. It was a conference presentation, not a final summation. The views of both authors would presumably have been well known. Samuelson was on record in Samuelson (1956) rather genially expressing his fears that the Republican Party would favour excessively tight money, and in Samuelson (1958) saying that the control of inflation should not be an absolute priority. Both would later be involved with the Kennedy administration and, as documented by Barber (1975), proponents of expansionary policy from an early stage. It should be remembered that in the world of the L-shaped supply curve, an expansionary policy is not an inflationary one.

5. Vanek (1962) and Morag (1962) similarly cited them as an authority for the impossibility of achieving price stability and full employment. Modigliani (1963, pp. 90–1) gave Samuelson and Solow as his example of authors who discussed the 'dilemma'. The orientation of Scitovsky and Scitovsky (1964, p. 429) is apparent from the fact that they quoted them only to show the extent of the problem. Morishima and Saito (1964) noted that Samuelson and Solow had studied the compatibility of full employment and price stability and quoted some of their results. Okun (1965c, p. xi) said 'they present us with a menu of policy choices that will not permit us to have our cake and eat it too . . . According to their analysis, the simultaneous pursuit of both full employment and price stability creates a very real dilemma.' Gilpatrick (1966, p. 204) noted they say 8 per cent unemployment would be required to keep wages from rising—something she clearly thinks a problem, but says this has been discounted in later work. Eagly (1967) regards it as the outcome of 'Phillips curve analysis' that price stability and full employment are incompatible—citing Samuelson and Solow amongst others.

6. Ackley (1961, p. 443) cited Samuelson and Solow in connection with his own discussion of cost-push, although they, along with Phillips (1958), are one of several 'see also' citations, and it is not clear exactly what point he takes from them. Hagger (1963b) referred to them in connection with the problem of distinguishing cost and demand inflation, as did Hagger (1964) and Douglas Smith (1970).

7. Pechman (1960, p. 220) said that he thought Samuelson and Solow were 'quite right in emphasizing that one of the major causes of inflation may be inflation itself'. They do say that, although one might doubt whether they really gave it much emphasis, but he is surely not drawing the conclusion that their curve is stable. Eckstein and Wilson (1962, p. 406) were denying the existence of an American Phillips curve and saw Samuelson and Solow as in accord with them, saying that they 'puzzled over the wide scatter of points' around the (purported) curve. Woods

and Ostry (1962), as well as noting that they took the view that the work done on determining whether inflation was cost-push or demand pull did not truly distinguish the hypotheses (p. 407), also cited them (p. 412) as authority for the instability of the curve. Kaliski (1964, p. 6, n. 11) cited them as an authority for the claim that the US curve was unstable, as did Sheahan (1967, p. 10) for the view that more explanatory variables were needed to account for wage change. Canterbery (1968, p. 33) noted that they said the curve had moved to the right, and drew the inference that it might be moved to the left as well. Liebling and Cluff (1969) noted that Samuelson and Solow observed the instability of the curve, and Howard and Tolles (1974) cite them as showing its empirical inadequacy.

8. Laidler (2003, pp. 26–7, n. 9) said that Lerner 'gently chides' Samuelson and Solow for *not* recommending high inflation as a means to low unemployment. If that is what he was doing then it clearly supports the view that he did not think they were inflationist. The remarks Laidler has in mind are as follows:

> One can apply the economic principle of equalizing marginal cost and marginal benefit, indulging in creeping inflation as long as the value of the additional output is greater than the damage from the additional inflation involved. As adjustment is made to the inflation it has to run faster and faster to keep output in the same place. When the damage done by marginal inflation becomes greater than the benefits from the marginal output, we have reached the point where the equalization of marginal social cost with marginal social benefit calls for currency reform. (p. 217)

On the other hand, I suspect he was joking since he continued by saying 'The cycle would then repeat. As long as rising prices and low employment are the only alternatives available, the orgies of inflation and the mornings-after of currency reform and devaluation are just what is prescribed by the sober application of the rational principles of maximization of benefits' (p. 217). The whole comment, although thoughtful, is written in a light-hearted manner.

9. Reynolds (1960) doubted there was much to be learned from their graph. Burtt (1963, p. 414), in his textbook of labour economics, noted that Samuelson and Solow said that if unemployment were pushed down to 3 per cent the consequence would be inflation, and suggested that the issue involved was a matter of value judgment. However, he went on immediately to assert that the Phillips curve was not stable, and particularly to point to the benefits of wage-price 'constraints' created by the government. Perry (1964, p. 296), and Perry (1966, p. 57), described their work as 'preliminary' and drew no conclusions from it. Blackburn (1966)—who could easily be read as himself treating the curve as stable—used Samuelson and Solow as the backdrop to emphasizing the *damage* done by inflation, and cited them for their estimate of the level of unemployment required to achieve price stability—a policy goal he clearly took seriously. A case that might initially seem to point in a different direction is that of Ross (1966a, p. 625) who said that Samuelson and Solow 'paired' 3 per cent unemployment with a 4 or 5 per cent price rise. But this was in a piece introducing a conference discussion and in the context of presenting conflicting views of the Phillips relation. It is certainly not an endorsement of Samuelson and Solow's 1960 paper, and beyond the point that the problem of estimating a Phillips relation is a difficult one no conclusion is drawn. Jacoby (1967a) thought they showed price stability and 4 per cent unemployment to be more or less attainable. Bodkin et al. (1967, p. 46) report Samuelson and Solow's result, drawing attention to the weakness of

the empirical work, and say (p. 80) that their correlation is not high. Bodkin et al. are something of a special case themselves since they are much more inflationist than most, so a notable point is that they gave no special weight to Samuelson and Solow's paper, made no comment on their policy views, and clearly regarded their work as inferior to that of others. Eckstein (1968) said Samuelson and Solow's work showed the inadequacy of annual data; John Adams (1968, p. 145) said they made estimates 'analogous' to Phillips', but went no further and does not appear to have regarded Phillips as an inflationist; and Lindauer (1968) said that they were concerned with identifying appropriate anti-inflation policies. Streit (1972, p. 616) suggested they were the originators of the view that the degree of labour market imperfection determines the location of the curve.

10. Those making this point, without saying much else about the paper, include Andersen and Carlson (1972), Zarnowitz (1985, p. 538), Richter and Diener (1987), Drobny (1988, p. 39), Chang (1997, p. 5), Gruen, Pagan, and Thompson (1999, p. 227), Ferri (2000, p. 97, n. 1), Fitchenbaum (2003, p. 47), Shepherd and Driver (2003, p. 183, n. 3), and Pearce and Hoover (1995, p. 205). Hillier (1986, p. 134) made the point whilst protesting about the resultant misuse of the expression 'Phillips curve'. Chiarella and Flaschel (2000, p. 180) went a step further and a step too far by saying that Samuelson and Solow *initiated* the view of prices that made them a 'simple static markup theory' of wages or costs.

11. Henneberry and Witte (1976) said that the Phillips curve was treated as being stable and Samuelson and Solow was the only example they gave, although what they actually said about those authors was that they are an example of an 'attempt' to interpret the curve as a structural relation. Desai (1981, p. 4), citing Samuelson and Solow, said: 'The argument was made that by controlling aggregate demand and therefore the level of unemployment, a government (on behalf of society) could choose the rate of inflation it felt was desirable', and suggested that idea was widely adopted from this source. Later in the book he was nearer to being right when he said they deployed the curve as 'a tool for fashioning an anti-inflation policy' (p. 59). (Elsewhere he took a slightly different view: Desai (1984, p. 261) gave Samuelson and Solow a special place in deploying the Phillips curve as 'a policy tool in the short run' but noted some of the limitations they saw in their analysis.) Walter Adams (1982, p. 6), and in exactly the same terms, Adams and Brock (1984, p. 195), clearly implied that the tradeoff was taken to be available through the 1960s at least, which is perhaps only an exaggeration. Ronald Johnson (1983, p. 191) said that Keynesian policy was based on belief in a stable tradeoff which was believed to be exploitable, citing Samuelson and Solow and Lipsey (1965). Coles and Chen (1990, p. 347) said that they interpreted a particular kind of Phillips curve as offering a policy choice. Paul Turner (1997 p.7), discussing the Lucas critique, said 'Phillips (1958), Lipsey (1960) and Samuelson and Solow (1960) purportedly found stable relationships' and obviously thought this was all that needed to be said to reveal their error. Barsky and Kilian (2001, p. 157, n. 10) clearly indicated that the interpretation of the curve as offering a stable tradeoff owes something to Samuelson and Solow. Paloviita (2008, p. 2260) said that they 'hypothesized' a stable relation, but the implication is that they also believed they had found it.

There are other, even stranger, contributions. Spulber (1989, p. 36), unusually, said that they both treated the curve as stable and suggested reasons it might shift. His reading does not appear to be close. Schettkat (1992, p. 3) had them presenting a 'menu for politicians', although his book is full of citation mistakes of various sorts. Richter (1994, p. 600) said that they 'deduced' a stable trade-off because they neglected the classical point that equilibrium in the labour market depends on the real wage, and immediately propounded the 'lesson': 'do not neglect previous theoretical knowledge!' At least one can applaud the sentiment. Mackie (1998, p. 163, n. 21) said very clearly and quite wrongly, 'The authors complied data from the twenty-five-year period following the Depression to demonstrate the stable relationship similar to that hypothesized by Phillips'.

12. Gittings (1979) noted that Samuelson and Solow thought the curve might move, but the implication of his piece is that they share responsibility, with Phillips, for the curve being regarded as stable and exploitable. Hughes (1980, p. 20) clearly regarded them as believing in an exploitable tradeoff (although it is not clear that he disapproved). Rosenbaum and Ugrinsky (1994, p. 617), discussing policymaking, said Samuelson and Solow named the curve, found the tradeoff to be 'within acceptable boundaries', and said that inflation associated with 4 per cent unemployment 'seemed manageable'. And they said that when the Kennedy administration chose 4 per cent as an unemployment target, this 'came straight from the results of the Samuelson/Solow research on the Phillips curve' (p. 618). Biven (2002, p. 124) made the same point before concluding that Samuelson and Solow said there was an exploitable tradeoff. Bernstein (2001, p. 278, n. 21) said they brought Phillips' work to attention in the United States, although there is a clear implication (pp. 155–6) that it was treated as a tradeoff from the beginning. Bellante (1994, p. 372) saw them as presenting 'a menu of choice facing national governments'.

13. Motivating one theme of Sargent's book is the claim that governments followed the idea of Samuelson and Solow. He noted that they had 'qualifications' elsewhere in their paper, quoted some of them, and said that he should not be judged unfair to them without a reading of chapter 10 of his book. But that chapter does not mention them. What he has said about them is not unfair, it is simply wrong. In any case, Cogley and Sargent (2005b, p. 263) say policymakers were 'seduced' by Samuelson and Solow's findings.

14. Winder (1968, p. 159) noted they made short-run estimates of a tradeoff but thought the long-run consequences of various policies unpredictable. Okun (1971) quoted them for the historical interest of their estimates, which by 1971 were clearly no longer correct. Kitching (1971) picked out their suggestions that low demand might lead to permanently high unemployment and the possibility that incomes policy would be useful. Tussing (1975) and Spooner (1978) presented them simply as having observed the existence of a policy dilemma, Laidler and Parkin (1975, p. 753) list them as one amongst 12 others in their text and another 12 in a footnote as providing 'seminal' contributions to the study of wage inflation. R. A. Gordon (1975) similarly discussed their work amongst others on the American Phillips curve, expressing a good deal of scepticism and describing their work as 'impressionistic'. Olson (1975) found the main interest in Samuelson and Solow's analysis of the controversy over cost-push and demand-pull inflation. Brunner and Meltzer (1976) is something of an oddity. The authors clearly believe that the existence of a tradeoff had been accepted, but indicate that they do not know how that happened, and they note that Samuelson and Solow thought policy might move the curve. They said,

> When offering their guesses, Samuelson and Solow pointed out that the shape of the Phillips curve depends on the policies pursued and that the position of the curve depends on the response to past experience.... They were unable to

predict the direction of shift following a period of sustained anti-inflation policy, however, and offered no conclusion about the long-run effects of expansive
or contractive policies. (Brunner and Meltzer 1976, p. 5)

Quite right.

   Eckstein and Girola (1978) listed them as previous analysts of wage determination. Parsley (1980, p. 26) mentioned them in passing as having studied wage
inflation in relation to a 'possible unemployment trade-off', but it is not clear what
he has in mind by that expression. Bayer (1990) is not a publication in a mainstream economics journal, and the author makes several historical mistakes, but
on Samuelson and Solow he was quite right, saying that they made some guesses
about the possibilities in the immediate future, and noting their prescience in
remarking on the difference between the short and long run, and on the importance of structural reform. Meltzer (1998) said they thought the curve unstable, as did Perry and Tobin (2000). Laurence Ball and Mankiw (2002) said: 'Even
Samuelson and Solow's (1960) classic discussion of the Phillips curve suggested
that the short-run menu of inflation-unemployment combinations would likely
shift over time' (p. 117). Mankiw (2006 p. 33) made the same point but also said
that the later literature 'forgot' the caveats.

15. Sheahan (1972) referred to their 'formulation' of the Phillips curve in terms of
    unemployment determining wage change, and productivity change then deter-
    mining price change. Hamermesh (1972a) said that they took the view that mar-
    ket power is not a cause of inflation, whereas Jonson, Mahar, and Thompson
    (1974, p. 82) felt that they had 'placed less emphasis on the role of labour market
    conditions' in the wage equation than had Phillips. Kraft and Kraft (1974) referred
    to them only in passing to note that later authors considered more sophisticated
    hypotheses. Soldofsky and Max (1975) merely said that they observed the exist-
    ence of a policy dilemma except that they reported that Samuelson and Solow
    found that 1.5 per cent inflation would be achieved with 9 per cent unemploy-
    ment, which is not even close to being correct. Kelley and Scheewe (1975, p. 46),
    writing from some distance away from the central concerns of macroeconomics,
    noted Samuelson and Solow's warning that an environment of rising prices would
    tend to shape expectations in that direction.

16. Abraham Wagner and Sufrin (1970) mentioned Samuelson and Solow (and
    Phillips), only to dismiss them. Flory (1974) seems to make them proponents of
    using the reciprocal of unemployment as a proxy for labour market conditions.
    Blair (1974) made them an authority on statistical methodology, but not in con-
    nection with macroeconomics. McNown (1975) mentioned them just to say that
    versions of the Phillips curve—like theirs—without import prices had been dis-
    credited. King and Watson (1994) had them finding a US curve over the same sort
    of time period as Phillips. Cencini and Baranzini (1996, p. 145) said Samuelson and
    Solow 'seized on' the Phillips curve as the 'missing link in the official Keynesian
    model'. Schuker (2003, p. 85) described the paper as a 'reply' to Phillips and sug-
    gested that the issue was whether, as Phillips said, it would have been possible to
    predict unemployment in 1925–9, with Samuelson and Solow casting doubt on
    that conclusion and therefore, presumably, on the stability of the curve. (Phillips
    (1958, p. 295) actually said the rate of wage change could have been predicted).
    Young, Leeson, and Darity (2004) seem to lose their way at some point: they noted
    that Samuelson and Solow contained various warnings (p. 97); then reported Lucas
    as saying Samuelson and Solow are responsible for inflationism without demur

(p. 115); before saying that Samuelson and Solow's paper was 'seminal' and that it included a role for expectations (p. 129). Leeson (1998a, p. 93) said Samuelson and Solow 'did not "forget"' about expectations, but Samuelson made a judgment that they should be excluded from the analysis, while Leeson (2000, p. 132) actually attributed the Lucas critique to them. He does not explain how he knows about Samuelson's judgment and it is not clear what he means by 'the Lucas critique' but whatever he has in mind it is difficult to see what consistent picture might emerge from all that. Guha and Visviki (2001, p. 448) seem to believe that it was Samuelson and Solow who discovered a relation between wages and inflation. Tabb (1999, p. 162), citing Leeson (1997b), said that the menu interpretation was 'influentially endorsed' by Samuelson and Solow and made it also the 'centerpiece of Samuelson's best selling introductory text' (p. 206). Waterman (2002, p. 33) noted they saw a problem about expectations, but said that the tradeoff was 'canonized' in the sixth edition of Samuelson's textbook (Samuelson, 1964a). In fact, in Samuelson (1961b, 1964a, 1967)—the three editions of the decade—the discussion of the Phillips curve is contained in an appendix and takes up less than a page. Boianovsky and Trautwein (2006, p. 893) attributed the canonization to Samuelson and Solow themselves. For Widmaier (2003) the paper was authority for the claim that neoclassical economics denied a commonality of interests; Widmaier (2004) and Widmaier (2005) said they advocated exploiting the tradeoff; Widmaier (2007) had the existence of the Phillips curve *diminishing* the need for price control, according to Samuelson and Solow. Best (2004, p. 390, n. 31) even said that they offered governments a 'precise' tradeoff, which is surely one thing they did not do. Roa, Vazquez, and Saura (2008) found the interest in the paper to be the idea that the curve becomes asymptotic as unemployment approaches zero.

CHAPTER 3

1. McGuire and Rapping (1966) raised statistical concerns about Eckstein and Wilson's testing of their hypothesis but produced no wage equation. McGuire and Rapping (1967) commented further and dismissed Eckstein and Wilson's work with econometric argument—although Eckstein and Wilson (1967) replied. But McGuire and Rapping (1968), using presumably a more satisfactory approach, gave a certain amount of cautious support to the 'key bargain' view. They gave more emphasis to 'supply and demand' or 'traditional' supply and demand variables, as they called them (p. 1016). In McGuire and Rapping (1970) they set themselves, and felt they had met, the rather limited objective of showing that 'local labor market conditions affect local wages' (p. 267). The point was they felt that 'bargaining' ideas like those of Eckstein and Wilson had been given too much emphasis and it was important to show the effect of supply and demand as well.

2. The Guideposts were indicative wage and price controls initiated by the Kennedy administration—the sort of thing that was called an 'incomes policy' in the United Kingdom. Pierson (1968), describing her work as 'patterned after' Perry's, found that in normal circumstances strong unions raised wages faster than weak ones, but that the Guideposts counteracted this thereby reducing inflation. She also noted that profits were not significant in Perry's equation over the longer period she was considering. Throop (1969) used the ideas about the union markup from Throop (1968) to call Perry's diagnosis of the Guideposts into question. These papers were thoroughly embedded in the old literature since they proceeded by estimating the determinants of the union wage markup, arguing that when that stopped growing,

cost-push inflation would cease. Anderson (1969) and Wachter (1969), meanwhile, alleged that Perry's equation was itself unstable—Perry (1969) criticized their analysis. Vroman (1970) sought to adjudicate between Perry and Simler and Tella, but in the end, mentioning (p. 166) that he had no startling conclusions, said that both the Guideposts and labour reserves played a role. Christian (1970) followed the general line of Kuh by including productivity rather than profit in industry-level wage equations and thought that this showed both the superiority of Kuh's approach and the ineffectiveness of the Guideposts. All of these were concerned with the simple question of whether the Guideposts worked; all considered price change, and none gave much attention to the question of expectations. None even mentioned Friedman (1968a).

3. Phillip Ross (1961) investigated wage change in the 84 'Standard Metropolitan Areas' of the United States, finding (p. 279) a very weak time-series relationship for his aggregated data, but saying that the cross-sectional relationship between unemployment and wage change produced 'a veritable milky way of points' (p. 279); he thought this cast doubt on 'Phillips' hypothesis'. Albrecht (1966) made a rather more thorough analysis of 73 such areas and noted 'a substantial variance' (p. 313) in responsiveness of wages to unemployment, feeling that this called into question the likely stability of an aggregate Phillips curve. Kaun (1965) investigated the existence of Phillips curves for the nine Appalachian states. He found that in six cases the coefficients on unemployment and the change in unemployment were 'negative and are larger than their respective standard errors' (p. 131) and that in the other three, wages were responsive to changes in unemployment. Those three cases did not disturb him, and as, unlike Albrecht, he was unruffled by the variability of results, he seemed to treat his work as confirming Phillips.

4. Ackley (1961, p. 444) presented a regression of wage change on unemployment and price change for the United States in the period 1946–58 in a footnote (others would have made a paper out of it). He concluded 'It is clear' that 'neither unemployment nor the change in the cost-of-living was the primary cause of wage rate changes during the period'. So he estimated a 'Phillips curve' to assert that it did *not* explain the data. Bowen and Berry (1963) also estimated simple Phillips curves for Britain and the United States, with just unemployment and the change in unemployment (p. 131) used to explain wage change; the omission of any other variables from their econometrics is mysterious in the light of Bowen's other work, but there it is. The orientation of Eagly (1965) is also slightly hard to understand. Like Behman he suggested that quit rates forecast wage change rather well, but instead of regarding that as offering an alternative to the Phillips curve, he seemed to take that as an established truth and—perhaps more modestly than others would have—merely said that he had discovered an 'intervening mechanism' (Eagly 1965, p. 48) in the Phillips analysis. He was also treating quit rates as more or less a measure of market power, whereas Behman had them more or less standing for excess demand. Morishima and Saito (1964) had a wage equation as part of a test of propositions about the Keynesian multiplier relating to the period before 1952—they made no reference to Phillips. Schultze and Tryon (1965) was a discussion of the wage equation in the Brookings–SSRC macroeconometric model. The authors themselves expressed doubts about it because it did not incorporate prices properly.

5. Cowling and Metcalf (1965) analysed the agricultural sector in England and Wales, giving consideration to profits, union activity, and wages policy, and in Cowling

and Metcalf (1966) sought to replicate it for Scotland, where unemployment in the sector had been much higher, but did not have data for profit and union activity. Cowling and Metcalf (1967) investigated the relationship between wage change and unemployment in English regions.

6. Jefferson, Sams, and Swann (1968) applied the same general approach as Perry to a linear adaptation of the equation of Lipsey (1960) to argue that the policy of voluntary income restraint adopted by the British government was not effective in 1965. (The bulk of their paper is non-econometric and has much to say about the political economy of incomes policy.) Smith (1968) also considered British incomes policy with results that were, at best, inconclusive; and Brechling (1972) was the delayed publication of a paper presented in 1966, offering a fairly mild suggestion of the effectiveness of incomes policy in the UK and the USA, in which the author modified the approach of Klein et al. (1961) in estimating a wage equation.

7. Eagly (1964) estimated a Phillips-type relation for Sweden (with unemployment and his 'intervening' quit rates—cf. note 4). Brownlie and Hampton (1967), noting that unemployment in New Zealand had been effectively zero estimated wage change as a function of the number of vacancies, regarding the results as more or less equivalent to a Phillips curve in those circumstances. They both identified Phillips as the key reference. O'Herlihy (1966) estimated a number of equations for Ireland, very much following the lead of British authors throughout, and found a kind of Phillips curve. Cowling (1966) started with O'Herlihy's work and set out to investigate the role of profits and unionization which that author had not considered, finding that their inclusion made unemployment less clearly significant.

8. Ian Hume (1970) worked on a South African data set and estimated separate curves for what he described as 'black' and 'white' workers. He faced some data difficulties, including the fact that there was no unemployment series for those classified by the race laws as 'black'; so he used the 'white' unemployment instead, hoping that they moved together. This led to the conclusion that the 'black' Phillips curve was upward sloping, and he decided that the Phillips hypothesis applied only to 'whites'. His objective in all this was to assess the likely macroeconomic effects of raising the (very low) wages of unskilled labour. William Bailey and Sackley (1970), in a straightforward estimation of a wage equation for the United States, reported that it is quite useful but a bit unstable. Rippe (1970) restricted his attention to the American steel industry, estimating amongst other things a variety of Phillips curve for that. Smyth (1971) is in a slightly different category because his 'Phillips curve' related price change to unemployment. He used the average rates of inflation, unemployment, and so on for 11 countries through the 1950s to estimate a 'cross-country Phillips curve' (one data point per country). He was impressed by the fit, noted the sharp convexity (in fact, to look at, it could just as well be an 'L' as a Phillips curve), and went on to argue for a rejection of the idea (said to be more or less equivalent to an idea from Lipsey) that where unemployment is volatile average inflation will be high; and to reject the claim he attributed to Perry that fast productivity-growth lowers inflation. All this took three and half pages. Siebert and Zaidi (1971), taking some inspiration from Kuh (1967), found both profit and productivity important in wage determination, but, beyond that, drew no conclusions. Others may be stragglers or may be pointedly ignoring Friedman. Boelaert (1973) considered five EEC countries, with mixed results. Eatwell, Llewellyn, and Tarling (1974) found 'key bargains' in the fastest-growing sectors to be principal determinants of overall wage change.

9. Gallaway, Koshal, and Chapin (1970) estimated a relation for South Africa; Koshal and Gallaway (1970) for Belgium; Koshal and Gallaway (1971) for West Germany; and Gallaway (1971, ch. 6) for the United States. They were all of a kind, using past, present, and future unemployment to explain wage change. In Koshal and Gallaway (1970) this was explained thus: 'On economic grounds we would argue that changes in money wage rates are influenced by what unemployment rates have been, what they are, and what they are expected to be' (p. 265), and they said that there were statistical advantages. In Koshal and Gallaway (1971, n. 2) this was described as a 'detailed justification' of the approach. They were criticized over their approach and whether the result could properly be called a Phillips curve by Streit (1972). Koshal and Gallaway (1971) is a response to Hoffman (1969), so it must have been written post-Friedman, but shows no sign of considering his arguments. Koshal and Shukla (1971) considered what they described as 'the five countries of the E.E.C.' but provided estimates for Belgium, 'Germany' (i.e. West Germany), Italy, the Netherlands, all of which were members of the EEC, and Denmark, which joined in 1972. France and Luxembourg, which were members from the creation of the EEC in 1958 were excluded because—so the authors said—data on unemployment and wage change was not available.

10. Their title identifies 'the inflation unemployment trade-off' as the literature considered, but in the body of the article they label it with Phillips' name (pp. 500, 513, 514) and it is certainly the most extensive survey, although when Lipsey and Scarth (2011, p. xvii) say it was 'exhaustive', that is not a misprint, but is an exaggeration—Santomero and Seater mentioned about one third of the papers considered earlier in this section. (They were considering a longer time period and theoretical as well as empirical issues.) Nevertheless, the point about the character of the literature is clear. Of those to whom I have given any priority, the author whose work is least like that of Phillips but is not considered by them is Behman. She is clearly integrated into the literature by the attention Eckstein (1968) gave her. Santomero and Seater did consider Eckstein and Wilson, Hines, and Kuh. They also, it might be added, have a good sense of which papers were widely cited and they focus on those. Since the most Phillips-like work was, as noted, generally weaker, it is no surprise that Santomero and Seater give it proportionately *less* attention than I do. (I have put most of it in endnotes, they put it nowhere.)

11. We might start with Phillips (1958), who suggested import price changes would matter, but only when sufficiently large. Bowen and Berry (1963, p. 164) explained their omission of price change with the point that if they included it they would face a problem of simultaneity in the price and wage equations. Kaun (1965, p. 135) said unapologetically and without explanation simply that he had not included price change.

   In McGuire and Rapping (1966, 1967) there is no role for price change because they are merely commenting on Eckstein and Wilson's methodology (cf. note 12); but McGuire and Rapping (1968, 1970) did not include price change, the former giving the explanation that it (and various other things) 'are impounded in the constant term' (McGuire and Rapping 1968, p. 1018). Cowling and Metcalf (1967) is a study of English regions. They explained the exclusion of prices (p. 32) by the absence of regional data. Some of those explanations are less than entirely convincing, and some are not really explanations at all. Surely, though, if the qualifications of the authors are not sufficient reassurance, these remarks reveal they have understood that there is an issue, even if they hope to brush it aside?

12. Eckstein and Wilson (1962, p. 392) said that 'rapid' inflation would affect wage bargains. But in other circumstances—the normal ones as far as they were concerned—they did not, because they affected neither the bargaining power of unions nor the ability to pay of employers. Eckstein (1968) retreated from that position and admitted price change. Levinson (1960) was a cross-sectional study, seeking correlations between industry wage change and such things as industry profits. Price change need not play a role in that, although Levinson did consider the relation of real and nominal profit. Philip Ross (1961) did present a time series—although a very short one for a period when prices were rather stable. But his main point—'the veritable milky way' (cf. note 3)—arises from cross-sectional analysis. Scott and McKean (1964) and Smyth (1971) were estimating price-change equations so the effect of inflation on wages was not at issue. Brownlie and Hampton (1967) tested for an effect of price change and rejected it. The institutional setting of their work was one of a high degree of regulation, and they took the regulated wage as an independent variable—presumably the price effect is incorporated there. The same sort of thing is true of Ian Hume (1970) who used minimum wages as an independent variable—that would presumably pick up the effect of price change. Throop (1968, 1969) did not consider price change, but he was measuring the ratio of union to non-union wages.

13. The case of Liebling and Cluff (1969) is quite clear. They excluded prices along with everything else, except unemployment. But, as noted, they actually suggested that the relation might have shifted because of changed expectations. For them, surely, their estimated equations were tools for organizing the data, not a complete solution to anything. They expected to leave a role for intelligent commentary, and price expectations appear in that. Behman (1964) is more problematic. She certainly understood the point since she discussed (p. 266) linking wages to prices, and she did include prices in later work, but she probably should have included them in her 1964 paper. Eagly (1964, 1965) said nothing about price change, but he was also working in terms of quit rates. That leaves only Lipsey and Steuer (1961). A speculation here is this: they were concerned exclusively with rejecting the claim that wage change was better explained by profit than unemployment. The exclusion of price change from both estimations might appear, to common sense, to leave the two explanations on an equal footing so that the test could properly proceed, and with the computing resources of the time, the effort saved would be worthwhile. There is an error there, but it is a failure to appreciate the importance of the issue of omitted, not real, variables. I am straying into econometrics: the matter of Lipsey's understanding of the issue, even at that time, is closed by the point that Lipsey (1960) noted the importance of price change.

14. Kaliski (1971, p. 13) may be taking a different view of it. Interestingly, Hines (1972) rejected the Archibald argument on technical grounds; Perry (1966, pp. 22–4) actually raised the point himself, and dismissed it on the basis that since perfect competition does not prevail, supply and demand will not be equalized by the equilibrium wage. He also said that on the assumption of perfect competition, price change would be included in the wage-change equation although with a fixed elasticity of 1. Santomero and Seater, interestingly, cite none of these three works.

15. Might there be an aspect of circularity in Santomero and Seater's construction of their picture? If we start with the presumption that the authors of the Phillips curve literature did not properly understand the relation of real and nominal variables, then it is natural to wonder why they included price change in the equation. Then,

indeed, the fact that some of them give no explanation raises a pseudo-puzzle. The resolution comes simply from waking up—of course these authors knew the meaning of real values. In consequence, the fact that the authors' explanations are brief (or indeed, non-existent) is no puzzle.

16. Lipsey (1960, p. 9) gave the explanation that price rises make 'trade unions more aggressive in demanding increases and employers and arbitrators more willing to grant them'. Perry (1966, p. 25) said that price changes were 'the most obvious' factor affecting wages, notably because so many wage contracts had explicit indexing clauses and there was plenty of evidence of cost-of-living increases affecting other bargains. Hines (1968) was surely right when he said, of the wage equation, 'The reasons for the inclusion of changes in the price level are well-known' (p. 65). It is no wonder, really, that others include it more or less without comment. I suppose some of these are vague, but does that really matter?

17. Ian Hume (1970 p. 241) puts it in deflationist terms, saying, of the Phillips curve, that it had 'enjoyed considerable (if controversial) use as a means of measuring the tradeoff between unemployment and wage-price stability . . . it is supposedly possible to find the degree of deflation of demand (measured in unemployment levels) which, on a given assumption about the rate of growth of productivity, would be consistent with any particular rate of wage-caused inflation.' Although a stable curve is presumed, the emphasis is on the *deflation* of demand, not the reduction of unemployment. That is the purpose of the analysis.

   Gillion (1968) described his work as 'an attempt to establish by regression analysis the form of the relationships which determine wage-rates and average earnings' (p. 52). Later he says, 'As in previous studies, the level of unemployment is found to have a strong influence [on wages]' (p. 65). That makes it clear that the issue is how unemployment determines wages, *not* how anything determines unemployment.

18. Koshal and Gallaway (1970) went to the trouble of calculating that Belgian policymakers might choose between 2 per cent unemployment at 22.3 per cent inflation, or 10 per cent unemployment at 2.9 per cent inflation. It would have been helpful to know how these results would have been modified by giving consideration to, for example, import prices. Gallaway, Koshal, and Chapin (1970) presented a table of alternative choices—although only up to a 1.51 per cent wage increase, which might not be inflationary at all, depending on productivity growth, although they do not mention that point. The conclusions in Koot (1969) only relate to the existence of a Phillips curve, although earlier calculations suggest he thinks a tradeoff is available. Edward Phillips and Singell (1970) said 'even with annual increases in the price level of four percent, a small amount of "hard core" unemployment would still exist'. That gives some hint that they feel a choice is available.

19. Nickell and Quintini (2003) doubted the importance of the matter, but not the fact of downward rigidity; Kahn (1997) found clear evidence of it and responded to some of the doubters. Strictly speaking, all that the argument made by Tobin requires is that real wages rise sufficiently more readily than they fall—there is no requirement of any degree of resistance specifically to nominal wage cuts, but the point is redundant in the face of clear evidence that there is resistance to those.

20. Even if we limit the enquiry to those specifically tracing the point to Schultze, this would include Burtt (1963, p. 323) and Siegel (1960), which were both textbooks. Pitchford (1963) is rather more than a textbook, as perhaps is Hagger (1964, pp. 77–80), but they both contain a clear discussion of the Schultze

argument. For Scitovsky and Scitovsky (1964)—a study for the Commission on Money and Credit—it was an important part of a broad treatment of inflation. That was published after the Report of the Commission itself (CMC 1961), which mentioned the argument and was reviewed by Smithies (1961), who also remarked briefly on it without mentioning Schultze. Cooper (1961) explained the argument and further used it to explain the difficulties of the American export sector. Zebot (1961) discussed it and other theories of inflation at length. For Woods and Ostry (1962, pp. 407–8), focusing on labour markets, and Smith (1966), on inflation, it was part of a broad overall picture important to Canadian policymaking. (Smith also discussed the effect of expectations on wage bargaining on pages 27 and 33.) Smith's is a dull work, but it is such works that say the things that everyone knows. Schultze must have had wide attention from the discussion by Morgan (1966, p. 9) in his Presidential Address to Section F of the British Association; Bodkin (1966, ch. 7) discussed it; Jacoby (1967b) discussed it in relation to the United States. Bowen and Masters (1964) specifically offered a test of the demand-shift explanation of inflation, identifying Schultze as the main advocate of that view. Hancock (1966b) followed them in that point, but doubted their results. Meanwhile, Ripley (1966) presented it in analysing the Eckstein–Wilson wage-determination model; Pierson (1967, p. 41) suggested Schultze had the most widely accepted explanation of inflation. Others gave briefer accounts, clearly showing their own awareness of the argument, if not really explaining it: Bodkin et al. (1967) were one.

There were also those who, one way or another, did not take a relaxed view of the kind of inflation described by Schultze, but nevertheless noted his argument. Segal (1961) disagreed with Schultze about the cause of inflation in the 1950s; Depodwin and Selden (1963) gave him a swipe with the back of the hand, but noted that his argument was significant; and Hutt (1963) deprecated him as an inflationist, but again, with the effect of confirming his standing (Hutt was not slow to take that attitude to any but the most orthodox of course). Jacoby (1967a, p. 59) drew the lesson that less downward rigidity would be desirable. Sohmen (1961) mentioned it, although he doubted the argument on the evidence and thought market power more important. Haberler (1961) likewise noted the argument but did not think it important in the 1950s. Johnson (1963a) noted it in an essay that was reprinted at least twice. Eckstein's (1964) careful discussion of inflation included it.

That is slightly more than two dozen, and it was easy.

21. The events of 'the Coyne affair' were described in Belanger (1970) and Rymes (1994). H. Scott Gordon (1961) published a severely critical work with the transparent title 'The economists versus the Bank of Canada', which published the text of a letter from 29 economists to the Minister of Finance. It said in part that recent public statements by Coyne displayed a reasoning which 'does not appear to us to approach that level of competence which is a necessary foundation for successful central bank policy' (p. VI) and called, in only lightly veiled terms, for the dismissal of the governor.

Gordon's account of the circumstances ranged over a number of matters including the constitutional position of the Bank of Canada, the role of Parliament in monetary policy, and some hints that the representations of the Bank were deceptive about the stance of policy. But on the matter of inflation and unemployment he said (p.14) that the governor had denied that monetary policy could be effective in reducing unemployment and that he apparently felt this denial left him free to pursue concretionary policy so that growing recession was met with tight money. The Bank, he said,

> has such a deep inflation fixation that it apparently believes that pretence and subterfuge are justified in its battle against this great enemy... Even the slight possibility of future price increases is regarded by the Bank as far more serious that the clear and present problem of widespread unemployment. (p. 14)

And he continued to say that the governor had advanced a theory that inflation was a major cause of unemployment but had offered no substantiation of this.

Indeed, this raises the 'tradeoff' issue and Coyne did, for example, in the 1958 Annual Report of the Bank, deny that it existed, saying,

> The idea that readiness to create or tolerate inflation can make a useful contribution to the problem of maintaining a high and expanding level of employment and output, is in danger of becoming the great economic fallacy of the day.

That might seem to be a denial of the existence of a Phillips-type tradeoff, but the immediately preceding remarks show it is something else. They were,

> Perhaps the greatest obstacle to the proper use of monetary policy is the spread of the theory that democracies cannot have both high employment and stable prices, that they must inevitably choose between unemployment and inflation, that high employment can only be achieved by the acceptance or even the deliberate creation of some degree of inflation. I am certain that these views are fundamentally wrong. (p. 9)

Coyne, then, was denying the existence of a problem. His point was that an exclusive concentration on price stability had no consequences for employment.

CHAPTER 4

1. Okun (1975) noted that Fellner (1959) had stated its essential elements; Hillier (1986, p. 146) observed that it is in Hicks (1967) but drew no conclusion. Gordon (1976a, p. 193) briefly noted that Johnson (1963a) suggested the curve might shift if a policymaker tried to pick a point on it, but on p. 190 of the same paper Gordon clearly regards Johnson's understanding as basically deficient, and seems to feel it was not until Lucas (1972b) that the point was properly made. Sumner (1984, p. 195) quoted Robertson (1955/1966) stating the argument and said that such warnings 'fell on deaf ears'; Young, Leeson, and Darity (2004) point to half a dozen sources they say contain the argument but show no interest in the point, whereas Leeson (1996b), reporting the same sources in almost the same words, says that they 'made little impression at the time' (p. 250). Howitt (2007) is one who noticed a single earlier statement of the argument—Lerner (1949)—in his case, but remarked that Lerner's account lacked 'coherent conceptual foundations' (Howitt, 2007, p. 208). Whether the problem was in their coherence or their conceptuality was not indicated, but Howitt had to say something since the whole piece is a Phelps hagiography. None of these say any more about how they know the authors made little impact, or what they think the explanation is. In a sense, they are right. None of them made any specific impact because the point they were making was an ordinary one—something everyone knew. Beggs (2010,

p. 43) appreciated the wide understanding of the argument in Australia, with no implication it was not understood elsewhere. Tobin (1995) is most unusual in saying that the argument was well known before Friedman and Phelps, but he, well, made no impact at the time.

2. Laidler (1997, n. 22) said of Haberler (1961) that he lacked realisation that acceleration would occur only if policy held unemployment below the natural rate. That seems to be incorrect. Haberler lacked the terminology of the 'natural rate' but he is clear in his argument that the inflation under discussion arises as a result of policy seeking to hold down unemployment. As far as the shape of the Phillips curve is concerned, nothing else is needed. Laidler may also have been trying too hard to avoid concluding that the expectations argument was old news, of course.

3. A slow adaptation to reality would allow a period of low unemployment while inflation rises, and require a period of high unemployment to bring it down. An institutional adjustment, such as the introduction of wage indexation, might allow the former, whilst allowing an immediate, costless disinflation. The arguments based on the alleged importance of 'credibility' along the lines suggested by Barro and David Gordon (1983) or, better, by Backus and Driffill (1985), would be a different case again. In these, since the private sector is presumed to be able to respond to policy before its effects are manifested, actual cognition of the future must be involved. I drew attention to the danger of confusion over this issue in Forder (2001) without then realising the historical resonance of the point and Posen (2011) followed a similar theme.

4. He considers only the adoption of a consistent policy leading to inflation, not such things as announcements of policy changes. In that context he says that full adjustment might take 'decades'. It is reasonable to interpret him as understanding the behaviour to be in the 'tropistic' sense. That sort of period is also the one suggested by Fisher (1930) in relation to the effect of inflation on nominal interest rates, although Rutledge (1974) has raised a question as to whether Fisher was thinking of the adjustment of expectations or of the adjustment of the whole economic system to the new rate of inflation. He suggests it was the latter and that this explains what would otherwise seem to be an unreasonably long adjustment period. But the idea that the process is meant to be 'tropistic' also has that advantage. It would still be possible, of course, to hypothesize that at higher rates of inflation, adjustment would be more conscious.

5. Ashenfelter, George Johnson, and Pencavel (1972) is a deep study of the relation of union and non-union wages. They—like so many earlier authors—thought union wages much less susceptible to the vicissitudes of the market in the short term, and mentioned Friedman's argument, late in the piece, saying (p. 48) that their study was not conclusive on the question of a vertical Phillips curve. A relative of the union/non-union study is the 'leading sector' study. Howard and Tolles (1974) considered the 'key bargain' approach that had had its first econometric outing in Eckstein and Wilson (1962). Considering eight major industry groups and the period from 1950 to 1964, and emphasizing the importance of union bargaining power in these industries, they rejected Eckstein and Wilson's 'wage rounds' but emphatically confirmed (p. 551) the idea that profits were more important than unemployment, and also said that past values of both were more important than current ones. On the other hand, their results for the period after 1964 were much less clear and the role of profit in particular was less—a difference they attributed to the Guideposts. These authors specifically excluded price change from their equation because they wished to

follow and thereby test the Eckstein–Wilson model. They certainly did not consider expected price change, therefore. Their argument clearly suggested that
emphasis on unemployment as a determinant of wage change was inappropriate. Flanagan (1976) considered the determination of contractual wages and the
relation of union to non-union wages, noting (p. 646) clearly enough the idea
that they were driven by expectations but pointing out in the 'general discussion' (p. 681) that actual earnings could drift from contractual wages, so that
his results carried no definite conclusion for the issue of the natural rate. The
relation of union and non-union wages was again considered by Mitchell (1978),
who made no mention of Friedman and offered only a few comments on accelerationism. Wachter (1974) was on the same sort of lines as the 1976 paper,
in particular reaching a pessimistic conclusion about the outcome for inflation
in 1975. Wachter and Wachter (1978) offered another discussion on the same
lines, benefiting from more work having been done on the nature and sources of
wage stickiness by, in particular, Wachter and Williamson (1978).

6. Again we could start with Phillips (1958) because he suggested that there was
    no separate response of wages to prices unless price increases were greater than
    his equation would otherwise make wage increases. Hamermesh (1970) found
    such a non-linearity, although he said nothing about expectations and is perhaps
    best thought of as a straggler from the 1960s. He also suggested that the effect of
    unemployment on wages to be so slight as to be 'unimportant', so this is not really
    a Phillips curve paper. In any case his conclusions related to what could be learned
    about the control of inflation. Aspects of his work were questioned by Gustman
    (1972) and he accepted parts of that in Hamermesh (1972b).

    Gordon (1972a) used a variable coefficient on inflation and found unit elasticity
    at 7 per cent. Spitäller (1975) introduced a threshold effect so that past inflation
    rates of more than 4 per cent could have a greater effect on current inflation than
    lower ones. Even then Phillips curve did not become vertical, although he imme-
    diately (pp. 789–90) expressed hesitation about that result. Pointing in a differ-
    ent direction, de Menil (1969) found that the sensitivity of wages to price change
    was greater the higher level of unemployment, and observed that the idea ran
    counter to the direction of argument in Keynes (1936) to the effect that wages
    are more rigid at high unemployment. Whether de Menil's equations are a proper
    interpretation of the point Keynes was making is another matter. Solow (1969)
    also considered a threshold effect.

7. Flanagan (1973) adopted the expectation view *arguendo* in trying to determine
    why the American Phillips curve was less favourably placed than others. Gramlich
    (1975) worked with an accelerationist model to address the issue of the optimal
    rate of disinflation; Eckstein and Girola (1978) made no mention of Friedman but
    found (p. 331) the Phillips curve to be more or less vertical below 4 per cent unem-
    ployment. Their main interest was in showing that data from 1891 to 1977 could
    be explained in a Phillips curve framework with shocks. Packer and Park (1973)
    said there was a long-run tradeoff and seemed to suggest (p. 22) that 4 per cent
    unemployment could be maintained at 2.6 per cent inflation with an incomes
    policy, although they probably gave more emphasis to the need for long-term
    structural improvement. Spitäller (1971) considered a number of countries and cal-
    culated 'steady-state relations' between inflation and unemployment and seemed
    to suggest (p. 548 and the chart on p. 549) that inflation of 3 per cent might be
    acceptable. Spitäller (1978) was another multi-country study, this time of seven
    countries. It was an attempt to bring some sophistication to the question of how

expectations of inflation are formed, such as by basing them on changes in prices and the quantity of money. Again the most striking outcome—although they did not particularly strike the author—is that the results for the seven countries were very different. This time, however, there was not even a hint of a policy conclusion.

8. The first was Parkin and Sumner (1972), which focused on incomes policy; the second, Laidler and Purdy (1974), also concerned labour markets; the third, consisting entirely of essays by Laidler on various topics in money and inflation, was Laidler (1975). There followed Parkin and Zis (1976a), Parkin and Zis (1976b), and Parkin and Sumner (1978). They are not as immediate in their discussion of prevailing circumstances as the *Brookings Papers*, nor or such consistent quality, although they are similarly self-referential. From the beginning it was fairly clear that the principal instigators had a fairly firm view that the money supply was crucial in the determination of inflation, so they were never likely to be sympathetic to incomes policy (and in fact they were not), although they were, naturally enough, well inclined towards the vertical Phillips curve.

9. Seeking to discover a stable relation, Taylor (1972) followed up Taylor (1970)—which was on the American economy—by correcting for 'labour hoarding' in the British data. This, together with the use of earnings rather than wage rates, and a measure of union militancy, resulted in the discovery of a stable relation for the period 1953–70. (There having been a sharp fall in labour hoarding in 1966.) He noted a low coefficient on price change, calling it 'disturbing' (1972, p. 198). Taylor (1974) was an advanced-textbook presentation of his ideas. Godfrey and Taylor (1973) has some resemblance in also considering labour hoarding. They tested two interpretations of the expectations view—one derived from Friedman, the other from Phelps, and greeted (p. 213) their rejection of both by expressing a worry about their measures of expectations. In any case, their policy conclusions were entirely concerned with preventing inflation.

Mulvey and Trevithick (1970) and Mulvey and Trevithick (1974), broadly in the manner of Eckstein and Wilson (1962), applied the idea of 'key bargains' to Irish data, but with the idea that something similar might be true in Britain. The behaviour of the electricians' unions was the principal driver of inflation in Ireland. Mackay and Robert Hart (1974, 1975) stated some concerns about the quality of data that had tended to be used in Phillips curve studies, and pointed to the importance of neglected aspects of labour market behaviour, such as the idea of 'internal' labour markets, as discussed by Doeringer and Piore (1971). Johnston and Timbrell (1973) tried to revive a debate about bargaining theories and denied the existence of the Phillips curve. Kraft and Kraft (1974) were fairly frank about being interested in using an estimation of the Phillips curve just to illustrate a particular idea in numerical analysis (viz. 'the cubic spline function').

10. Hines (1964) and (1968) seem initially to have attracted little attention—an impression confirmed by the fact that Johnson (1971a) noted that he included Hines (1971) in his conference volume because his comments during the conference 'excited wide interest among the participants' (Johnson 1971a, p. ix). That paper contains Hines' principal statement of the case for incomes policy. Meanwhile, Thomas and Stoney (1970) claimed the model of Hines (1964) is dynamically unstable, proposed a correction and re-estimated it, still finding unionization significant. Godfrey (1971, pp. 112–13) questioned whether they had understood the stability question correctly, but doubted that union membership changed sufficiently to have the effect Hines proposed for it. Purdy and Zis

(1973) criticized the Hines model in detail, earning an angry response from Dogas and Hines (1975). Hines treated the growth of union membership as an appropriate proxy for militancy. His stubbornness in sticking to that may be an explanation of the vehemence of the debate, but could also be a distraction. The point that may have been lost is that union growth was merely a *proxy* for militancy. The *theory* that militancy caused wage increases was not, as some of his critics seemed to suppose, a theory that union growth caused wage increases. One would not expect it to be argued that in all circumstances and all times, union growth measured militancy, but Hines' idea was that in the circumstances he was dealing with, this was the case. Indeed, Hines (1964, pp. 229–31) said that he was explaining what happened in a particular period. It is perhaps a pity that he seems later to have become anxious to defend more general claims, and for that reason, lost the argument. Another way of measuring militancy was through strike activity, but a militant union may be in a position to make a credible strike *threat* and so achieve a wage increase. It is a strength of the Hines approach that he was circumventing that problem. It is, I think, little noticed that Slichter (1954, p. 337) remarked on the association of union growth, strike activity, and rising wages in the United States in the 1930s; Holt (1970a, n. 25) also approved Hines' approach on this basis. A few later authors such as Ellis, Pearson, and Periton (1987) once again showed some interest in the idea.

11. Parkin (1970) sought to draw further conclusions from the paper, but it was criticized in rather a didactic piece by Wallis (1971). Hines (1971) and Godfrey (1971) also included criticism of Lipsey and Parkin (1970). Godfrey's reconsideration of the issue with a technique he preferred left standing only the points that wage change depended on price change and that union pushfulness, as proxied by strike activity, was an important determinant of wages. He described the coefficient on price change as having 'implications for the "expectations hypothesis"' (p. 114) and so must have been thinking of it as a measure of expected inflation. When his coefficient turned out very small and insignificant he was led to speculate on possible econometric failings that could have this result. A shorter version of the paper—Godfrey (1972)—repeated the substance of some of these conclusions. Burrows and Hitiris (1972) rejected Lipsey and Parkin's central conclusions on the basis that the Phillips relation had changed, as workers and employers came to expect full employment. Sumner (1972) rejected their results and presented a 'threshold' treatment of the effect of price change, with an argument about Phillips' insight on the matter being greater than previously reald. Taylor (1972) also said they were wrong. All of these criticisms (except Hines (1971)) were published or republished in Parkin and Sumner (1972), along with the original Lipsey and Parkin paper and a survey of the econometric of incomes policy literature by Parkin, Sumner, and Jones (1972) in which they accepted that the Lipsey–Parkin paper was flawed. (Lipsey (1997, p. xxviii) likewise accepted this, also on the occasion of the paper being republished.)

Despite this, the Lipsey–Parkin analysis continued to be cited occasionally in arguments against incomes policy—for example by Brittan and Lilley (1977), and Parkin (1978). The former presumably did not know of the authors' retraction. In the preface to the book in which the latter was published, Shenoy (1978) described the purpose of the publisher as being to provide 'a stream of reliable commentaries on economic and social issues presented by independent authors' (p. 11), and says 'These commentaries will elucidate principles, not grind particular axes.' Meanwhile, Mitchell (1970) assessed incomes policy before devaluation by the method of including a dummy variable, finding some effect, but not enough, obviously, to avert devaluation.

12. The idea that policy should favour employment in certain regions was an old one, but the 'National Plan' of 1965 noted that a better regional balance could improve growth, and in 1967 the 'Regional Employment Premium' was created to subsidize manufacturing employment in designated regions. Armstrong and Taylor (1985) is a textbook of regional economics well attuned to the issues of post-war British policy, and Parsons (1988) is outstandingly lucid and as captivating as any book on the political economy of regional policy is ever likely to be.

13. Thirlwall (1969) conducted a test similar to that of the earlier of the Archibald papers, with inconclusive results. Thirlwall (1970) suggested that the different slopes of (presumptively linear) regional Phillips curves was a problem and suggested that ending national bargaining would pay more dividends than regional subsidies. Cowling and Metcalf (1967) had given implicit support to the view that equalization of regional unemployment would lower inflation for given overall demand. Thomas and Stoney (1971) pointed to the aggregation effect but suggested that there might also be an inter-regional wage-leadership phenomenon, whereby wages agreed in one region could be carried over into others. They did not comment either on Thirlwall's paper or the prevalence of national bargaining. The appropriateness of their mathematical modelling was disputed by Sharot (1973), and Thomas (1973) responded. Thomas (1974) tried the effect of treating different industries separately, noting the point that it was important to consider the possibility of differently shaped Phillips curves in the different sectors. He also included effects of unionization and 'threshold' effects in wage adjustment in the manner of Eckstein and Brinner (1972). By basing his analysis on the comparison by industries, he avoided the need to consider the (presumably common) inflation expectations. His results were inconclusive but he is someone who left out the analysis of expectations without in any way suggesting they were unimportant. Brechling (1973) was a study of aggregation and leadership effects between American regions, but very much drawing its inspiration from the British literature and his care and insight was appreciated by Holt (1973).

14. Sparks and Wilton (1971), under the influence of Eckstein and Wilson (1962), made a 'disaggregated' study of Canadian wage bargaining, focusing on particular industries. They gave no systematic account of expectations, and ended up remarking on the similarity of their results to those of Bodkin et al. (1967), except that they noted that because of the data they had, they could not rely on them if inflation rose. Rowley and Wilton (1973a), Rowley and Wilton (1973b), and Rowley and Wilton (1974) were all principally concerned with statistical difficulties the authors felt were widespread in the literature and, in so far as they are relevant here, it is because they doubted the previous studies, the last cited focusing particularly on Canada. They, like Ashenfelter and Pencavel (1975), called the existence even of a short-run Phillips curve into question, although Riddell (1979) challenged that view.

15. Klein (1967) was obviously describing ongoing work. Rasche and Shapiro (1968, p. 147) clearly said their treatment of wage determination needs more work; Black and Kelejian (1970) was an attempt to give it much more attention but they were not concerned with anything like proposing policy. A number of those referred to were in the volume of Eckstein (1972), devoted to the econometrics of price determination. Some of the authors were interested in the nitty-gritty of that, but many seem to have thought of it is as a surrogate for arguing about the shape of

the Phillips curve. Lucas (1972b) struck the balance very well, presenting a serious argument about the econometrics of price determination generally, but also landing a heavy blow on the question of the shape of the curve. Heien and Popkin (1972) estimated a standard Phillips curve as part of a much larger project, noting, but substantially avoiding, the question about expectations, and were in any case greatly criticized by Gordon (1972b). Nordhaus (1972a) also revealed how determined he was to reject the vertical Phillips curve, but his argument was close, and very much evidence-based. Choudry et al. (1972, p. 40) said the wage equation conforms to 'standard Phillips curve analysis', that is, that wage change depended on unemployment and price change.

There were similar, although much less extensive, discussions of such models in a few other countries. Schott (1969) was a study of Australian wage change intended as part of a project directed by W. E. Norton to construct a macroeconometric model. It is typical of the 1960s literature in that it considered profits and prices. But it drew no policy conclusions. Norton and Henderson (1973) similarly found 'Average weekly earnings are explained by prices, unemployment and profits' (p. 59); in the same volume, Deane (1973, p. 101) considered the New Zealand economy, noting the poverty of data, and deferred to another occasion the matter of whether his model was, 'despite imperfections, likely to be a useful additional tool for the forecaster and policymaker'—wages depended fundamentally on prices and employment.

16. Thomas and Stoney (1971, p. 86) assumed that anticipated price change could be represented by changes in the aggregate price level. Artis (1971, pp. 11–12): 'a term in expected price change (usually represented in empirical work by the actual change in prices)'. Others who remarked on using actual price change as a measure of expected price change included, of course, as well as Lipsey and Parkin, Heien and Popkin (1972), and Godfrey (1971).

17. Brechling (1968) was written by invitation, as described by Meltzer (1968) to 'summarize and extend the analysis underlying the Phillips curve' (p. 661). He found insufficient evidence to conclude the Phillips curve was vertical, and thought the indications were against it. That led him to conclude that there was a tradeoff, and he clearly contemplated inflationary policy. Reuber (1968) was a discussant who supported that line, calculating the terms of tradeoffs implied by other studies of the Phillips relation as well. Meiselman (1968) on the other hand, savaged it, pointing out that key parts of the analysis were spurious, and, like Cagan (1968) was much more sympathetic to Friedman's position. Cukierman (1974) used adaptive expectations in rejecting the long-run curve, but the weight of his work is on presenting a more technical view than others of the relations between price and wage change and what conditions were required for the long-run curve to be vertical. R. A. Gordon (1975) was less specific than others about just what proposition he was testing and arrived at mixed results. McCallum (1975) considered the UK and McCallum (1976) the USA, giving qualified support to the vertical Phillips curve in both cases, as did Sargent (1973) for the USA.

18. Nevile (1970), as noted, was inflationist. Parkin also cited an unpublished version of Jonson, Mahar, and Thompson (1974), along with Hancock (1966a), Pitchford (1968), and Higgins (1973). As noted, Hancock and Pitchford were clearly concerned with understanding wage drift and price change respectively and gave no indication of thinking that inflationary policy was worth discussing. The published version of Jonson, Mahar, and Thompson said that there was no tradeoff. Higgins gave a technical description of a wage-price sector of a macroeconometric model.

CHAPTER 5

1. Both consisted of one-volume reports backed up by a large number of studies, to some of which reference has already been made—Schultze (1959) was a study for the Staff Report, and Klein and Bodkin (1964) for the Commission. The Commission study papers also included the famous Friedman and Meiselman (1963) paper, controversially alleging the demand for money to be more predictable than the Keynesian multiplier. In both cases a wide range of macroeconomic issues and related microeconomic questions were addressed so that other study papers were on quite different themes. The Report of the Commission perhaps did fall into the trap of seeking too far for consensus and was greatly criticized for its failure to state a clear case by Friedman (1962), Johnson (1963b), and Dewald (1965). Nevertheless, there are hundreds of references to the Report and studies and it is perhaps a curiosity that, except for Aliber (1972), its impact has not been more closely studied by later authors. The Staff Report and associated studies gave commentators more to work with in terms of agreeing or disagreeing.

2. It seems unlikely that he failed to appreciate that an inflationary policy might provoke more consumption or a flight from sterling, particularly as, at paragraph 10,679, he noted the expectations argument in the form it has been put by Robertson, so it is best to look elsewhere for an explanation of this remark. Arguments like Hamilton's were no doubt in his mind, as perhaps was the fact that there were extensive foreign currency controls and there are limits to the practical extent that households can protect themselves from inflation by bringing purchases forward. Indeed, events after 2008 showed it is perfectly possible for real interest rates to be negative without creating a consumption boom.

3. Bronfenbrenner and Holzman (1963) mentioned it, and it was fashionable enough to sometimes be questioned, as for example by Klein and Bodkin (1964, p. 372) who remark on it although they are not persuaded that it is important, and Clague (1965), who argued against it. That last, though, is important because it is a reprint in Okun (1965b)—a book certainly intended to enhance public understanding of economic issues and which also included Ruggles (1965) arguing for the importance of the bias—the original publications coming from the early 1960s. Perry (1966, pp. 60–1) was clearly aware of it and notes it again on page 123. The argument long pre-dated the 1960s since it was made by Slichter (1946) and Clark (1948, p. 131).

4. The argument was put by Clark (1945, p. 117): 'union leaders are under pressure to produce a gain for their membership every now and then, to earn their salaries and to justify the union dues and overhead'; by Hart (1952, pp. 236–7) and Baumol (1952/1964, ch. 7) at more length; and by Schlesinger (1957), who lacked the terminology of game theory but not the insight, saying,

> The parochial structure of collective bargaining possibly strengthens the tendency toward cost-inflation. Even though it may recognize the spillover effects on the price level, any individual union must act as if its particular wage level were more important than the general wage level. (pp. 17–18)

Rather later, Blackaby (1978b) made the same point.

5. (1) Since their customers object to nominal rises employers' resistance to wage claims is increasing in its anticipated real value *and* in its nominal value.

Alternatively, (2) the lag of prices behind wages, or the temporary fall in demand for a firm's product caused by a price increase, means that for large wage increases, layoffs result. This was argued by Pratten (1972, p. 12). Or, (3) the disutility of inflation to unions is increasing so that at some level of inflation they are deterred from making it even slightly worse. (It is to be recalled that in the days of key bargains, the influence of some unions on the rate of inflation was large.) Otherwise, (4) since all dislike inflation, whilst welcoming their own wage rises, the unions are in a repeated prisoner's dilemma with each other. The ideal collusive outcome at zero inflation is unavailable because the incentive to cheat would be too great, but it can still be available at some finite rate. The latter two arguments would certainly not have appealed to labour economists of the times, but their abundance of common sense would have taken them to the same conclusion. It is probably worth recalling that, from the union point of view, the link from wages to prices could be doubted. Goodwin (1975, p. 19) reported Walter Reuther (a leading American trade unionist) wanting higher real wages and Perry (1975, pp. 419–20) says unions thought profits should fall to give higher wages without inflation. So it might not be agreed that wage increases would cause price increases.

6. The remark about the fetish is one Leeson slightly misquoted (p. 471). Citing a reprint, he has Hansen saying the 'fetish of rigid price stability is an obstacle to growth'. More strangely, in discussing Hansen's view of the bottleneck problem from Hansen (1949) Leeson said 'It is tempting to see in this analysis an optimistic forerunner of the Phillips relation that would dominate New Frontier thinking' (Leeson (1997c, p. 470). That supposed domination arises from Leeson's idea about the influence of Samuelson and Solow (1960), discussed in Chapter 2, but Leeson seems not to have understood Hansen's argument. The effect of temporary bottlenecks is a one-time rise in affected prices. That would be measured, while ongoing, as 'inflation', and might lead a policymaker to contractionary policy. But when the bottleneck is cleared, high employment is maintained without inflation. Hansen (1960) is mildly inflationist, in that case resting the point squarely on the lubrication argument.

7. In Slichter (1947) he said that 10 per cent inflation would have a profound effect and continued 'Indeed, it could be a fact of profound significance if the expected rise were only 5 per cent per year' (p. 68). But in Slichter (1951, p. 398) the rate he is contemplating permitting is 2 per cent. In Slichter (1957) he gives no figure, but the whole discussion is about 'creeping inflation' and the figure for that tended to be put at about 2 per cent or less. The discussion from Section 3.4, indicates the magnitudes in question.

8. It would take far too long to respond to everything Leeson said, but here is part of a paragraph from Leeson (1997c p. 478). He referred to Slichter (1952a) and then said

> By 1952, Slichter was clearly an opponent of stable prices. Twenty years earlier, he had outlined the reasons why inflation was undesirable as an ongoing policy ([1932] 1961, 313). In 1950, his statistical analysis of interwar US data led him to propose a small but negative correlation between increases of *employment* and average hourly earnings ([1950] 1961, 376–77; 1945c, 221; 1946a, 308; [1948a] 1961, 90; [1942] 1961, 85; [1929] 1961, 186–7). Yet by 1952, Slichter's statistical analysis of inflation-output data led him to propose a *negatively* shaped

relation between *unemployment* and inflation, for the years 1889–1950 ([1952] 1961, 96–7).

In relation to the first sentence it should be noted that Leeson (1997c) never said what rate of inflation it was that Slichter proposed accepting, and gave the impression that a higher rate was proposed, but Slichter (1952a) presented a position in which rates of inflation of the order of 2 or 3 per cent did sufficiently little harm that the attempt to eliminate them would do more. There is no case to be made that he would have thought, other things equal, that price stability was a bad thing. The second sentence (Twenty years earlier...) gives entirely the wrong impression because although Slichter (1932/1961, p. 313) said, 'there are reasons why a slow inflation is undesirable as a steady policy', he gave no indication of what they were, and the remark is juxtaposed with comments on the infeasibility of other policies—if anything, he is accepting inflation might be tolerated (just as he did twenty years later). In any case the paper is on the topic of technological unemployment and is no place to look for detailed views on inflation. As to Leeson's next claim, about a proposal of a negative correlation, it is difficult to see why six sources over a period of more than two decades are helpful in establishing what was said in 1950; but taking the 1950 source (Slichter (1950/1961), we find that Slichter considered ('proposed', in Leeson's language), the rank correlation between the rate of growth of various industries and their levels of wages. It was not a time series correlation, and the question being addressed was about how management policy affected wages—not a piece of macroeconomics at all, much less anything to do with a tradeoff. In any case, Slichter did not seem to regard it as an interesting result and drew no further conclusion, such as about inflation policy. Although the contrast between this and Slichter's attitude in Slichter (1952b/1961) is made to seem dramatic, the latter discussion was actually on a different subject since there he was discussing macroeconomics. What he said, though, was not that there was a negative relationship between unemployment and inflation, as Leeson has it, but 'Periods of expanding production have usually (but not always) been accompanied by rising prices' (p. 96). In other words, business cycle upturns saw output and prices both rise. That was well known and there is nothing special in Slichter saying it, but in any case, if it was about unemployment at all, it was, despite Leeson's emphasis, about changing unemployment.

9. Lipsey (1965) used it, and furthermore later—in Lipsey (1981, p. 557, n. 16)—criticized himself, saying he had followed the lead of Samuelson and Solow in supposing the Phillips curve stable. This seems an uncharitable judgment. In the 1965 paper, Lipsey sought to distinguish 'structural' from 'demand-deficient' unemployment by saying that the latter could be eliminated without generating unacceptable inflation, and structural unemployment was therefore that which could only be eliminated, if at all, by moving the curve. Since the point he was making was about the nature of unemployment it is understandable that he did not discuss the explanation of inflation, but obviously he was aware of the reasons, considered earlier in this chapter, that targeting zero-measured inflation would not be optimal (indeed he used the lubrication argument precisely for the purpose of explaining the existence of the Phillips curve in Lipsey (1978)). He did not make anything out of the point that different rates of inflation might be chosen, and Vanderkamp (1966a) understood the point he was making perfectly and treated it as leading to a test of the view that structural unemployment had increased.

Bodkin (1968) commented on Gordon's (1967) use of the diagram, saying it is a good way of looking at the problem, and recognizing the importance of the weight put on manpower policy. Reuber (1964) used it. His work was considered in Chapter 3 and he was inflationist, of course. Kaliski (1964)—one of the non-inflationist Canadians—also used it, but he marked 'equilibrium' at zero wage change (and unlike Reuber did not call the curve a 'Phillips curve'). Fromm and Taubman (1968) might be added. As noted on page 100, their work was mainly concerned with advancing estimation technique and said that one would want to optimize policy, so there is some implication here of thinking in terms of accepting some inflation, but policy advocacy is not their prime concern.

10. Holt and David (1966) clearly highlighted the point that they thought of the curve as posing a problem and manpower policy being a possible solution. Cohen (1969) mentioned the possibility of moving along a Phillips curve, but said manpower policy was an alternative: the paper is about estimating its effects. Holt and Huber (1969) considered the use of computers in aiding job placement and mentioned the curve right at the end to say that if placement is too effective the quit rate might rise, moving the curve to the right. Meidner (1969) set his task as 'solving the well-known dilemma between high employment and inflation' (p. 161) and thought manpower policy could 'lower the Phillips curve'. It was about problem solving, not selecting an optimal tradeoff. In Ulman (1973) the case for manpower policy was put in terms of 'the Phillips curve' throughout but, as explained particularly on pages 60–3, this was based on a Schultze-type view. Mehmet (1970) put the same thing rather more in terms of a moveable tradeoff, but still saw the point as being to achieve an 'improved the reconciliation between price stability and unemployment' (p. 573).

11. That accounts for Hansen (1962) on the Economic Report of the President; Warren Smith (1962) on the Report of the Commission on Money and Credit; Phelps (1962) on Bowen (1960c); and Solow (1964b) on Harrod (1963). Delehanty (1966) said Lebergott (1964) did not discuss the Phillips curve, which I suppose suggests that he thought he should have done, but that is all he said. Blackman (1969) and Kruger (1969) both mentioned it despite reviewing books that did not; Malkiel (1965) used it to doubt the argument under review (which does not mention it). Thurow (1968) criticized Sheahan (1967) for not considering the optimal tradeoff. Sheahan in fact discussed and rejected (pp. 9–11) the Phillips curve, preferring the idea that the level of profit and rate of change unemployment were important determinants of wage change. Weber (1967) is in this category, although his point was to complain that Mabry (1966) gave the curve 'scant attention' (actually—none at all to Phillips, although he cited Samuelson and Solow (1960) on page 286 while discussing the rate of unemployment required to achieve price stability (p. 286)). Dillard (1968) said that the argument in Stewart (1967/1972) involves tradeoffs but notes that he did not use the Phillips curve. (It is not at all clear Dillard is right about the argument.)

12. Kuska (1966) and Rose (1967) made some abstruse points, seeming not to make a great impact even in their own time; Corry and Laidler (1967) doubted whether it should have a negative slope, and in Corry and Laidler (1968) replied to a comment by Vanderkamp (1968). Their concern arose from considering the effect of high levels of demand on the quit rate; Brechling (1967) used it in what became a well-cited paper to elucidate the problem of regional unemployment.

13. Eagly (1967) treated the curve as making a case for inflation, but that might just be to motivate his paper about the desirability of index bonds. Solow and Stiglitz

(1968) made use of the idea of a Phillips curve in theorizing about distribution; their model was far removed from current policy, but in any case they said 'Our analysis is limited strictly to the short run' (p. 538). Akerlof and Stiglitz (1969) linked wages, savings, and capital intensity in the determination of equilibrium employment; Akerlof (1969) built the importance of relative wages into a criticism of the natural rate; Brechling (1969) considered a variety of arguments about the existence of the natural rate, including the possibility of unemployment hysteresis; Nagatani (1969) felt he could explain the appearance of a Phillips curve in the data whilst making wage change depend (negatively) on real wages rather than the level of employment.

14. Romanis (1967), discussing incomes policy, disputed the existence of a stable curve; Bronfenbrenner (1967) used it to describe the intended effect of the Guideposts and suggested they had worked quite well until 1965 when demand started to become excessive. Sturmthal (1968) used it to discuss incomes policy and Gray (1968) to illustrate a point about how to improve competitiveness (i.e. relating to disinflationary policy), with incomes policy being one mechanism considered; Jones (1968), disputing its existence, mentioned it to say that in relation to a particular point it makes no difference whether it exists. Mitchell (1969) said that incomes policy might 'lower unemployment at a given rate of price increase' (p. 515), but his discussion makes it clear that this presumes it helps overcome imperfections of adjustment, not that it holds prices out of equilibrium.

15. Cooper (1967) mentioned the possibility of devising new policy tools to make full employment inflation compatible, and then elucidated this for his audience with a Phillips curve. Dobell and Ho (1967) used it for the idea of what would be meant by 'overfull employment', and Blackburn (1969) noted that they avoided issues about the relationship between inflation and unemployment. Nowicki (1968), like some of the book review authors, commented on some work in terms of the Phillips curve, but it is not mentioned in work under scrutiny. Marty (1968) used it in the context of observing that expectations might shift it. Tobin (1968b) employed it to illustrate a theoretical point about growth, and immediately said he doubts its appropriateness. Branson and Klevorick (1969) mentioned it briefly to say that their model rejects a hypothesis incorporating it. Sokol and Castle (1969) and Kenen (1969) used it to label a problem. Atkinson (1969) doubted its existence and Stephen Packer (1966) just reported that there has been work on trying to discover the relationship. Heller (1969) used it as a label for a tradeoff, but without presuming the tradeoff exists.

16. Modigliani (1964) referred to the Phillips curve once (p. 241) for the purpose of doubting its existence. Lester (1968) and Minsky (1968) drew attention to periods for which it predicted poorly. Gifford (1969) thought it arose from confusion on all fronts, although as John King and Millmow (2008) and Forder (2011) have agreed, he was not free of that condition himself. Mooney (1969) simply noted that some theories depended on the unsubstantiated idea of a stable Phillips curve and treated that as a rhetorical dismissal of them. In a variation on that, Wallich (1968, 1969a) had more time for it, but started from the presumption that the object under discussion was vertical. Reynolds (1969) doubted the usefulness of 'cross-country' Phillips curves.

17. Hutton and Hartley (1968) suggested regional policy could move the curve and there is a hint (p. 419) at analysing policy on the basis that it selects an optimal point on the curve, but it is not clear how seriously they took that idea. Martin (1969) had an idea for 'circumventing' it, and therefore sees it as a problem.

18. Shonfield (1967) mentioned it as indicating a way to control inflation; Christy (1968 p. 607) thought the point of Phillips was that inflation would start at 'much less than full employment'. Masters (1967, p. 389) used the expression 'optimal point on a Phillips curve' but he was not making a policy proposal, just trying to understand the relation of underemployment to unemployment. John Adams (1968) presumed a more-or-less stable relation and proposed studying public preferences in relation to it. He reported evidence of undergraduates accepting 3 per cent inflation when asked to choose from a tradeoff relation. Eckstein (1969) offered a discussion of attitudes taken to it and gave an informal statement of an idea more or less the same as the idea of rational expectations.

19. For Villard (1968) it was merely an example of an idea often misused by students and he had nothing to say about it himself. Gifford (1968) used it as an example of the misuse of the idea of statistical correlation; Burley (1969) saw Phillips (1958) as providing an idea about textile market research. Lawrence Smith (1972) offered 'a simple Phillip's curve specification' (p. 228), giving the rate of change of rent as a function of real estate rental vacancies; and Preston (1965) said the author he was reviewing described 'A kind of Phillips-curve for the business population, with birth and death rates of firms stated as functions of the (exogenous) rate of industry growth, among other variables' (p. 1239).

20. As of April 2014 there are in the region of ten times as many appearances of 'Phillips curve' in the 1970s as the 1960s in JStor, Google Scholar, or the database searched by http://books.google.com/ngrams. Electronic searches of *The Times*, *The New York Times*, and *The Economist* confirm the general picture of a very substantial increase in interest in the curve in the 1970s.

21. Holmes and Smyth (1970), Lipsey (1974), and Holmes and Smyth (1979) debated the derivations of the curve. Sometimes it was the theory of the loops—Grossman (1974) offered a theory, and Lipsey's was again disputed by Smyth (1979).

CHAPTER 6

1. British Conservative and Labour Party manifestos are all available online (<http://www.politicsresources.net/area/uk/man.htm>) and give a perfectly consistent picture. A Conservative government was in office from 1951 to 1964. In the election of 1959, the Labour manifesto blamed them for creating unemployment to stop inflation and said that the Labour plan for expansion without inflation required the co-operation of private industry. In 1964, still in Opposition, they blamed the Conservatives for slow growth resulting from periods of contractionary policy and said that more planning was required to prevent inflation. In 1966—this time in office—their manifesto declared that they had 'launched the first serious attack on the rising cost of living' and that the alternative was a 'cycle of inflation followed by deflation and unemployment'. In 1970, still in office, Labour said that 'the biggest challenge' was 'how to expand the economy without pushing up its costs'. Meanwhile, the Conservatives in 1959 said they wished to keep the cost of living 'as steady as possible'; in 1964 they said Britain had done better than most in achieving stable prices, that an incomes policy was necessary to growth without inflation, and that a Labour government would bring inflation. In 1966 it declared the importance of breaking from the 'pattern of inflation and stagnant production which has been created'. In 1970 the Conservative manifesto pointed out that Britain had had the worst inflation for 20 years and said curbing it was the first priority. It is difficult to see anyone thought there was a stable tradeoff there, but in the 1970s, when there was certainly serious inflation it was still seen only as a

problem, and never excused on account of its unemployment-reducing powers. The nearest hint to a connection is in the Conservative manifesto of 1955 when it said they have achieved full employment 'without continual inflation'—and that is not very near.

2. Brittan (1973) was specifically an enquiry into the character of the economic consensus and presented the results of questionnaires sent to economists about their views. Yet there is no mention of the Phillips curve, nor of expectations, nor of the optimal tradeoff between inflation and unemployment, nor yet of any other sense of the optimal rate of inflation. There is a question which draws out the point that expansionary policy lowers unemployment and raises inflation, but it does not seek views on whether or when that would be a good idea. Brittan (1975) actually gave an account of 'conventional wisdom' which, in effect, described the L-shaped view, and later used the Phillips curve as device to explain what went wrong, and that it was misunderstood as offering a menu, but stopped short of saying policymakers were motivated by it. In the 1980s, though, Brittan (1981) notably said that the Phillips curve motivated inflationary policy. It is Friedman (1968a) that Brittan (2000) reported changed his mind about economic policy, in particular by convincing him of the non-existence of a Phillips curve tradeoff, to the extent that, under a pseudonym, he wrote Shepherd (1970) to criticize Brittan (1969) for failing to appreciate this point.

3. Gwartney and Stroup (1997): 'even the prestigious annual *Economic Report of the President* argued that moderate inflation would reduce the unemployment rate. At the time, most economists thought the inflation-unemployment relationship was stable' (p. 363). King and Watson (1997): 'the conventional view in the late 1960s and early 1970s was that here was a much more favorable tradeoff between inflation and unemployment... Essentially the same tradeoff was suggested by the 1969 *Economic Report of the President*' (p. 92). McCallum (1989) cited the same diagram as showing the importance of the tradeoff in policymaking in a context where the implication was that it was understood as exploitable (although he does not suggest it led to inflationary policy). John Taylor (1997) said,

> there was a long-run Phillips curve, which appeared in the *Economic Report of the President* (for example, 1969, 95) and many textbooks, and which was widely discussed by the media. This idea indicated that the cost of an overheated economy would simply be higher inflation, rather than accelerating inflation. (p. 278)

Not only does Phillips curve does not appear in other reports but nor do textbooks of that time carry such a story, and mentions at least of 'the Phillips curve' in those terms in the media are very rare in the 1960s.

4. Wulwick (1989, p. 187) said that in 1967 Chancellor 'Jim Callaghan presented a budget designed to maintain unemployment at 2¼ percent' and quoted words attributing the idea to Paish and Phillips, citing *The Spectator*, 4 April 1967, and Blyth (1975, p. 306). Blyth does not say anything like that; the quoted words appear in *The Spectator* of 13 April, but they are a poor reflection of what Callaghan said. What he said can be found in Hansard, and it was that a lower pressure of demand would keep imports low. *The Spectator* seems to have construed this as amounting to saying that low demand would lower employment which would reduce inflation (Paish's point) and that this would reduce imports. As argued above (p. 144), Callaghan's point was about the quantity effect of lower demand, not any price

effect. Leeson (1994, p. 614) cited Wulwick for the claim that Callaghan 'invoked Phillips' name' to justify budget projections, which Callaghan did not do, and Wulwick did not say he did. Bollard (2011, pp. 7–8) said that 'At its most basic' the curve was interpreted so as to give a choice between 'preserve the pound' and 'go for growth', with the former being attractive to the Conservative Party and the latter to Labour (no citations, although it has a resemblance to the position taken by Leeson (1996a)), and that 'In 1964, Ted Callahan, Chancellor of the Exchequer, mentioned the Phillips curve in support of his expansionary budget of that year.' (No citations). There were two budgets that year – the first during the Conservative government was, Reginald Maudling's. His was said by Blackaby (1978c, p. 27) to have been mildly deflationary. The second, in November, was James Callaghan's. It was dominated by the problem of correcting a large current account deficit and neither Phillips nor his curve is mentioned.

CHAPTER 7

1. Ashenfelter, George Johnson, and Pencavel (1972), for example, studied short-run wage determination in manufacturing and described what they were doing in those terms. Similarly, it appears, such as in Tobin (1975), in theoretical discussions of why there should be any kind of Phillips relation; Feige (1972), for example, considered whether then-current policy would move the short-run curve downwards. Kenen (1971) denied the existence of a Phillips curve in the course of suggesting that wages respond powerfully to the change in unemployment, and noted that this has the potential to explain the rise in inflation in the 1960s. Andersen and Carlson (1970) actually referred to the 'standard short run Phillips curve' (p. 9) (whilst considering an alternative). Sargent (1971, p. 721) used the expression 'short-run' Phillips curve precisely to comment on the econometrics of testing the expectations hypothesis, and similarly Rothschild (1971, p. 266) used 'short-run Phillips curve' in theoretical exposition.

2. Considering the credit given to him, rather than his actual influence, Snodgrass (1963), Behman (1964), and Perry (1964, 1966) gave him priority; and Bodkin (1962) had him being 'already classic' (p. 12), but in his discussion of the literature, he began with the Americans, rather than Phillips. Others gave Phillips less credit: Bowen (1960c) gave Phillips no priority and little credit; Dicks-Mireaux and Dow (1959) and Kuh (1967) paired Brown (1955) with Phillips as originating the idea; Klein and Ball (1959) pointed to Dicks-Mireaux and Dow and Phillips; Eckstein and Wilson (1962) thought Lipsey the primary mover, saying he built on Phillips' work; France (1962) listed six European studies, including Phillips, in alphabetical order, followed by three American ones. He drew attention to some statistical ideas from Phillips and Lipsey that he followed but that does not make them originators of the economic ideas under investigation. Then Hines (1964) had Brown (1955), Phillips, and Lipsey as the key sources. Lipsey (1960) treated Phillips as special, but that was because he recognized the point about the very long period considered. The Phillips critics are, of course, excepted.

3. Spitäller (1971, p. 531) said Phillips was the first to 'expound' the relation between wage change and unemployment; Yamey (2000, n. 1) clearly implied the idea was more or less new in 1958. Cowling and Metcalf (1965, p. 179), Smith (1966, p. 27), Bhatia (1967), Parkin, Sumner, and Jones (1972, p. 3), and Brittan (1975, p. 83) called him pioneering, while Zaidi (1969) both did that and, exceptionally, noted the earlier investigations as well. Rothschild (1971) called the paper 'pioneer'. I take

it that it is so often 'pioneering' with Phillips because, whilst believing it to be original, the authors recognize that his paper was not very good.

4. Watanabe (1966) and others used the expression in the 1960s (see page 58); but it was much more common for a year or two after 1970: see Minami (1970), Toyoda (1972), Minami (1973), Otani (1975). The terminology, for some reason, was more common amongst Japanese and Canadian authors than others, Kaliski (1964) and Tandon and Tandon (1978) being Canadians. It was also used by Kaun and Spiro (1970), in a major survey article by Goldstein (1972), and by Phelps (1987). Hymans (1970) mentions the 'Phillips–Lipsey approach' (p. 153), distinguishing it from that of Kuh (1967). I have used it once or twice to distinguish work putting unemployment at the centre of the explanation of wage change.

5. Nor is it easy to see what Tobin had in mind by his allusion. Perhaps he was one-upping Phelps (1970a), who said, of agents in unemployment search models, 'Isolated and apprehensive, these Pinteresque figures construct expectations of the state of the economy...and maximize relative to that imagined world' (p. 22).

6. Consider a search model where producers are monopolistically competitive, purchasers of goods do not know the exact offers for sale available to them, and the opportunity cost of time spent searching is greater when unemployment is low. Then there is less search in booms and so equilibrium prices are higher. In upturns, then, effective monopoly power increases and prices rise.

7. Brechling (1968) considered a number of theoretical issues, but not that one, although his econometrics appeared to reveal the existence of a long-run tradeoff. Hymans (1970) gave no explanation of his result, whilst seeming to think there is a stable tradeoff and contemplating inflationist policy (up to nearly 3%). Similarly, Turnovsky and Wachter (1972) rejected the expectations hypothesis, but had nothing to offer about why it might be false. Nordhaus (1972b) is perhaps in something of a different category since he was overtly testing a number of theories, but again, the plausibility of the expectations hypothesis is displayed clearly enough. When it turns out (apparently) not to be true, no explanation regarding what it is that might be wrong with it is offered. Nordhaus (1972a, pp. 19–20) is exceptional in making the point that the natural rate hypothesis requires more than that expectations be correct (in the long run or otherwise), and noted that Phelps (1970b) recognized this but that Friedman appeared not to. His point was more sophisticated than the simple one about the lubrication argument although that would be sufficient. Even as late as Cukierman (1974), the expectations hypothesis is rejected, but discussion focuses on the superiority of the author's econometrics as compared to that of Solow (1969) and Gordon (1970). Arguing over the econometrics even when the results pointed in the same direction took priority over explaining the results. Eckstein and Brinner (1972) came closer. They found that there was complete adjustment to higher rates of inflation (attributing it to 'momentum' rather than 'expectations'), so they are not clearly denying Friedman's point. For lower rates of inflation they said, first of all, (p. 3) that whereas the coefficient on price change in the wage equation was only about 0.5, there were other right-hand-side variables, the effect of which was to keep real wages in line with productivity (that was what Dicks-Mireaux and Dow (1959) had said, as noted on page 66), and on page 13 suggested that the upward bias of the price index could make the difference at those rates of inflation.

REFERENCES

The references are cited in the text on the page numbers indicated in bold.

Ackley, G. (1961) *Macroeconomic Theory*. New York: Macmillan. **78, 224, 230**

Ackley, G. (1966a) 'The contribution of guidelines', in *Guidelines, Informal Controls, and the Market Place*, ed. G. P. Schultz and R. Z. Aliber. Chicago: Chicago University Press, 67–80. **188**

Ackley, G. (1966b) 'The contribution of economists to policy formation'. *Journal of Finance* 11(2): 169–77. **125, 132**

Adams, J. (1968) 'The Phillips curve, a "consensual trap" and national income'. *Western Economic Journal* 6(2): 145–9. **226, 248**

Adams, W. (1982) 'Economic theory and economic policy'. *Review of Social Economy* 40(1): 1–12. **226**

Adams, W. and J. W. Brock (1984) 'Countervailing or coalescing power—the problem of labor management coalitions'. *Journal of Post Keynesian Economics* 6(2): 180–97. **226**

Akerlof, G. (1969) 'Relative wages and the rate of inflation'. *Quarterly Journal of Economics* 83(3): 353–74. **174, 247**

Akerlof, G. (1982) 'Labor contracts as partial gift exchange'. *Quarterly Journal of Economics* 97(November): 543–69. **77**

Akerlof, G. (2002) 'Behavioral macroeconomics and macroeconomic behavior'. *American Economic Review* 92(3): 411–33. **164**

Akerlof, G. and R. J. Shiller (2009) *Animal Spirits*. Princeton: Princeton University Press. **222**

Akerlof, G. and J. E. Stiglitz (1969) 'Capital, wages and structural unemployment'. *Economic Journal* 79(314): 269–81. **247**

Akerlof, G. and J. Yellen (1990) 'The fair wage-effort hypothesis and unemployment'. *Quarterly Journal of Economics* 105(2): 255–83. **77**

Akerlof, G., W. Dickens, and G. L. Perry (1996) 'The macroeconomics of low inflation'. *Brookings Papers on Economic Activity* 27(1): 1–59. **184**

Albrecht, W. P. (1966) 'The relationship between wage changes and unemployment in metropolitan and industrial labour markets'. *Yale Economic Essays* 6(2): 279–341. **230**

Alchian, A. A. (1970) 'Information costs, pricing, and resource unemployment', in *Microeconomic Foundations of Employment and Inflation Theory*, ed. E. S. Phelps. London: Macmillan, 27–52. **134**

Aliber, R. Z. (1972) 'The Commission on Money and Credit ten years later'. *Journal of Money, Credit and Banking* 4(4): 915–29. **243**

Allais, M. (1969) 'Growth and inflation'. *Journal of Money, Credit and Banking* 1(3): 355–426. **117**

Allen, R. G. D. (1949) *Statistics for Economists*. London: Hutchinson's University Library. **15**

Allen, R. G. D. (1967) *Macro-Economic Theory*. New York: Macmillan.　　221

Amid-Hozour, E., D. Dick, and R. Lucier (1971) 'Sultan schedule and Phillips curve: An historical note'. *Economica* 38(151): 319–20.　　180

Andersen, L. C. and K. M. Carlson (1970) 'A monetarist model for economic stabilization'. *Federal Reserve Bank of St Louis Economic Review* 52: 7–25.　　250

Andersen, L. C. and K. M. Carlson (1972) 'An econometric analysis of the relation of monetary variable to the behaviour of prices and unemployment', in *The Econometrics of Price Determination*, ed. O. Eckstein. Washington, DC: Board of Governors of the Federal Reserve System.　　226

Anderson, P. S. (1969) 'Wages and the Guideposts: Comment'. *American Economic Review* 59(3): 351–4.　　230

Ando, A. K. and F. Modigliani (1969) 'Econometric analysis of stabilization policies'. *American Economic Review* 59(2): 296–314.　　99

Archibald, G. C. (1969) 'The Phillips curve and the distribution of unemployment'. *American Economic Review* 59(May): 124–34.　　62, 96, 184

Archibald, G. C. (1970) 'The structure of excess demand for labour', in *Microeconomic Foundations of Employment and Inflation Theory*, ed. E. S. Phelps. London: Macmillan, 212–23.　　183

Archibald, G. C., R. Kemmis, and J. Perkins (1974) 'Excess demand for labour, unemployment and the Phillips curve: A theoretical and empirical study', in *Inflation and Labour Markets*, ed. D. E. W. Laidler and D. L. Purdy. Manchester: Manchester University Press, 109–63.　　62, 96

Armstrong, H. and J. Taylor (1985) *Regional Economics and Policy*. London: Harvester Wheatsheaf.　　241

Arndt, H. W. (1998) 'From state to market'. *Asian Economic Journal* 12(4): 331–41.　　167

Arrow, K. J. (1967) 'Samuelson collected'. *Journal of Political Economy* 75(5): 730–7.　　134

Artis, M. J. (1971) 'Some aspects of the present inflation and the National Institute model', in *The Current Inflation*, ed. H. G. Johnson and A. R. Nobay. London: Macmillan, 3–37.　　242

Ascheim, J. (1955) 'Price-level stability at full employment'. *Oxford Economic Papers* 7(3): 265–71.　　219

Ashenfelter, O. C. and G. E. Johnson (1969) 'Bargaining theory, trade unions, and industrial strike activity'. *American Economic Review* 59(March): 35–49.　　113

Ashenfelter, O. C. and J. H. Pencavel (1975) 'Wage changes and the frequency of wage settlements'. *Economica* 42(3): 162–70.　　241

Ashenfelter, O. C., G. E. Johnson, and J. H. Pencavel (1972) 'Trade unions and the rate of change of money wage rates in United States manufacturing industry'. *Review of Economic Studies* 39(1): 27–54.　　237, 250

Ashworth, J. (1981) 'Wages, prices and unemployment', in *The Economics of Unemployment in Britain*, ed. J. Creedy. London: Butterworths.　　136

Atkinson, A. B. (1969) 'The timescale of economic models: How long is the long run?' *Review of Economic Studies* 36(2): 137–52.　　247

Attwood, T. (1831–2) 'Evidence before the select committee on the Bank of England Charter'.　　219

Bach, G. L. (1941) 'Rearmament, recovery and monetary policy'. *American Economic Review* 31(1): 27–41.　　24

Backhouse, R. E. (1985) *A History of Modern Economic Analysis*. Oxford: Basil Blackwell.　　47

Backhouse, R. E. and J. Forder (2013) 'Rationalizing incomes policy in Britain, 1948–1979'. *History of Economic Thought and Policy* (1): 17–35. **145**

Backus, D. and J. Driffill (1985) 'Rational expectations and policy credibility following a change in regime'. *Review of Economic Studies* 52: 211–21. **237**

Bacon, R. (1973) 'The Phillips curve: Another forerunner'. *Economica* 40(159): 314–15. **181**

Bailey, S. K. (1950) *Congress Makes a Law: The Story behind the Employment Act of 1946.* New York: Columbia University Press. **141**

Bailey, W. R. and A. Sackley (1970) 'An econometric model of worker compensation changes'. *Monthly Labor Review* 93: 32–8. **231**

Balassa, B. (1964) 'The purchasing power doctrine: A reappraisal'. *Journal of Political Economy* 72: 584–96. **120**

Balassa, B. (1973) 'Monetary integration in the European Common Market', in *Europe and the Evolution of the International Monetary System*, ed. A. K. Swoboda. Leiden: A. W. Sythoff, 93–128. **137**

Ball, L. and N. G. Mankiw (2002) 'The NAIRU in theory and practice'. *Journal of Economic Perspectives* 16(4): 115–36. **214, 228**

Ball, R. J. (1962) 'The prediction of wage-rate changes in the United Kingdom economy 1957–60'. *Economic Journal* 71(284): 27–44. **57**

Balogh, T. (1970) *Labour and Inflation.* London: Fabian Society. **138**

Balogh, T. (1982) *The Irrelevance of Conventional Economics.* London: Weidenfeld & Nicolson. **138**

Barber, W. J. (1975) 'The Kennedy years: Purposeful pedagogy', in *Exhortation and Control*, ed. C. D. Goodwin. Washington, DC: Brookings Institution, 135–93. **224**

Barkin, S. (1958) Statement to Evidence before the Joint Economic Committee, in *The Relationship of Prices to Economic Stability and Growth*, ed. Joint Economic Committee. Washington DC: Government Printing Office. **113**

Barnett, W. A. (2004/2007) 'MD interview: An interview with Paul A. Samuelson'. *Macroeconomic Dynamics* 8(4): 519–42. **48**

Barro, R. J. and S. Fisher (1976) 'Recent developments in monetary theory'. *Journal of Monetary Economics* 2(2): 133–67. **117**

Barro, R. J. and D. B. Gordon (1983) 'Rules, discretion and reputation in a model of monetary policy'. *Journal of Monetary Economics* 12: 101–21. **237**

Barry, B. (1985) 'Does democracy cause inflation? Political ideas of some economists', in *The Politics of Inflation and Economic Stagnation*, ed. L. N. Lindberg and C. Maier. Washington, DC: Brookings, 280–317. **184**

Barsky, R. B. and L. Kilian (2001) 'Do we really know that oil caused the great stagflation? A monetary alternative'. *NBER Macroeconomics Annual* 16: 137–83. **226**

Barton, C. A. and A. P. Thirlwall (1971) 'Inflation and growth: The international evidence'. *Banca Nazionale del Lavoro Quarterly Review* 24(3): 263–75. **117**

Baumol, W. J. (1952/1964) *Welfare Economics and the Theory of the State.* London: Longmans. **243**

Baumol, W. J. (1978) 'On the stochastic unemployment distribution model and the long-run Phillips curve', in *Stability and Inflation*, ed. A. Bergstrom, A. Catt, M. Peston, and B. Silverstone. Chichester: John Wiley & Sons, 3–21. **219**

Bayer, R. C. (1990) 'Do we want a Christian economics? The United States bishops' pastoral letter'. *Theological Studies* 51(4): 627–49. **228**

Beckerman, W. (1972) *The Labour Government's Economic Record.* London: Duckworth. **148**

Beeley, S. (1992) *A History of Bicycles*. London: Studio Editions Ltd.   **221**

Beggs, M. (2010) 'Inflation and the making of macroeconomic policy in Australia, 1945–85'. PhD thesis, University of Sydney.   **169**

Behman, S. (1964) 'Labor mobility, increasing labor demand and money wage rate increases in United States manufacturing'. *Review of Economic Studies* 31(4): 253–66.   **53, 59, 233, 250**

Belanger, M. D. (1970) 'The Coyne affair: Analysis and evaluation'. PhD thesis, University of Ottawa.   **235**

Bell, D. (1980) 'Models and reality in economic discourse', *The Public Interest*, Special Issue, 46–80.   **223**

Bell, D. (1982) *The Social Sciences since the Second World War*. New Brunswick, NJ: Transaction.   **223**

Bell, F. W. (1967) 'An econometric forecasting model for a region'. *Journal of Regional Science* 7(2): 109–28.   **56**

Bellante, D. (1994) 'The Phillips curve', in *The Elgar Companion to Austrian Economics*, ed. P. J. Boettke. Aldershot: Elgar, 372–7.   **227**

Bellerby, J. R. (1923) 'The controlling factor in trade cycles'. *Economic Journal* 33(131): 305–31.   **219**

Bernstein, M. A. (2001) *A Perilous Progress*. Princeton: Princeton University Press.   **227**

Best, J. (2004) 'Hollowing out Keynesian norms: How the search for a technical fix undermined the Bretton Woods regime'. *Review of International Studies* 30(3): 383–404.   **229**

Best, J. and W. Widmaier (2006) 'Micro- or macro-moralities? Economic discourses and policy possibilities'. *Review of International Political Economy* 13(4): 609–31.   **47**

Beveridge, W. H. (1944) *Full Employment in a Free Society*. London: George Allen & Unwin.   **12, 24**

Bewley, T. F. (1999) *Why Wages don't Fall in a Recession*. Cambridge, MA: Harvard University Press.   **77**

Bhatia, R. J. (1961) 'Unemployment and the rate of change of money earnings in the United States, 1900–1958'. *Economica* 28(August): 286–96.   **32**

Bhatia, R. J. (1967) 'Review of Perry "Unemployment, money wage rates, and inflation"'. *American Economic Review* 57(1): 316–18.   **250**

Biven, W. C. (2002) *Jimmy Carter's Economy: Policy in the Age of Limits*. Chapel Hill: North Carolina Press.   **227**

Black, S. W. and H. H. Kelejian (1970) 'A macro model of the US labor market'. *Econometrica* 38(5): 712–41.   **241**

Blackaby, F. T. (1971) 'Incomes policies and inflation'. *National Institute Economic Review* 58(1): 34–53.   **128**

Blackaby, F. T. (1976) 'The target rate of unemployment', in *The Concept and Measurement of Involuntary Unemployment*, ed. G. D. N. Worswick. London: George Allen & Unwin, 279–304.   **12**

Blackaby, F. T. (1978a) *British Economic Policy 1960–74*. Cambridge: Cambridge University Press.   **148**

Blackaby, F. T. (1978b) 'The reform of the wage bargaining system'. *National Institute Economic Review* 85(1): 49–54.   **114, 243**

Blackaby, F. T. (1978c) 'Narrative, 1960–74', in *British Economic Policy 1960–74*, ed. F. T. Blackaby. Cambridge: Cambridge University Press, 11–76.   **250**

Blackburn, J. O. (1966) 'The war in Viet Nam and the "war" on poverty'. *Law and Contemporary Problems* 31(1): 39–44.   **225**

Blackburn, J. O. (1969) 'An optimal unemployment rate: Comment'. *Quarterly Journal of Economics* 83(3): 518–20.   **247**

Blackman Jr, J. L. (1969) 'Review of Nelson "Unemployment insurance: The American experience"'. *Journal of Economic History* 29(4): 805–6. 246

Blair, J. P. (1974) 'Relative position, utility, and compensation principle: Comment'. *American Economist* 18(2): 124. 228

Blaug, M. (1980) *The Methodology of Economics: Or, How Economists Explain*. Cambridge: Cambridge University Press. 220

Blyth, C. A. (1975) 'A. W. H. Phillips'. *Economic Record* 51(135): 303–7. 13, 249

Blyth, C. A. (1987) 'A. W. H. Phillips', in *The New Palgrave Dictionary of Economics*, ed. J. Eatwell, M. Milgate, and P. Newman. London: Macmillan, 857–8. 13

Bodkin, R. G. (1962) *The Wage-Price-Productivity Nexus*. Discussion Paper no. 147. New Haven, CT: Cowles Foundation. 55, 250

Bodkin, R. G. (1966) *The Wage-Price-Productivity Nexus*. Philadelphia: University of Pennsylvania Press. 32, 55, 73, 75, 120, 138, 198, 235

Bodkin, R. G. (1968) 'Review of Gordon, the goal of full employment'. *American Economic Review* 58(4): 1003–6. 246

Bodkin, R. G., E. P. Bond, G. L. Reuber, and T. R. Robinson (1967) *Price Stability and High Employment: The Options for Canadian Economic Policy*. Ottawa: Queen's Printer. 58, 74, 162, 225, 241

Boelaert, R. (1973) 'Unemployment-inflation trade-offs in EEC countries'. *Review of World Economics* 109(3): 418–51. 231

Boianovsky, M. and H. M. Trautwein (2006) 'Price expectations, capital accumulation and employment: Lindahl's macroeconomics from the 1920s to the 1950s'. *Cambridge Journal of Economics* 30(6): 881–900. 229

Boland, L. A. (1992) 'Understanding the Popperian legacy in economics'. *Research in the History of Economic Thought and Methodology* 7: 273–84. 220

Bollard, A. E. (2011) 'Man, money and machines: The contributions of A. W. Phillips'. *Economica* 78: 1–9. 13, 250

Bordo, M. D. and A. J. Schwartz (1983) 'The importance of stable money: Theory and evidence'. *Cato Journal* 3(1): 63–82. 46

Boskin, M., E. Dulberger, R. J. Gordon, Z. Griliches, and D. W. Jorgenson (1996) *Toward a More Accurate Measure of the Cost of Living: Final Report to the Senate Finance Committee*. http://www.ssa.gov/history/reports/boskinrpt.html 120

Bowen, W. G. (1960a) '"Cost inflation" versus "demand inflation": A useful distinction?' *Southern Economic Journal* 26(3): 199–206. 37

Bowen, W. G. (1960b) *The Wage-Price Issue: A Theoretical Analysis*. Princeton: Princeton University Press. 54, 55, 59, 71, 115, 198

Bowen, W. G. (1960c) *Wage Behavior in the Postwar Period*. Princeton: Princeton University Press. 54, 71, 72, 199, 246, 250

Bowen, W. G. and R. A. Berry (1963) 'Unemployment conditions and movements of the money wage level'. *Review of Economic Studies* 45: 163–72. 32, 230, 232

Bowen, W. G. and S. H. Masters (1964) 'Shifts in the composition of demand and the inflation problem'. *American Economic Review* 54(6): 975–84. 235

Bowers, J. K., P. Cheshire, and A. Webb (1970) 'The change in the relationship between unemployment and earnings increase: A review of some possible explanations'. *National Institute Economic Review* 54(July/August): 44–63. 95

Branson, W. H. (1975) 'Monetarist and Keynesian models of the transmission of inflation'. *American Economic Review* 65(2): 115–19. 177

Branson, W. H. and A. K. Klevorick (1969) 'Money illusion and the aggregate consumption function'. *American Economic Review* 59(5): 832–49. 247

Brechling, F. P. R. (1967) 'Trends and cycles in British regional unemployment'. *Oxford Economic Papers* 19(1): 1–21. 246

Brechling, F. P. R. (1968) 'The trade off between inflation and unemployment'. *Journal of Political Economy* 76(4/2): 712–37.   **242, 251**

Brechling, F. P. R. (1969) 'Discussion'. *American Economic Review* 59(2): 161–2.   **87, 182, 247**

Brechling, F. P. R. (1972) 'Some empirical evidence on the effectiveness of prices and incomes policies', in *Incomes Policy and Inflation*, ed. M. Parkin and M. T. Sumner. Manchester: Manchester University Press, 30–47.   **231**

Brechling, F. P. R. (1973) 'Wage inflation and the structure of regional unemployment'. *Journal of Money, Credit and Banking* 5(1): 355–79.   **241**

Breit, W. and R. L. Ransom (1981) *The Academic Scribblers*. Chicago: Dryden Press.   **128, 223**

Brinner, R. E. (1977) 'The death of the Phillips curve reconsidered'. *Quarterly Journal of Economics* 91(August): 389–418.   **94, 104**

Brittan, S. (1964) *The Treasury under the Tories*. Harmondsworth: Penguin.   **156**

Brittan, S. (1969) *Steering the Economy: The Role of the Treasury*. London: Secker & Warburg.   **156, 249**

Brittan, S. (1971) *Steering the Economy: The Role of the Treasury*. (2nd edn) Harmondsworth: Penguin.   **155, 156, 157**

Brittan, S. (1973) *Is There an Economic Consensus?* London: Macmillan.   **249**

Brittan, S. (1975) *Second Thoughts on Full Employment Policy*. Chichester: Centre for Policy Studies.   **249, 250**

Brittan, S. (1981) *How to End the Monetarist Controversy*. London: Institute of Economic Affairs.   **249**

Brittan, S. (2000) 'Samuel Brittan', in *Exemplary Economists*, ed. R. E. Backhouse and P. Middleton. Cheltenham: Edward Elgar, 270–95.   **249**

Brittan, S. and P. Lilley (1977) *The Delusion of Incomes Policy*. London: Temple Smith.   **127, 240**

Britton, A. J. C. (1991) *Macroeconomic Policy in Britain 1974–1987*. Cambridge: Cambridge University Press/National Institute of Economic and Social Research.   **148**

Bronfenbrenner, M. (1955) 'Some neglected aspects of secular inflation', in *Post-Keynesian Economics*, ed. K. K. Kurihara. London: George Allen and Unwin.   **114**

Bronfenbrenner, M. (1963) 'A sample survey of the Commission on Money and Credit research papers'. *Review of Economics and Statistics* 65(February): 115–19.   **82**

Bronfenbrenner, M. (1967) 'A Guidepost-mortem'. *Industrial and Labor Relations Review* 20(4): 637–49.   **247**

Bronfenbrenner, M. and F. D. Holzman (1963) 'Survey of inflation theory'. *American Economic Review* 53(4): 593–661.   **42, 78, 162, 243**

Brothwell, J. F. (1972) 'An alternative theoretical explanation of the Phillips curve relationship'. *Bulletin of Economic Research* 24(2): 57–64.   **181**

Brown, A. J. (1955) *The Great Inflation*. London: Royal Institute of International Affairs/ Oxford University Press.   **18, 121, 162, 250**

Brownlie, A. D. and P. Hampton (1967) 'An econometric study of wage determination in New Zealand'. *International Economic Review* 8(3): 327–34.   **213, 233**

Brunner, K. (1968) 'The role of money and monetary policy'. *Federal Reserve Bank of St Louis Economic Review* (July): 9–24.   **88**

Brunner, K. and A. H. Meltzer (1976) 'The Phillips curve', in *The Phillips Curve and Labor Markets*, ed. K. Brunner and A. H. Meltzer. Amsterdam: North-Holland, 1–18.   **159, 227**

Buchanan, J. and R. Wagner (1977) *Democracy in Deficit: The Political Legacy of Lord Keynes*. New York: Academic Press.   **46, 160**

Burk, K. and A. Cairncross (1992) *Good-bye Great Britain: The 1976 IMF Crisis*. New Haven, CT: Yale University Press.   **152**

Burley, S. P. (1969) 'New econometric techniques for textile market research'. *Textile Research Journal* 39: 648–56.   **248**

Burns, A. F. (1957) *Prosperity without Inflation*. New York: Fordham University Press.   **108**

Burrows, P. and T. Hitiris (1972) 'Estimating the impact of incomes policy', in *Incomes Policy and Inflation*, ed. M. Parkin and M. T. Sumner. Manchester: Manchester University Press, 151–62.   **240**

Burtt, E. J. (1963) *Labor Markets, Unions and Government Policies*. New York: St Martin's Press.   **225**

Cagan, P. (1968) 'Theories of mild, continuing inflation: A critique and extension', in *Inflation: Its Causes, Consequences, and Control*, ed. S. W. Rousseas Wilton. Connecticut: Calvin K. Kazanjian Economics Foundation.   **87, 242**

Cairncross, A. (1992) *The British Economy since 1945*. Oxford: Blackwell.   **169**

Callaghan, Rt. Hon. J. (1987) *Time and Chance*. Glasgow: William Collins & Sons.   **152**

Calvo, G. A. (1983) 'Staggered prices in a utility maximising framework'. *Journal of Monetary Economics* 12(3): 383–98.   **177**

Canterbery, E. R. (1968) *Economics on a New Frontier*. Belmont, CA: Wadsworth.   **225**

Cantillon, R. (1755/1959) *Essai sur la nature du commerce en général*. London: Macmillan.   **219**

Carlaw, K. I. and R. G. Lipsey (2012) 'Does history matter? Empirical analysis of evolutionary versus stationary equilibrium views of the economy'. *Journal of Evolutionary Economics* 22(4): 735–66.   **214**

Carlos Meyer, A. (1964) 'Review of Friedman's "Inflation: Causes and cures"'. *Desarrollo Economico* 3(4): 635–9.   **78**

CEA (Council of Economic Advisers) (1962) *Economic Report of the President*. Washington, DC: US Government Printing Office.   **195**

CEA (Council of Economic Advisers) (1964) *Economic Report of the President*. Washington, DC: US Government Printing Office.   **145**

CEA (Council of Economic Advisers) (1968) *Report to Congress*. Washington, DC: US Government Printing Office.   **79**

CEA (Council of Economic Advisers) (1969) *Economic Report of the President*. Washington, DC: US Government Printing Office.   **167**

CEA (Council of Economic Advisers) (1970) *Economic Report of the President*. Washington, DC: US Government Printing Office.   **146**

CEA (Council of Economic Advisers) (1971) *Economic Report of the President*. Washington, DC: US Government Printing Office.   **146**

CEA (Council of Economic Advisers) (1975) *Report to Congress*. Washington, DC: US Government Printing Office.   **158, 161**

CEA (Council of Economic Advisers) (1982) *Economic Report of the President*. Washington, DC: US Government Printing Office.   **164**

Cencini, A. and M. Baranzini (1996) *Inflation and Unemployment: Contributions to a New Macroeconomic Approach*. London: Routledge.   **228**

Challen, D. W. and A. J. Hagger (1975) 'Another look at Australia's inflation-unemployment trade-offs'. *Australian Economic Papers* 14(25): 137–53.   **105**

Chamberlin, E. H. (1951) 'The monopoly power of labor', in *The Impact of the Union*, ed. D. M. Wright. New York: Harcourt Brace & Company, 168–87.   24

Chandler, L. V. (1960) 'Discussion'. *American Economic Review* 50(2): 212–15.   43

Chang, R. (1997) 'Is low unemployment inflationary?' *Federal Reserve Bank of Atlanta Economic Review* 82(1): 137–53.   226

Chapple, S. (1996) 'Phillips and the inflation-unemployment trade-off'. *New Zealand Economic Papers* 30(2): 219–28.   13, 208, 220

Chapple, S. (1998) "Bill Phillips's big trade-off." *History of Economics Review* 28(Summer): 72–86.   220

Chapple, S. (1999) "The challenge on Phillips." *History of Economics Review*: 29 (Winter) 107–110.   220

Chiarella, C. and P. Flaschel (2000) *The Dynamics of Keynesian Monetary Growth: Macro Foundations*. Cambridge: Cambridge University Press.   226

Choudry, N. K., Y. Kotowitz, J. A. Sawyer, and J. W. L. Winder (1972) *The Trace Econometric Model of the Canadian Economy*. Toronto: Univeristy of Toronto Press.   242

Christ, C. F. (1951) 'A test of an econometric model for the United States, 1921–47', in *Conference on Business Cycles*, ed. G. Haberler. New York: National Bureau of Economic Research, 35–106.   219

Christian, J. W. (1970) 'Bargaining functions and the effectiveness of the wage-price guideposts'. *Southern Economic Journal* 37: 51–65.   230

Christy, G. (1968) 'Real and monetary factors in interest rate determination'. *Southwestern Social Science Quarterly* 48(4): 602–12.   248

Clague, E. (1965) 'Computing the consumer price index', in *The Battle against Unemployment*, ed. A. M. Okun. New York: W. W. Norton, 83–8.   243

Clark, C. (1957) 'An international comparison of "over-employment" trends in money wages'. *Oxford Economic Papers* 9(2): 178–89.   12

Clark, C. (1960) 'The present position of econometrics: Further discussion'. *Journal of the Royal Statistical Society* 123(3): 287–8.   16

Clark, C. (1962) 'Economic growth', in *Economic Growth in Australia*, ed. J. Wilkes. Sydney: Angus and Robertson 1–29.   118

Clark, J. M. (1945) 'Financing high-level employment', in *Financing American Prosperity*, ed. P. T. Homan and F. Machlup. New York: Twentieth Century Fund, 71–125.   243

Clark, J. M. (1948) *Alternative to Serfdom*. New York: A. A. Knopf.   24, 243

Clark, J. M. (1951) 'Criteria of sound wage adjustments', in *The Impact of the Union*, ed. D. M. Wright. New York: Harcourt Brace & Company, 1–33.   79

Clark, J. M., A. Smithies, N. Kaldor, P. Uri, and E. R. Walker (1949) *National and International Measures for Full Employment*. Lake Success, NY: United Nations.   24, 108

Clower, R. W. (1964) 'Monetary history and positive economics'. *Journal of Economic History* 24(3): 364–80.   133

CMC (Commission on Money and Credit) (1961) *Money and Credit: Their Influence on Jobs, Prices, and Growth*. Englewood Cliffs, NJ: Prentice Hall.   235

Cogley, T. and T. J. Sargent (2005a) 'The conquest of US inflation: Learning and robustness to model uncertainty'. *Review of Economic Dynamics* 8(2): 528–63.   49

Cogley, T. and T. J. Sargent (2005b) 'Drifts and volatilities: Monetary policies and outcomes in the post WWII US'. *Review of Economic Dynamics* 8(2): 262–302.   227

Cogley, T., R. Colacito, and T. J. Sargent (2007) 'Benefits from US monetary policy experimentation in the days of Samuelson and Solow and Lucas'. *Journal of Money, Credit and Banking* 39(1): 67–99.   49

Cohen, M. S. (1969) 'The direct effects of federal manpower programs in reducing unemployment'. *Journal of Human Resources* 4(4): 491–507.   **246**

Coles, J. L. and P. Chen (1990) 'Preferences for unemployment versus inflation'. *Applied Economics* 22(3): 347–58.   **226**

Colombo, L. and G. Weinrich (2003) 'The Phillips curve as a long-run phenomenon in a macroeconomic model with complex dynamics'. *Journal of Economic Dynamics and Control* 28(1): 1–26.   **48**

Cooper, R. N. (1961) 'The competitive position of the United States', in *The Dollar in Crisis*, ed. S. E. Harris. New York: Harcourt, Brace & World, 137–64.   **235**

Cooper, R. N. (1967) 'National economic policy in an interdependent world economy'. *Yale Law Journal* 76(7): 1273–98.   **247**

Corden, W. M. (1972) *Monetary Integration*. Princeton: International Finance Section, Princeton University.   **137**

Corden, W. M. (1976) 'Inflation and the exchange rate regime'. *Scandinavian Journal of Economics* 78(2): 370–83.   **178**

Corry, B. (1995) 'Politics and the natural rate hypothesis: A historical perspective', in *The Natural Rate of Unemployment*, ed. R. B. Cross. Cambridge: Cambridge University Press, 362–73.   **47**

Corry, B. (2002) 'Some myths about Phillips's curve', in *Money, Macroeconomics and Keynes*, ed. P. Arestis, M. Desai, and S. Dow. London: Routledge, 163–72.   **220**

Corry, B. and D. E. W. Laidler (1967) 'The Phillips relation: A theoretical explanation'. *Economica* 34: 189–97.   **246**

Corry, B. and D. E. W. Laidler (1968) 'The Phillips relation: A theoretical explanation. Reply to Vanderkamp'. *Economica* 35: 184.   **246**

Council on Prices, Productivity and Incomes (1958a) *First Report*. London: HMSO.   **14, 84**

Council on Prices, Productivity and Incomes (1958b) *Second Report*. London: HMSO.   **79**

Council on Prices, Productivity and Incomes (1961) *Fourth Report*. London: HMSO.   **118**

Cowling, K. (1966) *Determinants of Wage Inflation in Ireland*. Dublin: The Economic Research Institute.   **231**

Cowling, K. and D. Metcalf (1965) 'An analysis of the determinants of wage inflation in agriculture'. *Manchester School* 33(2): 179–204.   **230, 250**

Cowling, K. and D. Metcalf (1966) 'Determinants of wage inflation in Scottish agriculture, 1948–63'. *Manchester School* 34: 189–95.   **230–231**

Cowling, K. and D. Metcalf (1967) 'Wage-unemployment relationships: A regional analysis for the UK 1960–65'. *Bulletin of the Oxford University Institute of Economics and Statistics* 29(1): 31–9.   **231, 232, 241**

Cross, R. B., H. Hutchinson, and S. Yeoward (1990) 'The natural rate versus the hysteresis hypothesis: A century of prices and unemployment in the United States and UK'. *Weltwirtschaftliches Archiv-Review of World Economics* 126(1): 156–64.   **220**

Cukierman, A. (1974) 'A test of the "No trade-off in the long run" hypothesis'. *Econometrica* 42(6): 1069–80.   **242, 251**

Dale, E. L. J. (1957) 'Basic inquiry into a baffling inflation'. *New York Times Magazine*, 25 August: 9, 38, 42, 44, 47.   **122**

Deane, R. S. (1973) 'Macroeconometric relationships within New Zealand: A preliminary examination', in *Econometric Studies of Macro and Monetary Relations*, ed. A. A. Powell and R. A. Williams. Amsterdam: North-Holland, 85–114.   **242**

Delehanty, G. E. (1966) 'Review of Lebergott, "Men without work: The economics of unemployment"'. *Journal of Business* 39(1): 83–4.   **246**

DeLong, B. (1997) 'America's peacetime inflation: The 1970s', in *Reducing Inflation*, ed. C. D. Romer and D. H. Romer. Chicago: University of Chicago Press, 247–80.   **116**

Depodwin, H. J. and R. T. Selden (1963) 'Business pricing and inflation'. *Journal of Political Economy* 71(2): 116–27.   **235**

Desai, M. (1973) 'Growth cycles and inflation in a model of the class struggle'. *Journal of Economic Theory* 6(6): 527–45.   **219**

Desai, M. (1975) 'The Phillips curve: A revisionist interpretation'. *Economica* 42: 2–19.   **15**

Desai, M. (1981) *Testing Monetarism*. London: Pinter.   **226**

Desai, M. (1984) 'Wages, prices and unemployment', in *Econometrics and Quantitative Economics*, ed. D. Hendry and K. F. Wallis. Oxford: Blackwell, 253–73.   **220**

Desai, M. (1995) 'The natural rate of unemployment: A fundamentalist Keynesian view', in *The Natural Rate of Unemployment*, ed. R. Cross. Cambridge: Cambridge University Press, 346–61.   **220**

Desai, M. (2000) 'Meghnad Desai', in *Exemplary Economists*, ed. R. E. Backhouse and P. Middleton, 350–67.   **220**

Dewald, W. G. (1965) 'Commission on Money and Credit research studies'. *Journal of Political Economy* 73(1): 83–93.   **243**

Dickens, C. (1861) *Great Expectations*. London: Chapman & Hall.   **221**

Dicks-Mireaux, L. A. (1961) 'The interrelationship between cost and price changes, 1964–1959: A study of inflation in post-war Britain'. *Oxford Economic Papers* 13(3): 267–92.   **57**

Dicks-Mireaux, L. A. and J. C. R. Dow (1959) 'The determinants of wage inflation: United Kingdom, 1946–1956'. *Journal of the Royal Statistical Society* 122(2): 146–74.   **18, 56, 59, 60, 65, 66, 70, 148, 207, 219, 220, 250, 251**

Dillard, D. (1968) 'Review of Stewart, Keynes and after; and Slesinger, national economic policy'. *Journal of Economic History* 28(4): 740–1.   **246**

Dobell, A. R. and Y. C. Ho (1967) 'An optimal unemployment rate'. *Quarterly Journal of Economics* 81: 675–83.   **247**

Doeringer, P. B. and M. J. Piore (1971) *Internal Labor Markets and Manpower Analysis*. Lexington, MA: D. C. Heath and Company.   **239**

Dogas, D. and A. G. Hines (1975) 'Trade unions and wage inflation in the UK: A critique of Purdy and Zis'. *Applied Economics* 7(3): 195–211.   **240**

Donner, A. W. (1972) 'Labour turnover, expectations and the determination of money wage changes in US manufacturing'. *Canadian Journal of Economics* 5(1): 16–34.   **87**

Donner, A. W. and J. F. McCollum (1972) 'The Phillips curve: An historical note'. *Economica* 155(39): 323–4.   **180**

Dornbusch, R. (1976) 'Expectations and exchange rate dynamics'. *Journal of Political Economy* 84(December): 1161–76.   **221**

Dornbusch, R. and S. Fischer (1978) *Macroeconomics*. Tokyo: McGraw-Hill.   **161, 195**

Dornbusch, R. and J. A. Frenkel (1973) 'Inflation and growth: Alternative approaches'. *Journal of Money, Credit and Banking* 5(1): 141–56.   **117**

Dow, J. C. R. (1956) 'Analysis of the generation of price inflation: A study of cost and price changes in the United Kingdom, 1946–54'. *Oxford Economic Papers* 8(3): 252–301.   **15, 56, 60**

Dow, J. C. R. (1964) *The Management of the British Economy 1945–60*. Cambridge: NIESR.   **84, 148**

Downs, A. (1957) *An Economic Theory of Democracy*. New York: HarperCollins.   **136**

Draghi, M. (2013) ECB press conference, 7 November. www.ecb.europa.eu.　　**202**

Drobny, A. (1988) *Real Wages and Employment: Keynes, Monetarism, and the Labour Market*. London: Routledge.　　**226**

Duesenberry, J. (1980) 'Discussion of Perry (1980), Inflation in theory and pratice'. *Brookings Papers on Economic Activity* (1): 258.　　**93**

Dunlop, J. T. (1944) *Wage Determination under Trade Unions*. New York: Macmillan.　　**30**

Dunlop, J. T. (1947) 'A review of wage-price policy'. *Review of Economics and Statistics* 29(3): 154–60.　　**28**

Dunlop, J. T. (1948) 'Productivity and the wage structure', in *Income, Employment and Public Policy*, ed. L. A. Metzler. New York: Norton. 341–62.　　**29**

Dunlop, J. T. (1957/1966) 'The task of contemporary wage theory', in *The Theory of Wage Determination*, ed. J. T. Dunlop. London: Macmillan, 123–35.　　**26**

Eagly, R. V. (1964) 'Market power, unemployment, and the rate of change in money wage in Sweden, 1914–57'. *Ekonomisk Tidskrift* 66(3): 171–85.　　**231, 233**

Eagly, R. V. (1965) 'Market power as an intervening mechanism in Phillips curve analysis'. *Economica* 32: 48–64.　　**230, 233**

Eagly, R. V. (1967) 'On government issuance of an index bond'. *Public Finance* 22: 268–84.　　**224, 246**

Eatwell, J., J. Llewellyn, and R. Tarling (1974) 'Money wage inflation in industrial countries'. *Review of Economic Studies* 41(4): 515–23.　　**231**

Eckstein, O. (1958) 'Inflation, the wage-price spiral and economic growth', in *The Relationship of Prices to Economic Stability and Growth*, ed. Joint Economic Committee. Washington, DC: Government Printing Office, 361–75.　　**118**

Eckstein, O. (1959) *Staff Report on Employment, Growth, and Price Levels ('The Eckstein Report')*. Washington, DC: Joint Economic Committee.　　**78, 118**

Eckstein, O. (1964) 'A theory of the wage-price process in modern industry'. *Review of Economic Studies* 31(4): 267–86.　　**235**

Eckstein, O. (1968) 'Money wage determination revisited'. *Review of Economic Studies* 35(2): 133–43.　　**53, 226, 232, 233**

Eckstein, O. (1969) 'Discussion'. *American Economic Review* 59(2): 161–7.　　**248**

Eckstein, O. (ed.) (1972) *The Econometrics of Price Determination*. Washington, DC: Board of Governors of the Federal Reserve System.　　**241**

Eckstein, O. and R. E. Brinner (1972) 'The inflation process in the United States'. Study prepared for the Joint Economic Committee. Washington DC: Government Printing Office.　　**93, 104, 241, 251**

Eckstein, O. and G. Fromm (1959) 'Steel and the postwar inflation', in *Employment Growth and Price Levels*, Study Paper no. 2, ed. Joint Economic Committee. Washington, DC: Government Printing Office.　　**113**

Eckstein, O. and J. A. Girola (1978) 'Long-term properties of the price-wage mechanism in the United States, 1891–1977'. *Review of Economics and Statistics* 60(3): 323–33.　　**196, 228, 238**

Eckstein, O. and T. A. Wilson (1962) 'The determination of money wages in American industry'. *Quarterly Journal of Economics* 76(3): 379–414.　　**52, 59, 68, 215, 224, 233, 237, 239, 241, 250**

Eckstein, O. and T. A. Wilson (1967) 'Reply'. *Quarterly Journal of Economics* 81(4): 690–4.　　**229**

Eichengreen, B. (1996) 'Institutions and economic growth: Europe after World War II', in *Economic Growth in Europe since 1945*, ed. N. C. R. Crafts and G. Toniolo. Oxford: Oxford University Press, 38–72.　　**25**

Ellis, I. A., J. M. Pearson, and P. D. Periton (1987) 'Trade unions and wage inflation in the United Kingdom: A re-estimation of Hines' model'. *Applied Economics* 19(5): 597–608.   240

European Central Bank (2003) *Monthly Bulletin* July 2003 Frankfurt: European Central Bank.   202

European Central Bank web page. Definition of Price Stability. https://www.ecb. europa.eu/mopo/strategy/pricestab/html/index.en.html (accessed 17 April 2014).   202

Evans, M. K. and L. R. Klein (1968) *The Wharton Econometric Forecasting Model*. Philadelphia: Wharton School.   100

Fand, D. I. (1969) 'Keynesian monetary theories, stabilization policy, and the recent inflation'. *Journal of Money, Credit and Banking* 1(3): 556–87.   154

Farrell, M. J. (1965) *Fuller Employment?* London: IEA.   126, 132, 194

Feige, E. L. (1972) 'The 1972 report of the president's council of economic advisers: Inflation and unemployment'. *American Economic Review* 62(4): 509–16.   250

Feldstein, M. S. (1979) 'The welfare cost of permanent inflation and optimal short-run economic policy'. *Journal of Political Economy* 87(4): 749–68.   164

Feldstein, M. S. (1981) 'Inflation and the American economy'. *Empirica* 8(2): 155–68.   46

Felix, D. (1956) 'Profit inflation and industrial growth: The historic record and contemporary analogies'. *Quarterly Journal of Economics* 70(3): 441–63.   119

Fellner, W. J. (1959) 'Demand inflation, cost inflation, and collective bargaining', in *The Public Stake in Union Power*, ed. P. Bradley. Charlottesville, VA: University of Virginia Press, 225–54.   8, 236

Fellner, W. J. (1971) 'Phillips-type approach or acceleration?' *Brookings Papers on Economic Activity* 2: 469–83.   138

Fellner, W. J. (1976a) 'Lessons from the failure of demand-management policies: A look at the theoretical foundations'. *Journal of Economic Literature* 14(1): 34–53. 184

Fellner, W. J. (1976b) *Towards a Reconstruction of Macroeconomics: Problems of Theory and Policy*. Washington, DC: American Enterprise Institute.   93

Fellner, W. J. (1976c) 'Guide to the volume', in *Contemporary Economic Problems*, ed. W. J. Fellner. Washington, DC: American Enterprise Association, 1–16.   128

Fellner, W. J., M. Gilbert, B. Hansen, R. Kahn, F. A. Lutz, and P. de Wolff (1961) *The Problem of Rising Prices*. Paris: OECD.   108, 116, 118

Ferri, P. (2000) 'Wage dynamics and the Phillips curve', in *Macroeconomics and the Real World*, vol. 2: *Keynesian Economics, Unemployment, and Policy*, ed. R. E. Backhouse and A. Salanti. Oxford: Oxford University Press, 97–112.   226

Fisher, I. (1926) 'A statistical relation between unemployment and price changes'. *International Labour Review* (13): 785–92.   11, 180

Fisher, I. (1930) *The Theory of Interest*. New York: Macmillan.   237

Fisher, I. (1973) 'I discovered the Phillips curve'. *Journal of Political Economy* 81(2): 496–502.   181

Fisher, J. D. M. (2008) 'Phillips curve (new views)', in *The New Palgrave Dictionary of Economics*, ed. S. N. Durlauf and L. E. Blume. Basingstoke: Palgrave Macmillan.   48

Fisher, M. R. (1976) 'Professor Hicks and the Keynesians'. *Economica* 43(171): 305–14.   184

Fitchenbaum, R. (2003) 'Is there a natural level of capacity utilization'. *Forum for Social Economics* 33(1): 45–62.   226

Flanagan, R. J. (1973) 'The US Phillips curve and international unemployment rate differentials'. *American Economic Review* 63(1): 114–31.   238

Flanagan, R. J. (1976) 'Wage interdependence in unionized labor markets'. *Brookings Papers on Economic Activity* 3: 635–73.   **238**

Fleming, J. M. (1971) 'On exchange rate unification'. *Economic Journal* 81: 467–88.   **137**

Fleming, J. M. (1972) 'Concluding observations', in *Inflation as a Global Problem*, ed. R. Hinshaw. Baltimore, MD: Johns Hopkins University Press, 150–3.   **135**

Flory, L. J. (1974) 'Stability of Phillips curve and accelerationist hypothesis: Recent microeconomic evidence'. *Quarterly Review of Economics and Business* 14(3): 35–45.   **228**

Forder, J. (2001) 'The theory of credibility and the reputation bias of policy'. *Review of Political Economy* 13(1): 5–25.   **237**

Forder, J. (2005) 'Why is central bank independence so widely approved?' *Journal of Economic Issues* 39(4): 843–65.   **216**

Forder, J. (2010a) 'Friedman's Nobel lecture and the Phillips curve myth'. *Journal of the History of Economic Thought* 32(3): 329–48.   **2**

Forder, J. (2010b) 'The historical place of the "Friedman–Phelps" expectations critique'. *European Journal of the History of Economic Thought* 17(3): 493–511.   **82, 179**

Forder, J. (2011) 'One more word on J. K. Gifford'. *History of Economics Review* 54(Summer): 151–4.   **247**

Forder, J. (2013a) 'The balance of payments and the Phillips curve in post-war British policy'. mimeo Balliol College Oxford.   **143**

Forder, J. (2013b) 'Textbooks on the Phillips curve'. mimeo. Balliol College Oxford.   **161**

Forder, J. (2013c) 'Macroeconomics and the L-shaped aggregate supply curve', in *Handbook of Post-Keynesian Economics* (vol. 2), ed. G. C. Harcourt and P. Kriesler. Oxford: Oxford University Press, 245–64.   **222**

Forder, J (2014) 'Hall and Hart on Samuelson and Solow: Some comments'. mimeo. Balliol College Oxford.   **224**

France, R. R. (1962) 'Wages, unemployment and prices in the United States, 1890–1932, 1947–1957'. *Industrial and Labor Relations Review* 15: 171–90.   **32, 54, 61, 84, 250**

Freedman, C., G. C. Harcourt, and P. Kriesler (2004) 'Has the long-run Phillips curve turned horizontal?', in *Growth, Distribution and Effective Demand: Alternatives to Economic Orthodoxy*, ed. G. Argyrous, M. Forstater, and G. Mongiovi. Armonk, NY: M. E. Sharpe, 144–62.   **214**

Freeman, R. (1988) 'Does the new generation know more than the old?', in *How Labor Markets Work*, ed. B. E. Kaufman. Lexington, MA: D. C. Heath and Company, 205–32.   **30**

Friedman, M. (1951) 'Some comments on the significance of labor unions for economic policy', in *The Impact of the Union*, ed. D. M. Wright. New York, Harcourt Brace & Company, 204–34.   **24**

Friedman, M. (1951/1966) 'The effects of a full-employment policy on economic stability'. *Economie Appliquée* 4(July–December): 441–56. Reprinted in Freidman, M. (ed) *Essays in Positive Economics*. Chicago: Chicago University Press, 117–32.   **221**

Friedman, M. (1953/1966) 'The methodology of positive economics', in *Essays in Positive Economics*, ed. M. Friedman. Chicago: Chicago University Press, 3–43.   **211**

Friedman, M. (1956) 'The quantity theory of money: A restatement', in *Studies in the Quantity Theory of Money*, ed. M. Friedman. Chicago: University of Chicago, 3–21.   **178**

Friedman, M. (1958) 'The supply of money and changes in prices and output', in *The Relationship of Prices to Economic Stability and Growth*, ed. Joint Economic Committee. Washington, DC: Government Printing Office, 241–56.   **85, 88**

Friedman, M. (1962) 'An essay in petitio principii'. *American Economic Review* 52(2): 291–301.   **243**

Friedman, M. (1963/1968) *Inflation: Causes and Consequences*. Bombay: Asia Publishing House.   **88**

Friedman, M. (1966a) 'Comments', in *Guidelines, Informal Controls, and the Market Place*, ed. G. P. Schultz and R. Z. Aliber. Chicago: Chicago University Press, 55–61.   **82, 88, 182**

Friedman, M. (1966b) 'What price Guideposts?', in *Guidelines, Informal Controls, and the Market Place*, ed. G. P. Schultz and R. Z. Aliber. Chicago: Chicago University Press, 17–40.   **85, 89, 112, 187**

Friedman, M. (1966c) 'An inflationary recession'. *Newsweek*, 17 October, 92.   **88**

Friedman, M. (1968a) 'The role of monetary policy'. *American Economic Review* 58: 1–17.   **1, 5, 39, 50, 52, 58, 59, 62, 63, 65, 67, 76, 79, 80, 82, 83, 86, 88, 133, 153, 154, 171, 172, 173, 174, 184, 186, 189, 190, 192, 193, 194, 195, 204, 208, 209, 211, 230, 249**

Friedman, M. (1968b) *Dollars and Deficits*. Englewood Cliffs, NJ: Prentice Hall.   **89**

Friedman, M. (1971/1974) 'A theoretical framework for monetary analysis', in *Milton Friedman's Monetary Framework*, ed. R. J. Gordon. Chicago: University of California, 1–62.   **22**

Friedman, M. (1975a) *Unemployment versus Inflation?* London: Institute of Economic Affairs.   **9, 158, 161, 177, 195**

Friedman, M. (1975b) *Milton Friedman in Australia*. Sydney: Constable & Bain.   **161**

Friedman, M. (1977) 'Nobel lecture: Inflation and unemployment'. *Journal of Political Economy* 85: 451–72.   **2, 6, 51, 60, 61, 142, 152, 160, 161, 167, 172, 177, 178, 179, 201, 211, 217**

Friedman, M. and D. I. Meiselman (1963) 'The relative stability of monetary velocity and the investment multiplier in the United States, 1897–1958', in *Stabilization Policies* Englewood Cliffs, NJ: Commission on Money and Credit/Prentice Hall. 165–268.   **243**

Frisch, H. (1977) 'Inflation theory 1963–1975: A "second generation" survey'. *Journal of Economic Literature* 15(4): 1289–317.   **34, 45, 163, 182**

Frisch, H. (1983) *Theories of Inflation*. Cambridge: Cambridge University Press.   **34**

Fromm, G. and P. Taubman (1968) *Policy Simulations with an Econometric Model*. Washington, DC: Brookings.   **100, 246**

Funk, P. and B. Kromen (2010) 'Inflation and innovation-driven growth'. *Journal of Macroeconomics* 10(1): 1–52.   **117**

Fuss, H. (1926) 'Unemployment in 1925'. *International Labour Review* 14: 202–31.   **219**

Galbraith, J. K. (1952/1956) *American Capitalism: The Concept of Countervailing Power*. Boston: Houghton Mifflin.   **113**

Galbraith, J. K. (1957) 'Market structure and stabilisation policy'. *Review of Economics and Statistics* 39(2): 124–33.   **113**

Galbraith, J. K. (1960) *The Liberal Hour*. New York: Houghton Mifflin.   **108**

Galbraith, J. K. (1975/1976) *Money: Whence it Came, Where it Went*. New York: Bantam/ Houghton Mifflin.   **138**

Galbraith, J. K. (1997) 'Time to ditch the NAIRU'. *Journal of Economic Perspectives* 11(1): 93–108.   **48, 215**

Galenson, W. (ed.) (1973) *Incomes Policy: What Can We Learn from Europe.* New York: New York State School of Industrial and Labor Relations.　　**127**

Gallaway, L. E. (1963) 'Labor mobility, resource allocation, and structural unemployment'. *American Economic Review* 53(4): 694–716.　　**133**

Gallaway, L. E. (1971) *Manpower Economics.* Homewood, IL: Richard D. Irwin.　　**232**

Gallaway, L. E., R. K. Koshal, and G. L. Chapin (1970) 'The relationship between the rate of change in money wage rates and unemployment levels in South Africa'. *South African Journal of Economics* 38(4): 262–7.　　**232, 234**

Gifford, J. K. (1968) 'Correlationism: A virulent disease in economic science'. *Journal of Political Economy* 76(5): 1091–5.　　**248**

Gifford, J. K. (1969) 'Critical remarks on the Phillips curve and the Phillips hypothesis'. *Weltwirtschaftliches Archiv* 102: 77–96.　　**247**

Gilbert, C. L. (1976) 'The original Phillips curve estimates'. *Economica* 43(169): 51–7. **15**

Gilbert, M. (1961) 'Quality changes and index numbers'. *Economic Development and Cultural Change* 9(3): 287–94.　　**120**

Gillion, C. (1968) 'Wage-rates, earnings, and wage-drift'. *National Institute Economic Review* (46): 52–67.　　**57, 61, 207, 234**

Gilpatrick, E. G. (1966) *Structural Unemployment and Aggregate Demand.* Baltimore: Johns Hopkins.　　**133, 224**

Gittings, T. A. (1979) 'The inflation-unemployment tradeoff'. *Federal Reserve Bank of Chicago Economic Perspectives* (October): 3–9.　　**227**

Glezakos, C. (1978) 'Inflation and growth: A reconsideration of the evidence from the LDCs'. *Journal of Developing Areas* 12(2): 171–82.　　**117**

Godfrey, L. (1971) 'The Phillips curve: Incomes policy and trade union effects', in *The Current Inflation,* ed. H. G. Johnson and A. R. Nobay. London: Macmillan, 99–124.　　**239, 240, 242**

Godfrey, L. (1972) 'Some comments on the estimation of the Lipsey–Parkin inflation model', in *Incomes Policy and Inflation,* ed. M. Parkin and M. T. Sumner. Manchester: Manchester University Press, 138–50.　　**240**

Godfrey, L. and J. Taylor (1973) 'Earnings changes in the United Kingdom 1954–1970: Excess labour supply, expected inflation and union influence'. *Oxford Bulletin of Economics and Statistics* 35: 197–216.　　**239**

Goldstein, M. (1972) 'Trade-off between inflation and unemployment: Survey of econometric evidence for selected countries'. *International Monetary Fund Staff Papers* 19(3): 647–98.　　**45, 136, 162, 182, 151**

Goldthorpe, J. (1978) 'The current inflation: Towards a sociological account', in *The Political Economy of Inflation,* ed. J. Goldthorpe and F. Hirsch. Cambridge, MA: Harvard University Press.　　**114**

Goodhart, C. A. E. and R. Bhansali (1970) 'Political economy'. *Political Studies* 18(1): 43–106.　　**136**

Goodwin, C. D. (1975) *Exhortation and Controls: The Search for a Wage-price Policy.* Washington, DC: Brookings.　　**145, 149, 244**

Goodwin, C. D. and R. S. Herren (1975) 'The Truman administration: Problems and policies unfold', in *Exhortation and Control,* ed. C. D. Goodwin. Washington, DC: Brookings Institution, 9–94.　　**219**

Goodwin, R. M. (1967) 'A growth cycle', in *Socialism, Capitalism and Economic Growth,* ed. C. H. Feinstein. Cambridge: Cambridge University Press, 54–8.　　**219, 246**

Gordon, D. F. (1976) 'A neo-classical theory of Keynesian unemployment', in *The Phillips Curve and Labor Markets,* ed. K. Brunner and A. H. Meltzer. New York: North-Holland.　　**181**

Gordon, H. S. (1961) *The Economists versus the Bank of Canada*. Toronto: Ryerson Press.   235

Gordon, R. A. (1967) *The Goal of Full Employment*. New York: John Wiley & Sons.   126

Gordon, R. A. (1975) 'Wages, prices, and unemployment, 1900–1970'. *Industrial Relations* 14(3): 273–301.   227, 242

Gordon, R. J. (1970) 'The recent acceleration of inflation and its lessons for the future'. *Brookings Papers on Economic Activity* 1: 8–41.   102, 155, 182, 190, 195, 251

Gordon, R. J. (1971a) 'Inflation in recession and recovery'. *Brookings Papers on Economic Activity* 1: 105–58.   102, 103, 104, 191

Gordon, R. J. (1971b) 'Steady anticipated inflation: Mirage or oasis?' *Brookings Papers on Economic Activity* (2): 499–510.   104, 128

Gordon, R. J. (1971c) 'Steady inflation: An exaggerated menace', in *The 1971 Midyear Review of the Economy, Hearings before the Joint Economic Committee, 92 Cong. 1 Sess*. Washington, DC: Government Printing Office.   104

Gordon, R. J. (1972a) 'Wage-price controls and the shifting Phillips curve'. *Brookings Papers on Economic Activity* (2): 385–421.   104, 238

Gordon, R. J. (1972b) 'Discussion of papers in session II', in *The Econometrics of Price Determination*, ed. O. Eckstein. Washington, DC: Board of Governors of the Federal Reserve System.   242

Gordon, R. J. (1973a) 'The response of wages and prices to the first two years of controls'. *Brookings Papers on Economic Activity* 4(3): 765–79.   104

Gordon, R. J. (1973b) 'The welfare cost of higher unemployment'. *Brookings Papers on Economic Activity* 4(1): 133–95.   103, 191

Gordon, R. J. (1975a) 'The impact of aggregate demand on prices'. *Brookings Papers on Economic Activity* 6(3): 613–62.   104

Gordon, R. J. (1975b) 'The demand for and supply of inflation'. *Journal of Law and Economics* 18: 807–36   137

Gordon, R. J. (1976a) 'Recent developments in the theory of inflation and unemployment'. *Journal of Monetary Economics* 2(2): 185–219.   158, 182, 236

Gordon, R. J. (1976b) 'Aspects of the theory of involuntary unemployment: A comment'. *Carnegie Rochester Conference Series on Public Policy* 1: 98–110.   184

Gordon, R. J. (1977) 'Can the inflation of the 1970s be explained?' *Brookings Papers on Economic Activity* 8: 253–77.   102, 104

Gordon, R. J. (2011) 'The history of the Phillips curve: Consensus and bifurcation'. *Economica*: 78(309):10–50.   165

Graham, L. and D. J. Snower (2008) 'Hyperbolic discounting and the Phillips curve'. *Journal of Money, Credit and Banking* 40(2–3): 427–48.   48

Gramlich, E. M. (1975) 'The optimal timing of unemployment in a recession'. *Brookings Papers on Economic Activity* 1975(1): 167–81.   238

De Grauwe, P. (1994) *The Economics of Monetary Integration*. Oxford: Oxford University Press.   137

Gray, H. P. (1968) 'Depreciation or incomes policy?' *Manchester School* 36: 49–61.   44

Griffin, K. B. (1962) 'A note on wages, price and unemployment'. *Bulletin of the Oxford University Institute of Economics and Statistics* 24(3): 379–85.   17, 35

Griliches, Z. (1968) 'The Brookings model volume: a review article'. *Review of Economics and Statistics* 50(2): 215–34.   100

Grossman, H. I. (1974) 'The cyclical pattern of unemployment and wage inflation'. *Economica* 41(164): 403–13.   248

Grubel, H. G. (1970) 'The theory of optimum currency areas'. *Canadian Journal of Economics* 3(2): 318–24.   137

Gruen, D., A. Pagan, and C. Thompson (1999) 'The Phillips curve in Australia'. *Journal of Monetary Economics* 44(2): 223–58.   226

Guha, D. and D. Visviki (2001) 'What determines inflation in the US, job growth or unemployment?' *International Journal of Forecasting* 17(3): 447–58.   229

Gustman, A. (1972) 'Wage bargains, threshold effects, and the Phillips curve: A reexamination'. *Quarterly Journal of Economics* 86(2): 332–8.   238

Gwartney, J. D. and R. Stroup (1997) *Economics: Private and Public Choice*. Fort Worth: Dryden.   249

Haberler, G. (1960) *Inflation: Its Causes and Cure*. Washington, DC: American Enterprise Institute.   82, 155

Haberler, G. (1961) *Inflation: Its Causes and Cure*. Washington, DC: American Enterprise Institute.   220, 235, 237

Haberler, G. (1966a) 'Adjustment, employment, and growth', in *Maintaining and Restoring Balance in International Payments*, ed. W. J. Fellner, F. Machlup, and R. Triffin. Princeton: Princeton University Press/OECD, 123–35.   133

Haberler, G. (1966b) *Inflation: Its Causes and Its Cure* (rev. and expanded edn). Washington, DC: American Enterprise Association.   155

Haberler, G. (1971) *Incomes Policies and Inflation: An Analysis of Basic Principles*. Washington, DC: American Enterprise Institute.   155

Haberler, G. (1972) 'Incomes Policies and Inflation: Some Further Reflections'. *American Economic Review* 62(1/2): 234–41.   155, 156, 157, 187

Haberler, G. (1985) *The Problem of Stagflation: Reflections on the Microfoundations of Macroeconomic Theory and Policy*. Washington, DC: American Enterprise Institute for Public Policy Research.   46

Hagger, A. J. (1963a) 'Some gaps in the theory of the inflationary process'. *Economic Record* 39(86): 166–86.   162

Hagger, A. J. (1963b) 'Inflation types'. *Economia Internazionale* (May): 224.   224

Hagger, A. J. (1964) *The Theory of Inflation*. Melbourne: Melbourne University Press.   162, 224, 234

Hagger, A. J. (1977) *Inflation Theory and Policy*. London: Macmillan.   162

Hahn, F. H. (1982) *Money and Inflation*. Oxford: Blackwell.   192

Haldane, A. and D. Quah (1999) 'UK Phillips curves and monetary policy'. *Journal of Monetary Economics* 44(2): 259–78.   47

Hall, R. E. (1970) 'Why is the unemployment rate so high at full employment?' *Brookings Papers on Economic Activity* 1970(3): 369–403.   91

Hall, R. E. (1974) 'The process of inflation in the labor market'. *Brookings Papers on Economic Activity* 1974(2): 343–93.   91, 182, 184

Hall, R. E. (1976) 'The Phillips curve and macroeconomic policy', in *The Phillips Curve and Labor Markets*, ed. K. Brunner and A. H. Meltzer. North-Holland.   92

Hall, T. E. (2003) *The Rotten Fruits of Economic Controls and the Rise from the Ashes, 1965–1989*. Lanham, MD: University Press of America.   223

Hall, T. E. and W. R. Hart (2012) 'The Samuelson–Solow Phillips curve and the great inflation'. *History of Economics Review* 54: 62–72.   223

Hall, V. B. (1976) 'Inflation in a small, fixed exchange rate, open economy: A model for New Zealand', in *Inflation in Open Economies*, ed. M. Parkin and G. Zis. Manchester: Manchester University Press, 259–79.   98

Hamada, K. (1977) 'On the political economy of monetary integration: A public economic approach', in *Political Economy of Monetary Reform*, ed. R. Z. Aliber. London: Macmillan, 12–31.   137

Hamermesh, D. S. (1970) 'Wage bargaining, threshold effects, and the Phillips curve'. *Quarterly Journal of Economics* 84(3): 501–17.   **238**

Hamermesh, D. S. (1972a) 'Market power and wage inflation'. *Southern Economic Journal* 39(2): 204–11.   **228**

Hamermesh, D. S. (1972b) 'Reply'. *Quarterly Journal of Economics* 86(2): 339–41.   **238**

Hamilton, E. J. (1929) 'American treasure and the rise of capitalism (1500–1700)'. *Economica* (27): 338–57.   **116**

Hamilton, E. J. (1952) 'Prices as a factor in business growth: Prices and progress'. *Journal of Economic History* 12(4): 325–49.   **116**

Hancock, K. (1966a) 'Earnings drift in Australia'. *Journal of Industrial Relations* 8: 128–57.   **98, 242**

Hancock, K. (1966b) 'Shifts in demand and the inflation problem: Comment'. *American Economic Review* 56(3): 517–22.   **235**

Hansen, A. H. (1947) *Economic Policy and Full Employment*. New York: McGraw-Hill.   **24**

Hansen, A. H. (1949) *Monetary Theory and Fiscal Policy*. New York: McGraw-Hill.   **244**

Hansen, A. H. (1954) Testimony in Hearings on the 1954 Economic Report of the President Joint Economic Committee. Washington DC: Government Printing Office.   **219**

Hansen, A. H. (1957) *The American Economy*. New York: McGraw-Hill.   **118, 123, 132**

Hansen, A. H. (1960) *Economic Issues of the 1960s*. New York: McGraw-Hill.   **42, 244**

Hansen, A. H. (1962) 'Some reflections on the Annual Report of the Council of Economic Advisers'. *Review of Economics and Statistics* 44(3): 337–9.   **246**

Hansen, B. (1957) 'Full employment and wage stability', in *The Theory of Wage Determination*, ed. J. T. Dunlop. London: Macmillan, 66–78.   **162**

Hansen, B. (1970) 'Excess demand, unemployment, and wages'. *Quarterly Journal of Economics* 84(1): 1–23.   **100, 138**

Hansen, B. and G. Rehn (1956) 'On wage drift: A problem of money wage determinants', in *Twenty-five Economic Essays in Honour of Erik Lindahl*. Stockholm.   **219**

Harcourt, G. C. (1992) 'Is Keynes dead?' *History of Economics Review* 18: 1–9.   **47**

Harris, D. J. (1967) 'Inflation, income distribution and capital accumulation in a two-sector model of growth'. *Economic Journal* 77(308): 814–33.   **58**

Harrod, R. F. (1939) *International Economics*. London: Nisbet.   **120**

Harrod, R. F. (1963) *The British Economy*. New York: McGraw-Hill.   **246**

Harrod, R. F. (1972) 'The issues: Five views', in *Inflation as a Global Problem*, ed. R. Hinshaw. London: Johns Hopkins University Press, 43–5.   **114**

Hart, A. G. (1942) 'Use of flexible taxes to combat inflation'. *American Economic Review* 32(1): 87–102.   **79**

Hart, A. G. (1952) *Money, Debt and Economic Activity*. New York: Prentice Hall.   **114, 243**

Hawtrey, R. G. (1930) 'Money and index numbers'. *Journal of the Royal Statistical Society* 93(1): 64–85.   **13**

Heien, D. and J. Popkin (1972) 'Price determination and cost-of-living measures in a disagggregated model of the US economy', in *The Econometrics of Price Determination*, ed. O. Eckstein. Washington, DC: Board of Governors of the Federal Reserve System.   **242**

Heller, W. W. (1965) 'The future of our fiscal system'. *Journal of Business* 38(3): 235–44.   **128**

Heller, W. W. (1969) 'Has monetary policy been oversold?', in *Monetary vs Fiscal Policy*, ed. M. Friedman and W. Heller. New York: W. W. Norton, 13–42.   **247**

Hendry, D. and K. F. Wallis (eds) (1984) *Econometrics and Quantitative Economics*. Oxford: Blackwell.   **57**

Hendry, D. F. and G. E. Mizon (2000) 'The influence of A. W. Phillips on econometrics', in *A. W. H. Phillips: Collected Works in Contemporary Perspective*, ed. R. Leeson. Cambridge: Cambridge University Press, 353–64.   **221**

Henneberry, B. and J. G. Witte (1976) 'Stabilization-policies: Complications of balance of payments constraints'. *Weltwirtschaftliches Archiv–Review of World Economics* 112(2): 231–59.   **226**

Henry, S. G. B., M. C. Sawyer, and P. Smith (1976) 'Models of inflation in the United Kingdom: An evaluation'. *National Institute Economic Review* (77): 60–71.   **95**

Hibbs, D. A. (1977) 'Political parties and macroeconomic policy'. *American Political Science Review* 71(4): 1467–87.   **136**

Hicks, J. R. (1955) 'Economic foundations of wages policy'. *Economic Journal* 65(259): 388–404.   **29, 62, 84**

Hicks, J. R. (1967) *Critical Essays in Monetary Theory*. Oxford: Oxford University Press.   **236**

Hicks, J. R. (1974) *The Crisis in Keynesian Economics*. Oxford: Blackwell.   **114**

Higgins, C. I. (1973) 'A wage-price sector for a quarterly Australian model', in *Econometric Studies of Macro and Monetary Relations*, ed. A. A. Powell and R. A. Williams. Amsterdam: North-Holland, 115–47.   **242**

Hillier, B. (1986) *Macroeconomics: Models, Debates and Developments*. Oxford: Blackwell.   **226**

Hineline, D. R. (2010) 'Long-run impacts of inflation across sectors in a small sample of countries'. *Applied Economics* 42(10): 1197–207.   **117**

Hines, A. G. (1964) 'Trade unions and wage inflation in the United Kingdom, 1893–1966'. *Review of Economic Studies* 31(4): 221–52. **57, 68, 95, 207, 239, 240, 250**

Hines, A. G. (1968) 'Unemployment and the rate of change of money wages in the United Kingdom, 1862–1963'. *Review of Economics and Statistics* 50: 60–7.   **57, 59, 95, 215, 234, 239**

Hines, A. G. (1969) 'Wage inflation in the United Kingdom 1948–1962: A disaggregated study'. *Economic Journal* 79(313): 66–89.   **57**

Hines, A. G. (1971) 'The determinants of the rate of change of money wage rates and the effectiveness of incomes policy', in *The Current Inflation*, ed. H. G. Johnson and A. R. Nobay. London: Macmillan, 143–75.   **239, 240**

Hines, A. G. (1972) 'The Phillips curve and the distribution of unemployment'. *American Economic Review* 62(1/2): 155–60.   **233**

Hirsch, A. A. (1972) 'Price simulations with the OBE econometric model', in *The Econometrics of Price Determination*, ed. O. Eckstein. Washington, DC: Board of Governors of the Federal Reserve System, 237–76.   **100, 160**

Hoffman, W. (1969) 'Die "Phillips-curve" in Deutschland'. *Kyklos* 22(2): 219–31.   **232**

Holmes, J. M. and D. J. Smyth (1970) 'The relation between unemployment and excess demand for labour: An examination of the theory of the Phillips curve'. *Economica* 37(147): 311–15.   **248**

Holmes, J. M. and D. J. Smyth (1979) 'Excess demand for labor, unemployment, and theories of the Phillips curve'. *Journal of Macroeconomics* 1(4): 347–72.   **248**

Holt, C. C. (1969) 'Improving the labor market trade-off between inflation and unemployment'. *American Economic Review* 59(2): 135–46.   **127, 178**

Holt, C. C. (1970a) 'Job search, Phillips' wage relation, and union influence', in *Microeconomic Foundations of Employment and Inflation Theory*, ed. E. S. Phelps. Macmillan: London, 53–123.   **127, 183, 240**

Holt, C. C. (1970b) 'How can the Phillips curve be moved to reduce both inflation and unemployment', in *Microeconomic Foundations of Employment and Inflation Theory*, ed. E. S. Phelps. New York: W. W. Norton, 224–56.   **127, 183**

Holt, C. C. (1973) 'Wage inflation and the structure of regional unemployment: A comment'. *Journal of Money, Credit and Banking* 5(1): 380–81.   **241**

Holt, C. C. (2000) 'Interactions with a fellow research engineer-economist', in *A. W. H. Phillips: Collected Works in Contemporary Perspective*, ed. R. Leeson. Cambridge: Cambridge University Press, 308–14.   **17**

Holt, C. C. and M. H. David (1966) 'The concept of vacancies in a dynamic theory of the labor market', in *Measurement and interpretation of job vacancies*. Washington, DC: NBER   **246**

Holt, C. C. and G. P. Huber (1969) 'A computer-aided approach to employment service placement and counselling'. *Management Science* 15(11): 573–94.   **246**

Holzman, F. D. (1959) 'Creeping inflation'. *Review of Economics and Statistics* 41(3): 324–9.   **121**

Horwich, G. and P. H. Hendershott (1969) 'The appropriate indicators of monetary policy', in *Savings and Residential Financing*, ed. D. P. Jacobs and R. T. Pratt. Chicago: US Savings and Loan League, 33–52.   **88**

Howard, W. A. and N. A. Tolles (1974) 'Wage determination in key manufacturing industries'. *Industrial and Labor Relations Review* 27(4): 543–59.   **225, 237**

Howitt, P. (2007) 'Edmund Phelps: Macroeconomist and social scientist'. *Scandinavian Journal of Economics* 109(2): 203–24.   **236**

Hughes, B. (1980) *Exit Full Employment*. London: Angus & Robertson.   **227**

Hughes Hallett, A. J. (2000) 'Aggregate Phillips curves are not always vertical: Heterogeneity and mismatch in multiregion or multisector economies'. *Macroeconomic Dynamics* 4: 534–46.   **213**

Hume, D. (1752/1987) 'Of money', in *Essays Moral, Political and Literary*. Indianapolis: Liberty Classics. Ed Eugene F Miller.   **11**

Hume, I. (1970) 'Notes on South African wage movements'. *South African Journal of Economics* 38(3): 240–56.   **44, 231, 233, 234**

Humphrey, T. M. (1973) 'Changing views of the Phillips curve'. *Federal Reserve Bank of Richmond Monthly Review* 59(July): 2–13.   **157, 160**

Humphrey, T. M. (1976) 'Some current controversies in the theory of inflation'. *Federal Reserve Bank of Richmond Monthly Review*: July 8–19.   **160**

Humphrey, T. M. (1978) 'Some recent developments in Phillips curve analysis'. *Federal Reserve Bank of Richmond Economic Review* 63: 15–23.   **160**

Humphrey, T. M. (1985) 'The early history of the Phillips curve'. *Federal Reserve Bank of Richmond Economic Review* 71: 17–24.   **46, 219**

Hutchinson, T. W. (1938) *The Significance and Basic Postulates of Economic Theory*. London: Macmillan.   **220**

Hutchinson, T. W. (1968) *Economics and Economic Policy in Britain 1946–1966*. London: George Allen & Unwin.   **148**

Hutt, W. H. (1963) *Keynesianism—Retrospect and Prospect: A Critical Restatement of Basic Economic Principles*. Chicago: Henry Regnery Company.   **235**

Hutton, J. P. and K. Hartley (1968) 'A regional payroll tax'. *Oxford Economic Papers* 20(3): 417–26.   **247**

Hymans, S. H. (1970) 'The trade off between unemployment and inflation: Theory and measurement', in *Readings in Money, National Income and Stabilization Policy*, ed. W. L. Smith and R. L. Teigen. Washington, DC: Irwin Dorsey.   **251**

Hymans, S. H. (1972) 'Prices and price behavior in three US econometric models', in *The Econometrics of Price Determination*, ed. O. Eckstein. Washington, DC: Board of Governors of the Federal Reserve System, 309–24.   **160**

Isachsen, A. J. (1977) 'A note on wage drift: The case of Sweden'. *Scandinavian Journal of Economics* 79(3): 366–74.   **98**

Ito, T. (1996) 'General discussion of Akerlof, Dickens and Perry'. *Brookings Papers on Economic Activity*: 171–2.   **78**

Jackson, D. A. S., H. A. Turner, and S. F. Wilkinson (1975) *Do Trade Unions Cause Inflation?* Cambridge: Cambridge University Press.   **114**

Jacobsson, L. and A. Lindbeck (1969) 'Labor market conditions, wages and inflation: Swedish experiences 1955–67'. *Swedish Journal of Economics* 71(2): 64–103.   **98**

Jacobsson, L. and A. Lindbeck (1971) 'On the transmission mechanism of wage change'. *Swedish Journal of Economics* 73(3): 273–93.   **98**

Jacoby, N. H. (1957) 'The threat of inflation'. *Harvard Business Review* 35(3): 15–16, 22–3, 24, 26, 28, 30, 32, 160–2.   **87**

Jacoby, N. H. (1967a) 'Wage-price Guideposts as an instrument to attain US economic goals', in *Government Wage Price Guideposts in the American Economy*, ed. A. L. Gitlow. New York: New York University Press.   **120, 131, 225, 235**

Jacoby, N. H. (1967b) in *Government Wage-Price Guideposts in the American Economy*, ed. G. Meany, R. M. Blough, and N. H. Jacoby.   **235**

Jacoby, S. (2008) *The Age of American Unreason*. New York: Pantheon.   **205**

Jay, P. (1974) 'Do trade unions matter?', in *Inflation: Causes, Consequences, Cures*, ed. L. Robbins. London: IEA, 27–34.   **152**

Jay, P. (1976) *A General Hypothesis of Employment, Inflation, and Politics*. London: IEA.   **151, 152**

Jefferson, C. W., K. I. Sams, and D. Swann (1968) 'The control of incomes and prices in the United Kingdom, 1964–1967: Policy and experience'. *Canadian Journal of Economics* 1(2): 269–94.   **58, 96, 231**

Johnson, H. G. (1962) 'Monetary theory and policy'. *American Economic Review* 52(3): 335–84.   **132, 208**

Johnson, H. G. (1963a) 'A survey of theories of inflation'. *Indian Economic Review* 6(4): 29–69.   **126, 133, 235, 236**

Johnson, H. G. (1963b) 'Objectives, monetary standards, and potentialities'. *Review of Economics and Statistics* 65(February): 137–44.   **243**

Johnson, H. G. (1968) 'Problems of efficiency in monetary management'. *Journal of Political Economy* 76(5): 971–90.   **88**

Johnson, H. G. (1970) 'Recent developments in monetary theory: A commentary', in *Money in Britain* 1959–1969, ed. D. R. Croome and H. G. Johnson. Oxford: Oxford University Press, 83–114.   **10, 155, 175**

Johnson, H. G. (1971a) 'Introduction', in *The Current Inflation*, ed. H. G. Johnson and A. R. Nobay. London: Macmillan, vii–xi.   **239**

Johnson, H. G. (1971b) 'The Keynesian revolution and the monetarist counter-revolution'. *American Economic Review* 62(2): 1–14.   **196**

Johnson, R. (1983) 'Supply-side economics: The rise to prominence'. *Review of Black Political Economy* 12(2): 189–202.   **226**

Johnson, S. R. (1973) 'Phillips curve, expectations, and stability'. *Quarterly Review of Economics and Business* 13(3): 85–91.   **182**

Johnston, J. and M. Timbrell (1973) 'Empirical tests of a bargaining theory of wage rate determination'. *Manchester School* 41(2): 141–67.   **239**

Joint Economic Committee (1960) 'Employment, growth and price levels'. Washington, DC: Government Printing Office.   **118**

Jones, A. (1968) 'Prices and incomes policy'. *The Economic Journal* 78(312): 799–806.
247

Jonson, P. D., K. L. Mahar, and G. J. Thompson (1974) 'Earnings and award wages in Australia'. *Australian Economic Papers* 13(22): 80–98.   **106, 228, 242**

Jorgenson, D. W. (1966) 'Rational distributed lag functions'. *Econometrica* 34(January): 135–49.   **101**

Jossa, B. and M. Musella (1998) *Inflation, Unemployment and Money*. Cheltenham: Edward Elgar.   **48, 220**

Kahn, S. (1997) 'Evidence of nominal wage stickiness from microdata'. *American Economic Review* 87(5): 993–1008.   **234**

Kahneman, D., J. Knetsch, and R. Thaler (1986) 'Fairness as a constraint on profit seeking'. *American Economic Review* 76(4): 728–41.   **77**

Kaldor, N. (1957) 'A model of economic growth'. *Economic Journal* 67(268): 591–624.
221

Kaldor, N. (1959a) 'Economic growth and the problem of inflation, part 2'. *Economica* 26(November): 287–98.   **16, 56**

Kaldor, N. (1959b) *Evidence to the Radcliffe Committee*. London: HMSO.   **118, 132**

Kaldor, N. (1967) *Strategic Factors in Economic Development*. Ithaca, NY: Cornell University Press.   **118**

Kalachek, E. and R. Westebbe (1961) 'Rates of unemployment in Great Britain and the United States 1950–60'. *Review of Economics and Statistics* 43(4): 340–50.   **220**

Kaliski, S. F. (1964) 'The relation between unemployment and the rate of change of money wages in Canada'. *International Economic Review* 5: 1–33.   **58, 225, 246, 251**

Kaliski, S. F. (1971) 'Is the Phillips curve still with us?', in *Inflation and the Canadian Experience*, ed. N. Swan and D. Wilton. Kingston, ON: The Industrial Relations Centre, Queen's University, 9–18.   **135, 233**

Kaliski, S. F. (1972) *The Trade-off between Inflation and Unemployment: Some Explorations of the Recent Evidence for Canada*. Ottawa: Information Canada.   **105**

Karanassou, M., H. Sala, and D. J. Snower (2008) 'Long-run inflation-unemployment dynamics: The Spanish Phillips curve and economic policy'. *Journal of Policy Modeling* 30(2): 279–300.   **213**

Karmel, P. H. (1959) 'Some reflections on inflation, productivity and growth'. *Economic Record* 35(72): 349–70.   **84**

Kaufman, B. E. (1988) 'The postwar view of labor markets and wage determination', in *How Labor Markets Work*, ed. B. E. Kaufman. Lexington, MA: D. C. Heath and Company.   **222**

Kaufman, B. E. (1993) *The Origins and Evolution of the Field of Industrial Relations in the United States*. Ithaca, NY: Cornell University.   **222**

Kaun, D. E. (1965) 'Wage adjustments in the Appalachian states'. *Southern Economic Journal* 32: 127–36.   **230, 232**

Kaun, D. E. and M. H. Spiro (1970) 'The relation between wages and unemployment in US cities 1955–1965'. *Manchester School* 38(1): 1–14.   **251**

Kelley, E. J. and L. R. Scheewe (1975) 'Buyer behavior in a stagflation-shortages economy'. *Journal of Marketing* 39(2): 44–50.   **228**

Kendrick, J. W. (1967) 'Review of Shultz and Aliber "Guidelines: Informal controls and the market place"'. *American Economic Review* 57(4): 927–30.   **89**

Kenen, P. B. (1969) 'The new fiscal policy: Comment'. *Journal of Money, Credit and Banking* 1(3): 503–5.   **247**

Kenen, P. B. (1971) 'The role of unions, management and government in a viable incomes policy'. *Antitrust Law Journal* 40(2): 270–81.   **250**

Keohane, R. (1978) 'Economics, inflation, and the role of the state: Political implications of the McCracken Report'. *World Politics* 31: 108–28.   **109**

Kerr, C. (1950) 'Labor markets, their character and consequences'. *American Economic Review* 40(2): 278–91.   **28**

Kessel, R. A. and A. A. Alchian (1960) 'The meaning and validity of the inflation-induced lag of wages behind prices'. *American Economic Review* 50(1): 43–66.   **119**

Keynes, J. M. (1930a) *Treatise on Money* (vol. 2). London: Macmillan.   **116**

Keynes, J. M. (1930b) 'Discussion of Mr Hawtrey's paper'. *Journal of the Royal Statistical Society* 93(1): 86–8.   **13**

Keynes, J. M. (1936) *The General Theory of Employment, Interest and Money*. London: Macmillan.   **24, 28, 209, 221, 238**

Keynes, J. M. (1940) *How to Pay for the War*. London: Macmillan.   **221**

Keynes, J. M. (1946/1972) 'Newton, the man', in *Collected Writings of John Maynard Keynes* (vol. 10). London: Macmillan, 363–74 ed D. E. Moggridge.   **208**

Kindleberger, C. P. (1967) *Europe's Post-war Growth: The Role of the Labor Supply*. Cambridge, MA: Harvard University Press.   **42**

King, J. E. and A. Millmow (2008) 'Crank or proto-monetarist? J. K. Gifford and the cost-push inflation fallacy'. *History of Economics Review* 47(1): 54–71.   **247**

King, R. G. and M. W. Watson (1994) 'The post-war US Phillips curve: A revisionist econometric history'. *Carnegie Rochester Conference Series on Public Policy* 41: 157–219.   **228**

King, R. G. and M. W. Watson (1997) 'Testing long-run neutrality'. *Federal Reserve Bank of Richmond Economic Quarterly* 83(3): 69–101.   **249**

Kirshner, J. (2001) 'The political economy of low inflation'. *Journal of Economic Surveys* 15(1): 41–70.   **48**

Kitching, B. (1971) 'Possibility of an inflation-recession trap with no tradeoff'. *Rivista Internazionale di Scienze Economiche E Commerciali* 18(8): 814–23.   **227**

Klamer, A. (1984) *The New Classical Macroeconomics: Conversations with New Classical Economists and their Opponents*. Brighton: Wheatsheaf Books.   **41**

Klein, L. R. (1950) *Economic Fluctuations in the United States*. New York: Wiley.   **12**

Klein, L. R. (1967) 'Wage and price determination in macroeconometrics', in *Prices: Issues in Theory, Practice, and Public Policy*, ed. A. Phillips and O. E. Williamson. Philadelphia: University of Pennsylvania Press, 82–100.   **241**

Klein, L. R. (2000) 'The Phillips curve', in *A. W. H. Phillips: Collected Works in Contemporary Perspective*, ed. R. Leeson. Cambridge: Cambridge University Press, 288–95.   **17**

Klein, L. R. and R. J. Ball (1959) 'Some econometrics of the determination of absolute prices and wages'. *Economic Journal* 69(275): 465–82. **18, 56, 60, 70, 207, 250**

Klein, L. R. and R. G. Bodkin (1964) 'Empirical aspects of the trade-offs among three goals: High level employment, price stability, and economic growth', in *Inflation, Growth and Employment: Studies Prepared for the Commission on Money and Credit*, ed. B. Fox. Englewood Cliffs, NJ: Prentice Hall, 367–428.   **58, 71, 243**

Klein, L. R. and A. S. Goldberger (1955) *An Econometric Model of the United States, 1929–1952*. Amsterdam: North-Holland.   **12, 18, 159**

Klein, L. R. and Y. Shinkai (1963) 'An econometric model of Japan, 1930–59'. *International Economic Review* 4(1): 1–28.   **58**

Klein, L. R., R. J. Ball, A. Hazlewood, and P. Vandome (1961) *An Econometric Model of the United Kingdom*. Oxford: Blackwell. **57, 59, 70, 231**

Knowles, K. G. J. C. and C. B. Winsten (1959) 'Can the level of unemployment explain changes in wages?' *Bulletin of the Oxford University Institute of Economics and Statistics* 21(2): 113–20. **16**

Koot, R. S. (1969) 'Wage changes, unemployment, and inflation in Chile'. *Industrial and Labor Relations Review* 22(4): 568–75. **234**

Koshal, R. K. and L. E. Gallaway (1970) 'The Phillips curve for Belgium'. *Tijdschrift voor Economie* 3: 263–71. **232, 234**

Koshal, R. K. and L. E. Gallaway (1971) 'The Phillips curve for West Germany'. *Kyklos* 24(2): 346–9. **232**

Koshal, R. K. and V. Shukla (1971) 'Unemployment and changes in wage rates in member countries of European economic community'. *Rivista Internazionale di Scienze Economiche E Commerciali* 18(6): 603–7. **232**

Kotowitz, Y. (1971) 'Review of price stability and high employment: The options for Candian economic policy, by Bodkin, Bond, Reuber, and Robinson'. *Journal of Economic Literature* 9(3): 839–40. **74**

Kraft, A. and J. Kraft (1974) 'A re-estimation of the Phillips curve for the United Kingdom'. *Applied Economics* 6(3): 215–27. **228, 239**

Kruger, A. (1969) 'Review of Smith "The labour market and inflation"'. *Industrial and Labor Relations Review* 22(4): 617–18. **246**

Krugman, P. (2007) 'Who was Milton Friedman?' *New York Review of Books*, 15 February. 54(2): 27–30. **165**

Kuh, E. (1960) 'Profits, profit markups, and productivity', in *Employment, Growth, and Price Levels*, Study Paper No. 15, ed. Joint Economic Committee. Washington, DC: Government Printing Office. **43**

Kuh, E. (1967) 'A productivity theory of wage levels: An alternative to the Phillips curve'. *Review of Economic Studies* 34: 333–60. **53, 59, 207, 215, 231, 250, 251**

Kuska, E. A. (1966) 'The simple analytics of the Phillips curve'. *Economica* 33: 462–7. **246**

Kydland, F. and E. Prescott (1977) 'Rules rather than discretion: The inconsistency of optimal plans'. *Journal of Political Economy* 85: 473–91. **136**

Laffer, A. B. and R. D. Ranson (1971) 'A formal model of the economy'. *Journal of Business* 44(3): 247–70. **138**

Laidler, D. E. W. (1971) 'The Phillips curve, expectations and incomes policy', in *The Current Inflation*, ed. H. G. Johnson and A. R. Nobay. London: Macmillan, 75–98. **176**

Laidler, D. E. W. (1975) *Essays on Money and Inflation*. Manchester: Manchester University Press. **239**

Laidler, D. E. W. (1978) 'Review: Towards full employment and price stability'. *Journal of Economic Literature* 16(3): 1040–4. **109**

Laidler, D. E. W. (1984) 'Harry Johnson as a macroeconomist'. *Journal of Political Economy* 92(4): 592–615. **133**

Laidler, D. E. W. (1997) 'The emergence of the Phillips curve as a policy menu', in *Trade, Technology and Economics*, ed. B. C. Eaton and R. G. Harris. Cheltenham: Edward Elgar, 88–106. **74, 157, 237**

Laidler, D. E. W. (2003) 'The role of the history of economic thought in modern macroeconomics', in *Monetary History, Exchange Rates and Financial Markets: Essays in Honour of Charles Goodhart* (vol. 2), ed. P. Mizen. Cheltenham: Elgar, 12–29. **47, 225**

Laidler, D. E. W. and M. Parkin (1975) 'Inflation: A survey'. *Economic Journal* 85(December): 741–809. **105, 162, 227**

Laidler, D. E. W. and D. L. Purdy (eds) (1974) *Inflation and Labour Markets*. Manchester: Manchester University Press. **239**

Larkin, P. (1974) *High Windows*. London: Faber and Faber. **208**

Leavis, F. R. (1962) 'Two cultures? The significance of CP Snow'. *Spectator*, 9 March. **20**

Lebergott, S. (ed.) (1964) *Men without Work*. Englewood Cliffs, NJ: Prentice Hall. **246**

Lee, F. S. (1984) 'The marginalist controversy and the demise of full cost pricing'. *Journal of Economic Issues* 18(4): 1107–32. **26**

Leeson, R. (1994) 'A. W. H. Phillips, MBE (Military Division)'. *Economic Journal* 104(424): 605–18. **208, 250**

Leeson, R. (1996a) 'The rise and fall of the Phillips curve in British policy-making circles'. *History of Economics Review* (25): 232–48. **167, 168, 169, 250**

Leeson, R. (1996b) 'The rise of the natural-rate of unemployment model'. *History of Economics Review: Special Keynes Centenary Issue* (25): 249–64. **167, 236**

Leeson, R. (1997a) 'The trade-off interpretation of Phillips's dynamic stabilization exercise'. *Economica* 64(253): 155–71. **223**

Leeson, R. (1997b) 'The political economy of the inflation-unemployment trade-off'. *History of Political Economy* 29(1): 117–56. **34, 41, 219, 222, 223, 229**

Leeson, R. (1997c) 'The eclipse of the goal of zero inflation'. *History of Political Economy* 29(3): 447–96. **123, 124, 128, 244, 245**

Leeson, R. (1998a) 'Early doubts about the Phillips curve trade-off'. *Journal of the History of Economic Thought* 20(1): 83–102. **220, 229**

Leeson, R. (1998b) 'The demise of the high inflation trade off interpretation: A reply to Chapple'. *History of Economics Review* 28: 87–103. **220**

Leeson, R. (1999) 'The Phillips controversy: A further reply to Chapple'. *History of Economics Review* 29: 97–106. **220**

Leeson, R. (2000) 'Inflation, disinflation and the natural rate of unemployment: A dynamic framework for policy analysis', in *The Australian Economy in the 1990s*, ed. D. Gruen and S. Shrestha. Reserve Bank of Australia 124–75. **229**

Leijonhufvud, A. S. B. (1968) 'Comment: Is there a meaningful trade-off between inflation and unemployment?' *Journal of Political Economy* 76(July): 738–43. **174**

Lekachman, R. (1967) 'Review of Schultz and Aliber "Guidelines: Informal controls and the market place"'. *Political Science Quarterly* 82(3): 495–6. **89**

Lerner, A. P. (1949) 'The inflationary process: Some theoretical aspects'. *Review of Economics and Statistics* 31(3): 193–200. **83, 121, 236**

Lerner, A. P. (1951) *Economics of Employment*. New York: McGraw-Hill. **129, 219**

Lerner, A. P. (1958) 'Inflationary depression and the regulation of administered prices', in The Relationship of Prices to Economic Stability and Growth, ed. Joint Economic Committee. Washington, DC: Government Printing Office, 257–68. **79**

Lerner, A. P. (1960) 'Discussion'. *American Economic Review* 50(2): 215–18. **43**

Lerner, A. P. (1967) 'Employment theory and employment policy'. *American Economic Review* 57(2): 1–18. **129**

Lester, R. A. (1941) *Economics of Labor*. New York: Macmillan. **26**

Lester, R. A. (1946) 'Shortcomings of marginal analysis for wage-employment problems'. *American Economic Review* 36(1): 63–82. **26**

Lester, R. A. (1952) 'A range theory of wage differentials'. *Industrial and Labor Relations Review* 5: 483–500. **27**

Lester, R. A. (1968) 'Negotiated wage increases, 1951–1967'. *Review of Economics and Statistics* 50(2): 173–81.   247

Leudicke, H. (1957/1957) 'Editorial'. *Journal of Commerce*, 13 February. Reprinted in *Creeping Inflation* Twin Coast Newspapers Inc: 7–11.   82

Levinson, H. M. (1960) 'Postwar movement of prices and wages in manufacturing', in The Relationship of Prices to Economic Stability and Growth, Study Paper No. 21, ed. Joint Economic Committee. Washington, DC: Government Printing Office.   52, 233

Levy, M. E. (1966) 'Full employment and inflation: A "trade-off" analysis'. *Conference Board Record* (December): 17–27.   55, 69

Lewis, A. (1959) 'Saulnier urges some price cuts'. *New York Times*, 26 August. 1, 30.
                                                                                                                                                                              120

Lewis, H. G. (1963) *Unionism and Relative Wages*. Chicago: University of Chicago Press.
                                                                                                                                                                           68–69

Liebling, H. I. and A. T. Cluff (1969) 'US postwar inflation and Phillips curves'. *Kyklos* 22: 232–50.   56, 70, 225, 233

Lindauer, J. (ed.) (1968) *Macroeconomic Readings*. New York: Free Press.   226

Lindblom, C. E. (1948) 'The union as monopoly'. *Quarterly Journal of Economics* 62(5): 671–97.   114

Lipsey, R. G. (1960) 'The relation between unemployment and the rate of change of money wage rates in the United Kingdom, 1882–1957: A further analysis'. *Economica* 27(105): 1–31.   **14, 15, 16, 18, 20, 31, 51, 56, 57, 78, 96, 101, 105, 136, 172, 176, 177, 183, 184, 211, 219, 226, 231, 233, 234, 250**

Lipsey, R. G. (1961) 'Is inflation explosive?' *The Banker* (October): 2–12.   121

Lipsey, R. G. (1962) 'Can there be a valid theory of wages?' *Advancement of Science* (19): 105–12.   21, 178, 211

Lipsey, R. G. (1963) *An Introduction to Positive Economics*. London: Weidenfeld & Nicolson.   20, 221

Lipsey, R. G. (1964) 'Positive economics in relation to some current trends'. *Journal of the Economics Association* 5: 365–71.   20

Lipsey, R. G. (1965) 'Structural and deficient-demand unemployment reconsidered', in *Employment Policy and the Labor Market*, ed. A. M. Ross. Berkeley and Los Angeles: University of California Press, 210–55.   136, 226, 245

Lipsey, R. G. (1966) *An Introduction to Positive Economics*. (2nd edn). London, Weidenfeld & Nicolson.   79, 211, 221

Lipsey, R. G. (1974) 'The micro theory of the Phillips curve reconsidered: A reply to Holmes and Smyth'. *Economica* 41(161): 62–70.   248

Lipsey, R. G. (1978) 'The place of the Phillips curve in macroeconomic models', in *Stability and Inflation*, ed. A. R. Bergstrom, A. Catt, M. H. Peston, and B. D. J. Silverstone. Chichester: John Wiley & Sons, 49–76.   18, 22, 245

Lipsey, R. G. (1981) 'The understanding and control of inflation: Is there a crisis in macro-economics?' *Canadian Journal of Economics* 14(4): 545–76.   173, 245

Lipsey, R. G. (1997) 'Introduction: An intellectual autobiography', in *Microeconomics, Growth and Political Economy: The Selected Essays of Richard Lipsey*, ed. R. G. Lipsey.   17, 221, 240

Lipsey, R. G. (2000) 'The famous Phillips curve article', in *A. W. H. Phillips: Collected Works in Contemporary Perspective*, ed. R. Leeson. Cambridge: Cambridge University Press, 232–42.   15, 17, 219

Lipsey, R. G. (2009) 'Some legacies of Robbins' "An essay on the nature and significance of economic science"'. *Economica* 76(s1): 845–56.   221

Lipsey, R. G. and M. Parkin (1970) 'Incomes policy: A reappraisal'. *Economica* 37(146): 115–38. **96, 100, 196, 240**

Lipsey, R. G. and B. Scarth (eds) (2011) *Inflation and Unemployment: The Evolution of the Phillips Curve*. Cheltenham: Elgar. **232**

Lipsey, R. G. and M. D. Steuer (1961) 'The relation between profits and wage rates'. *Economica* 28(110): 137–55. **20, 56, 212, 219, 233**

Lipton, M. (1968) *Assessing Economic Performance*. London: Staples Press. **148**

Little, I. M. D. (1952) 'Fiscal policy', in *The British Economy, 1945–1950*, ed. G. D. N. Worswick and P. H. Ady. Oxford: Clarendon Press, 159–87. **148**

Little, I. M. D. (1962) 'Fiscal policy', in *The British Economy in the 1950s*, ed. G. D. N. Worswick and P. H. Ady. Oxford: Oxford University Press, 231–300. **148**

Lohani, P. and E. A. Thompson (1971) 'Optimal rate of secular inflation'. *Journal of Political Economy* 79(5): 962–82. **45**

Lomax, K. S. (1966) 'Wages, prices, profits and inflation'. *Transactions of the Manchester Statistical Society*. March: 1–22. **57, 61**

Lucas, R. E. (1972a) 'Expectations and the neutrality of money'. *Journal of Economic Theory* 4: 103–24. **160, 242**

Lucas, R. E. (1972b) 'Econometric testing of the natural rate hypothesis', in *The Econometrics of Price Determination*, ed. O. Eckstein. Washington, DC: Board of Governors of the Federal Reserve System. **102, 236**

Lucas, R. E. (1973) 'Some international evidence on output-inflation tradeoffs'. *American Economic Review* 63(3): 326–34. **102, 138**

Lucas, R. E. (1976) 'Econometric policy evaluation: A critique', in *The Phillips Curve and the Labor Market: Carnegie-Rochester Series on Public Policy* (vol. 1), ed. K. Brunner and A. H. Meltzer. Amsterdam: North-Holland, 19–46. **159, 160**

Lucas, R. E. and L. A. Rapping (1969a) 'Price expectations and the Phillips curve'. *American Economic Review* 59(3): 342–50. **87, 101, 154, 174**

Lucas, R. E. and L. A. Rapping (1969b) 'Real wages, employment, and inflation'. *Journal of Political Economy* 77(5): 721–54. **134**

Lucas, R. E. and T. J. Sargent (eds) (1978) *After the Phillips Curve: Persistence of High Inflation and High Unemployment*. Boston: Federal Reserve Bank of Boston. **7, 160**

Lundberg, E. (1952) 'General survey of some issues of wage policy', in *Wages Policy under Full Employment*, ed. R. Turvey. London: William Hodge & Company Limited, 1–15. **13**

Lundborg, P. and H. Sacklen (2006) 'Low-inflation targeting and long-run unemployment'. *Scandinavian Journal of Economics* 108(3): 397–418. **48**

Mabry, B. D. (1966) *Labor Relations and Collective Bargaining*. New York: Ronald Press. **246**

McCaffree, K. M. (1963) 'A further consideration of wages, unemployment, and prices in the United States, 1948–1958'. *Industrial and Labor Relations Review* 17(1): 60–74. **54**

McCallum, B. T. (1975) 'Rational expectations and the natural rate hypothesis: Some evidence for the United Kingdom'. *Manchester School* 43(1): 55–67. **242**

McCallum, B. T. (1976) 'Rational expectations and the natural rate hypothesis: Some consistent estimates'. *Econometrica* 44(January): 43–52. **242**

McCallum, B. T. (1989) *Monetary Economics: Theory and Policy*. New York: Macmillan. **249**

McCracken, P. W., G. Carli, H. Giersch, A. Karaosmanoglu, R. Komiya, A. Lindbeck, R. Marjolin, and R. Matthews (1977) *Towards Full Employment and Price Stability* ('The McCracken Report'). Paris: OECD. **109, 110, 120**

McDonald, J. (1975) 'Wages and prices in Australia: On the short and long-run trade-offs between inflation and unemployment'. *Australian Economic Papers* 14(25): 154–70.   **105**

MacDougall, D. G. A. (1959) 'Inflation in the United Kingdom'. *The Economic Record* 35(72): 371–88.   **132**

McGuire, T. W. and L. A. Rapping (1966) 'Interindustry wage change dispersion and the "spillover" hypothesis'. *American Economic Review* 61(June): 493–501.   **229, 232**

McGuire, T. W. and L. A. Rapping (1967) 'The determination of money wages in American industry: Comment'. *Quarterly Journal of Economics* 81: 684–94.   **229, 232**

McGuire, T. W. and L. A. Rapping (1968) 'The role of market variables and key bargains in the manufacturing wage determination process'. *Journal of Political Economy* 76: 1015–1036.   **229, 232**

McGuire, T. W. and L. A. Rapping (1970) 'The supply of labor and manufacturing wage determination in the United States: An empirical examination'. *International Economic Review* 11(2): 258–68.   **229, 232**

Machlup, F. (1960) 'Another view of cost-push and demand-pull inflation'. *Review of Economics and Statistics* 42(2): 125–39.   **79, 112**

Mackay, D. I. and R. A. Hart (1974) 'Wage inflation and the Phillips relationship'. *Manchester School* 42(2): 136–61.   **239**

Mackay, D. I. and R. A. Hart (1975) 'Wage inflation and regional wage structure', in *Contemporary Issues in Economics*, ed. M. Parkin and A. R. Nobay. Manchester: Manchester University Press, 88–116.   **239**

Mackie, C. D. (1998) *Canonizing Economic Theory: How Theories and Ideas are Selected in Economics*. New York: M. E. Sharpe.   **227**

McNamara, K. (1998) *The Currency of Ideas*. Ithaca, NY: Cornell University Press. **167**

McNown, R. (1975) 'Impact of currency depreciation and international markets on United States inflation'. *Quarterly Review of Economics and Business* 15(4): 7–14.   **228**

Magee, B. (1973) *Popper*. Glasgow: Fontana.   **220**

Magnifico, G. (1973) *European Monetary Unification*. Basingstoke: Macmillan.   **137**

Malkiel, B. G. (1965) 'Review of Hansen: "The dollar and the international monetary system"'. *Journal of Finance* 20(4): 758–60.   **246**

Maloney, J. (2011) 'Straightening the Phillips curve, 1968–1976'. *European Journal of the History of Economic Thought* 18(3): 407–40.   **166**

Mankiw, N. G. (1996) 'Comment on Akerlof, Dickens and Perry'. *Brookings Papers on Economic Activity* 1: 66–70.   **184**

Mankiw, N. G. (2006) 'The macroeconomist as scientist and engineer'. *Journal of Economic Perspectives* 20(4): 29–46.   **228**

Mankiw, N. G. and M. P. Taylor (2011) *Economics*. Andover: South-Western Cengage Learning.   **166**

De Marchi, N. (1988a) 'Popper and the LSE economists', in *The Popperian Legacy in Economics*, ed. N. de Marchi. Cambridge: Cambridge University Press, 139–66.   **18, 211**

De Marchi, N. (1988b) *The Popperian Legacy in Economics*. Cambridge: Cambridge University Press.   **220**

Marczewski, J. (1978) *Inflation and Unemployment in France: A Quantitative Analysis*. New York: Praeger.   **98**

Marget, A. W. (1962) 'The applicability of "orthodox monetary remedies" to developed and under-developed countries', in *Inflation*, ed. D. C. Hague. New York: St Martin's Press Inc.   **108**

Marin, A. (1970) 'Review of Solow, "Price expectations and the behavior of the price level"'. *Economica* 37(148): 430–1.   101

Martin, L. R. (1969) 'Discussion: Demographic and social dimensions of rural economic policy'. *American Journal of Agricultural Economics* 51(2): 444–7.   247

Martineau, H. (1832/2004) *Illustrations of Political Economy: Selected Tales.* Peterborough, ON: Broadview Press.   219

Marty, A. L. (1968) 'The optimal rate of growth of money'. *Journal of Political Economy* 76(4): 860–73.   247

Marx, K. (1867/2003) *Capital* (vol. 1). London: Lawrence and Wishart.   219

Masters, S. H. (1967) 'The behavior of output per man during recessions: An empirical study of underemployment'. *Southern Economic Journal* 33(3): 388–94.   248

Matthijs, M. (2012) *Ideas and Economic Crises in Britain from Attlee to Blair.* Abingdon: Routledge.   153, 167

Mayer, T. (1997) 'What remains of the monetarist counter-revolution?', in *Reflections on the Development of Modern Macroeconomics*, ed. B. Snowdon and H. Vane. Cheltenham: Elgar, 78–102.   166

Maynard, G. W. (1955) 'Import prices and inflation: The experience of the United Kingdom 1950–2'. *Oxford Economic Papers* 7(3): 241–58.   15

Maynard, G. W. and W. van Ryckeghem (1976) *A World of Inflation.* London: Batsford.   135

Meade, J. E. (1958) *The Control of Inflation.* Cambridge: Cambridge University Press.   84

Means, G. C. (1935) *Industrial Prices and their Relative Flexibility.* Washington, DC: Government Printing Office.   113

Means, G. C. (1959) *Administrative Inflation and Public Policy.* Washington, DC: Anderson Kramer Associates.   113

Mehmet, O. (1970) 'A critical appraisal of the economic rationale of government-subsidized manpower training'. *Relations Industrielles–Industrial Relations* 25: 568–80.   146

Meidner, R. (1969) 'Active manpower policy and the inflation unemployment dilemma'. *Swedish Journal of Economics* 71(3): 161–83.   219, 246

Meiselman, D. I. (1968) 'Money-wage dynamics and labor-market equilibrium and the trade-off between inflation and unemployment: Comment'. *Journal of Political Economy* 76(4/2): 743–50.   242, 243

Meltzer, A. H. (1968) 'Introduction'. *Journal of Political Economy* 76(4): 661–3.   242

Meltzer, A. H. (1998) 'Monetarism: The issues and the outcome'. *Atlantic Economic Journal* 26(1): 8–31.   228

De Menil, G. (1969) 'Nonlinearity in a wage equation for United States manufacturing'. *Review of Economics and Statistics* 51(2): 202–6.   238

De Menil, G. and J. Enzler (1972) 'Prices and wages in the FR-MIT-Penn econometric model', in *The Econometrics of Price Determination*, ed. O. Eckstein. Washington, DC: Board of Governors of the Federal Reserve System, 277–308.   99, 160

Merry, D. H. and G. R. Bruns (1945) 'Full employment: The British, Canadian and Australian White Papers'. *The Economic Record* 21(2): 223–35.   141

Metcalf, D. (1971) 'The determinants of earnings changes: A regional analysis for the UK, 1960–1968'. *International Economic Review* 12(2): 273–82.   96

Mill, J. S. (1844/1974) 'Of the influence of consumption upon production', in *Essays on Some Unsettled Questions of Political Economy*. Clifton, NJ: Augustus M. Kelley.   83

Minami, R. (1970) 'Further considerations on the turning point in the Japanese economy (II)'. *Hitotsubashi Journal of Economics* 11: 18–60.   251

Minami, R. (1973) 'Wage adjustments in postwar Japan: An alternative approach to the Phillips–Lipsey curve'. *Hitotsubashi Journal of Economics* 14: 44–55.   252

Minsky, H. P. (1961) 'Employment, growth and price levels: A review article'. *Review of Economics and Statistics* (42): 3–6.   78

Minsky, H. P. (1968) 'Effects of shifts of aggregate demand upon income distribution'. *American Journal of Agricultural Economics* 50(2): 328–39.   78, 247

Mitchell, D. J. B. (1969) 'A simplified approach to incomes policy'. *Industrial and Labor Relations Review* 22(4): 512–27.   247

Mitchell, D. J. B. (1970) 'British incomes policy, the competitive effect and the 1967 devaluation'. *Southern Economic Journal* 37(1): 88–92.   240

Mitchell, D. J. B. (1978) 'Union wage determination: Policy implications and outlook'. *Brookings Papers on Economic Activity* 1978(3): 537–82.   238

Mitchell, W. C. (1951) *What Happens during Business Cycles*. New York: National Bureau of Economic Research.   119

Mittra, S. (1971) *Dimensions of Macroeconomics: A Book of Readings*. New York: Random House.   88

Modigliani, F. (1963) 'The monetary mechanism and its interaction with real phenomena'. *Review of Economics and Statistics* 45(1/2): 79–107.   224

Modigliani, F. (1964) 'Some empirical tests of monetary management and of rules versus discretion'. *Journal of Political Economy* 72(June): 211–45.   247

Modigliani, F. (1974) 'The 1974 Report of the President's Council of Economic Advisers: A critique of past and present prospective policies'. *American Economic Review* 64(September): 544–77.   151

Modigliani, F. (1977) 'The monetarist controversy or, should we forsake stabilization policies'. *American Economic Review* 67(2): 1–19.   9

Modigliani, F. and L. Papademos (1975) 'Targets for monetary policy in the coming years'. *Brookings Papers on Economic Activity* 1: 141–65.   94

Modigliani, F. and E. Tarantelli (1973) 'A generalization of the Phillips curve for a developing country'. *Review of Economic Studies* 40(2): 203–23.   97

Mooney, J. D. (1969) 'Urban poverty and labor force participation: Reply'. *American Economic Review* 59(1): 194–8.   247

Morag, A. (1962) 'For an inflation-proof economy'. *American Economic Review* 52(1): 177–85.   224

Morgan, E. V. (1966) 'Is inflation inevitable?' *Economic Journal* 76(301): 1–15.   235

Morishima, M. and M. Saito (1964) 'A dynamic analysis of the American economy, 1902–1952'. *International Economics Review* 5(2): 125–64.   224, 230

Mortensen, D. T. (1970) 'A theory of wage and employment dynamics', in *Microeconomic Foundations of Employment and Inflation Theory*, ed. E. S. Phelps. Macmillan: London, 167–211.   92, 134

Morton, W. A. (1950) 'Trade unionism, full employment, and inflation'. *American Economic Review* 40(March): 13–39.   82

Moulton, H. G. (1958) *Can Inflation be Controlled?* Washington, DC: Anderson Kramer Associates.   114

Mulvey, C. and M. Gregory (1977) 'The Hines wage inflation model'. *Manchester School* 45(1): 29–40.   96

Mulvey, C. and J. A. Trevithick (1970) 'Wage inflation: Causes and cures'. *Central Bank of Ireland Quarterly Bulletin*: 111–22.   239

Mulvey, C. and J. A. Trevithick (1974) 'Some evidence on the wage leadership hypothesis'. *Scottish Journal of Political Economy* 21(1): 1–11.   239

Mundell, R. A. (1963) 'Inflation and real interest'. *Journal of Political Economy* 71(3): 280–3. **88, 117**

Mundell, R. A. (1972) 'The issues: Five views', in *Inflation as a Global Problem*, ed. R. Hinshaw. Baltimore: Johns Hopkins University Press, 46–50. **157**

Nagatani, K. (1969) 'A monetary growth model with variable employment'. *Journal of Money, Credit and Banking* 1(2): 188–206. **247**

Nash, J. (1950) 'The bargaining problem'. *Econometrica* 18(2): 155–62. **27**

Nell, E. (1977) 'Inflation, market power, and monetary restraint'. *Challenge* 20(2): 62–3. **114**

Nelson, E. (2004) 'News-magazine monetarism', in *Money Matters*, ed. P. Minford. Cheltenham: Edward Elgar, 123–47. **48**

Nelson, E. (2005a) 'Paul Samuelson and monetary analysis'. *Federal Reserve Bank of St Louis Monetary Trends* April 1. **169**

Nelson, E. (2005b) 'The great inflation of the seventies: What really happened?' *Advances in Macroeconomics* 5(1): Article 3. **169**

Nelson, E. (2009) 'An overhaul of doctrine: The underpinning of UK inflation targeting'. *Economic Journal* 119(538): 333–68. **169**

Netherlands Central Statistical Office (1933) 'De wisselwesking tusschen loon en werkgelegenheid'. *De Nederlandsche Conjunctuur*: 10–26. **12**

Nevile, J. W. (1970) *Fiscal Policy in Australia*. Melbourne: Cheshire. **98, 242**

Nevile, J. W. (1975) 'A comment on short-run and long-run trade-offs between inflation and unemployment in Australia'. *Australian Economic Papers* 14(24): 132–6. **105**

Nevile, J. W. (1977) 'Domestic and overseas influences on inflation in Australia'. *Australian Economic Papers* 16: 121–9. **106**

Newton-Smith, W. H. (1981) *The Rationality of Science*. London; Routledge & Kegan Paul. **221**

Nickell, S. and G. Quintini (2003) 'Nominal wage rigidity and the rate of inflation'. *Economic Journal* 113(490): 762–81. **234**

Nobay, A. R. and H. G. Johnson (1977) 'Monetarism: Historic-theoretic perspective'. *Journal of Economic Literature* 15(2): 470–85. **45**

Nordhaus, W. D. (1972a) 'Recent developments in price dynamics', in *The Econometrics of Price Determination*, ed. O. Eckstein. Washington, DC: Board of Governors of the Federal Reserve System, 16–49. **176, 242, 251**

Nordhaus, W. D. (1972b) 'The worldwide wage explosion'. *Brookings Papers on Economic Activity* (2): 431–65. **101, 175, 251**

Nordhaus, W. D. (1975) 'The political business cycle'. *Review of Economic Studies* 42: 169–90. **136**

Norton, W. E. and J. F. Henderson (1973) 'The structure of a model of the Australian economy', in *Econometric Studies of Macro and Monetary Relations*, ed. A. A. Powell and R. A. Williams. Amsterdam: North-Holland, 49–84. **242**

Nowicki, A. (1968) 'Discussion of Soper and Webb'. *American Economic Review* 58(2): 284–92. **247**

O'Herlihy, C. S. J. (1966) *A Statistical Study of Wages, Prices and Employment in the Irish Manufacturing Sector*. Dublin: Economics Research Institute. **231**

OECD (Organisation for Economic Co-operation and Development) (1970) *Inflation: The Present Problem*. Paris: OECD.

OECD (Organisation for Economic Co-operation and Development) (1971) *Present Policies against Inflation*. Paris: OECD.

Okun, A. M. (1965a) 'The role of aggregate demand in alleviating unemployment', in *Unemployment in a Prosperous Economy*, ed. H. R. Bowen and F. H. Harbison. Princeton, 67–81.   **126**

Okun, A. M. (ed.) (1965b) *The Battle against Unemployment*. New York: Norton.   **243**

Okun, A. M. (1965c) 'Introduction', in *The Battle against Unemployment*, ed. A. M. Okun. New York: W. W. Norton, vii–xvii.   **224**

Okun, A. M. (1970) 'Inflation: The problems and prospects before us', in *Inflation*, ed. A. L. Gitlow. New York: New York University Press. 1–53.   **126, 132**

Okun, A. M. (1971) 'The mirage of steady inflation'. *Brookings Papers on Economic Activity* 1971(2): 485–98.   **128, 227**

Okun, A. M. (1975) 'Inflation: Its mechanics and welfare costs'. *Brookings Papers on Economic Activity* 1975(2): 351–90.   **236**

Olivera, J. H. G. (1960) 'La teoría no monetaria de la inflación'. *El Trimestre Económico* 27(108): 616–28.   **78**

Olivera, J. H. G. (1964) 'On structural inflation and Latin-American structuralism'. *Oxford Economic Papers* 16: 321–32.   **78**

Olson, M. (1975) 'Demand for and supply of inflation: Comment'. *Journal of Law & Economics* 18(3): 859–69.   **227**

Oppenheimer, P. M. (1970) 'Muddling through: The economy, 1951–1964', in *The Age of Affluence 1951–1964*, ed. V. Bogdanor and R. Skidelsky. London: Macmillan. 117–67.   **136**

Orcutt, G. H. (1950) 'Measurement of elasticities in international trade'. *Review of Economics and Statistics* 32: 117–32.   **70**

Ormerod, P. (1994) *The Death of Economics*. London: Faber and Faber.   **47**

Otani, I. (1975) 'Some empirical evidence on the determinants of wage and price movements in Japan, 1950–73'. *IMF Staff Papers* 22: 469–93.   **251**

Packer, A. H. and S. H. Park (1973) 'Distortions in relative wages and shifts in the Phillips curve'. *Review of Economics and Statistics* 55: 16–22.   **238**

Packer, S. B. (1966) 'Monetary policy: A current perspective'. *Financial Analysts Journal* 22(6): 107–14.   **247**

Paish, F. W. (1948) 'Reducing internal demand'. *The Listener*, 4 March.   **151**

Paish, F. W. (1958/1966) 'Inflation in the United Kingdom'. *Economica* 25(98): 94–105. Reprinted in Paish, F. W. (ed) *Studies in an inflationary economy*. London: Macmillan, 105–19.   **151**

Paish, F. W. (1964/1966) 'The limits of incomes policies', in *Policy for Incomes: Hobart Paper No. 29*, ed. F. W. Paish and J. Hennessy. (2nd edn). London: IEA.   **151**

Paish, F. W. (1968/1970) 'How the economy works'. *Lloyds Bank Review* (April). Reprinted in Paish, F. W. (ed) *How the economy works & other essays*. London: Macmillan 129-62.   **151**

Paldam, M. (1973) 'An empirical analysis of the relationship between inflation and economic growth in 12 countries, 1950–1969'. *Scandinavian Journal of Economics* 75(4): 420–27.   **117**

Paloviita, M. (2008) 'Comparing alternative Phillips curve specifications: European results with survey-based expectations'. *Applied Economics* 40: 2259–70.   **226**

Parkin, M. (1970) 'Incomes policy: Some further results on the determination of the rate of change of money wages'. *Economica* 37(148): 386–401.   **240**

Parkin, M. (1973) 'The short-run and long-run trade-offs between inflation and unemployment in Australia'. *Australian Economic Papers* 12(21): 127–44.   **105**

Parkin, M. (1975a) 'The politics of inflation'. *Government and Opposition* 10: 189–202.   **162**

Parkin, M. (1975b) 'Reply to "A comment on short-run and long-run trade-offs between inflation and unemployment in Australia" by John Nevile'. *Australian Economic Papers* 14(24): 136–8.　　　　　　　　　　　　　　　　　　　　　　**106**

Parkin, M. (1976) 'Yet another look at Australia's short-run and long-run trade-offs between inflation and unemployment'. *Australian Economic Papers* 15(26): 127–44.　　　　　　　　　　　　　　　　　　　　　　　　　**106**

Parkin, M. (1978) 'Britain 1951–72: The lessons unlearned', in *Wage-price Control: Myth and Reality*, ed. C. G. F. Simkin. Turramurra: Centre for Independent Studies, 145–74.　　　　　　　　　　　　　　　　　　　　　　　　**240**

Parkin, M. (1998) 'Unemployment, inflation and monetary policy'. *Canadian Journal of Economics* 31(5): 1003–32.　　　　　　　　　　　　　　　　**12**

Parkin, M. and M. T. Sumner (eds) (1972) *Incomes Policy and Inflation*. Toronto: University of Toronto Press.　　　　　　　　　　　　　　　　　　　**239**

Parkin, M. and M. T. Sumner (eds) (1978) *Inflation in the United Kingdom*. Manchester: Manchester University Press.　　　　　　　　　　　　**239**

Parkin, M. and G. Zis (eds) (1976a) *Inflation in the World Economy*. Manchester: Manchester University Press.　　　　　　　　　　　　　　　**239**

Parkin, M. and G. Zis (eds) (1976b) *Inflation in Open Economies*. Manchester: Manchester University Press.　　　　　　　　　　　　　　　　**239**

Parkin, M., M. T. Sumner, and R. A. Jones (1972) 'A survey of econometric evidence of the effects of incomes policy on the rate of inflation', in *Incomes Policy and Inflation*, ed. M. Parkin and M. T. Sumner. Manchester: Manchester University Press, 1–29.　　　　　　　　　　　　　　　　　**240, 250**

Parsley, C. J. (1980) 'Labor union effects on wage gains: A survey of recent literature'. *Journal of Economic Literature* 18(1): 1–31.　　　　　　　　**228**

Parsons, W. (1988) *The Political Economy of British Regional Policy*. London: Routledge.　　　　　　　　　　　　　　　　　　　　　　　　**241**

Parsons, W. (1989) *The Power of the Financial Press*. Aldershot: Edward Elgar.　**152**

Peacock, A. T. (1972) 'Fiscal means and political ends', in *Essays in Honour of Lord Robbins*, ed. M. H. Peston and B. Corry. London: Weidenfeld & Nicolson, 82–98.　　　　　　　　　　　　　　　　　　　　　　　　**136**

Pearce, K. A. and K. D. Hoover (1995) 'After the revolution: Paul Samuelson and the textbook Keynesian model'. *History of Political Economy* 27: 183–216.　**130, 226**

Pechman, J. A. (1960) 'Discussion'. *American Economic Review* 50(2): 218–22.　**224**

Pencavel, J. H. (1971) 'A note on the comparative predictive performance of wage inflation models of the British economy'. *Economic Journal* 81(321): 113–19.　**57**

Perry, G. L. (1964) 'The determinants of wage rate changes and the inflation-unemployment trade-off for the United States'. *Review of Economic Studies* 31: 287–308.　　　　　　　　　**52, 73, 173, 225, 250**

Perry, G. L. (1966) *Unemployment, Money Wage Rates, and Inflation*. Cambridge, MA: The MIT Press.　**52, 53, 59, 61, 73, 75, 133, 198, 207, 215, 225, 233, 234, 243, 250**

Perry, G. L. (1967) 'Wages and the Guideposts'. *American Economic Review* 57(4): 897–904.　　　　　　　　　　　　　　　　　　　　　　**56, 96**

Perry, G. L. (1969) 'Wages and the Guideposts: Reply'. *American Economic Review* 59(3): 365–70.　　　　　　　　　　　　　　　　　　　　**230**

Perry, G. L. (1970) 'Changing labor markets and inflation'. *Brookings Papers on Economic Activity* 3: 411–48.　　　　　　　　　　　　　　　**92, 104**

Perry, G. L. (1971) 'After the freeze'. *Brookings Papers on Economic Activity* 1971(2): 445–9.　　　　　　　　　　　　　　　　　　　　　　　**92**

Perry, G. L. (1973) 'The success of anti-inflation policies in the United States'. *Journal of Money, Credit and Banking* 5(1): 569–93.   92

Perry, G. L. (1975) 'Determinants of wage inflation around the world'. *Brookings Papers on Economic Activity* 1975(2): 403–47.   **176, 244**

Perry, G. L. (1976) 'Stabilization policy and inflation', in *Setting National Priorities: The Next Ten Years*, ed. H. Owen and C. L. Schultze. Washington, DC: Brookings, 271–321.   169

Perry, G. L. (1978) 'Slowing the wage-price spiral: The macroeconomic view'. *Brookings Papers on Economic Activity* 1978(2): 259–99.   **92, 169**

Perry, G. L. (1980) 'Inflation in theory and practice'. *Brookings Papers on Economic Activity* 1980(1): 207–48.   93

Perry, G. L. and J. Tobin (eds) (2000) *Economic Events, Ideas, and Policies: The 1960s and After*. Washington, DC: Brookings.   228

Peston, M. H. (1971) 'The microeconomics of the Phillips curve', in *The Current Inflation*, ed. H. G. Johnson and A. R. Nobay. London: Macmillan, 125–42.   44

Phelps, E. S. (1962) 'Review of William G. Bowen, Wage behavior in the postwar period, an empirical analysis. Princeton: Industrial Relations Section, 1960'. *Journal of the American Statistical Association* 57(297): 221–2.   246

Phelps, E. S. (1967) 'Phillips curves, expectations of inflation and optimal unemployment over time'. *Economica* 34(135): 254–81.   **1, 63, 81, 82, 85, 92, 134, 172**

Phelps, E. S. (1968) 'Money wage dynamics and labor market equilibrium'. *Journal of Political Economy* 76(4): 678–711.   **92, 134**

Phelps, E. S. (1969) 'The new microeconomics in inflation and employment theory'. *American Economic Review* 59(2): 147–60.   87

Phelps, E. S. (ed.) (1970a) *Microeconomic Foundations of Employment and Inflation Theory*. New York: Norton.   **127, 134, 251**

Phelps, E. S. (1970b) 'Introduction: The new microeconomics in employment and inflation theory', in *Microeconomic Foundations of Employment and Inflation Theory*, ed. E. S. Phelps. Macmillan: London, 1–26.   **134, 251**

Phelps, E. S. (1970c) 'Money wage dynamics and the labor market equilibrium', in *Microeconomic Foundations of Employment and Inflation Theory*, ed. E. S. Phelps. Macmillan: London, 124–66.   **88, 134, 154, 200**

Phelps, E. S. (1971) 'Inflation, expectations and economic theory', in *Inflation and the Canadian Experience*, ed. N. Swan and D. Wilton. Kingston, ON: The Industrial Relations Centre, Queen's University, 31–47.   135

Phelps, E. S. (1972a) 'The 1972 Report of the President's Council of Economic Advisers: Economics and Government'. *American Economic Review*. 62(4) 539–633.   135

Phelps, E. S. (1972b) *Inflation Policy and Unemployment Theory: The Cost-benefit Approach to Monetary Planning*. New York: W. W. Norton.   **92, 102**

Phelps, E. S. (1987) 'Phillips curve', in *New Palgrave Dictionary of Economics*, ed. J. Eatwell, M. Milgate, and P. Newman. London: Macmillan.   251

Phelps Brown, E. H. (1961) 'Review of Bowen "The wage-price issue"'. *Economica* 28(109): 82–3.   72

Phelps Brown, E. H. (1968) *Pay and Profits*. Manchester: Manchester University Press.   95

Phelps Brown, E. H. (1971) 'The analysis of wage movements under full employment'. *Scottish Journal of Political Economy* 18(3): 233–43.   **114, 138**

Phillips, A. W. H. (1954) 'Stabilization policy in a closed economy'. *Economic Journal* 64: 290–323.   **18, 22, 209**

Phillips, A. W. H. (1957) 'Stabilization policy and the time forms of lagged responses'. *Economic Journal* 67: 265–77.   **209**

Phillips, A. W. H. (1958) 'The relation between unemployment and the rate of change of money wage rates in the United Kingdom, 1861–1957'. *Economica* 25(100): 283–99.   **1, 4, 9, 10, 11, 40, 48, 51, 65, 74, 78, 88, 125, 138, 147, 159, 172, 177, 179, 185, 186, 197, 199, 207, 208, 211, 220, 224, 228, 232, 238, 248**

Phillips, A. W. H. (1959/2000) *Wage Changes and Unemployment in Australia, 1947–1958*. In Leeson, R (ed) A. W. H. Phillips: Collected Works in Contemporary Perspective, Cambridge: Cambridge University Press ch 28, 269–81.   **98, 209, 220**

Phillips, A. W. H. (1962) 'Employment, inflation and growth'. *Economica* 29(113): 1–16.   **13, 44, 132, 209**

Phillips, E. L. and L. D. Singell (1970) 'The simple analytics of hard core unemployment'. *Rocky Mountain Social Science Journal* 7(1): 51–87.   **234**

Pierson, F. C. (1967) *Unions in Postwar America: An Economic Assessment.* New York: Random House.   **235**

Pierson, G. (1968) 'Effect of union strength on the US Phillips curve'. *American Economic Review* 58: 456–67.   **229**

Pigou, A. C. (1944) *Lapses from Full Employment.* London: Macmillan.   **219**

Pitchford, J. D. (1957) 'Cost and demand elements in the inflationary process'. *Review of Economic Studies* 24: 139–48.   **113**

Pitchford, J. D. (1963) *A Study of Cost and Demand Inflation.* Amsterdam: North-Holland.   **84, 98, 162, 234**

Pitchford, J. D. (1968) 'An analysis of price movements in Australia, 1947–1948'. *Australian Economic Papers* 7(11): 111–35.   **98, 242**

Polanyi, K. (1944) *The Great Transformation.* New York: Farrar & Rinehart.   **82**

Poole, W. (1978) 'Summary and evaluation', in *After the Phillips Curve: Persistence of High Inflation and High Unemployment.* Boston: Federal Reserve Bank of Boston, 210–15.   **164**

Popper, K. R. (1959) *The Logic of Scientific Discovery*. London: Hutchinson & Co.   **19, 20, 220**

Popper, K. R. (1963) *Conjectures and Refutations.* London: Routledge & Kegan Paul. **220**

Posen, A. (2011) 'The soft tyranny of inflation expectations'. *International Finance* 14(3): 541–66.   **237**

Pratten, C. F. (1972) *Lloyds Bank Review.* No 103: 12–24.   **244**

Preston, L. E. (1965) 'Review of Wedervang "Development of a population of industrial firms: The structure of manufacturing industries in Norway 1930–1948"'. *American Economic Review* 55(5): 1238–9.   **248**

Purdy, D. L. and G. Zis (1973) 'Trade unions and wage inflation in the UK: A reappraisal', in *Essays in Modern Economics*, ed. M. Parkin. London: Longman, 294–327.   **239–240**

Qin, D. (2011) 'The Phillips curve from the perspective of the history of econometrics', in *Histories on Econometrics*, ed. M. Boumans, A. Dupont-Kieffer, and D. Qin. Durham, NC: Duke University Press, 283–308.   **7, 57**

Raimon, R. L. (1964) 'Labor mobility and wage inflexibility'. *American Economic Review* 54(3): 133–44.   **133**

Rasche, R. H. and H. T. Shapiro (1968) 'The FRB-MIT econometric model: Its special features'. *American Economic Review* 58(2): 123–49.   **241**

Reder, M. W. (1948) 'The theoretical problems of a national wage-price policy'. *Canadian Journal of Economics* 14(1): 46–61.   **83**

Reder, M. W. (1952) 'The theory of union wage policy'. *Review of Economics and Statistics* 34(February): 34–45.   **30**

Rees, A. (1950) 'Labor unions and the price system'. *Journal of Political Economy* 58(3): 254–63.   **79**

Rees, A. (1958) 'Price level stability and economic policy', in The Relationship of Prices to Economic Stability and Growth, ed. Joint Economic Committee. Washington, DC: Government Printing Office.   **122**

Rees, A. (1961) 'Review of Bowen "The wage-price issue"'. *Journal of Political Economy* 69(2): 205–7.   **71**

Rees, A. (1962) *The Economics of Trade Unions*. Chicago: Chicago University Press.

Rees, A. (1970) 'The Phillips curve as a menu for policy choice'. *Economica* 37(147): 227–38.   **79, 87, 99, 184**

Rees, A. (1973) *The Economics of Work and Pay*. New York: Harper & Row.   **222**

Rees, A. (1993) 'The role of fairness in wage determination'. *Journal of Labor Economics* 11(1): 243–52.   **222**

Rees, A. and M. T. Hamilton (1967) 'The wage-price-productivity perplex'. *Journal of Political Economy* 75: 63–70.   **138**

Reuber, G. L. (1962) *The Objectives of Monetary Policy: Working Paper Prepared for the Royal Commission on Banking and Finance*. Ottawa: The Queen's Printer.   **58, 74**

Reuber, G. L. (1964) 'The objectives of Canadian monetary policy, 1949–1961: Empirical "trade-offs" and the reaction function of the authorities'. *Journal of Political Economy* 72: 109–32.   **58, 74, 155, 246**

Reuber, G. L. (1968) 'Comment: The specification and stability of estimated price-wage-unemployment adjustment relationships'. *Journal of Political Economy* 76(4): 750–4.   **120, 242**

Reuber, G. L. (1970) 'Wage adjustments in Canadian industry, 1953–66'. *Review of Economic Studies* 37(4): 449–68.   **97**

Reynolds, L. G. (1951) *The Structure of Labor Markets*. New York: Harper.   **28, 30**

Reynolds, L. G. (1960) 'Wage-push and all that'. *American Economic Review* 50(2): 195–204.   **225**

Reynolds, L. G. (1966) *Economics: A General Introduction*. Homewood, IL: Richard D. Irwin.   **79**

Reynolds, L. G. (1969) 'The content of development economics'. *American Economic Review* 59(2): 401–8.   **247**

Richter, R. (1994) 'Methodology from the viewpoint of the economic theorist: 30 years on'. *Zeitschrift Für Die Gesamte Staatswissenschaft–Journal of Institutional and Theoretical Economics* 150(4): 589–608.   **227**

Richter, R. and F. Diener (1987) 'Phillips curves in West Germany 1975–1985: On the role of the Deutsche-Bundesbank as an expectation determining institution'. *Weltwirtschaftliches Archiv–Review of World Economics* 123(2): 346–53.   **226**

Riddell, W. C. (1979) 'The empirical foundations of the Phillips curve: Evidence from Canadian wage contract data'. *Econometrica* 47(1): 1–24.   **105, 241**

Ripley, F. C. (1966) 'An analysis of the Eckstein–Wilson wage determination model'. *Quarterly Journal of Economics* 80(1): 121–36.   **235**

Rippe, R. D. (1970) 'Wages, prices, and imports in the American steel industry'. *Review of Economics and Statistics* 52(1): 34–46.   **231**

Roa, M. J., F. J. Vazquez, and D. Saura (2008) 'Unemployment and economic growth cycles'. *Studies in Nonlinear Dynamics and Econometrics* 12(2): 1–21.   **229**

Robbins, L. (1932/1984) *The Nature and Significance of Economic Science*. London: Macmillan.   **19, 211, 215**

Robbins, L. (1972) 'Inflation: An international problem', in *Inflation as a Global Problem*, ed. R. Hinshaw. Baltimore: Johns Hopkins University Press, 10–25.   **150**

Robbins, L. (1974) *Aspects of Post-War Economic Policy*. London: IEA.   **150**

Roberts, J. M. (1995) 'New Keynesian economics and the Phillips curve'. *Journal of Money, Credit and Banking* 27(4): 975–84.   **177**

Robertson, D. H. (1955/1966) 'Creeping inflation'. *The Times Review of Industry*. Reprinted in Robertson, D (ed) Essays in money and interest. London Collins 245–56.   **122, 202, 236**

Robertson, D. H. (1957) *Lectures on Economic Principles* (vol. 3). London: Staples.   **13**

Robinson, J. V. (1937) *Essays in the Theory of Employment*. New York: Macmillan.   **24**

Robinson, J. V. (1972) 'The second crisis of economics'. *American Economic Review* 62(1/2): 1–10.   **138**

Robinson, J. V. (1973) 'What has become of the Keynesian revolution?', in *After Keynes*, ed. J. V. Robinson. Oxford: Blackwell 1-11.   **138**

Robinson, R. (1960) 'Employment, growth and price level: The Joint Economic Committee Report'. *American Economic Review* 50(5): 996–1010.   **77**

Romanis, A. (1967) 'Cost inflation and incomes policy in industrial countries'. *IMF Staff Papers* 14(1): 169–209.   **247**

Romanis Braun, A. (1971) 'Wages in the United Kingdom: Has there been a shift in the Phillips curve?'. *IMF Staff Papers* 28: 136–80.   **95**

Romer, C. D. and D. Romer (2002) 'The evolution of economic understanding and postwar stabilization policy', in *Rethinking Stabilization Policy*, ed. T. M. Hoenig. Kansas City: Federal Reserve Bank of Kansas City, 11–78.   **166**

Rose, H. (1967) 'On the non-linear theory of the business cycle'. *Review of Economic Studies* 34: 153–73.   **246**

Rosenbaum, H. D. and A. Ugrinsky (1994) *The Presidency and Domestic Policies of Jimmy Carter*. London: Greenwood Press.   **227**

Ross, A. M. (1948) *Trade Union Wage Policy*. Berkeley: California University Press.   **29, 30**

Ross, A. M. (1966a) 'Where we are and why'. *Monthly Labor Review* 89: 624–9.   **225**

Ross, A. M. (1966b) 'Guideline policy: Where we are and how we got here', in *Guidelines, Informal Controls, and the Market Place*, ed. G. P. Schultz and R. Z. Aliber. Chicago: Chicago University Press, 97–142.   **131**

Ross, P. (1961) 'Labor market behavior and the relationship between unemployment and wages'. *Proceedings of the Industrial Relations Research Association* 14: 275–88.   **230, 233**

Ross, S. and M. L. Wachter (1973) 'Wage determination, inflation, and industrial structure'. *American Economic Review* 63(4): 675–92.   **184**

Rothschild, K. W. (1971) 'The Phillips curve and all that'. *Scottish Journal of Political Economy* 18(3): 245–80.   **45, 136, 162, 178, 182, 250**

Rothschild, K. W. (1974) 'Friedman, expectations and the Phillips trade-off: A reply'. *Scottish Journal of Political Economy* 21(3): 303–8.   **136**

Routh, G. (1959) 'The relation between unemployment and the rate of change of money wage rates: A comment'. *Economica* 26(104): 299–315.   **9, 16, 35**

Routh, G. (1986) *Unemployment: Economic Perspectives*. London: Macmillan.   **9**

Rowley, J. C. R. and D. A. Wilton (1973a) 'The empirical sensitivity of the Phillips curve'. *The American Economist* 17(2): 90–112.   **241**

Rowley, J. C. R. and D. A. Wilton (1973b) 'Quarterly models of wage determination: Some new efficient estimates'. *American Economic Review* 63(3): 380–9.   **241**

Rowley, J. C. R. and D. A. Wilton (1974) 'Empirical foundations for Canadian Phillips curve'. *Canadian Journal of Economics* 7(2): 240–59.   **178, 241**

Rowthorn, R. E. (1975) 'What remains of Kaldor's law'. *Economic Journal* 85(337): 10–19.   **199**

Rowthorn, R. E. (1977) 'Conflict, inflation and money'. *Cambridge Journal of Economics* 1(3): 215–39.   **114, 194, 200**

Ruggles, R. (1965) 'The problems of our price indexes', in *The Battle against Unemployment*, ed. A. M. Okun. New York: W. W. Norton.   **243**

Rutledge, J. (1974) *A Monetarist Model of Inflationary Expectations*. Lexington, MA: Lexington Books.   **237**

Rymes, T. K. (1994) 'On the Coyne–Rasminsky directive and responsibility for monetary policy in Canada', in *Varieties of Monetary Reforms: Lessons and Experiences on the Road to Monetary Union*, ed. P. L. Siklos. Boston/Dordrecht/London: Kluwer Academic Publishers, 351–67.   **235**

Samuelson, P. A. (1948) *Economics*. New York: McGraw-Hill.   **131**

Samuelson, P. A. (1951) 'Economic theory and wages', in *The Impact of the Union*, ed. D. M. Wright. New York: Harcourt Brace & Company, 312–43.   **27**

Samuelson, P. A. (1955) *Economics* (3rd edn). New York: McGraw-Hill.   **131**

Samuelson, P. A. (1956) 'The economics of Eisenhower'. *Review of Economics and Statistics* 38(4): 371–3.   **130, 224**

Samuelson, P. A. (1958) 'Has inflation been built into our economic structure?', in *Problems of United States Economic Development*, ed. Committee for Economic Development. New York: Committee for Economic Development, 63–5.   **224**

Samuelson, P. A. (1960) 'Reflections on monetary policy'. *Review of Economics and Statistics* 42(3): 263–9.   **130**

Samuelson, P. A. (1961a) *Economics* (5th edn). New York: McGraw-Hill.   **9, 79, 130, 132, 173**

Samuelson, P. A. (1961b) *Prospects and Policies for the 1961 American Economy*. Report to President Elect Kennedy. Reprinted in Paul Samuelson, Collected Works, vol. 2, 1478–92.   **130, 224, 229**

Samuelson, P. A. (1963) 'A brief survey of post-Keynesian developments', in *Keynes' General Theory: Reports of Three Decades*, ed. R. Lekachman. New York: Macmillan, 331–47.   **130**

Samuelson, P. A. (1964a) *Economics* (6th edn). New York: McGraw-Hill.   **224, 229**

Samuelson, P. A. (1964b) 'Theoretical notes on trade problems'. *Review of Economics and Statistics* 46: 145–54.   **120**

Samuelson, P. A. (1965) 'The new economics in the US faces some old problems'. *Financial Times*, 3 December: 9.   **133, 182**

Samuelson, P. A. (1967) *Economics* (7th edn). New York: McGraw-Hill.   **224, 229**

Samuelson, P. A. (1973) Testimony in *The 1973 Midyear Review of the Economy*, ed. Joint Economic Committee. Washington, DC: US Government Printing Office.   **128, 132**

Samuelson, P. A. and R. M. Solow (1960) 'Analytical aspects of anti-inflation policy'. *American Economic Review* 50(2): 177–94.   **1, 4, 9, 33, 34, 40, 41, 43, 55, 74, 130, 132, 160, 163, 167, 169, 172, 179, 198, 199, 223, 225, 226, 228, 244, 245, 246**

Santomero, A. M. and J. J. Seater (1978) 'The inflation-unemployment trade-off: A critique of the literature'. *Journal of Economic Literature* 16(2): 499–544. **7, 15, 17, 51, 59, 62, 160, 162, 208, 233**

Sargan, J. D. (1964) 'Wages and prices in the United Kingdom: A study in econometric methodology', in *Econometric Analysis for National Economic Planning*, ed. P. E. Hart, G. Mills, and J. K. Whitaker. London: Butterworths, 25–54.   **57, 61, 67, 95**

Sargent, T. J. (1971) 'A note on the "accelerationist" controversy'. *Journal of Money, Credit and Banking* (3): 721–5. **102, 250**

Sargent, T. J. (1973) 'Rational expectations, the real rate of interest, and the natural rate of unemployment'. *Brookings Papers on Economic Activity* 1973(2): 429–80. **242**

Sargent, T. J. (1999) *The Conquest of American Inflation*. Princeton: Princeton University Press. **34, 47**

Sargent, T. J. (2008) 'Evolution and intelligent design'. *American Economic Review* 98(1): 5–37. **49**

Saulnier, R. J. (1963) *The Strategy of Economic Policy*. New York: Fordham University Press. **111**

Schettkat, R. (1992) *The Labor Market Dynamics of Economic Restructuring: The United States and Germany in Transition*. New York: Praeger. **226**

Schlesinger, J. R. (1957) 'The role of the monetary environment in cost-inflation'. *Southern Economic Journal* 23(3): 12–27. **243**

Schmidt, E. P. (1957) 'Full employment as a cause of inflation'. *Proceedings of the Academy of Political Science* 26(3): 9–26. **219**

Schott, K. E. (1969) *An Equation for Average Weekly Earnings*. Reserve Bank of Australia Research Discussion Paper no. 7. Sydney: R. B. o. A. Reserve Bank of Australia. **242**

Schuettinger, R. (1978) 'Wage-price control: The first 5000 years', in *Wage-price Controls: Myth and Reality*, ed. C. G. F. Simkin. Turamurra: The Centre for Independent Studies. **29**

Schuker, S. A. (2003) 'The gold-exchange standard: A reinterpretation', in *International Financial History in the Twentieth Century*, ed. M. Flandreau, C.-L. Holtfrerich, and H. James. Cambridge: Cambridge University Press, 77–94. **228**

Schultze, C. L. (1959) 'Recent inflation in the United States', in *Employment, Growth and Price Levels*, Study Paper No. 1, ed. Joint Economic Committee. Washington, DC: Government Printing Office. **76, 77, 78, 113, 119, 126, 136, 141, 243**

Schultze, C. L. (1960) *Prices Costs and Output for the Postwar Decade*. New York: Committee for Economic Development. **76**

Schultze, C. L. and J. L. Tryon (1965) 'Prices and wages', in *The Brookings Quarterly Econometric Model of the US*, ed. J. S. Duesenberry. Chicago: Rand McNally, 281–334. **230**

Schwarzer, J. A. (2012) 'A. W. Phillips and his curve: Stabilization policies, inflation expectations and the "menu of choice"'. *European Journal of the History of Economic Thought* 19(6):976–1003. **220**

Schwier, A. (2000) 'Playing around with some data', in *A. W. H. Phillips: Collected Works in Contemporary Perspective*, ed. R. Leeson. Cambridge: Cambridge University Press, 24–5. **13**

Scitovsky, T. (1940–1) 'Capital accumulation, employment and price rigidity'. *Review of Economic Studies* 8(2): 69–88. **82**

Scitovsky, T. (1978) 'Market power and inflation'. *Economica* 45: 221–33. **113**

Scitovsky, T. and A. Scitovsky (1964) 'Inflation versus unemployment: An examination of their effects', in *Inflation, Growth and Employment: Studies Prepared for the Commission on Money and Credit*, ed. B. Fox. Englewood Cliffs, NJ: Prentice Hall, 429–70. **224, 235**

Scott, R. H. and J. R. McKean (1964) 'A "cross-section" look at employment, growth, and inflation'. *Economic Inquiry* 3(1): 1–6. **43, 55, 68, 233**

Seers, D. (1962) 'A theory of inflation and growth in underdeveloped countries'. *Oxford Economic Papers* 15: 173–95. **78**

Segal, M. (1961) 'Unionism and wage movements'. *Southern Economic Journal* 28(2): 174–81.   **235**

Selgin, G. (1997) *Less than Zero: The Case for a Falling Price Level*. London: Institute of Economic Affairs.   **13**

Sharot, T. (1973) 'Unemployment dispersion as a determinant of wage inflation in the UK 1925–66: A note'. *Manchester School* 41(2): 225–8.   **241**

Sheahan, J. (1967) *The Wage-price Guideposts*. Washington, DC: Brookings Institution.   **145, 246**

Sheahan, J. (1972) 'Incomes policies'. *Journal of Economic Issues* 6(4): 9–26.   **228**

Shenoy, S. R. (1978) 'Preface', in *Wage-price Control: Myth and Reality*, ed. C. G. F. Simkin. Turramurra: Centre for Independent Studies, 11–14.   **240**

Shepherd, A. S. B. (1970) 'Review of Brittan, Steering the economy'. *The Banker* 120: 99–105.   **249**

Shepherd, D. and C. Driver (2003) 'Inflation and capacity constraints in Australian manufacturing industry'. *Economic Record* 79(245): 182–95.   **226**

Shonfield, A. (1967) 'Stabilization policies in the West: From demand management to supply management'. *Journal of Political Economy* 75(4): 433–45.   **42, 248**

Shultz, G. P. and R. Z. Aliber (1966) 'Introduction', in *Guidelines, Informal Controls and the Market Place*, ed. G. P. Shultz and R. Z. Aliber. Chicago: University of Chicago Press, 1–14.   **89**

Shupp, F. R. (1976) 'Optimal policy rules for a temporary incomes-policy'. *Review of Economic Studies* 43(2): 249–59.   **184**

Sidrauski, M. (1967) 'Rational choice and patterns of growth in a monetary economy'. *American Economic Review* 57(2): 534–44.   **117**

Siebert, C. D. and M. A. Zaidi (1971) 'The short-run wage price mechanism in US manufacturing'. *Economic Inquiry* 9(3): 278–88.   **231**

Siegel, B. N. (1960) *Aggregate Economics and Public Policy*. Homewood, IL: Richard D. Irwin.   **234**

Simler, N. and A. Tella (1968) 'Labour reserves and the Phillips curve'. *Review of Economics and Statistics* 50: 32–49.   **53, 69, 92, 230**

Simons, H. C. (1936) 'Rules versus authorities in monetary policy'. *Journal of Political Economy* 44(1): 1–30.   **82**

Sleeman, A. G. (2011) 'Retrospective. The Phillips curve: A rushed job?'. *Journal of Economic Perspecgtives* 25(1): 223–38.   **17**

Slichter, S. H. (1932/1961) 'Technological unemployment—Lines of action, adaptation, and control'. *American Economic Review* 22(1): 41–54. Reprinted in John T. Dunlop (ed.) *Potentials of the American Economy*. Cambridge MA: Harvard University Press, 301–16.   **245**

Slichter, S. H. (1946) 'Wage-price policy and employment'. *American Economic Review* 36(2): 304–18.   **243**

Slichter, S. H. (1947) 'The danger in spiraling prices'. *New York Times Magazine*, 14 September, 12, 67–8.   **244**

Slichter, S. H. (1950/1961) 'Notes on the structure of wages'. *Review of Economics and Statistics* 32(1): 80–91. Reprinted in John T. Dunlop (ed.) *Potentials of the American Economy*. Cambridge MA: Harvard University Press, 360–78.   **28, 245**

Slichter, S. H. (1951) 'The integrity of the dollar'. *Proceedings of the Academy of Political Science* 24: 99–116.   **244**

Slichter, S. H. (1952a) 'How bad is inflation?' *Harper's Magazine* 205(1227): 53–7.   **124, 125, 132, 244, 245**

Slichter, S. H. (1952b/1961) 'How stable is the economy?' *Commerical and Financial Chronicle*, 23 October. Reprinted in John T. Dunlop (ed.) *Potentials of the American Economy*. Cambridge MA: Harvard University Press, 95–111.   **245**

Slichter, S. H. (1954) 'Do the wage fixing arrangements in the American labor market have an inflationary bias?' *American Economic Review* 44(2): 322–46.   **124, 240**

Slichter, S. H. (1957) 'Thinking ahead'. *Harvard Business Review* (September/October): 15–169.   **124, 125, 131, 244**

Slichter, S. H. (1959) 'Statement of Sumner Slichter', in *Hearings before the Joint Economic Committee on Employment, Growth, and Price Levels, 1st Session, Part 1, Washington 1958*. Washington, DC: Government Printing Office.   **125**

Slichter, S. H. (1959/1961) 'Inflation: A problem of shrinking importance'. *Commercial and Financial Chronicle*, 23 April: 134–49.   **124**

Slichter, S. H. (1961) *Economic Growth in the United States*. Baton Rouge, LA: State University Press.   **124**

Smith, D. A. (1970) 'Collective bargaining results'. *Relations Industrielles–Industrial Relations* 25(1): 46–54.   **224**

Smith, D. C. (1966) *Income Policies: Some Foreign Experiences and their Relevance for Canada*. Ottawa: Queen's Printer.   **147, 235, 250**

Smith, D. C. (1968) 'Incomes policy', in *Britain's Economic Prospects*, ed. R. Caves and L. B. Krause. Washington, DC: Brookings, 104–46.   **231**

Smith, L. (1972) 'Real estate: Discussion'. *Journal of Finance* 27(2): 227–30.   **248**

Smith, W. L. (1960) 'Monetary policy, 1957–1960: An appraisal'. *Review of Economics and Statistics* 42(3): 269–72.   **78**

Smith, W. L. (1962) 'The report of the Commission on Money and Credit'. *American Economic Review* 52(2): 302–10.   **246**

Smithies, A. (1961) 'The Commission on Money and Credit'. *Quarterly Journal of Economics* 75(4): 544–68.   **235**

Smithies, A. (1962) 'Review of Fellner et al., The problem of rising prices'. *American Economic Review* 52(3): 535–8. Smyth, D. J. (1971) 'Unemployment and inflation: Cross-country analysis of Phillips curve'. *American Economic Review* 61(3): 426–9.   **109**

Smyth, D. J. (1971) "Unemployment and inflation - Cross-Country Analysis of Phillips curve." *American Economic Review* 61(3): 426–9.   **44, 231, 233**

Smyth D. J. (1979) 'Unemployment dispersion and Phillips loops: A direct test of the Lipsey hypothesis'. *Oxford Bulletin of Economics and Statistics* 41(3): 227–33.   **248**

Snider, D. A. and R. D. Irwin (1971) *Introduction to International Economics*. Homewood, IL: Irwin.   **79**

Snodgrass, D. R. (1963) 'Wage changes in 24 manufacturing industries, 1948–59: A comparative analysis'. *Yale Economic Essays* (Spring): 171–222.   **55, 250**

Snow, C. P. (1956) 'The two cultures'. *New Statesman*, 6 October.   **20**

Snow, C. P. (1959) *The Two Cultures and the Scientific Revolution*. Cambridge: Cambridge University Press.   **20**

Snowdon, B. and H. R. Vane (1999) *Conversations with Leading Economists*. Cheltenham: Elgar.   **41, 48**

Snowdon, B. and H. R. Vane (2005) *Modern Macroeconomics: Its Origins, Development and Current State*.Cheltenham: Edward Elgar.   **165**

Soffer, B. (1959) 'The effects of recent long-tem wage agreements on general wage level movements: 1950–1957'. *Quarterly Journal of Economics* 73(1): 36–60.   **87**

Sohmen, E. (1961) 'The dollar and the mark', in *The Dollar in Crisis*, ed. S. E. Harris. New York: Harcourt, Brace & World, 183–200.   **235**

Sokol, M. and L. Castle (1969) 'Observations on economic development'. *Eastern European Economics* 8(1): 3–19.   **247**

Soldofsky, R. M. and D. F. Max (1975) 'Securities as a hedge against inflation: 1910–1969'. *Journal of Business Research* 3(2): 165–72.   **228**

Solow, R. M. (1956) 'A contribution to the theory of economic growth'. *Quarterly Journal of Economics* 70(1): 65–94.   **26**

Solow, R. M. (1962) 'A policy for full employment'. *Industrial Relations* 2(1): 1–14.   **40**

Solow, R. M. (1964a) *The Nature and Sources of Unemployment in the United States: The Wicksell Lectures, 1964*. Stockholm: Almqvist & Wiksell.   **40**

Solow, R. M. (1964b) 'Review of Harrod "The British economy"'. *The Economic Journal* 74(293): 149–51.   **41, 246**

Solow, R. M. (1966a) 'Comments', in *Guidelines, Informal Controls, and the Market Place*, ed. G. P. Schultz and R. Z. Aliber. Chicago: Chicago University Press, 62–5.   **187**

Solow, R. M. (1966b) 'The case against the case against Guideposts', in *Guidelines, Informal Controls, and the Market Place*, ed. G. P. Schultz and R. Z. Aliber. Chicago: Chicago University Press, 41–54.   **89, 188**

Solow, R. M. (1968) 'Recent controversy on the theory of inflation: An eclectic view', in *Inflation: Its Causes, Consequences, and Control*, ed. S. W. Rousseas. Wilton, CT: Calvin K. Kazanjian Economics Foundation.   **41, 101, 175, 188, 189, 195**

Solow, R. M. (1969) *Price Expectations and the Behaviour of the Price Level*. Manchester: Manchester University Press.   **101, 190, 238, 251**

Solow, R. M. (1973) 'What happened to full employment?' *Quarterly Review of Economics and Business* 13(2): 7–20.   **40**

Solow, R. M. (1975) 'The intelligent citizen's guide to inflation'. *Public Interest* (38): 39–49.   **41**

Solow, R. M. (1978) 'Down the Phillips curve with gun and camera', in *Inflation, Trade and Taxes*, ed. D. A. Belsley, E. J. Kane, P. A. Samuelson, and R. M. Solow. Columbus, OH: Ohio State University Press, 3–22.   **39, 223**

Solow, R. M. (1979a) 'What we know and don't know about inflation'. *Technology Review* 81(3): 30–44.   **39, 40, 223**

Solow, R. M. (1979b) 'Another possible source of wage stickiness'. *Journal of Macroeconomics* 1(1): 79–82.   **77**

Solow, R. M. (1988/2005) 'My evolution as an economist: A lecture delivered at Trinity University, San Antonio, Texas', in *Lives of the Laureates*, ed. W. Breit and B. T. Hirsch. Boston: The MIT Press, 153–70.   **41**

Solow, R. M. (2002) 'Analytical aspects of anti-inflation policy after 40 years', in *Paul Samuelson and the Foundations of Modern Economics*, ed. K. Puttaswamaiah. New Brunswick, NJ: Transaction, 71–7.   **41**

Solow, R. M. and J. E. Stiglitz (1968) 'Output, employment, and wages in the short run'. *Quarterly Journal of Economics* 82(4): 537–60.   **246–247**

Soule, G. (1960) 'Review of employment, growth, and price levels'. *Journal of Economic History* 20(2): 349–52.   **77**

Sparks, G. R. and D. A. Wilton (1971) 'Determinants of negotiated wage increases: An empirical analysis'. *Econometrica* 39(5): 739–50.   **241**

Spinelli, F. (1976) 'The determinants of price and wage inflation: The case of Italy', in *Inflation in Open Economies*, ed. M. Parkin and G. Zis. Manchester: Manchester University Press, 201–36.   **97**

Spitäller, E. (1971) 'Prices and unemployment in selected industrial countries'. *IMF Staff Papers* 18: 528–69. **238, 250**

Spitäller, E. (1975) 'Inflationary expectations and the trade-off between unemployment and inflation in the United States'. *IMF Staff Papers* 22(3): 775–90. **238**

Spitäller, E. (1978) 'A model of inflation and its performance in the seven main industrial countries, 1958–76'. *IMF Staff Papers* 25(2): 254–77. **238**

Spooner, F. C. (1978) '3 functions of money: Accounts, exchanges, and assets'. *Diogenes* (101): 105–37. **227**

Spulber, N. (1989) *Managing the American Economy from Roosevelt to Reagan*. Bloomington, IN: Indiana University Press. **226**

Stedman Jones, D. (2012) *Masters of the Universe*. Princeton: Princeton University Press. **167**

Stein, H. (1958) 'A general view of the inflation problem', in *The Relationship of Prices to Economic Stability and Growth: Compendium of Paper Submitted by Panelists Appearing before the JEC 85th Congress, 2d Sess, Mar 31 1958*. Washington, DC: Government Printing Office, 665–9. **83**

Stein, H. (1962) 'Reducing unemployment: With or without inflation?' *Industrial Relations* 2(1): 15–27. **84**

Stein, H. (1969) *The Fiscal Revolution in America*. Chicago: University of Chicago. **149, 156**

Stein, H. (1984) *Presidential Economics*. New York: Simon & Schuster. **156**

Stekler, H. O. (1968) 'Forecasting the GNP price deflator'. *Journal of Business* 41(4): 431–8. **55**

Stewart, M. (1967/1972) *Keynes and After*. London: Penguin. **12, 246**

Stigler, G. J., D. S. Brady, E. F. Denison, P. J. McCarthy, A. Rees, R. Ruggles, and B. C. Swerling (1961) *The Price Statistics of the Federal Government*. Washington, DC: National Bureau of Economic Research. **120**

Storm, S. and C. W. M. Naastepad (2012) *Macroeconomics beyond the NAIRU*. Cambridge, MA: Harvard University Press. **214**

Streit, M. E. (1972) 'Phillips curve: Fact or fancy? The example of West Germany'. *Weltwirtschaftliches Archiv* 108(4): 609–33. **226, 232**

Sturmthal, A. (1968) 'Income policies and international experience: Further comments'. *Relations Industrielles–Industrial Relations* 23: 221–36. **247**

Suits, D. B. (1962) 'Forecasting and analysis with an econometric model'. *American Economic Review* 52: 104–32. **99**

Sultan, P. E. (1957) *Labor Economics*. New York: Holt. **18, 180**

Sumner, M. T. (1972) 'Aggregate demand, price expectations and the Phillips curve', in *Incomes Policy and Inflation*, ed. M. Parkin and M. T. Sumner. Manchester: Manchester University Press, 163–81. **240**

Sumner, M. T. (1984) 'The history and significance of the Phillips curve', in *Surveys in Economics: Macroeconomics*, ed. D. Demery. London: Longman, 169–225. **163, 220, 236**

Tabb, W. K. (1999) *Reconstructing Political Economy: The Great Divide in Economic Thought*. London: Routledge. **229**

Tandon, B. B. and K. K. Tandon (1978) 'Inflation-unemployment trade-off: The Canadian experience'. *Indian Journal of Industrial Relations* 13(3): 277–93. **251**

Tatemoto, M., T. Uchida, and T. Watanabe (1967) 'A stabilization model for the postwar Japanese economy: 1954–62'. *International Economic Review* 8(1): 13–44. **58**

Taylor, J. (1970) 'Hidden unemployment, hoarded labor and the Phillips curve'. *Southern Economic Journal* 37(1): 1–16. **239**

Taylor, J. (1972) 'Incomes policy, the structure of unemployment and the Phillips curve: The United Kingdom experience 1953–1970', in *Incomes Policy and Inflation*, ed. M. Parkin and M. T. Sumner. Manchester: Manchester University Press, 182–200.   **239, 240**

Taylor, J. (1974) *Unemployment and Wage Inflation*. Harlow: Longman.   **239**

Taylor, J. B. (1997) 'Comment on DeLong, America's peacetime inflation', in *Reducing Inflation: Motivation and Strategy*, ed. C. D. Romer and D. H. Romer. Chicago: University of Chicago Press, 276–80.   **166, 249**

Teigen, R. L. (1975) 'Interpreting recent world inflation'. *American Economic Review* 65(2): 129–32.   **176**

Temple, J. (2000) 'Inflation and growth: Stories short and tall'. *Journal of Economic Surveys* 14(4): 395–426.   **116**

Thirlwall, A. (1969) 'Demand disequilibrium in the labour markets and wage rate inflation in the United Kingdom'. *Yorkshire Bulletin of Economics and Social Research* 21(1): 66–76.   **79, 241**

Thirlwall, A. (1970) 'Regional Phillips curves'. *Bulletin of the Oxford University Institute of Economics and Statistics* 32(1): 19–32.   **241**

Thirlwall, A. (1972) 'The Phillips curve: An historical note'. *Economica* 39(155): 325.   **180**

Thirlwall, A. (1980) 'Rowthorn's interpretation of Verdoorn's law'. *The Economic Journal* 90(358): 386–8.   **119**

Thomas, R. L. (1973) 'Unemployment dispersion as a determinant of wage inflation in the United Kingdom, 1925–1966: Rejoinder'. *Manchester School* 41(3): 229–34.   **241**

Thomas, R. L. (1974) 'Wage inflation in the UK: A multi-market approach', in *Inflation and Labour Markets*, ed. D. E. W. Laidler and D. L. Purdy. Manchester: Manchester University Press, 227–53.   **241**

Thomas, R. L. and P. Stoney (1970) 'A note on the dynamic properties of the Hines inflation model'. *Review of Economic Studies* 37(2): 286–94.   **239**

Thomas, R. L. and P. Stoney (1971) 'Unemployment dispersion as a determinant of wage inflation in the United Kingdom, 1925–1966'. *Manchester School* 39(2): 83–116.   **241, 242**

Thornton, H. (1802) *An Enquiry into the Nature and Effects of the Paper Credit of Great Britain*. London: John Hatchard.   **219**

Thorp, W. L. and R. E. Quandt (1959) *The New Inflation*. New York: McGraw-Hill.   **122**

Throop, A. W. (1968) 'The union-nonunion wage differential and cost-push inflation'. *American Economic Review* 58(1): 79–99.   **55, 68, 229, 233**

Throop, A. W. (1969) 'Wages and the Guideposts: Comment'. *American Economic Review* 59(3): 358–65.   **229, 233**

Thurow, L. C. (1968) 'Review of Sheahan The Wage-Price Guideposts'. *Journal of Finance* 23(4): 702–3.   **246**

Tinbergen, J. (1937) *An Econometric Approach to Business Cycle Problems*. Paris: Hermann.   **12, 18**

Tinbergen, J. (1939) *Statistical Testing of Business-cycle Theories: Business Cycles in the United States of America 1919–1932*. Geneva: League of Nations Economic Intelligence Service.   **12**

Tinbergen, J. (1951) *Business Cycles in the United Kingdom, 1870–1914*. Amsterdam: North-Holland.   **12, 181**

Tobin, J. (1965) 'Money and economic growth'. *Econometrica* 33(4): 671–84.   **117**

Tobin, J. (1966) *The Intellectual Revolution in US Policy-making*. London: Longmans, Green & Co. Ltd.   **131, 149, 156, 204**

Tobin, J. (1967) 'Unemployment and inflation: The cruel dilemma', in *Prices: Issues in Theory, Practice, and Public Policy*, ed. A. Phillips and O. E. Williamson. Philadelphia: University of Pennsylvania Press, 101–7.   **184**

Tobin, J. (1968a) 'Comment during discussion', in *Inflation: Its Causes, Consequences, and Control*, ed. S. W. Rousseas. Wilton, CT: Calvin K. Kazanjian Economics Foundation, 59.   **184**

Tobin, J. (1968b) 'Notes on optimal monetary growth'. *Journal of Political Economy* 76(4): 833–59.   **247**

Tobin, J. (1972a) *The New Economics One Decade Older*. Princeton: Princeton University Press.   **156, 157, 161, 195**

Tobin, J. (1972b) 'Inflation and unemployment'. *American Economic Review* 62(1): 1–18.   **76, 79, 157, 195, 200**

Tobin, J. (1975) 'Keynesian models of recession and depression'. *American Economic Review* 65(2): 195–202.   **250**

Tobin, J. (1978) 'Harry Gordon Johnson, 1923–77'. *Proceedings of the British Academy* 63: 443–58.   **133**

Tobin, J. (1995) 'The natural rate as new classical macroeconomics', in *The Natural Rate of Unemployment*, ed. R. B. Cross. Cambridge: Cambridge University Press, 32–42.   **237**

Tobin, J. and L. Ross (1971) 'Living with inflation'. *New York Review of Books* 16(8): 23–6.   **157, 186**

Tobin, J. and L. Ross (1972) 'A reply to Gordon Tullock'. *Journal of Money, Credit and Banking* 4(2): 431–6.   **186**

Toyoda, T. (1972) 'Price expectations and the short-run and long-run Phillips curves in Japan'. *Review of Economics and Statistics* 54(3): 267–74.   **98, 251**

Tullock, G. (1972) 'Can you fool all of the people all of the time? Comment'. *Journal of Money, Credit and Banking* 4(2): 426–30.   **186**

Turner, H. A. (1959) 'Employment fluctuations, labour supply and bargaining power'. *Manchester School* 27(2): 175–202.   **16**

Turner, H. A. and F. Wilkinson (1971) 'Real new incomes and the wage explosion'. *New Society*, 25 February: 309–10.   **114**

Turner, P. (1997) 'The Phillips curve, parameter instability and the Lucas critique'. *Applied Economics* 29(1): 7–10.   **226**

Turnovsky, S. J. (1978) 'Macroeconomic dynamics and growth in a monetary economy: A synthesis'. *Journal of Money, Credit and Banking* 10(1): 1–26.   **117**

Turnovsky, S. J. and M. L. Wachter (1972) 'A test of the "expectations hypothesis" using directly observed wage and price expectations'. *Review of Economics and Statistics* 54(1): 47–54.   **101, 251**

Turvey, R. (1951) 'Some aspects of the theory of inflation in a closed economy'. *Economic Journal* 61(243): 531–43.   **114**

Tussing, A. D. (1975) *Poverty in a Dual Economy*. New York: St Martin's Press.   **227**

Ulman, L. (ed.) (1973) *Manpower Programs in the Policy Mix*. Baltimore: Johns Hopkins University Press.   **246**

Ulman, L. (1998) 'The Kennedy and Johnson Guideposts'. *Proceedings of the Industrial Relations Research Association*: 168–81.   **169**

Ulman, L. and R. J. Flanagan (1971) *Wage Restraint: A Study of Incomes Policies in Western Europe*. Berkeley, CA: University of California Press.   **127, 145**

Usher, D. (2012) 'Bargaining unexplained'. *Public Choice* 151(1/2): 23–41.   **27**

Valavanis-Vail, S. (1955) 'An econometric model of growth: USA 1869–1953'. *American Economic Review* 35: 208–21.   **219**

Vanderkamp, J. (1966a) 'An application of Lipsey's concept of structural unemployment'. *Review of Economic Studies* 33(3): 221–5.   245

Vanderkamp, J. (1966b) 'Wage and price level determinants: An empirical model for Canada'. *Economica* 33(130): 194–218.   58, 74

Vanderkamp, J. (1968) 'The Phillips relation: A theoretical explanation—a comment'. *Economica* 35(138): 179–83.   246

Vanderkamp, J. (1972) 'Wage adjustment, productivity and price change expectations'. *Review of Economic Studies* 39(1): 61–72.   105

Vanek, J. (1962) *International Trade*. Homewood, IL: Irwin.   224

Verdoorn, P. J. (1949) 'Fattori che regolano lo sviluppo della produttività del lavoro'. *L'Industria* 1: 3–10.   118

Vickrey, W. S. (1955) 'Stability through inflation', in *Post-Keynesian Economics*, ed. K. K. Kurihara. London: Macmillan, 89–122.   82

Villard, H. H. (1968) 'Discussion'. *American Economic Review* 58(2): 483–91.   248

Viner, J. (1936) 'Mr Keynes on the causes of unemployment'. *Quarterly Journal of Economics* 51(1): 147–67.   24

Viner, J. (1937) *Studies in the Theory of International Trade*. New York: Harper.   120

Viner, J. (1950) 'Full employment at whatever cost'. *Quarterly Journal of Economics* 64(3): 385–407.   24

Vroey, M. de (1998) 'Accounting for involuntary unemployment in neoclassical theory: Some lessons from sixty years of uphill struggle', in *Economics and Methodology*, ed. R. E. Backhouse, D. M. Hausman, U. Mäki, and A. Salanti. Houndmills: Palgrave, 177–224.   192

Vroman, W. (1970) 'Manufacturing wage behavior with special reference to the period 1962–1966'. *Review of Economics and Statistics* 52(2): 160–7.   230

Wachter, M. L. (1969) 'Wages and the Guideposts: Comment'. *American Economic Review* 59(3): 354–8.   230

Wachter, M. L. (1970) 'Cyclical variation in the interindustry wage structure'. *American Economic Review* 60(1): 75–84.   90

Wachter, M. L. (1974) 'The wage process: An analysis of the early 1970s'. *Brookings Papers on Economic Activity* 1974(2): 507–25.   238

Wachter, M. L. (1976a) 'Some problems in wage stabilization'. *American Economic Review* 66(2): 65–71.   174, 184

Wachter, M. L. (1976b) 'The changing cyclical responsiveness of wage inflation'. *Brookings Papers on Economic Activity* 1976(1): 115–67.   90, 213

Wachter, M. L. and S. M. Wachter (1978) 'Institutional factors in domestic inflation', in *After the Phillips Curve: Persistence of High Inflation and High Unemployment*. Boston: Federal Reserve Bank of Boston, 124–55.   238

Wachter, M. L. and O. E. Williamson (1978) 'Obligational markets and the mechanics of inflation'. *Bell Journal of Economics* 9(2): 549–71.   238

Wagner, A. and S. C. Sufrin (1970) 'Discontinuous relations and economic regulation'. *Rivista Internazionale di Scienze Economiche E Commerciali* 17(11): 1081–94.   228

Wallich, H. C. (1958) 'Postwar United States monetary policy appraised', in *United States Monetary Policy*, ed. N. H. Jacoby. New York: The American Assembly, 91–117.   119

Wallich, H. C. (1966) 'The Employment Act objectives after 20 years', in *Twentieth Anniversary of the Employment Act of 1946: Hearing before the Joint Economic Committee Congress of the United States*. Washington, DC: US Government Printing Office, 12–19.   182

Wallich, H. C. (1968) 'The American Council of Economic Advisers and the German Sachverstaendigenrat: A study in the economics of advice'. *Quarterly Journal of Economics* 82(3): 349–79.   **247**

Wallich, H. C. (1969a) 'The spotty economy'. *Financial Analysts Journal* 25(4): 21–4.   **247**

Wallich, H. C. (1969b) 'Comment on Fand's "Keynesian monetary theories, stabilization policy, and the recent inflation"'. *Journal of Money, Credit and Banking* 1(3): 590–5.   **154**

Wallich, H. C. (1969c) 'Money and growth: A country cross-section analysis'. *Journal of Money, Credit and Banking* 1(2): 281–302.   **117**

Wallis, K. F. (1971) 'Wages, prices and incomes policies: Some comments'. *Economica* 38(151): 304–10.   **240**

Watanabe, T. (1966) 'Price changes and the rate of change of money wage earnings in Japan 1955–1962'. *Quarterly Journal of Economics* 80: 31–47.   **58, 69, 251**

Waterman, A. M. C. (1966) 'Some footnotes to the "Swan diagram": Or how dependent is a dependent economy?'. *Economic Record* 42: 447–64.   **133**

Waterman, A. M. C. (2002) 'The new political economy then and now'. *American Journal of Economics and Sociology* 61(1): 13–51.   **229**

Weber, A. R. (1967) 'Review of Mabry, "Labor relations and collective bargaining"'. *Industrial and Labor Relations Review* 20(4): 702–3.   **246**

Weintraub, S. (1959) *A General Theory of the Price Level, Output, Income Distribution and Economic Growth*. Philadelphia: Chilton.   **54**

Weintraub, S. (1968) 'Supplement: Theoretical economics'. *Annals of the American Academy of Political and Social Science* 380: 145–62.   **54**

White Paper (1944) *Employment Policy*, Cmnd 6527. London: HMSO.   **141**

Widmaier, W. (2003) 'The Keynesian bases of a constructivist theory of the international political economy'. *Millennium: Journal of International Studies* 32(1): 87–107.   **229**

Widmaier, W. W. (2004) 'The social construction of the "impossible trinity": The intersubjective bases of monetary cooperation'. *International Studies Quarterly* 48(2): 433–53.   **229**

Widmaier, W. W. (2005) 'The meaning of an inflation crisis: Steel, Enron, and macroeconomic policy'. *Journal of Post Keynesian Economics* 27(4): 555–73.   **229**

Widmaier, W. W. (2007) 'Where you stand depends on how you think: Economic ideas, the decline of the Council of Economic Advisers and the rise of the Federal Reserve'. *New Political Economy* 12(1): 43–59.   **229**

Wiles, P. (1973) 'Cost inflation and the state of economic theory'. *Economic Journal* 83(330): 377–98.   **114**

Williams, J. H. (1945) 'Free enterprise and full employment', in *Financing American Prosperity*, ed. P. T. Homan and F. Machlup. New York: Twentieth Century Fund, 337–93.   **119**

Winch, D. (1969/1972) *Economics and Policy*. London: Hodder & Stoughton/Fontana. **149**

Winder, J. W. L. (1968) 'Structural unemployment', in *The Canadian Labour Market: Readings in Manpower Economics*, ed. A. Kruger and N. Meltz. Toronto: University of Toronto Press, 135–220.   **227**

Wonnacott, P. (1960) 'Employment, growth, and price levels'. *Political Science Quarterly* 75(4): 560–71.   **78**

Woods, H. D. and S. Ostry (1962) *Labour Policy and Labour Economics in Canada*. Toronto: Macmillan.   **224–225, 235**

Worswick, G. D. N. (1952) 'Introduction: The British economy, 1945–50', in *The British Economy, 1945–1950*, ed. G. D. N. Worswick and P. H. Ady. Oxford: Clarendon Press, 1–34. **79**

Worswick, G. D. N. and P. H. Ady (eds) (1952) *The British Economy, 1945–1950*. Oxford: Oxford University Press. **148**

Worswick, G. D. N. and P. H. Ady (1962) *The British Economy in the 1950s*. Oxford: Oxford University Press. **148**

Woytinsky, W. S. (1949) *Labor and Management Look at Collective Bargaining*. New York: Twentieth Century Fund. **87**

Wulwick, N. J. (1987) 'The Phillips curve: Which? Whose? To do what? How?' *Southern Economic Journal* 53(4): 834–57. **223**

Wulwick, N. J. (1989) 'Phillips' approximate regression'. *Oxford Economic Papers* 41: 170–88. **15, 249**

Yamey, B. (2000) 'The famous Phillips curve article: a note on its publication', in *A. W. H. Phillips: Collected Works in Contemporary Perspective*, ed. R. Leeson. Cambridge: Cambridge University Press, 335–8. **17, 250**

Young, W., R. Leeson, and W. A. Darity (2004) *Economics, Economists, and Expectations*. London: Routledge. **228, 236**

Zaidi, M. A. (1969) 'The determinants of money wage rate changes and unemployment-inflation "trade-offs" in Canada'. *International Economic Review* 10(2): 207–19. **58, 74, 250**

Zarnowitz, V. (1985) 'Recent work on business cycles in historical-perspective: A review of theories and evidence'. *Journal of Economic Literature* 23(2): 523–80. **226**

Zebot, C. A. (1961) 'Toward an integrated theory of inflation in the United States'. *Weltwirtschaftliches Archiv* 87: 351–71. **235**

INDEX

Printed and bound by CPI Group (UK) Ltd, Croydon, CR0 4YY